Empathy in Psychotherapy

Empathy in Psychotherapy

How Therapists and Clients
Understand Each Other

FRANK-M. STAEMMLER

For the English language version translated by Elizabeth J. Hamilton and Deirdre Winter © 2011
Frank-M. Staemmler—The translation of this work was funded by *Geisteswissenschaften International—Translation Funding for Humanities and Social Sciences from Germany*, a joint initiative of the Fritz Thyssen Foundation, the German Federal Foreign Office, the collecting society VG WORT, and the Börsenverein des Deutschen Buchhandels (German Publishers & Booksellers Association).

Springer Publishing Company, LLC
11 West 42nd Street
New York, NY 10036
www.springerpub.com

Acquisitions Editor: Jennifer Perillo
Production Editor: Michael Lisk
Composition: Manila Typesetting Company

ISBN: 978-0-8261-0902-6
ebook ISBN: 978-0-8261-0934-7

11 12 13 14 / 5 4 3 2 1

The author and the publisher of this Work have made every effort to use sources believed to be reliable to provide information that is accurate and compatible with the standards generally accepted at the time of publication. The author and publisher shall not be liable for any special, consequential, or exemplary damages resulting, in whole or in part, from the readers' use of, or reliance on, the information contained in this book. The publisher has no responsibility for the persistence or accuracy of URLs for external or third-party Internet websites referred to in this publication and does not guarantee that any content on such websites is, or will remain, accurate or appropriate.

Library of Congress Cataloging-in-Publication Data
Staemmler, Frank-M., 1951-
  [Geheimnis des Anderen. English]
  Empathy in psychotherapy : how therapists and clients understand each other / Frank-M. Staemmler.
— 1st ed.
    p. cm.
  Includes bibliographical references and indexes.
  ISBN 978-0-8261-0902-6 (alk. paper) — ISBN 978-0-8261-0934-7 (ebook) 1. Empathy. 2. Psychotherapy.
3. Psychotherapist and patient. I. Title.
  RC489.E46S73 2012
  616.89'14—dc23
                                                                                    2011039318

Printed in the United States of America by Gasch Printing.

Dedicated to Barbara,
my life partner and a master of loving compassion in "real life"
and to Lynne,
my soul mate and teacher in committed empathy in psychotherapy.

Contents

1

Introduction
The Mystery of the Other

"Encountering a human being means being kept awake by an enigma" (Lévinas, 1983, p. 120).[1]
"The mystery of the person lures us for its own sake into ever new and deeper attempts at understanding" (Dilthey, 2002, p. 233).

When I was considering, about 35 years ago, whether I should seriously pursue the idea that I had first had some years previously of becoming a psychotherapist, I found myself faced with an interesting dilemma. The quandary arose from a very simple preconceived notion I had, namely that psychotherapists want to and must empathize with their clients and understand as best they can what moves them.

However, after this initial assumption, I soon realized that things were not so clear-cut. On the one hand, I began to doubt whether it is in fact even possible to "put oneself *into* someone else's shoes." Is it not the case that the other's subjective experience always remains his or her "mystery," as Lévinas (1889, p. 48) puts it? Or can it be unveiled? If so, to what extent? How do we know whether we have been successful? On the other hand, this is precisely the point where I began to become curious. Is there anything more interesting than the different experiential worlds of other people? What other profession could be more varied, continually enabling the practitioner to make new discoveries? Where else does one have the opportunity to get so close to other people on a daily basis?

The dilemma in which I found myself at the time is a well-known one. "Ultimately one is always alone," runs an old German saying. The poet John Donne (1623) saw it differently: "No man is an island."[2] There

---

1 Quotes from German sources which had not previously been translated into English have been translated by the translators of this book.
2 Ziman (2006) expresses the same idea in the terms of scientific philosophy.

is an element of truth in both viewpoints. They should not be seen as antitheses, but as poles between which human existence oscillates. Martin Buber speaks of two "movements" which together constitute the "twofold principle" of human existence. One of them he calls "the primal setting at a distance" and the other "entering into relation" (Buber, 1957, p. 97).

BOX 1

MARTIN BUBER (1878–1965), was a Jewish philosopher of religion. His central thesis was that encounters between human beings and also between human beings and God are unmediated or direct. He therefore placed an emphasis on dialogue, for example in one of his major works, *I and Thou* (1958). He exerted a strong influence on modern education, psychiatry and psychotherapy, including gestalt therapy in particular (see Doubrawa & Staemmler, 2003; Staemmler, 1993a). Buber's main statement in this essay is "Through the *Thou* a man becomes *I*" (1958, p. 28—original italics). For a biography of Buber see Wehr (1991).

We experience both movements frequently: I feel drawn to one person and repelled by another. I have close friendships with some people, while remaining more or less indifferent to others. Whereas with one person I experience intense closeness, I have an aversion to another. I get on well with some people from the start, and yet I am completely unable to understand others, however hard I try.

How well we understand each other (and thus get on with each other) and how much of a riddle we remain to each other (and thus do not want to have much to do with each other) appears to be a decisive dimension of experiencing that spans the gap between "distance" and "relation." In other words, the more two people are able to relate empathically to each other, the more probable it is that the relationship between them will be successful and endure. Without empathic understanding, there is no closeness, and even business relationships or superficial, everyday encounters, in busy road traffic, for example (see Bernieri & Rosenthal, 1991, p. 401), become difficult or even problematic if there is not a minimum of empathy between those involved. Empathy is therefore considered to be a central aspect of emotional intelligence, "a type of emotional information processing that includes accurate appraisal of emotions in oneself and others, appropriate expression of emotion, and adaptive regulation of emotion in such a way as *to enhance living*" (Mayer, DiPaolo, & Salovey, 1990, p. 772—original italics; see also Goleman, 1995). Ziman is even of the opinion that "the human sciences depend, ultimately, on an *empathic intersubjectivity* . . . The primary research data of the human sciences are nothing other than *frozen records of intersubjectivity in action*" (2006, pp. 29f.—original italics).

For this book, at all events, this is true: It is based on a multitude of my own experiences as a psychotherapist.

Heinz Kohut hit the nail on the head when he wrote: "The empathic understanding of the experiences of other human beings is as basic an endowment of man as his vision, hearing, touch, taste, and smell" (1977, p. 144), and for the person who receives it is "a psychological nutriment without which human life as we know it and cherish it could not be sustained" (1980, p. 84). Ickes considers human empathy, which, interestingly, can be extended not only toward other human beings, but also toward animals, to be "the second greatest achievement of which the mind is capable, consciousness itself being the first" (1997, p. 2). If we are to believe the infancy researcher and intersubjectivist Colwyn Trevarthen, empathy and consciousness are closely related: "The core of every human consciousness appears to be an immediate, unrational, unverbalized, conceptless, totally atheoretical potential for rapport of the self with another's mind" (1993, p. 121).

Because that is so, people who are not able to empathize with the situation of other people, or have great difficulty in doing so, are considered to be particularly severely mentally disturbed (see Soderstrom, 2003). They used to be called "psychopaths"; today, we prefer to use the term "antisocial personality disorder." However, human behavior that is devoid of all empathy toward others does not only occur when people are severely mentally disturbed, but can also be strongly dependent on the prevailing situational, cultural, and historico-political conditions in which "*good people turn evil*" (Zimbardo, 2007). This has been demonstrated not only by Milgram's (1974) sensational experiments, but also, for example, by the death of Kitty Genovese[3] (see Rosenthal, 1999) and the subsequent studies on the behavior of "*bystanders*" — those passersby who see somebody get into a situation of distress and have to decide whether they will go to their aid or whether they would rather not get involved (see for example, Darley & Latané, 1968). The desensitization caused by repeatedly watching crime films and series on television and even playing computer games like *Ego Shooter* to excess (see Staemmler & Merten, 2006, p. 10) is one of the current cultural influences that is likely to have serious consequences. Those who frequently indulge in such pastimes may well lose their ability

---

3 "In 1964 a young woman was attacked early one morning in New York. People were woken by her screams. They appeared at the windows of various houses but did not actively intervene. The woman was severely injured and was killed by the last thrusts of the knife into her defenseless body after her attacker had attempted to rape her. The crime went on for 35 minutes. A total of 36 people watched it from their windows. They saw each other. None of them went to help the young woman and none of them phoned the police" (Bonn, 2008, p. 192).

to empathize. However, the constant commercialization of sickness, hunger, violence, war, and death by the mass media (see Moeller, 1999) is also likely to promote numbing and fatigue of the human capacity for compassion. The most extreme and unfathomable example of empathic indifference ever experienced was the unresponsive behavior shown by most Germans to the Holocaust as it was taking place before their very eyes (see Dean, 2004). This was a form of indifference that can, under certain historico-political circumstances, affect almost a whole people. It is to be hoped that it will never be repeated.

However, empathy constitutes the "barrier to inhumanity" (Gruen, 1997). It implies "a moral perception of another being as a sentient being, as a being capable of suffering, and therefore deserving of moral consideration" (Thompson in de Waal, Thompson, & Proctor, 2005, p. 39). Its positive significance is seen in a special way in psychotherapy. Since Luborsky's large-scale studies on therapeutic outcomes (1988, pp. 152ff.), psychotherapists' ability to understand their clients has been considered the second most important healing factor in all therapies, since it has a strong influence on the client-therapist relationship (for more recent research results on the efficacy of empathy see also Norcross, 2002; Watson, 2001, pp. 449ff.). A therapeutic relationship without empathy is hardly conceivable. How could therapists respond to their clients' mental situations if they were not, to a certain extent, able to enter into their subjective worlds? "Once and for all we have to recognize the fact that the first wish of a patient is to be *understood*" (Balint, 1968, p. 93).[4] Thus, anybody who goes to a psychotherapist expects—and I believe rightly so—the therapist to be willing and able to empathize.

Sometimes this expectation is expressed in a way that shows signs of both idealization and paranoia. Some clients imagine that their therapists have "X-ray" eyes and are thus able to see "right into them" and wrest from them the secret of their private thoughts and feelings. Consequently, their longing to be understood is mixed with a fear of the embarrassment of being "seen through" and caught out. However, behind such an expectation is the central human wish to be seen and recognized lovingly as the person that one essentially is. When this wish is fulfilled, it feels highly agreeable and often leads to change (see Beisser's "Paradoxical Theory of Change," 1970; see also Beisser, 1989[5]).

---

4 It is one of the extraordinary facts about psychotherapy that I shall later discuss under the heading of "one-sidedness" that complementary needs often remain unmentioned: "Although the need to be understood is often emphasized, the need to understand others also is important for most people" (Jordan, 1997, p. 345). In my experience, that also applies to clients.

5 This book is Beisser's autobiography—a lived paradox of change.

> ## BOX 2
>
> **ARNOLD BEISSER (1925–1991),** was a gestalt therapist who was confined to a wheelchair after suffering from severe polio. He became well-known through his "paradoxical theory of change," according to which
>
> > *change occurs when one becomes what he is, not when he tries to become what he is not.* Change does not take place through a coercive attempt by the individual or by another person to change him, but it does take place if one takes the time and effort to be what he is—to be fully invested in his current positions (Beisser, 1970, p. 77—original italics).
>
> This is often only possible in the presence of someone who is fundamentally benevolent and present (see Buber's dialogics).

The experience of empathic contact frees us as human beings from the isolation in which we can remain locked when this contact is lacking, even in the physical presence of other people. Empathy connects us and not infrequently culminates in our liking the other person. In the 35 years or more in which I have been doing my best to be accessible and present for my clients, I have often found myself getting to like even those people whom I had not liked at all to begin with. This always happened in cases where—sometimes after a faltering start—I had managed to be open for them and to engage with them in such a way that I could vividly imagine their experiential worlds.

This liking and the compassion that usually develops at the same time do not, of course, mean that I go along with everything that the other person says or does, but the moment their secret is aired, even partially, a human connection develops in which the fundamental similarity to and equality with the other become directly experienceable. Perhaps I should rather say that it is through empathic contact that the human connectedness that derives from our fundamental similarity and equality and thus defines our very existence becomes clearly perceptible. This is so even if we are temporarily unable to perceive it due to a lack of such contact.

All relationships between concrete human beings are dependent on our empathically engaging with the other and on our compassion and connectedness with her.[6] But this is not all. They are also the basis of the feeling of solidarity with human beings of whose situations we are aware,

---

6 To avoid cumbersome repetitions I have decided to use both the male and female forms randomly, and so as not to pathologize unnecessarily, I have elected to use the term "clients" rather than "patients."

even if we do not know them personally. Thus, no one would donate to the surviving victims of an earthquake or tsunami who live far away if they were not able to imagine what it means to be involved in such a natural disaster. Without empathy, compassion, and other social emotions

> There would have been no spontaneous exhibition of the innate social responses. . . . In the absence of the feelings of such emotions, humans would not have engaged in a negotiation aimed at finding solutions for problems faced by the group, e.g., identification and sharing of food resources, defense against threats, or disputes among its members. . . . It is unlikely that humans without basic social emotions and feelings would ever have created a religious system in the first place (Damasio, 2003, pp. 157f.).

Empathy, therefore, also has a dimension that goes beyond individual commitment to the other. It not only makes humane political actions possible, but it is also an important prerequisite for spirituality as symbolized by the Bodhisattva of Compassion, Avalokiteśvara, in the Buddhist tradition—a spirituality that is based on a comprehensive consciousness of our connectedness with the animate and inanimate world. I shall come back to this in Chapter 5.

BOX 3

AVALOKITEŚVARA, the Bodhisattva of Compassion, is seen as the personification of the boundless compassion of the Buddhas. In Mahayana Buddhism, it plays a central role and is considered to be the patron deity of Tibet. The thousand-armed manifestation of Avalokiteśvara symbolizes his active compassion for all living creatures (see Midal, 2002).

However, I shall begin by outlining the main features of those conceptions of empathy that have been most influential in psychotherapy to date. In Chapter 2, I shall therefore give a retrospective overview of some of these conceptualizations formulated by, for example, Carl Rogers for client-centered therapy, Heinz Kohut for his psychoanalytic self psychology and Frederick Perls for gestalt therapy. However, it is not my intention to give a comprehensive description of each of these approaches, but to compare and contrast them briefly to demonstrate how widely (and in some cases, how radically) they diverge on some points. On the other hand, at the same time, I will show how similar some of their prior assumptions nonetheless are. These similarities are even more important for the further development of my ideas than are the differences between them.

Three of the prior assumptions on which they agree would seem to me to be both fundamental and problematic. I shall discuss these in Chapter 3. To begin with, I shall address what I would describe as the implicit "one-sidedness" of the existing psychotherapeutic ideas of empathy. Many authors write about empathy as if it were a capacity that many therapists have, but not their clients. This would appear to me to be not only elitist, but also demonstrably false. If empathy is a basic human capacity, we must also credit people who seek psychotherapeutic help with the ability to empathize. This is not altered by the relatively rare exceptional cases of people who show signs of having an antisocial personality disorder (see above).

The second point that I consider worthy of criticism concerns the "disembodiment" that prevails in the conception of empathy that has been widespread to date. I am referring to the idea that the psyche somehow exists almost without a body and puts itself in the position of another psyche—purely mentally, so to speak. Here, notwithstanding the efforts of schools of "body-oriented" psychotherapy for example, the influence of Descartes' mind/body dualism is still evident in psychotherapy. Its traces are recognizable even within these efforts. Thus, the term *"body*-oriented *psycho*therapy" is an attempt to connect the very things that it simultaneously also continues to separate.

> ### BOX 4
>
> **RENÉ DESCARTES' (1596–1650)** dualistic philosophy has exerted a lasting influence on European thought in the modern era. His fundamental distinction between the *res cogitans* (thinking substance, mind) and *res extensa* (extended substance, matter) led him to believe that the body was a mindless machine that contrasted with and was more or less unconnected to the God-like mind. His statement, *"Cogito, ergo sum"* ("I think, therefore I am"), became famous and, with time, also notorious. It resulted from the assumption that
>
> > I was a substance whose whole essence or nature consists only in thinking, and which, that it may exist, has need of no place, nor is dependent on any material thing; so that 'I,' that is to say, the mind by which I am what I am, is wholly distinct from the body . . . , and as such, that although the latter were not, it would still continue to be all that it is (1924/2008, p. 31).

In both recent philosophy, for example phenomenology, and the modern neurosciences Cartesian dualism is now seen as *Descartes' Error* (Damasio, 1994). With this theory of "somatic markers"[7] (Damasio, 1994),

---

7 This term refers to traces of memories of bodily states that are linked to certain experiences.

Damasio has shown that thinking and decision making—and also social behavior—would be impossible if they were not anchored in the body. At the time when he wrote this book, he was as yet unable to integrate into his theory building the recent discovery of what are known as "mirror neurons," which was not made until after his book was published. This discovery impressively underscores how the body and mind interpenetrate each other and how both are intertwined with social reality. (I say more about this in Chapter 4.2.) A new conceptualization of empathy must therefore also attempt to leave Descartes' error behind: "Social cognition is not only *thinking* about the contents of someone else's mind" (Gallese, Keysers, & Rizzolatti, 2004, p. 401—original italics).

The third point of my critique of the traditional concept of empathy, which I will present in Chapter 3, has to do with an aspect that seems to me to be equally as important as the first two; I call it "individualism." In this view, both therapist and client appear to be in a vacuum. It looks as if there is no context surrounding them. Just as the relationship between them is seen as being one-sided, and their bodies as separated from their minds, they are apparently disconnected from the rest of the world. The traditional conceptualizations of empathy do not even include an *immediate* context surrounding and influencing the individuals in question. This is, of course, also an illusion. However, illusions may well on occasion have real consequences, and these may not necessarily always be desirable, as we shall see.

The critique presented in Chapter 3 is not intended to show that the traditional concepts of empathy are completely wrong and useless. However, their limitations will become clear. Empathy can be much more if it is released from the prison of the individualistic ideology on which my three points of criticism are based. As Foucault (1970) has demonstrated, psychotherapy as a whole resulted from the tendencies toward individualization that characterize the views of the world and the human being that predominate in our culture. This also applies, of course, to the central concepts of psychotherapy. Because of the way in which cultural backgrounds work, their prior assumptions become so much part of our flesh and blood that they often seem to us to be no longer culture, but almost nature—that is, if we are aware of them at all, since our "worldviews lay down the framework of fundamental concepts within which we interpret everything that appears in the world in a specific way as something" (Habermas, 1984, p. 58). Thus, basically, it is only possible for us to become aware of the dimensions of this framework to a limited extent.

To try to analyze and clearly describe what goes on when we understand in this sense is impossible, not because the process in some way "transcends" or is "beyond" normal experience, is some special act of magical divination not describable in the language of ordinary experience; but for the opposite reason, that it enters too intimately into our most normal experience, and is a kind of automatic integration of a very large number of data too fugitive and various to be mounted on the pin of some scientific process, one by one, in a sense too obvious, too much taken for granted, to be enumerable (Berlin 1996, p. 24).

Hermeneutic efforts can never achieve more than approximations. In Chapter 3, I will therefore attempt, as far as I can and without laying any claim to completeness, to delineate some of the basic characteristics of the individualistic ideology that are concealed within the traditional concept of empathy and contribute to its limitations.

BOX 5

THE CONCEPT OF HERMENEUTICS is derived from the Ancient Greek *hermēneuein*, a verb which referred to the process of "bringing to understanding," with its three dimensions: to express, to convey, and to translate or interpret. The word contains the name of the messenger of the gods, Hermes, whose task was to bring the gods' messages to the human beings, i.e., to bear the responsibility for creating understanding between the worlds. Hermeneutics thus refers in general to that segment of philosophy that is concerned with issues of understanding. The key words of hermeneutics are interpretation, understanding, and meaning. Hermeneutics deals with the understanding of the culturally transmitted worldviews that determine our everyday lives.

After developing a critique of the traditional conceptualization of empathy and its background, I will use it as a basis for exploring the alternatives. This will be the subject of Chapter 4, which is divided into three subsections corresponding to the three points of the critique. In Chapter 4.1, I put forward the view that *empathy exists only in the plural*.[8] One must relate empathically to others to some degree at least if one is to be able to take note of and use how other people relate empathically to oneself — and not simply for purely pragmatic reasons. In fact, empathizing with somebody who has just empathized with oneself is one of the most important interpersonal experiences that one can have. This alone leads to that kind of intersubjectivity that enables us to be aware of how our own experience comes back to ourselves, but in the form that it

---

8 I have borrowed this phrase from Olaf-Axel Burow, who used it similarly as a subtitle for one of his books (see Burow, 1999).

has assumed as a result of the other person's empathy. We see ourselves "through the eyes of the other."

Empathy thus has something to do with mutual attunement, tuning in to each other. Human beings are already capable of a certain form of attunement, checking back or referencing when they are only a few months old, as I shall demonstrate with studies from infant research. In this context, we become involved with the concept of "social referencing," which plays no small role in developmental and social psychology.

Chapter 4.2 is concerned with the *bodily* aspect of empathy, which I shall present from several different viewpoints, i.e., from the perspective of academic psychology, the perspective of phenomenological philosophy, and the perspective of recent neuroscientific findings (the above-mentioned discovery of the "mirror neurons" will be discussed in detail).

BOX 6

PHENOMENOLOGY is a philosophical discipline which was founded by Edmund Husserl (1859–1938) and has since been expanded by numerous scholars. The aim of phenomenology is to approach things as far as possible without prior assumptions, as their main characteristics appear in consciousness, and to describe them as exactly as possible.

This method reveals, for example, that human consciousness is always conscious *of* something and always refers *to* something in the world. This is what is meant by the term "intentionality." However, consciousness does not—in contrast to Descartes' view—exist independently of the body. Rather, as Merleau-Ponty says, "the body is the vehicle of being in the world," and "it is through my body that I understand other people" (1962, pp. 82, 186).

One later development of this philosophical movement is "New Phenomenology" ("Neue Phänomenologie"), which was developed (and given its distinctive shape) by the German philosopher Hermann Schmitz (who was born in 1928). Some of Schmitz's concepts will be of special importance for my considerations.

If we view these disciplines in context, there can be hardly any doubt that empathic relating between human beings (and in some cases even between apes) is an embodied process. (The term used by German phenomenologists is *leiblich*—of the lived body.) Most empathic processes take place much too fast for the participants involved to have sufficient time to develop mental theories about the experience of the other person. The processes that help us to find a way of getting along with others in numerous everyday situations are much more intuitive, embodied processes, which have more to do with simulation than with theory building. In analogy to the word "Einfühlung" (empathy, literally: feeling one's way into—see Box 9), Hermann Schmitz has coined the term "Ein*leib*ung" (literally "feeling into the living or feeling body," or encorporation), which is a good description for many such processes.

Schmitz and Gurwitsch (1979) before him, also employ another term which I will use in Chapter 4.3 to capture the context within which human beings who empathize with each other move: the "joint situation." It provides the frame, a larger whole, which encompasses the persons involved and is not only *more* than, but also something *different* from the sum of these persons. Psychologically informed readers will recognize the basic tenet of Gestalt psychology.

BOX 7

GESTALT PSYCHOLOGY defines itself as a holistic psychology (as opposed to elementarist or associationist trends). According to this theory, it is not the sum of the elements of a whole that determines its character, but vice versa. The whole (e.g., a melody) is more than and different from the sum of its parts (the individual notes). For example, one can transpose a melody on to a different scale. All of the elements change, but the character of the whole remains unaltered.

Some leading Gestalt psychologists were Max Wertheimer (1880–1943), Wolfgang Köhler (1887–1967), Kurt Koffka (1886–1941), and Kurt Lewin (1890–1947).

I shall show how the joint situation contains typical features of a dance or game played by the participants. A game depends not only on the individual players *doing* something specific, but also essentially on their allowing themselves to get involved in the game with its rules and inherent dynamic—even being determined by it and becoming *completely absorbed in it*, the more involved they become (see Gadamer, 1989). One would then sometimes be equally justified in saying "The game is playing the players" as "The players are playing a game." The players learn something from each other because they are parts of the same game, and they not only empathize with the other players, but also empathize or "feel (their way) into" the joint situation of the game. Looking at it, this way opens up new ways of understanding empathy and our relationships with each other.

Equipped with the terms and insights resulting from the first three subsections of Chapter 4, I will then summarize the main points of my own understanding of empathy in a further subsection, Chapter 4.4. Here I will propose a definition which draws together the main threads of the material I have gathered in a systematic way.

In Chapter 5, I shall enter somewhat uncertain territory. Here I want to address some issues which, while they lie somewhat on the peripheries of the subject, seem to me to be too important and interesting to neglect. Parapsychology lies "on the periphery" of psychology. I shall address some aspects of this field and also the partially related area of altered states of consciousness such as can be induced by the practice of meditation, for instance. This is an area that has elements which touch on parapsychology.

I became interested in the scientific form of parapsychology at the beginning of my undergraduate course in psychology in Freiburg. At the time, the only professor for this subject was Hans Bender. I attended his lectures and seminars, and he was my examiner in my preliminary degree examinations. I learned from him that phenomena that initially appear incredible and incomprehensible can be investigated on a rational level, using methods that can be considered scientifically valid, and that the theoretical explanations hypothesized for such phenomena can be just as rationally tested (and disproven) as theories about "normal" events (see Bauer & von Lucadou, 1983).

If empathy is understood as I shall propose, it also becomes possible to get a grasp of such phenomena as telepathy or clairvoyance, i.e., events that occur more frequently in the context of altered states of consciousness. I shall show how some of these phenomena can be seen as special cases of empathy and need not necessarily be considered to belong to an area that is peripheral to psychology. I shall also present evidence indicating that certain forms of meditation—in particular the Tibetan Buddhist meditation of compassion (see Avalokiteśvara, above) and Zen meditation— can lead to significant increases in our capacity to empathize.

Finally, in Chapter 6, I shall present a few tentative ideas as to why the experience of empathy is often felt to be so agreeable and healing. My main objective throughout this book is to improve our understanding of the immense therapeutic potential that the human capacity for empathy holds and thus improve our use of it in the practice of psychotherapy. In doing so, I shall draw on concepts developed by the great Russian psychologist Lev Vygotsky which, while he referred to them by such cumbersome terms as "interiorization" and "zone of proximal development," nonetheless fit in well with my considerations.

BOX 8

LEV VYGOTSKY (1896–1934) is seen as the founder of "cultural-historical psychology." When he died at an early age, he left a legacy of over "270 texts whose innovative force made him world-famous as an art, language and developmental psychologist, with ideas that still remain pathbreaking today" (Petzold & Sieper, 2005, p. 489; see also Vygodskaja & Lifanova, 2000). The individual psyche is formed as cultural influences are internalized. To put it another way: Human beings develop only in constant exchanges with other persons. It is a certain form of human contact that makes the next developmental step possible (Keiler, 2002; Koelbl, 2006).

The publication dates of the empirical and theoretical data to which I refer and on which I base my considerations vary, some being less recent than others, and this will be evident from the dates given in the bibliographical references. In order to make this clearer, I have integrated a large number of references in the body of the text and quote numerous authors verbatim. I find it stimulating to tune into their words and get a grasp of the way they think. However, my main object in giving the references and quotations is to give an idea of the theoretical environment in which I move and to show what has influenced my understanding of psychotherapy in general and empathy in particular. I do this out of respect for the achievements of many people who have not only had thoughts, but have made the effort to write them down and share them with others. It is important for me to show my recognition of this, both for them and for myself, since in this way, I feel connected with them and a part of a community of people who have contributed and continue to contribute to better understanding between human beings.

The sources I mention are accessible to anyone. However, I imagine that the content of a number of them will be new for some readers and may therefore arouse their interest. I also hope that the way in which I have put together, structured, and interpreted the individual pieces of information creates a new whole that is worth reading.

To conclude this introduction, I would like to express my thanks and add a note about the layout of this book. My thanks go to all those who have provided me with help as I was writing this book—in the form of support and encouragement, and also suggestions and criticism. I am thinking in particular of Barbara Staemmler, Werner Bock, Doris Köhler, Rolf Merten, and Olaf Axel-Burow and also of many other colleagues at home and abroad[9] who have discussed my ideas in a constructive way at lectures and seminars that I have given.

With regard to the layout, I would like to add a brief explanation about the boxes which appear throughout. They complement the actual text, explain certain terms and concepts, or provide further details about persons to whom I have referred. My aim is not to achieve encyclopedic completeness, but to mention certain aspects of theories and personalities which or who have had a special influence on my own thinking and to explain concepts that may not necessarily be familiar to all readers.

---

9 The participants of the Winter Residential Program run by the Pacific Gestalt Institute (Los Angeles) in the spring of 2005 deserve particular mention as do those who took part in "Gestalt-Begegnung," a conference that took place at the Zentrum für Gestalttherapie in Würzburg in October 2006.

I shall also use a second category of boxes that begins with the word "Example" to illustrate my theoretical considerations with concrete examples.

Now I hope that you will enjoy what you read and find ample food for thought.

2

Retrospective

How Empathy Has Been Understood in Psychotherapy to Date

As a rule, all deliberations on a subject begin with definitions. Reading them can be tedious if one has the impression that the focus is on words alone. However, this is by no means always the case. If a definition is well thought through and expressed in a meaningful way, it will contain references to the theory behind it. Thus, a definition also formulates a theoretical position and leads right into the important issues about the subject itself. This is where it fast becomes particularly interesting. It also applies to the definition of empathy.

BOX 9

EXAMPLES If you look on the internet for definitions of "empathy" you will find numerous entries, two of which I would like to quote here (retrieved July 27, 2010).

(1) "Empathy, which literally translates as *in feeling*, is the capability to share another being's emotions and feelings" (http://en.wikipedia.org/wiki/Empathy—original italics).

(2) "Empathy . . . is (a) the intellectual identification of the thoughts, feelings, or state of another person; (b) the capacity to understand another person's point of view or the result of such understanding" (http://en.wiktionary. org/wiki/empathy).

It is evident that in the first definition, the *emotional* component ("share emotions") comes first. In the second definition, the *cognitive* component ("*understand* another person's *point of view*") has priority. The first definition therefore points toward a theory of empathy in which the emotional components are stressed, and the second definition to a theory in which cognitive processes play a more important role.

Irrespective of their differing focuses, these two definitions have a common element. Both of them describe empathy as consisting of at least two components, namely a "primary emotional reaction . . . , where the insight lies in the quality of the empathic *feeling* itself" (Bischof-Köhler, 2001, p. 321—italics added) and, second cognitive perspective taking. It is "a purely rational mechanism in which one *imagines* oneself in the position of the other person without being emotionally affected" (Bischof-Köhler, p. 321—original italics).

These two components and their relative impacts will continue to be of interest as we go on, since they are important for what I shall call the "*traditional* understanding of empathy." In this chapter, I shall give some examples of statements by well-known psychotherapists to give an idea of how empathy has traditionally been understood *within psychotherapy*. I would like to start with Carl Rogers and Heinz Kohut, who, in particular, made the concept of empathy almost their trademarks.

Rogers adhered to the tradition of "Humanistic Psychology," which at the time was still in its infancy and on which he had a decisive influence. For Rogers, the therapist's empathic relating—along with her congruence and unconditional positive regard—was one of the three "necessary and sufficient conditions" for any therapeutic success to which it is the therapist's task to contribute (Rogers, 1957).[10]

BOX 10

CARL R. ROGERS (1902–1987) founded *client-centered therapy* (Rogers, 1951), also known as "person-centered" or "non-directive" psychotherapy, which he saw as being clearly different from the behaviorist and psychoanalytic approaches. He placed the client-therapist relationship, which he believed should be as equal as possible, in the center of his conceptualization of psychotherapy, which he saw as being more a "developmental project" and less a treatment of mental disorders.

Rogers' approach was based on the client's "tendency to self-actualization" and believed that all that was required was for the therapist to provide suitable conditions for it to become effective. There is then no need to exert any direct influence on the client or to guide her in a certain direction. This "non-directive" attitude is reflected in the name "client-centered therapy."

---

10 In addition to the three above-mentioned attitudes of the therapist, which rank third and fifth in Rogers' listing, he also named three other factors. Number 1 is in a sense trivial: "Two persons are in psychological contact" (1957, p. 96). Number 2 states: "The first, whom we shall term the client, is in a state of incongruence, being vulnerable or anxious" (1957, p. 96). I shall say more about the sixth condition in the next chapter.

Heinz Kohut was a psychoanalyst, an approach with a much longer tradition. With his innovations, the most important of which was the analyst's empathic behavior, he established a new trend within the psychoanalytic movement. His "self psychology" was not only highly successful itself, but also created a basis for many further innovations introduced in the years that followed and led, for instance, to the development of "relational" and "intersubjective" psychoanalysis (see, for example, Orange, 1995; Stolorow, Brandchaft, & Atwood, 1987).

> ### BOX 11
>
> **HEINZ KOHUT (1913–1981)** was the founder of psychoanalytic *self psychology* and is well-known in particular for his work on narcissism (Kohut, 1971). It was his therapeutic experience with the psychodynamics of this constellation of mental characteristics that led him to lay the main emphasis on the therapist's empathy (and the client's "mirror transferences") because he was convinced that a healthy "coherence of the self" could only be achieved in this way.
>
> His concept of the "self" shows that he intended his psychology to go beyond traditional psychoanalytic drive theory and ego psychology and that he wanted to develop them further in a more holistic framework. This was manifested in his clinical psychotherapeutic work, in which he accorded the "phase of understanding" absolute (temporal and systematic) priority over explanatory interpretations.

For Kohut, the ability to meet another person with empathy was not only a "basic human endowment" (1977, p. 144). He also considered empathy to be extremely important from the opposite point of view, i.e., with regard to what it means to a person when another person gives them empathic attention: "The child that is to survive psychologically is born into an empathic-responsive human milieu . . . just as he is born into an atmosphere that contains an optimal amount of oxygen if he is to survive physically" (Kohut, 1977, p. 253). Thus, in his view, parents' failures to be empathic toward their children and the resulting disturbances in the parent-child relationship are one of the main reasons for the subsequent development of mental disorders in adults.

For him, empathy was therefore much more than a mere method which one can use to collect information on the mystery of the other; he also saw it as "a powerful emotional bond between people" (Kohut, 1984, p. 84):

> Empathy is not just a useful way by which we have access to the inner life of man—the idea itself of an inner life of man, and thus of a psychology of complex mental states, is unthinkable without our ability to know via vicarious introspection—my definition of empathy . . . —what

the inner life of man is, what we ourselves and what others think and feel (Kohut, 1977, p. 306).[11]

Carl Rogers' position on empathy was centered less on such thoughts that are almost anthropological in nature and oriented more toward therapeutic practice. His attempts to define empathy were much more detailed than those of Kohut. He continually revised his understanding of empathy right up to the end of his career (e.g., in 1975). However, he worked longest with the following definition, and it is also the one which became the most widely known and accepted and remained so for the longest time.

> The state of empathy, or being empathic, is to perceive the internal frame of reference of another with accuracy, and with the emotional components and meanings which pertain thereto, as if one were the other person, but without ever losing the "as if" condition. Thus, it means to sense the hurt or the pleasure of another as he senses it and to perceive the causes thereof as he perceives them, but without ever losing the recognition that it is *as if* I were hurt or pleased, etc. If this "as if" quality is lost, then the state is one of identification (1959, pp. 210f.—original italics).

According to Rogers, the therapist's task is

> to assume, in so far as he is able, the internal frame of reference of the client, to perceive the world as the client sees it, to perceive the client himself as he is seen by himself, to lay aside all perceptions from the external frame of reference while doing so, and to communicate something of the empathic understanding to the client (1951, p. 29).

In the dialog between Carl Rogers and Martin Buber, Rogers emphasized, as elsewhere, that this must take place "without losing my own personhood or separateness in that" (Buber, 1965, p. 170).

It is striking how strongly Rogers emphasizes his separateness and the as-if quality of empathy and thus endeavors to distance himself from the state of identification. Other client-centered authors also give a similar warning: "If, on the whole, the therapist has the feeling that he

---

11 Kohut had to defend this conviction against the objections of psychoanalytic colleagues who were of a quite different opinion: "I would regret it if psychoanalysis were to accept empathy as its tool . . . because we would then relinquish our place among the sciences altogether" (Shapiro, 1981, p. 429). Others asked anxiously, for example, whether empathy was "regressive or mature" and "Does it not undermine the rule of abstinence?" (Basch, 1983, p. 102).

understands the client completely and 'only too well,' he is no longer able to introduce new aspects and thus to stimulate further development in the client" (Becker & Sachse, 1998, p. 49f). Bohart and Greenberg draw attention to additional dangers:

i.e., Codependency

> To feel the same feelings, in fact, might be dangerous. It could lead to the therapist's emotionally overidentifying with the client. This could lead to counterproductive attempts to "rescue" the client or to a failure to differentiate the client's experience from that of the therapist, with the therapist imposing his or her view of the situation on the client (1997, p. 25).

This emphasis on "separateness" and differentness as experienced by the therapist and client is worth noting and cannot necessarily be taken for granted. There are other conceptualizations of empathy that attach little importance to it. I would like to mention just two examples. Macann, a phenomenological philosopher, defines "'empathy' as a primordial situation in which the self *lives the life of the other as his own*"[12] (1995, p. 98—original italics). Mahrer describes empathy as an "alignment" of the therapist with the client, thus positively making the identification a requirement.

> There is little or no conscious awareness of being you, a therapist, with your own identity and self, and that you are being with a patient who is over there. There is, in other words, a washing away of the self-other distinction . . . It is as if the two of you now occupy the same physical space . . . , and you literally take on the experiencing identity or self that is the other person (1997, p. 200).

However, in Rogers' conceptualization, it is very important that I and Thou remain differentiated, however deep the empathic understanding. What Rogers refers to as the "as if" quality is also included in Kohut's definition of empathy as "vicarious introspection." We will frequently encounter this vicarious "as if" later on, when it will also assume greater significance, since on closer scrutiny, it leads us to ask how it can be possible "to sense the hurt or the pleasure of another as he senses it without losing the as-if stance." It almost seems like a contradiction. Either one feels *exactly* as the other person, or one is aware of one's *own* position, which may then also be associated with other sensations and feelings. In very simple terms, one could say that *either* one is different *or* one is empathic and identifies with the other person.

---

12 Note that Macann does not write merely "*experiences* . . . as his own," but "*lives* . . . as his own"!

This seems to have been the opinion of Frederick Perls, the founder of gestalt therapy. I present his understanding of empathy as a third example (after Kohut and Rogers), not only because I consider myself to be a gestalt therapist—although I differ from Perls on a number of points—but also because at first glance, Perls' viewpoint seems to stand in strong contradiction to those of Kohut and Rogers. However, if we look more closely, we can discern a certain agreement between them. This juxtaposition of contradiction and agreement leads us to an interesting phenomenon which will be important for my ideas on the traditional approach to empathy.

BOX 12

FREDERICK ("FRITZ") S. PERLS (1893–1970), was initially an "orthodox analyst," as he described himself retrospectively, and later founded gestalt therapy together with his wife Lore Perls (née Posner, 1905–1990) and the social critic Paul Goodman (1911–1972) (see Perls, Hefferline, and Goodman, 1951). Like client-centered therapy, gestalt therapy was part of Humanistic Psychology, the "third force" which formed in North America in the 1950s in response to the "duoculture" of behaviorism and psychodynamic therapy (see Quitmann, 1985), and it revolutionized psychotherapy.

The practice of gestalt therapy focuses on interventions that are oriented toward direct experience and experimental and existential procedures (see Fuhr, 1999) on the basis of a dialogical relationship (see Buber, 1958; Staemmler, 1993a).

Perls had a tendency to exaggerate (and not merely with regard to the issue of empathy). In his view, empathy was "a kind of identification with the patient which excludes the therapist himself from the field and thus excludes half the field" (1973, p. 104). In this view, a therapist who is identified with his patient gives up his own perspective and "disappears" from the situation (in Perls' language "from the field").[13] In Perls' view, he no longer appears as an independent protagonist and thus becomes therapeutically ineffective. "If the therapist withholds himself, in empathy, he deprives the field of its main instrument, his intuition and sensitivity to the patient's on-going processes" (Perls, 1973, p. 105).

For Perls, "good contact" between therapist and client was central. By *good* contact, he meant an interaction in which the individuality and independence of the respective persons were as pronounced as possible. "Contact is the appreciation of differences" (Perls, 1969, unpaginated). He felt that this recognition of differences was missing in empathy, which he

---

13 For a discussion of the concept of "field" in gestalt therapy, see Staemmler (2006).

understood to be identification and frequently referred to as "confluence" (we will encounter this term often in what follows). Perls therefore came to the conclusion: "There can be no true contact in empathy. At its worst it becomes confluence" (1973, p. 106).

Joseph Zinker, a leading gestalt therapist of the second generation, has a similar understanding:

"Codependency" w/ client

> The therapist's greatest enemy is that state in which he finds himself deeply identified with his client . . . The psychological boundaries . . . begin to merge. This state is called confluence: the loss of differentiation between two people. The characteristic result is that they can no longer disagree and rub against each other. Creative conflict, or simply good contact, is sacrificed for routine interactions which are flat, static, and safe. (1977, p. 46).

BOX 13

CONFLUENCE is a term used in gestalt therapy. It refers to an indistinct experiencing of differences.

> When the individual feels no boundary at all between himself and his environment, when he feels that he and it are one, he is in *confluence* with it. . . . The person in whom confluence is a pathological state cannot tell what he is, and he cannot tell what other people are. He does not know where he leaves off and others begin. As he is unaware of the boundary between himself and others, he cannot make good contact with them (Perls, 1973, p. 38—original italics).

yes.

Since for Perls empathy was almost *synonymous* with identification and confluence, he came to a much more radical conclusion than Rogers and Kohut, for whom it was sufficient to point out the *dangers* of identification. However, irrespective of this, it can be said that all three were motivated by the *same* concern: They wanted the therapist to maintain her autonomy and separateness from the client. For this reason, Kohut stressed the "vicarious" perspective of the therapist, whom he saw as temporarily carrying out the introspection that is actually the main task of the client and that was originally the client's own responsibility. For the same reason, Rogers emphasized the "as if" nature of empathy, through which *this* the therapist acts as if she could assume the client's perspective. *seems*

Perls evidently felt that this balancing act was too risky. In his view, *rigid* anyone who attempted it was in danger of identifying with the client. He *to* attempted to deal with this risk by categorically rejecting all confluent or *me* empathic attitudes of the therapist, advocating instead "good contact."[14] In order to understand why he preferred this concept to empathy, it is necessary to consider the theory of the dialogical relationship in gestalt therapy, which was influenced by Martin Buber.

As mentioned in the Introduction, Buber spoke of a "twofold principle of human life" or a "twofold movement," which he referred to as the "primal setting at a distance" and "entering into relation," and was of the opinion "that the first movement is the presupposition of the other is plain from the fact that one can enter into relation only with a being which has been set at a distance, more precisely, has become an independent opposite" (Buber 1957, p. 97—see also Box 1). For him, distance was a *prerequisite* for relationship.

It is in this context that Perls' position is to be seen. His conceptualization of relationship was expressed in his idea of "good contact." Like Perls, Buber was not a supporter of the concept of empathy. He preferred to develop his own, new concept to describe his idea of how persons who have become "independent opposites" for each other can "enter into relation" in a personal and committed way. He called this "inclusion."

I would like to add a fourth example, which illustrates Buber's concept of "inclusion." A well-known Buber scholar, Maurice Friedman, summarized Buber's position as follows:

> Buber distinguishes between inclusion and empathy. Empathy literally means to feel into the other. It means you leave your ground and you go over to the other. . . . True confirmation, in contrast, has to be bipolar: it has to be both sides simultaneously. . . . The therapist has to be there and here at the same time. Inclusion is this bold swinging, through an intense stirring of one's whole being, through which one can, to some extent, concretely imagine what the other is thinking, feeling and willing (1990, pp. 22f.).

This example from Buber also reveals what was apparent from the other three examples. All of the cited authors' views on empathy (or inclusion) keep coming back to the question as to *how empathy can be possible* while at the same time *avoiding confluence.* However, they drew different conclusions. Kohut and Rogers were in favor of the concept of empathy and warned about the possibility of confluence, while Perls and Buber were *opposed* to empathy, Perls favoring "good contact" and Buber advo-

---

14 For Perls, there was only "one exception. The empathetic, non-frustrating technique is helpful in the initial phase of treatment of psychosis" (1973, p. 106).

cating "inclusion." This is the interesting phenomenon I referred to above. It is an important starting point for the ideas I shall develop later on.

Whether one calls it "good contact," "inclusion," or "empathy",[15] what is meant is an activity by means of which the therapist attempts to open up the mystery of the other and to make present to herself—on the basis of the verbal and nonverbal communications she receives from the client—the client's subjective experience. In other words, she *imagines* how it is to perceive and experience the world as the client is doing, *without* actually experiencing it that way herself. Mentally, she takes the role (see Mead, 1934/1963) of the client, but retains an awareness of the fact that she is only doing it temporarily and is not identified with this role, but remains an independent person, even as she is seeing herself in the role. I would like to call this the "traditional understanding" of empathy, and I shall keep coming back to it in the following chapters. I have summarized it once again in the following box.

BOX 14

THE TRADITIONAL UNDERSTANDING OF EMPATHY IN PSYCHOTHERAPY Empathy is a mode of attending to the client whereby the therapist strives to capture the client's experiential world as accurately as possible without losing her awareness of the boundary between self and other.

While "attending" in this way requires a certain feeling of goodwill toward or at least interest in the other person, without which one would hardly become empathically involved with him,[16] it is not the same as *liking*. "Liking" includes not only being attentive, but also *affection*. It is a positively emotionally colored attitude which can remain superficial and does not necessarily require an appreciable degree of empathic involvement. When we like another person, we do not necessarily want to discover their mystery, and sometimes our liking even depends on their remaining mysterious. However, if empathic attention is sustained over an extended period of time, liking often also develops—and vice versa. It is often easier to empathize with people whom one likes, for example, friends, than with strangers (Colvin, Vogt, & Ickes, 1997).

---

15 The concept of *"empathy"* found its way into English from translations of German-language literature, into which it had been introduced, probably by Lipps (1913).
16 It is also possible to be interested *without* feeling goodwill, which can also lead to empathic engagement, e.g., when a swindler skillfully exploits his ability to empathize with the situation of his victim with the intention of extracting money from him. However, I think this exception can be disregarded in the context of psychotherapy.

Nor is empathy identical with *compassion*.[17] There are also different

kinds of compassion. Some are focused on a particular person or group who suffers and go together with empathy—that is, imagining vividly the feeling that the other is experiencing. Some are related to a state of benevolence that pervades the mind and is accompanied by a complete readiness to act for the benefit of others without necessarily trying to "feel" the suffering of others (Ricard in Harrington & Zajonc, 2006, p. 167).

Thus, the first kind of compassion develops when one empathizes mainly with a certain aspect of the experiential world of another person, i.e., with the particular aspect with which that person is dissatisfied or which is the source of their suffering, and when one also sincerely wishes that the other's suffering may be relieved. "Compassion is . . . a concerned, heartfelt caring, wanting to do something to relieve the person's suffering" (Goleman, 2003, p. 61; see also Blum, 1980; Eisenberg, 2000). This kind of compassion thus refers to *part* of what can be empathized with. However, it does not stop there, but in a sense takes a *stand*, for example by comforting.

The second kind of compassion is less personal, but at the same time goes further. It does not simply apply to a concrete person whose specific suffering one witnesses and then wishes to relieve. It is more a basic attitude toward *all* sentient beings (i.e., not only human beings, but also animals), which leads one to try to live in a way that has a positive effect on the general conditions of life of these beings, in that it both reduces current suffering and contributes to less suffering occurring in the first place. This is symbolized by Avalokiteśvara.

The goal of empathy is to understand the other person. The goal of compassion is to achieve the well-being of the other (or at least to improve their condition) (Wispé, 1986). Thus, the traditional understanding of empathy and compassion as described above have something in common and also differ. This relationship between the two concepts would, of course, immediately be altered if the understanding of empathy or compassion (or both) were to change. I shall come back to this idea in Chapter 5, when I have developed a new notion of empathy.

---

17 Empathy is also not the same as a problematic variation of compassion, i.e. *pity*, which controls the other's suffering and behaves condescendingly toward him or exploits him for other selfish reasons.

3

A Critique of the Traditional Concept of Empathy

One-sidedness, Disembodiment, and Individualism

The traditional understanding of empathy as I described it in the previous chapter has served me well in my therapeutic work. Rogers' version, especially, with which I became acquainted during my training in client-centered therapy in the 1970s, was of great help to me in assuming a dialogical attitude toward my clients. They often told me how good it was to realize that someone was making an active effort to understand their problems from their own perspective instead of viewing them from outside with a quasi-objective diagnostic eye and seeing them as belonging to some pathological category (see Staemmler, 1993a, 1989).

Assessing another person objectively (and thus also objectifying them) may be of value for other purposes, but it is not useful when it comes to fathoming the mystery of another person's subjective experiencing. In his famous essay with the amusing title "What is it like to be a bat?," Nagel (1974) used the bat as an example to explain that what it is *like* for another person to have a certain experience can never be rendered objectively accessible:

> If the subjective character of experience is fully comprehensible only from one point of view [i.e. from the perspective of the subject in question—F.-M. St.], then any shift to greater objectivity—that is, less attachment to a specific viewpoint—does not take us nearer to the real nature of the phenomenon: it takes us farther away from it (Nagel, 1974, pp. 444f.).

Both Rogers and Kohut consistently put this important and valuable insight into practice, which is why I have such great respect for their historical achievements. However, I also gradually became more and more aware of the limitations of this view of empathy. I am intentionally speaking of "limitations" and not, for example, of "errors," since I still believe that the traditional concept of empathy is accurate and useful *for the sphere that it describes*. I see its deficits more in the fact that it fails to capture many aspects and therefore leaves them out of the picture. These are aspects that should be included in our understanding of empathy because they allow a more comprehensive view of the therapeutic situation. As I describe it in this way, I have an image in my mind of two large circles of different sizes, the smaller of which represents the traditional concept of empathy and is contained inside the larger one, which represents my current view of empathy.

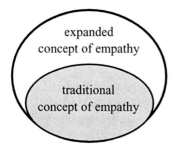

FIGURE 1
Sketch showing the relationship between the traditional and expanded understandings of empathy in psychotherapy

The white area inside the large circle, which is *not* covered by the smaller circle, still remains to be filled with the content of the new understanding of empathy. Both areas together cover what I now believe empathy can be overall. Thus, the old concept can continue to exist, but it needs to be complemented with a new concept. In this chapter, the next step in the development of my ideas is to draw attention to what it is about the traditional understanding of empathy that makes it too narrow. In the following chapters, we can then look at how these deficits can be compensated for.

I am mainly interested in three characteristics.

3.1   ONE-SIDEDNESS

I call the first characteristic "one-sidedness." It has to do with the fact that in the traditional understanding of empathy, clients are seen mainly as objects and hardly at all as subjects. They are objects of empathic activity which apparently comes from the therapist alone. While the clients must supply their therapists with information by talking about their personal experiential worlds and accompany their verbal communications with nonverbal messages, all this information serves the *therapists* as material which enables *them, the therapists,* to empathize with the clients. For example, Bozarth describes empathy explicitly and unreservedly as "an activity of the *therapist*" (1997, p. 87—italics added.)

Commenting on this view of empathy in his book *Demystifying Therapy*, Ernesto Spinelli was quite right to write: "While valid and valuable, this attempt at empathy is also limited in that while it may succeed in 'capturing' the experience in isolation, it fails to grasp it within its relational context to the being . . . who experiences" (1996, p. 339). The clients themselves do not appear as empathic persons in this conceptualization.[18] They are suppliers of information and recipients of therapeutic suggestions and responses, but they themselves are seemingly not people who behave empathically toward their therapists and contribute to the therapeutic process. Thus, the therapists and their experiential worlds seem to remain strangers to the clients, who do not behave in an actively empathic way. Conventionally, empathy has been seen as a one-way street, a view which reflects the tradition of what has been labeled the "one-person psychology," which fails to do justice to the intersubjective character of psychotherapy (and of human beings in general).

BOX 15

INTERSUBJECTIVITY "*Videor, ergo sum!* I am seen, therefore I am." This is the common denominator that Altmeyer (2003, p. 261), both in allusion to and diverging from Descartes, suggests for the concept of intersubjectivity. Both developmentally and in principle, the self is always secondary, the other is always primary. In the words of Martin Buber, "through the *Thou* a man becomes I" (1958, p. 28—original italics). The other is therefore always already contained in the self.

Being a self, or subjectivity, is based on relatedness to the other and always comes into being and develops in relation to her. Conversely, of course, the other, who from her own perspective is also a self, only becomes the self she is in interaction with the other. Self and other only exist reciprocally:

> In your gaze, as that of the second person who speaks to me as a first person, I become aware of myself not only as a conscious subject but also as a unique individual. The subjectifying gaze of others possesses an individuating power (Habermas, 2008, p. 15).

In the traditional understanding of empathy, the therapists empathize with the clients, and the clients are only the "object" of the therapeutic empathy. One might even say that in this conceptualization, the clients

---

18 This is true even of a recent study, although its title ("Empathy as an interpersonal phenomenon"—Hakansson & Montgomery, 2003) led me to expect something different.

are transparent and the therapists remain invisible. The clients' mystery is exposed, while that of the therapists remains untouched.

> This cloaks the assumption that the therapist *does* something to the patient so that the patient is fixed or cured. "Doing to" establishes the patient as the object of the therapist's action rather than as a collaborator in a joint venture. This model of treatment grows out of a one-person psychology, where the patient is the object of study of a detached observer (Buirski & Haglund, 2001, p. 25—original italics).

For me, the unequal nature of this relationship is strongly reminiscent of the situation in the confessional: On the one side, the "poor" sinner who is in the limelight, burdened with problems and required to confess his transgressions as unreservedly as possible, and on the other, the "good" confessor, who is hidden in darkness, only dimly visible to the sinner, and who remains *incognito* as a person. He gets an idea of his "black sheep's" offenses and then gives him instructions as to how to put things right again.

It is doubtlessly no coincidence that such a comparison should occur to me, since psychotherapy is still full of "cryptoreligious ideas" (Petzold & Orth, 1999, p. 238) and relicts of clerical traditions, of which Bert Hellinger's (1998) reactionary ideology and his (hardly empathic) procedures are an extreme example (see Goldner, 2003). However, the image of the confessional is not merely indicative of a link with such traditions and their contemporary offshoots; as a metaphor for the one-sidedness of the traditional understanding of empathy; it is also indicative of an elitist mentality often found among therapists, the precursors of which are to be found not only in the haughtiness of priests, but also no doubt in the arrogance of doctors.

The one-sided concept of empathy may also derive partly from a link between two outdated views, i.e., the idea of the child as a *passive* recipient of maternal and paternal care and the orthodox psychoanalytic model of the therapeutic relationship as a purely (or at least mainly) *transferential* relationship in which early patterns of parent-child interaction are repeated. These two notions together then conjure up the image of a more or less passive client to whom the transference figure of the therapist attends empathically—an image which can, incidentally, easily be squared with the traditions of medical treatment or pastoral care.

The assumption that infants or toddlers are passive, to start with, "does not concur with the facts as we know them today, thanks to a flood of new research results" (Downing, 1996, p. 143; see also Dornes, 1993, for example). The idea of transferential dynamics, in which early childhood patterns are, as it were, transferred to the therapeutic relationship on a

[handwritten marginal note: Wahoo! Bent noted! ·]

one-to-one basis, is also inconsistent with all more recent insights (see, for example, Fosshage, 1994; Lachmann & Beebe, 1998). The current view is that there are at least "four vectors of experience, . . . both the patient's experience of being influenced by the analyst as well as influencing the analyst, *and* reciprocally the analyst's experience of being influenced by the patient as well as influencing the patient" (Beebe & Lachmann, 2002, p. 211 — original italics).

I do not consider it justifiable to ascribe empathic behavior to the therapist alone. In my experience, the same potential for empathy is to be found among clients as among therapists. How should it be otherwise, if Kohut's assertion (above) that it is "as basic an endowment of man as his vision, hearing, touch, taste, and smell" (1977, p. 144) is correct? There are, of course, clients whose problems include finding it difficult to put themselves in other people's shoes. However, there are just as many clients who empathize to excess. They try to attune to their therapists to such an extent that they hardly like to confront them with their problems, but act as if they were "easy-care" so as not to overburden the therapist. They manage, often amazingly accurately, to sense where the therapist's sensitive points are and where his limits are, and then they take care to go easy on him.

narciss [handwritten margin note]

BOX 16

EXAMPLE Louis J. Cozolino reports on a depressed patient, a mother of two children. She worked part-time, and her unemployed husband made no effort to find a job nor did he help in the house, while she worked herself to death to support the family.

During our first few sessions, I noticed that Suzanne would always ask me questions about how I was feeling. She seemed very sensitive to my facial expressions, movements, and gestures. A couple of times she asked me if I was eating right and getting enough rest. She then began bringing me coffee and a muffin because she thought I was not eating enough. One day, when I had to change the time of an appointment, she responded very quickly by saying that we could skip the session if I was too busy or tired to see her that week. It became clear that despite the fact that she paid me to take care of her, she, in fact, had made it her job to be *my* caretaker. She had added me to her list of responsibilities (2006, p. 205—original italics).

I would like to go even further and claim that one of the requirements for the success of psychotherapy is that the client be empathic enough to be able to make use of what the therapist has to offer. It was to this prerequisite that Rogers presumably was referring when he formulated the sixth of his "necessary and sufficient conditions of therapeutic personality change": "The communication to the client of the therapist's empathic understanding and unconditional positive regard is to a minimal degree achieved" (1957, p. 96). The client must experience the therapist's empathy as such if it is to develop its effect, and the client can only do so with the aid of his own empathic activity, i.e., if he is not only the object, but also the subject of the empathy.

Occasionally, although remarkably rarely, some authors have noted the one-sidedness of the traditional understanding of empathy. Thus, Petzold, for example, speaks of "reciprocal empathy" and demands that the analyst be "prepared to encounter the patient 'in a natural way' (Heimann, 1978); he must be willing to allow empathic reactions in the patient, as empathic analysts do (see Greenson, 1966, pp. 282ff.); more than that, he must make such reactions possible and support them" (1986, p. 329). Such demands are only to be welcomed, even if they do not, in my view, go far enough. They remain bound to the assumption of one-sidedness in that they are seen as something that the analyst must "allow" and "make possible" — as if the patient did not bring his empathic abilities with him to his analysis from the start. In my view, it is much more a case of acknowledging and valuing the patient's existing skills, especially as these are resources that contribute to the quality of the therapeutic relationship and thus to the success of the therapy.

As mentioned above, without the client's empathy, the therapist's empathy cannot take effect. But this is not all. Many of the general basic conditions of therapy, suggestions, interpretations, and experiments would remain incomprehensible and ineffective if Rogers' sixth condition were not fulfilled. The client on the couch, for example, must be able to discover, at least roughly, what is going on inside the analyst who is invisible to her, in order to be able to arrive at a meaningful understanding of his interpretations in the given context. The client of a gestalt therapist must be able to sense what the therapist means when he suggests that the client talk to an empty chair (see Staemmler, 1995). It is often necessary for client and therapist to adjust to each other with respect to situative or more basic matters that require both of them to place themselves in the position of the other.

BOX 17

EXAMPLE The following brief verbal exchange from a therapy session that Carl Rogers conducted with a client called Jan illustrates how each participant adjusts to the other.

CARL: You can take all the time you want, because I feel I'm getting acquainted with that frightened little Jan that is inside.

JAN: So the more I talk, the more I'm helping you to get through to me, is that right? (Rogers, 1951, p. 249)

*he expresses
empathy*

she expresses empathy

3.2   DISEMBODIMENT

The second dimension of what I believe is missing from the traditional understanding of empathy has to do with the embodied nature of those involved. In order to make clear what I mean, I would like to mention a debate that has been carried on between philosophers and psychologists for some time, sometimes with considerable vehemence, about what is referred to as the *"theory of mind."*[19] It asks how it is possible at all to come to know something about the mystery of the other and exactly how people actually gain access to the mental experiencing of other people.[20] As so often occurs in such debates, there are two opposing camps (and a few more moderate, mediating positions in between the two extremes).[21]

One camp supports the *simulation theory*, according to which people gain access to others by producing mental states in themselves which are similar to those with which they are empathizing. Edgar Allen Poe evidently made use of this strategy. He wrote

When I wish to find out how wise, or how stupid, or how good, or how wicked is any one, or what are his thoughts at the moment, I fashion the expression of my face, as accurately as possible, in accordance with the expression of his, and then wait to see what thoughts or sentiments arise in my mind or heart, as if to match or correspond with the expression (1902, p. 41).

In the psychological literature, one also occasionally finds conceptions of empathy which are evidently decisively influenced by the

---

19 Confusingly, in the context of research on empathy, this term is also used in a different sense, i.e., as the capacity to "mentalize" (see below), i.e., to ascribe mental states such as wishes, convictions, and intentions to other people. All this, in turn, has nothing to do with the term *philosophy of mind*, which refers to general philosophical considerations about the characteristics and functions of the human mind.

20 For overviews of these debates, see, for example, Carruthers and Smith (1996), Davies and Stone (1995), Lenzen (2005), Moore (1996), and Whiten (1991).

21 Other approaches are, for example, the "interaction theory" (Gallagher, 2005, p. 206ff.) and the "modularity theory" (Segal, 1996).

simulation theory. Thus, Eisenberg, Valiente, and Champion define empathy as

> an affective response that stems from the apprehension or comprehension of another's emotional state or condition, and which is similar to what the other person is feeling or would be expected to feel. Thus, if someone views a sad person and consequently feels sad, that person is experiencing empathy (2004, p. 387).[22]

Similarly, de Vignemont and Singer lay down four conditions that they believe must be fulfilled if we are to speak of empathy:

> (i) one is in an affective state; (ii) this state is isomorphic to another person's affective state; (iii) this state is elicited by the observation or imagination of another person's affective state; (iv) one knows that the other person is the source of one's own affective state (2006, p. 435).

The other camp supports what is amusingly referred to as the *theory theory*. According to this theory, people gain access to the experience of others by developing a folk psychology (*quasi*-scientific) theory that enables them to develop plausible assumptions as to the subjective experience of other persons in connection with certain observations.

BOX 18

THEORY THEORY AND SIMULATION THEORY are two different theories about how people develop an idea of what is going on in other people's minds.

The main difference between theory theory and simulation theory is that according to the simulation theory, a folk psychologist experiences *similar mental states* to those of the person to be understood, whereas according to the theory theory, the mental states that a folk psychologist experiences are the object of those of the person to be understood, i.e., s/he thinks about them (Lenzen, 2005, p. 88—italics added).

To begin with, the theory theory and the simulation theory are opposing *theories*, each of which has a number of arguments in support of itself and also a number of arguments against the other. However, I do

---

22 Evidently, empirical researchers such as Eisenberg et al. can more easily afford to allow their views of empathy to come close to identification and confluence than psychotherapists. Their personal distance is guaranteed by the research design.

not believe that it is useful to ask which of these theories is correct and which is not. In my experience, people do *both*—they simulate, *and* they develop theories. There is substantial plausible evidence in support of this (e.g., Perner, 1996)—and there are suitable situations for each method of empathizing.

> It is often considered that the recognition of the emotional state of others is a sort of direct, automatic process that does not require psychological inference and metarepresentation. Although this may be true for the recognition of basic emotions, more complex ones, such self-conscious[23] emotions, are likely to require cognitive processing (Decety & Jackson, 2004, p. 74).

I would therefore prefer to say that they are two different *modes* of bringing to mind. *Both* are valuable in their own right, and in encounters between adults, the two are often used together.

> Mature adult empathy is a two-step process. The first step involves an emotional resonance that is immediate, holistic, and nonverbal. This emotional resonance probably involves unconscious coordinations at a presymbolic sensorimotor level.[24] The second step consists in the assignment of meaning to the resonance via complex cognitive affective and conceptual structures. This step presupposes verbal capacity (Sucharov, 1998, p. 278).

Of course, the relative contributions of these two steps (or, as I prefer to say, these two modes) vary from one situation to another, and sometimes the best one can do is to switch back and forth between the two. Thus, while as a rule, the first is a prerequisite for the second, the theoretical mode can be useful when the simulation mode does not work for some reason. It does not replace it, but it may make it possible to gain access to the other person temporarily, which is better than none at all and may, in the next step, bridge the gap to the simulation mode, thus restoring direct access.

If in later chapters I lay more emphasis on simulation, it is because, from a developmental and chronological point of view, it is *primary* (Trevarthen, 1993, p. 122) and because it is nonetheless accorded too little attention in the traditional understanding of empathy and has been

---

23 Shame, for instance, is considered to be one of the "self-conscious emotions."
24 It will become clear what is meant by this in Chapter 4.2.

pushed into the background by an increased emphasis on cognitive understanding processes (see Figure 1).[25]

> Many of the more standard cognitive approaches give us an incomplete and potentially misleading picture. It is a powerful and useful picture but it has not yet incorporated what one might call the affective theory of mind—a theory of mind that is more spontaneous—based on the primary process affective dance between infant and caretaker with direct interchange of feelings, so evident in play (Panksepp in Gallagher, 2008, p. 118),

and evident also in many spontaneous interactions between adults. The simulation mode is usually activated spontaneously. It takes place mostly when one is *in direct contact*, as one *participates* in an encounter. Developmentally speaking, it is also the older mode, already being present from birth onward. For this and other reasons, Hobson argues that

> in order to have and apply a theory, an individual must know what it is to theorize, and for this he or she must *already* have a concept of his or her own theory-holding mind. In order to avoid an infinite regress, therefore, we should have to acknowledge that a person needs to begin by acquiring a concept of mind on some 'non-theoretical' basis (1991, p. 36—original italics).

Not until the second half of the second year of life does a child gradually become aware that other people have mental states such as convictions, wishes, feelings, and intentions. Some authors call this development "mentalizing"—in my view somewhat ineptly.

> The ability to mentalize, which can be seen as the central mechanism of "social *(or mental) reality testing*," is therefore a developmental achievement that unfolds through the gradual sensitization to and learning about the mental significance of relevant expressive, behavioral, verbal, and situational cues that indicate the presence of mind states in persons (Fonagy, Gergely, Jurist, & Target, 2002, pp. 347f.—original italics).

Only when this developmental step takes place do children gradually acquire the capacity to develop a theory about other people since it is now that children realize that other people have a mind (which is sometimes called

---

25 This is also confirmed by Decety and Jackson, who write, "The perception of a given behavior in another individual automatically activates one's own representations of that behavior. . . . These processes are functionally intertwined—that is, perception is a means to action, and action is a means to perception, and they operate right after birth" (2004, p. 75).

theory of mind abbreviated as "ToM," see also footnote 19). Following the primary capacity to simulate, a second skill, i.e., that of "mentalizing," has now developed. The fact that, from now on, the two can actually exist side-by-side and complement each other is due precisely to the difference between them.

> The capacity to understand other people's emotions by *sharing* their affective states is fundamentally different in nature from the capacity to *mentalize*. Thus, sharing the grief of a close friend feels fundamentally different than understanding what this person is having as thoughts and intentions, the latter lacking a bodily sensation (Singer, 2006a, p. 856—italics added).[26]

Singer calls the latter "ToM." It is the empirical reference point for the theory theory. The first she calls "empathy." It provides the empirical justification for the simulation theory. The former mode can also be activated in direct contact. If it is the *predominant* mode used, however, it means that one is, partially at least, distancing oneself from the other person[27]—that is, if on the experiencing level one does not participate fully, but rather thinks *about* the other person from the position of an observer (as one can and usually does *in retrospect*, for example, when one remembers an encounter and thinks about what the other person might have been experiencing). Here Frith and Frith (2003) speak of "decoupling," in the sense that what one recalls by this means may not necessarily have anything to do with the *current* reality or with reality at all. By decoupling, we can also play out purely *speculative* versions of the other person's possible experience in our imagination.

If the simulation mode is to be reactivated in other situations *later* on, e.g., during supervision, certain aids such as role plays are required to reactivate the original situation as far as is possible (see under "process activation," below). In this way, we can attempt to simulate the other person and, like an actor, imagine ourselves in his "role" so vividly that we actually experience feelings which are (presumably) similar to his. In contrast, in the theory-building mode, we would attempt to develop a hypothesis about what the other person may have experienced on the basis of our knowledge of human nature and mental life and also of what we have perceived externally in the other person and can still remember.

---

26 In the same article, Singer refers to the respective neuronal structures involved: "ToM . . . relies on structures of the temporal lobe and the pre-frontal cortex. In contrast, empathy . . . relies on sensorimotor cortices as well as limbic and para-limbic structures" (2006a, p. 855).
27 The above-mentioned "antisocial personality disorder" is an extreme form of this distancing. According to a theory put forward by Mealy (1995), the inability of people labeled as "sociopaths" to participate in the experience of other people and their corresponding ability to exploit other people's situations scrupulously for their own purposes have to do with the fact that, on the one hand, their ability to simulate is impaired, while on the other, their capacity to develop a theory has remained intact.

The core difference between theory theory and simulation theory, in our view, is that theory theory depicts mind reading[28] as a thoroughly "detached" theoretical activity, whereas simulation theory depicts mind reading as incorporating an attempt to replicate, mimic, or impersonate the mental life of the target agent (Gallese & Goldman, 1998, p. 497).

Lenzen (2005, p. 87) therefore calls simulation the "hot method" because a person who uses it does not remain "out in the cold" like someone who employs the "cold method" of developing a theory about the other person.[29] In contrast, anyone who simulates the mental processes of other people in himself is personally affected and emotionally involved. He *feels* something and does not simply think.

BOX 19

EXAMPLE

It was my first session with a new analyst. I was in the process of interviewing analysts to find one with whom to work. I was already in tears, describing the recent death of one who was very dear to me. I felt shattered, lost, and was struggling to regain my footing in the difficult aftermath of this person's death. At one moment, the analyst sighed and said with great feeling, "What a nightmare!" I was surprised and warmed by the vehemence of his remark. The affective tone was certainly attuned to my story and my state of mind. But more, he seemed to be expressing a spontaneous reaction of the impact of my story upon him. His remark did not seem to be aimed solely at communicating to me what he thought was my state of mind. Rather, he seemed to be balanced between being attuned to my state of mind and expressing *his* state of mind as he was affected by being immersed in empathic listening (Jacobs, 1998, pp. 197f.—original italics).

Some authors therefore refer to the "cold" form of empathy as the "cognitive" or "hermeneutic" form, and to the "hot" form of empathy as "affective" or "experiential." The former

> can be understood as a mental, thinking act, in which one person attempts to imagine how it is to perceive and experience the world as another person. . . . By contrast, "affective empathy" involves "responding with the same emotion to another person's emotion" (Gladstein, 1983,

---

28 The term "mind reading" can easily be misunderstood. Whiten thus considered it necessary to begin the preface to his book with a warning: "This book is not about telepathy! It is about the kind of everyday mindreading which we take for granted, which we use throughout our daily lives, explaining and predicting others' behavior by reference to their inner mental states: their desires, expectations and a host of other psychological concepts" (1991, p. v).
29 Mahrer, Boulet, and Fairweather refer to this mode of gaining access to other people as the "external model of empathy" (1994, p. 184).

p. 468). That is, rather than *seeing* the world as another person does, affective empathy involves *feeling* the same way as another person does (Cooper, 2001, p. 219—original italics).

In some situations, this kind of emotional identification (or confluence) can, of course, be experienced as stressful.[30] If we empathize with unpleasant or even painful experiences of another person, we need not only a willingness to identify emotionally, but also a well-developed capacity to regulate our emotions.

If we now compare these two theories with the traditional understanding of empathy, which bends over backward to avoid identifying with the other person and attempts rather to maintain the differentiation between I and Thou whatever happens, we get the impression that this view of empathy is more similar to the theory theory (or to cognitive empathy) than to the simulation theory (or affective empathy), despite the fact that Rogers' term "as if" is somewhat reminiscent of simulation. However, he was more concerned with *mental* simulation. The "as if" was intended to create *distance*, to avoid confluence and identification and thus to prevent it becoming "hot" for the therapist. The therapist was supposed to be attentive and show positive regard, but not to be personally affected or emotionally involved, and rather to remain in the theory-building mode.

Although the researcher Barbara T. Brodley found, to her surprise, in her thorough analysis of Rogers' style of intervention, that only 24% of his therapeutic responses referred to his clients' feelings (Brodley, 1991; Brodley & Brody, 1990), to be fair, one must add that Rogers' proximity to the theory theory was not particularly pronounced. Moreover, the older he became, the more he moved away from it (see Neville, 1995; I will come back to Rogers' later views further on). The classical psychoanalytic model, which follows Freud's metaphor of the surgeon and supplies the patient with interpretations from a distance is probably the form of therapeutic practice that comes closest to a consistently applied theory theory:

> I cannot advise my colleagues too urgently to model themselves during psychoanalytic treatment on the surgeon, who puts aside all his feelings, even his human sympathy, and concentrates his mental forces on the single aim of performing the operations as skillfully as possible. . . . The justification for requiring this emotional coldness is that it creates the most advantageous conditions for both parties: for the doctor a desirable protection for his own emotional life and for the patient the

---

30 If the actual or expected degree of stress is too high, the motivation to protect oneself can be activated and lead to the phenomenon of "empathy avoidance" (Batson, Ahmad, & Stocks, 2004, pp. 373ff.—see Box 58).

largest amount of help that we can give him today (Freud 1912/1958, p. 115).[31]

Although it was evidently Freud's intention to provide "for the patient the largest amount of help" (I will refrain from commenting on the second motive, the "desirable protection" of the analyst's feelings), this practice has since proved to be a "deprivation experiment" (Moser, 1979, p. 71) with few positive effects and more negative ones. Moser's term "deprivation experiment" not only draws attention to the social and emotional vacuum of the classical psychoanalytic setting with its many risks and side effects, but also to the associated *sensory* deprivation. The analysand can only hear the analyst, who is sitting behind the top of the couch. The analyst can see the analysand, but only from an angle that severely restricts her view of the analysand's face. Thus, the empathic process in this situation is doubly burdened. First, both participants miss out on important impressions of each other's facial expressions; I will say more about their special importance further on. Second, the richness of the sensory impressions is diminished, although it could, precisely in its holistic entirety, contribute something important to the empathic understanding, since

> within certain limits, we can see the soul or capture it with our other senses. . . . We perceive many attitudes, moods, and sensations. We see that someone is waiting impatiently, that he is annoyed, that he is in pain. We frequently perceive that someone is annoyed or excited just as easily and well as we perceive what he is doing (Scholz, 1999, p. 92).

My criticism of the original psychoanalytic setting brings me to speak of another form of empathic access to other people besides the simulation theory and theory theory, a form which is not particularly mysterious, which may be why it is sometimes forgotten. I am referring to immediate perception that allows us to infer much about the other person directly, as phenomenology has demonstrated in great detail. "Thus, by his walk, posture, and his every movement, we also 'see' 'how he feels,' his vigor, sluggishness, etc." (Stein, 1917/1964, p. 64). To this, also, I shall return later on.

With regard to the classical psychoanalytic setting, I would like to add that it is well known that it is now no longer often practiced.[32] Modern

---

31 Freud, who was committed to the cause of rendering the unconscious conscious, evidently overlooked the fact that his metaphor of the surgeon had implications that were quite the opposite of what he was trying to achieve, i.e., it requires that the patient be rendered unconscious by an anesthetic.
32 As well as a few psychoanalysts who have remained true to the orthodox tradition, the exceptions also include, for example, an "experiential" psychotherapist: "To help me see

psychoanalysts even see Freud's distanced attitude (which he regarded as serving an objectivity that has since been recognized as an unattainable goal) as realizing the "myth of the isolated mind" à la Descartes, which they criticize for being "a form of defensive grandiosity" (Stolorow et al., 1997, p. 439). It was intended as a defense against the vulnerability associated with the social interdependence of human beings. At all events, in the context of my considerations about empathy, Freud's comparison of the work of the analyst with that of the surgeon makes it obvious that in extreme cases, the therapist who adheres to the traditional understanding of empathy reduces himself to practicing a purely intellectual activity through which he reconstructs the mystery of the client in his own mind, from the latter's verbal and (tell-tale) nonverbal utterances.

> A man's states of mind are manifested, almost without exception, in the tensions and relaxations of his facial muscles, in the adaptations of his eyes, in the amount of blood in the vessels of his skin, in the modifications in his vocal apparatus and in the movements of his limbs and in particular of his hands. The concomitant physical changes are for the most part of no advantage to the person concerned; on the contrary, they often stand in his way if he wishes to conceal his mental processes from other people. But they serve these other people as trustworthy indications from which his mental processes can be inferred and in which more confidence can be placed than in any simultaneous verbal expressions that may be made deliberately (Freud, 1905/1975, p. 286).

As a phenomenon, this attitude is not only associated with the psychoanalytic tradition, but can also be found in other schools of therapy to this very day. Therapeutic understanding is seen, for example (note the wording), "as complex information processing, as a *process in which the therapist creates mental models about his clients*" (Becker & Sachse, 1998, p. 13—italics added). In my view, this creation of *mental* models *about* the client is much closer to Freud's metaphor of the surgeon than to a live human encounter. "There is a real danger that one's cognitive and imaginative capacities will become so sophisticated that one has ceased sharing the experiences of real people" (Kohn, 1990, p. 119).

If a therapist creates models that are mainly *in his mind*, this can be seen as resulting from a Cartesian *cogito*, that is separated as far as possible from all corporeality relating to the other person, i.e., the client, who

---

what is out there, and to feel and experience what the person is feeling or experiencing, and to minimize all the interferences and problems of two people looking directly at each other, I close my eyes throughout the whole session. I also invite the person to do the same" (Mahrer, 1997, p. 200).

is considered to have simply a *body* that is at most the transmitter of non-verbal signals and not a *lived body*, which is the foundation and medium[33] of his entire existence. However,

> in this way, the body expresses *total* existence, not because it is an external accompaniment to that existence, but because existence realizes itself in the body. This incarnate significance is the central phenomenon of which body and mind, sign, and significance are abstract moments (Merleau-Ponty, 1962, p. 166—italics added).

However, in a mentalistic understanding of empathy, when the client's emotions, which she can feel in her body, enter into the therapist's mental models, they assume the nature of boxes in diagrams which are associated with other elements of his mental model in a more or less mechanical way. Here, the client's vital emotions and moods that are rooted in her lived body are not present in her facial expressions, in her gestures, in her habitus, in her gaze, or in her "bodily stirrings" (Schmitz, 1985, pp. 79f.) as significant sensations and movements that make an impression on the therapist and *touch* him (in both the literal and figurative senses of the word). In this view, they are seen more as irrational cognitions which enter into the therapist's mental model as variables. It is not two humans, made of flesh and blood, who encounter each other, but one *res cogitans* representing the other *res cogitans*. The therapist's cognitive act represents that of the client. As a result of the dualistic thinking, the bodies of the participants remain in the status of a mechanical *res extensa*; they are only granted a subordinate role, if any at all.

> According to this [mentalistic] supposition, this is a problem of access because other minds are hidden away, closed in, behind the overt behavior that we can see. This seems to be a Cartesian supposition about the very nature of what we call "the mind." The mind is conceived as an inner realm, in contrast to behavior, which is external and observable, and which borrows its intentionality from the mental states that control it (Gallagher, 2005, p. 209).[34]

---

33 "The lived body is of the nature of a *medium*. In contrast to an instrument, a medium is both the means and the conveying itself. As a medium, my body cannot be separated from me like a pair of binoculars that I am looking through, but I myself am also the *medium*" (Fuchs, 2000, p. 71—original italics).

34 In his book *The Concept of Mind*, Ryle analyzed the "category-mistake" behind this assumption. "The traditional theory of the mind has misconstrued the type-distinction between disposition and exercise into its mythical bifurcation of unwitnessable mental causes and their witnessable physical effects" (1949/2002, p. 33).

Thus, the impulses of the *res extensa* also cannot be seen as independent carriers of meaning, since meaning and significance are ascribed exclusively to the domains of the *res cogitans*. This unfortunately leaves no room for a concept that could overcome mind-body dualism, such as Gendlin's inspired concept of "felt sense." However, it is so useful that I would like to describe it briefly.

BOX 20

FELT SENSE

Your bodily feeling state (Befindlichkeit) in the moment, the bodily mood that you can feel when you bring your attention to the center of your body . . . A felt sense forms out of the body's experiencing in a situation . . . A felt sense of anything and anyone that you are currently paying attention to can form within you as a bodily resonance, as it were. Thus, felt sense is the subjective, bodily feeling of the situation. Felt sense is implicit (felt, but not yet known) experience (Gendlin, 1994, p. 33).

In the felt sense, the mind and the body are integrated (see Chapter 4.3)—that is, they are embedded in a *situation* and thus directly related to the world. Felt sense is thus a concept that is compatible with the phenomenological concept of embodiment.[35]

BOX 21

EMBODIMENT

When I see the Other, I see his body and grasp him in an understanding way as a human being . . . The body is grasped not only as a body . . ., but also as a lived body, and the lived body also includes a psychical dimension (Husserl, 1973, p. 341).

---

35 Damasio's "somatic markers" (see above) are presumably also connected with the felt sense. In my opinion, this is indicated by the results of a study by Bar-On, Tranel, Denburg, and Bechara (2003) according to which people whose neuronal circuits for somatic markers are impaired have a significantly lower emotional and social intelligence than unimpaired persons, although no meaningful differences in cognitive intelligence (as measured by IQ tests) or psychopathological symptoms (according to DSM-IV criteria) were found.

The body of a human being is not simply a physical mass that she possesses, but the "vehicle of being in the world," as Merleau-Ponty (1962, p. 82) put it. That is, human beings are intentionally directed toward an experienced world. They experience the world through their bodies—through its senses and proprioception, through its gestures and movements, and through the individual perspectives that are defined by their bodies, etc.

The "lived body" is a phenomenological term that refers to the living body as it is experienced. The concept of the lived body serves to overcome Cartesian dualism (see Leder, 1998; see also Box 4 on Descartes and Box 6 on phenomenology).[36]

The traditional understanding of empathy is contaminated with the Cartesian legacy. The neglect of human embodiment is inherent in it, to varying degrees and in different ways, depending on the author. However, if the bodily dimension is not included, empathy remains anemic and has an unworldly quality, "because my existence as subjectivity is merely one with my existence as a body and with the existence of the world, and because the subject that I am, when taken concretely, is inseparable from this body and this world" (Merleau-Ponty, 1962, p. 408). A purely mentalistic conception of empathy fails to live up to the requirements of a modern psychotherapy that strives to understand human beings holistically and to enter into contact with them in a holistic "dialogue" that is *not* merely verbal (see Staemmler, 2003a).

The therapeutic dialog must not be allowed to degenerate into an exchange of words between "talking dummies" (Moser, 1987), since it derives its efficacy in part from processual activation (see Grawe, 2002; Staemmler, 1999a), i.e., from the activation of the behaviors and modes of experiencing that are to be changed: "In a comprehensive meta-analysis by Orlinsky, Grawe, and Parks (1994) on all process-outcome connections being found so far in empirical research, 'experiential confrontation' turned out to be one of the most efficient therapeutic interventions of all" (Grawe, 2002, p. 106). Experiential confrontation refers to a central therapeutic strategy used to draw the client's attention to nonverbal processes in the current therapeutic situation, for example, to his tone of voice, pattern of breathing, or posture. He may not initially be aware of these but can, in principle, become so if he directs his attention toward them. This gentle "confrontation" is intended to activate a psychic process. The rationale for using it is

---

36 "Thus, dualism arises from a double disembodiment. On the one hand, the lived body is externalized into a body that becomes lost in a world of things, and on the other, the embodied ego is raised up to become a pure ego that withdraws from the situation" (Waldenfels, 2000, p. 264).

that only what is happening processually can be changed. . . . Change manifests itself in the current experience and behavior. Talking about experiencing and behavior without either of these processes actually going on can be useful for preparing the ground for change, but the change itself materializes in the moment of the actual experiencing. . . . In experimental outcome research, all those procedures which explicitly promote the immediate experiencing in the treatment of the problems did particularly well (Grawe, 2002, p. 75).

Grawe emphasizes that, a "somewhat paradoxical conclusion arises from this: The therapist has to activate what he wants to eliminate in order to change it" (Grawe, 2002, p. 196). In gestalt therapy terms, it is a question of the "here and now" (see Staemmler, 2002a), of orienting the process toward immediate experience. The therapeutic situation is given the character of a "safe emergency" (Perls et al., 1951, p. 286) in which, on the one hand, the problem of the client that is being focused on is activated as a process so that it can be worked on effectively, and on the other, a protective setting and the therapist's friendly support ensure that instead of simply repeating the old patterns, a new way of dealing with the old distress that has been re-activated is opened up[37] (see Box 2 on Beisser's "paradoxical theory of change" and Box 12 on Frederick Perls).

It is not enough for the therapist and client simply to *talk* together *about* a problem of the client; the problem that needs working on must be "actualized," i.e., it must be rendered *directly experienceable* for the client as if it were actually happening in the present, using suitable therapeutic techniques such as "experiments" (see Staemmler, 1999b). "Conversations about psychological processes or problems that remain mere contents and are not transformed into processual events produce no changes" (Grawe, 2002, p. 103).

However, this is not the only disadvantage if there is no processual activation. I think another aspect is almost more important when we are considering empathy and, that is, that if the client only verbalizes the issue that is problematic for her, and it is not actualized, the therapist too will usually fail to experience the clear *bodily* resonance that the problem can trigger in situations in which the client experiences it directly. For most therapists (and most other people too), it makes a real difference whether the client or other person only *says*, for example, that she is sad or whether she also *weeps* as

---

37 The intensity of the experiencing should preferably remain within a *medium* range. If the intensity is too low (too much safety, too little "emergency"), the level of activation will be too low, and therefore, the threshold for new learning will not be reached. Too high an intensity (too little safety, too much "emergency") easily leads to emotional flooding and regressive processes, during which the client becomes unable to access necessary resources (see Staemmler, 1997a).

she does so. One could almost say that the processual activation in the client stimulates the empathic activation of the therapist. In contrast, if the client simply verbally communicates and fails to experience the required reactivation, this tends rather to invite the therapist to simply think about her.

The therapist's reactions will differ correspondingly. A client who talks about his sadness will tend to elicit a verbal response from the therapist,[38] while a client who cries may also stimulate the therapist to put his arm around him, and this is—notwithstanding some prudish demands for the therapist to remain "abstinent" (see Bauriedl, 1998)—sometimes both a human and a therapeutic exigency. Moser has shown quite clearly "that exclusively verbal understanding, even in the form of non-interpretative empathy, can also be traumatizing if the patient is refused concrete bodily support in certain phases" (Moser, 1989, p. 109).[39]

Both client and therapist must be able to sense each other as lived bodies and be mutually accessible in an unmediated way. Direct touch, as Moser describes, is only one of many levels—and not even the most important (see Staemmler, 1981, 1998, 2003b). "Only an encounter between incarnated beings whose worlds interpenetrate each other can be seen as successful communication" (Fuchs, 2000, p. 24). If both the client's and the therapist's embodiment are taken into account and integrated in a way that is commensurate with the therapeutic endeavor and consistent with professional ethics, this can enable both participants to overcome the isolation that imprisons them if they relate to each other exclusively through the medium of "verbalizing" (see Perls et al., 1951, pp. 320ff.).

3.3   INDIVIDUALISM

The word "isolation" is a stepping stone to the third dimension that I believe to be problematic in the traditional concept of empathy. I call this

---

38 Or he may even get tired and be in danger of falling asleep. Unfortunately, Zwiebel does not discuss in his book on the *Der Schlaf des Analytikers* (*The Sleep of the Analyst*, 1992) whether this form of "countertransference," as he calls it, might have something to do with a lack of processual activation, although he does, like Winnicott, consider it important to contribute to the analyst's liveliness (Zwiebel, 1992, p. 145). I think this gap in Zwiebel's analysis is a good illustration of the fact "that the term [countertransference] itself obscures more than it clarifies, and that we should stop using it" (Bacal, 1998b, p. 163; see also Staemmler, 1993a, pp. 158ff.).

39 Warnings against harmful forms of physical contact in therapy, for example, those that violate boundaries, are widespread, whereas the fact that *refusing* physical contact can have a negative effect is hardly ever discussed. "As sparse as the literature is about the positive and negative effects of touch in the therapeutic relationship, it is not surprising that almost nothing has been written on the effects of the *lack* of touch during psychotherapy. Yet it is clear that the absence or withholding of touch can have intense meaning" (Hunter & Struve, 1998, p. 102—original italics).

dimension "individualism." Individualism is a corollary of philosophical and political developments in history. Philosophically, the starting point was the Enlightenment, while politically, it was the French Revolution.[40]

> The individual attained independence for the first time in history when bourgeois societies came into being after the French Revolution in 1789. Since then all persons have had to be responsible for their own acts. It was now no longer possible to invoke old traditions, rigid societal norms or some otherworldly point of reference. God, the form of government and life had become relativizable quantities whose significance depended mainly on the perception of the *individual* (Scotti, 2001, p. 20—italics added).

As is generally known, for the individual, this development brought with it a substantial degree of emancipation from the dependencies and heteronomies that had existed hitherto. From then on, "liberty, equality, and fraternity" were the order of the day, or at least they were the ideal, as were also equal opportunities to participate actively in public life, to develop personal skills and attain affluence. Individualism can thus initially be understood as a view according to which human beings are

> loosely linked individuals who view themselves as independent of collectives; are primarily motivated by their own preferences, needs, rights, and the contracts they have established with others; give priority to their personal goals over the goals of others; and emphasize rational analyses of the advantages and disadvantages to associating with others (Triandis, 1995, p. 2).

BOX 22

INDIVIDUALISM The term individualism refers to a view of humankind that has been highly influential in Western cultures over the last few centuries. It is almost the antithesis of the concept of intersubjectivity (see Box 15). According to this conception,

> the individual should prove himself to be an individual by developing his individuality in total isolation and independently of influence from other individuals. Only retrospectively—one might say when he has become an inherently fully consummate individual—can he enter into a relationship with other individuals, out of which collaborative action can then gradually develop. (Pieper, 2003, p. 61/7).

---

40 Taylor (1992) has shown that the historical beginnings go much further back than this.

Via the staging post of Romanticism (see Berlin, 1996, pp. 168ff.), this conception of the human being has also become widespread in psychotherapy. "Individualism within the social sciences is not a passing fad or merely a minor offshoot. It has played an extremely important role in psychology" (Etzioni, 1997, p. 43). It has led, broadly speaking, mainly to two convictions: First, individuals are seen as *initially* separate beings. Second, these individuals are conceived of as initially somehow existing in a vacuum, as if they were not embedded in concrete interpersonal situations and larger social, cultural and ecological and political contexts. They only enter into these situations and conditions *secondarily* because they expect to benefit from them and decide to do so of their own free will.

> *Psychological individualism* is characterized by the opinion that every individual represents a distinctive autarchic entity whose distinctiveness is rooted in the mental sphere and remains identical with itself over time. This uniqueness is attained through a self-referential examination of the individual's own history, so that his own distinctive identity forms and maintains itself until (or even beyond) death. Natural and cultural determinants are held to be irrelevant for the development of psychological uniqueness and disregarded. In this form of individualism the autarchic distinctiveness of the individual is seen as being intrapsychically constituted.
>
> Psychological individualism had its heyday as the doctrine of the autarchic uniqueness of the individual in the Romantic era. Psychological individualism could therefore also be called romantic or esthetic individualism. Starting with Novalis and Schlegel and continuing through to Nietzsche, an individualism came into its own which celebrated individual distinctiveness in almost cult fashion and remained quite oblivious to the "objective" cultural and natural conditions of its constitution (Hastedt, 1998, pp. 17ff.—original italics).

In the 1930s, 1940s, and 1950s, the voices of an increasing number of theorists who did not share the individualist viewpoint made themselves heard, including, for example, Harry Stack Sullivan[41] and George Herbert Mead, whom I mentioned above.

---

41 In Sullivan's view, "scientific psychiatry has to be defined as the study of interpersonal relations" (1953, p. 368).

BOX 23

GEORGE HERBERT MEAD (1863–1931) was an influential North American sociologist, social psychologist, and philosopher and also the founder of what was later to become known as "symbolic interactionism." According to this approach, both the human mind and each individual self are emergent from the social process of meaningful communication ("gestures") and are neither logical nor biological preconditions of these interactions.

> The self is something which has a development; it is not initially there, at birth, but arises in the process of social experience and activity, that is, develops in the given individual as a result of his relations to that process as a whole and to other individuals within that process (Mead, 1934/1963, p. 135).

This self consists of two components or phases, the "me" and the "I." The former reflects the attitudes of the ("generalized") other, and the latter is the response of the person to these attitudes. The "me" is the totality of adopted attitudes and internalized roles that the self has acquired, while the "I" is the sum of the original reactions to the "me." Intrapsychically, the two are in a dialectical relationship.

However, at the same time, the horrors of collectivism and totalitarianism committed during this period also led to renewed individualistic tendencies, which were probably mainly directed toward defending human rights and in particular freedom (of thought) and at not permitting the individual to escape his moral responsibility (see Sartre, 1948[42]).

In Frederick Perls, who was a German Jew and a socialist (see Box 12), we can see one personal example of how these partly contradictory historical forces made their mark on contemporary psychotherapeutic modalities. It was probably Perls' own individualist tendencies that helped him survive the Holocaust because they enabled him to let go of his ties and emigrate (see Bocian, 2010). In addition to his individualistic side, which weakened his affiliations to fellow leftists and heightened his aversion to the Fascist hordes, he probably also had a side to him that could—in contradistinction to individualism—perhaps be called "relational." From this point of view, he considered it "deceptive to think of the 'individuals' as primitive and combined in social relations, for there is no doubt that the existence of 'individuals' comes about as the result of a very complicated society" (Perls et al., 1951, p. 315).

---

42 Sartre is frequently considered to have a purely individualistic stance; however, that does not do justice to him. "And, when we say that man is responsible for himself, we do not mean that he is responsible only for his own individuality, but that he is responsible for all men" (Sartre, 1948, p. 12; see also Hasenhüttl, 2006; Merten, 2008).

It is in this very relational sense that I wish my critical attitude toward individualist-oriented psychology and psychotherapy to be understood. "Due to its social nature, the self is richer and . . . refined; it is the nonsocial self which is prevented from developing because it suffers from a dearth of diverse positive attachments" (Etzioni, 1997, p. 54). The concepts that I suggest as alternatives to "individualism" are therefore not "collectivism," "totalitarianism," or any other "-ism" that stands for an attitude which violates the dignity and human rights of the individual, but "relatedness," "connectedness," and "intersubjectivity" as the basic requirements for individuality to come into being and as conditions that are conducive to its development.

Hastedt (1998) also refers to an individualist attitude with which the individual no longer sees herself as a being that is embedded in communities, as the narcissistic "aberration of individualism." It is characterized by the fact that

in individualistic cultures, people are more detached from their collectives. They feel autonomous, and their social behavior maximizes enjoyment and depends on interpersonal contracts. If the goals of the collective do not match their personal goals, they think it is "obvious" that their personal goals have precedence. If the costs of relationships are greater than their enjoyments, they drop the relationships. They change relationships often, and when they get married, they do it on the basis of personal emotions, which often change over time, and thus, divorce is frequent. They raise their children to be independent of their collectives. Freedom from the influence of the collective is a very important value (Triandis, 1995, p. xiii).

BOX 24

EXAMPLES of behaviors that are more individualistic (even numbers in the following list) and more community-oriented (odd numbers):

1 In Brazil, a waiter brings one menu for four people and gives it to the "senior" member of the group, who orders the same food for all.

2 In France, each member of the group orders a different entree at a restaurant.

3 In India, a senior engineer is asked to move to New York, at a salary that is 25 times his salary in New Delhi, but he declines the opportunity.

4 In California, a senior engineer is asked to move to New York, at a salary that is 50% higher than his salary in Los Angeles, and he accepts.

5 On a street in Moscow, an older woman scolds a mother she does not know because she thinks the mother has not wrapped her child warmly enough.

6 In New York, a woman asks for help from passersby to escape from the beatings that her boyfriend is giving her, but no one helps.

7 In Japan, a supervisor knows a great deal about the personal life of each subordinate and arranges for one of his subordinates to meet a nice girl he can marry.

8 In England, a subordinate does not mention to his supervisor that his father has just died.

9 In Germany, a man walks on the grass in a public park and is reprimanded by several passersby.

10 In Illinois, a man marries a woman his parents disapprove of (Triandis, 1995, p. 1).

Many of the forms of psychology and psychotherapy that are widespread in our culture follow this predominantly individualistic tradition. Thus, for example, "the psychological birth of the human infant" (Mahler, Pine, & Bergman, 1975) is often understood as a step out of "symbiosis" toward "individuation." Such a position leads to the view that "maturation is a continuous process of transcending environmental support and developing self-support, which means an increasing *reduction* of dependencies" (Perls et al., 1951, p. v—italics added). There is seldom any discussion of how development might also be seen differently. One could regard it as an "expansion" of initially relatively simple social relations, which are to begin with limited to the primary significant other(s), but then develop toward increasingly *diversified* and *complex* interpersonal relationships and networks.[43]

Thus viewed, psychological development would not consist mainly in a person's growing independence from support provided by others; it would be characterized more by the increasing differentiation and broadening of supportive social networks on which the person can draw and on which she herself also comes to have a shaping influence, for example, by taking on more and more supportive functions for others. Then, the developmental line would not run from dependency to independence, but from simpler forms of interdependence to more differentiated and more complex ones. What Mahler construed as a transition from symbiosis to individuation and Perls as a transformation from external support into self-support would also not be seen as increasing independence of the

---

[43] In his cumulative developmental model, Stern speaks of "domains of relatedness" (1985) that develop one after the other, but unlike "phases" do not supersede each other, but *supplement* each other (see Staemmler, 1997a).

individual, but—similarly to the way Vygotsky described it (see Box 8 and Chapter 6)—as a process of internalizing interdependent social systems and their supportive functions. This internalization would then *not* mean that the individual disengages or even isolates himself, but rather that he has the others "inside" or "with" him, i.e., that he remains connected to them even when he is alone.[44]

We could also, like Waldenfels (and other phenomenologists), consider even more radically whether

> the very question "How can I gain access to the other?" is not in fact wrongly expressed. If I put it in this way, I feel imprisoned in my own internal space and then have to think how I can reach the other person outside. My psyche is described as an internal space, and the others are seen as being in an external space (2000, p. 216).

Thus, in a certain sense, the way in which the question is put actually creates the problem that it is supposed to solve. For Heidegger, this question does not therefore arise, since for him "Dasein's Being-in-the-world is essentially constituted by Being-with" (1962, p. 156):

> Being-with is an existential characteristic of Dasein even when factically no Other is present-at-hand or perceived. Even Dasein's Being-alone is Being-with in the world. The Other can *be missing* only *in* and *for* a Being-with. Being-alone is a deficient mode of Being-with; its very possibility is the proof of this (Heidegger, 1962, pp. 156f.—original italics).

Thus, "even the explicit disclosure of the Other ... grows only out of one's primarily Being with him in each case" (Heidegger, 1962, p. 161)—and thus, I come back to my question, namely: If Being-with is *primary*, must it

---

44 Here I am thinking of concepts like Stern's "evoked companion" (1985) and Mead's "generalized other" (1934/1963). Bråten's (1992) concept of the "virtual other," which is still in the process of development, should perhaps also be mentioned in this context. Dornes summarizes it as follows: "In this theory we have not a monad which has inborn social, communicative or drive-related needs and therefore enters into contact with another person, but a monad that is inherently intersubjectively or dialogically structured, i.e. is born with expectations that an other will be there and what he should be like. The monad is thus not a monad at all, or only for an external observer. In actual fact it is a dyad, right from the start even, but initially only an internal one. The other who exists inside it is a virtual other, but in Bråten's view this virtual presence of an other in the subject, even before she comes into contact with a real other, is necessary for the actual contact, when it happens in a certain way, to be experienced as satisfying" (Dornes, 2006, p. 79f.; see also Trevarthen 1998). I do not know whether Bråten (or Dornes) is aware of how similar his concept of the "virtual other" is to Buber's anthropology (see Box 1). Buber talks of the "*a priori* of relation, *the inborn Thou*" and declares that "The inborn *Thou* is realized in the lived relations with that which meets it" (1958, p. 27—original italics).

not first be created by empathy? Then empathy would in fact seem to be merely its self-evident derivative. Put in even more basic terms, would the I of the individual not then be the starting point from which the mystery of the Thou can be painstakingly rendered accessible? The We would be the point of departure from which first the Thou, and then the I would emerge with increasing clarity, without ever being able to leave the Being-with behind them.

The developmental psychologist Peter Hobson puts this pertinent question from the standpoint of his own discipline and then responds in a manner reminiscent of Mead.

> We need to explain how she becomes aware of herself and others as beings who have and who can adopt perspectives.
>
> It sounds baffling, but in order to do all this, she first has to take a perspective on herself and her own attitudes. It is only by doing this, by taking a view on her own ways of construing the world, that she can begin to *think* in terms of her own and others' perspectives.
>
> This happens through a particular species of identification: The child identifies with others' attitudes toward the child's own attitudes and actions. Once more, the child is lifted out of her own stance and is drawn into adopting another perspective—this time, a perspective on herself and what she is feeling and doing. She becomes self-aware through others (2002, p. 106—original italics).

Waldenfels gives an example:

BOX 25

EXAMPLE

How do you learn . . . what anger means? Do you know what you look like when you are angry? Look at yourself in the mirror when you are angry—or have you learned what you look like when you are angry? You have never seen many of your own gestures—you see them mainly in others. The movement of the understanding of expressions does not go from the inside to the outside, but vice versa, from the other to me, and only then from myself to the other (Waldenfels, 2000, p. 221).

Within the broader context of such critical reflections on individualism, the above-mentioned positions of the authors who subscribe to the traditional understanding of empathy are problematic because they are based exclusively on the individual. They fail to mention either the direct interactions with other persons that precede the development of the self or the broader social frame of reference within which human beings encounter each other—as if there were no cultural context or, if one existed, it had no appreciable significance.

With regard to this broader frame of reference, I would like to mention just one of many possible examples to show that a viewpoint that isolates human beings from their wider social context is unsatisfactory. The literature on the *Zeitgeist* (e.g., that of the postmodern era) and its influence on the consciousness of the individual and on forms of individual lifestyles and individual mental disorders fills entire libraries. One well-known author of such literature, Zygmunt Bauman, writes: "*The hub of postmodern life strategy is not identity building, but the avoidance of being fixed*" (1997, p. 89—original italics). Elsewhere he writes,

> one needs to be capable of being seduced by the infinite possibility and constant renewal promoted by the consumer market, of rejoicing in the chance of putting on and taking off identities, of spending one's life in the never ending chase after ever more intense sensations and even more exhilarating experience (Bauman, 1997, p. 14)

If there is any truth in this diagnosis of a "new fluidity" in our times, this will also be evidenced in psychotherapy practices, hospitals for psychosomatic disorders, and psychosocial counseling centers, and it will also affect the relationships between the clients and practitioners who encounter each other there. It is likely to affect the personal experiences and modes of experiencing with which they will have to empathize if they want to understand each other, and it will probably also have an influence on the extent to which they can empathize with each other.

However, the individualist view of humankind not only results in the omission from the traditional concept of empathy of the "broader'" cultural and sociological contexts, i.e., those that exert an influence on the therapeutic situation from *outside* of it, so to speak. This also results in an astonishing neglect of situative and relational connections *within* the therapeutic space—since the individualist worldview is based on the assumptions outlined above:

1. that the individual is prior to relationship, and exists in some essential way apart from relational context and connection, and
2. that relationships themselves are therefore secondary, and in some sense less real than the individuals who enter into them, who after all were already there, fully formed, and can come and go from one

relationship to another as their own needs and circumstances dictate, presumably without altering their own essential nature. . . .

The fundamental separation of one individual's *experience* from that of another . . . follows directly from these assumptions (Wheeler, 2000, p. 53—original italics).

Since in the individualistic paradigm there is no *direct* connection between persons, and the experiential world of the other is not *directly* accessible—and indeed, it is also not supposed to be (due to the risk of confluence and identification)—the subject thus conceived (correspondingly) has a problem. It "is master in its own house (its 'psyche,' its consciousness, its own private internal world), but does not know how it is supposed to get out of it" (Schmitz, 2003, p. 493). It must bridge the gap that exists between it and the other in the way that the theory theory describes: The individual constructs for herself a mental model of the experience of the other, to which she actually has no access.

BOX 26

EXAMPLE An excerpt from the autobiography of Frederick Perls can be taken as an example of this view of human beings.

The privacy of your experiences is unknown to me
Except for revelations.
There is no bridge from man to man.
I guess, imagine, empathize, whatever this may mean.
For strangers we are, and strangers we stay (1969, unpaginated).

Thus, this individual manages, with considerable difficulty, to more or less maintain his ideal of independence and at the same time to more or less keep in check the danger of the complete isolation in which he constantly finds himself due to his fear of the complementary threat of confluence. This view of the human condition is then reflected in the traditional view of empathy.

Characteristic of early . . . conceptions of empathy is an egocentric image of two separate individuals wherein one—the therapist—attempts to discern something happening within the skin of the other—the client. . . . As if suspicious of any psychic organization not based on the modernist ideal of individuation, psychologists from analytic, existential, and humanistic traditions have characteristically insisted that empathy be clearly differentiated from the more regressive process that Buie calls 'merging' (O'Hara, 1997, pp. 300f.).

Merging and confluence are undesirable because they appear to call into question the delimited self that is allegedly to be developed and sustained. However, it proves to be impossible to keep insisting on fixed boundaries, since "'finding oneself' is not something one does alone" (Bellah, Madsen, Sullivan, Swidler, & Tipton, 1985, p. 85). This even affects the result: *What* the person who finds herself in the course of psychotherapy is *like* is not independent of the *person with whom* she has undertaken the search for herself.

done w/in community!!

> The individuality of the individual is . . . never something that exists in isolation, but has always to a great extent been related to the individuality of other . . . individuals. The individual needs . . . the recognition of others who confirm him in his way of being and who can, in turn, only become individuals through being recognized by him. . . . The individual can only grasp himself as a subject if he has an object against which to define himself and only experiences himself as a self in a dialogical relation to another self (Pieper, 2003, 61/4; p. 6).

It is not possible to become who one is alone—and this is not a deficit, as some individualists with their idea of *self* actualization may perhaps think, but a natural and (for me, at least) welcome consequence of the intersubjectivity through which a human being becomes a human being in the first place[45] or, as Buber says, through which he becomes a *person*. By this, Buber means much more than he does by the word *individual*, which in his view emphasizes mainly the capacity to be unique and independent.

> But a person, I would say, is an individual living really with the world. And *with* the world, I don't mean *in* the world—just in *real contact*, in real reciprocity with the world in all the points in which the world can meet man. . . . This is what I would call a person and if I may say expressly Yes and No to certain phenomena, I'm *against* individuals and *for* persons (Buber, 1965, p. 184—original italics).

Stern even considers intersubjectivity to be "a condition of humanness" and believes

> that it is also an innate, primary system of motivation, essential for species survival, and has a status like sex or attachment. The desire for

---

45 The capacity for language, the ability to laugh and walk upright, and many other characteristics are, of course, also involved.

intersubjectivity is one of the major motivations that drive a psycho-therapy forward. Patients want to be known and to share what it feels like to be them (2004, p. 97).

The desire for *"self* actualization" inevitably leads us to enter into personal contact with the other. I cannot see any convincing alternative to Taylor's statement that

> the search for pure subjective expressive fulfilment may make life thin and insubstantial, may ultimately undercut itself. . . . But that by itself does nothing to show that subjective fulfillment is not a good. It shows only that it needs to be part of a "package," to be sought within a life which is also aimed at other goods (1992, p. 511),

especially that of relating to the other, without whom there would be no "person" in Buber's sense of the word. This other, who relates to me and empathizes with me is, one could say, following Stern (1985, p. 102)—and not only with regard to infants—always an other who forms my self.

> If this is so, the mature human self is not essentially a center of mono-logical consciousness . . . Rather the self is a scene or locus of dialogue. In this view, what I centrally *am* is an interplay or conversation among vari-ous voices, commitments, identifications, or points of view (Richardson, Fowers, & Guignon, 1999, p. 264—original italics).

Mikhail Bakhtin has put it in even more radical terms: "The *I* hides in the other and in others, it wants . . . to enter completely into the world of others as an other, and to cast from itself the burden of being the only *I* (*I-for-myself*) in the world" (1986, p. 147—original italics). As Bråten as-serts "Cartesian and Leibnizian assumptions about monadic subjects and disembodied and self-centered minds without windows to each other except as mediated by constructed or symbolic representations" (Bråten, 2007a, p. 2) can no longer be upheld as valid.

3.4 SUMMARY OF CHAPTER 3

First, the traditional concept of empathy sees empathy in psychotherapy as a *one-sided* activity that is practiced by the therapist. Second, it under-stands this activity as being *primarily* a mental one, in which the therapist imagines in his mind the contents of the client's mind. The dimension of the body or lived body is more or less neglected. Third, the traditional concept of empathy presents empathy as an *individualistic* phenomenon in which there is no intersubjectivity between client and therapist nor are they embedded in a social and cultural context.

This is summarized in Figure 2.

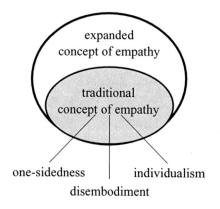

FIGURE 2
Sketch of the relationship between the traditional and expanded concepts of empathy showing three important aspects of the traditional concept

Thus, in my view, the traditional concept of empathy covers only a *segment* of the phenomenon and neglects other important aspects that are also part of it, since

> I apprehend the other, not as a thing but as another subjectivity similar to mine as alter ego. It is through his/her body that I am linked to the other, first as an organism similar to mine, but also perceived as an embodied presence, site and means of an experiential field. This double dimension of the body (organic/lived; *Körper/Leib*) is part and parcel of *empathy*, the royal means of access to social conscious life, beyond the simple interaction, as fundamental intersubjectivity (Varela, 1999, p. 81—original italics).

This intersubjectivity, which is expressed in mutual empathy between human beings, does not take place in a vacuum, but is embedded in the natural and social world which always surrounds people's encounters with each other in the form of present *situations*. "It is only with the information obtained in situations via our own observations that we arrive at a valid picture of the external world" (Magnusson, 1978, p. 2) and of other people.

An expanded understanding of empathy should therefore take into consideration the mutuality of empathic processes and the embodiment, intersubjectivity, and sociality of human beings.

write on the specifically Christian lens in reading this ... & how his view in actuality aligns w/ those "naughty"

4

Toward a New Concept of Empathy

4.1 EMPATHY IN THE PLURAL—SOCIAL REFERENCING

I will happily admit that I was overdoing it a little when I stated in the introduction that I intended to demonstrate that empathy is only possible "in the plural." This statement was a slight exaggeration and is not absolutely true. Nevertheless, I chose it because I wanted to highlight a viewpoint that stands in contradiction to the one-sidedness of the traditional concept of empathy that I have been taking issue with. In the previous Chapter (3.1), I drew an analogy with the tradition of the confessional. However, I do not intend to argue in general against the existence of more or less one-sided empathic processes. The confessional is still in existence today, just as there are therapists who, while they empathize with their clients, still want to remain as anonymous as possible themselves. This is often justified by the well-meaning idea that it meets the needs of the clients with as much objectivity as possible. However,

> it has not been possible to sustain the idea that therapists can take on the role of objective observers . . . of their patients' mental worlds, since it has been shown that they cannot avoid reacting to the way the patient experiences them and to the type of relationships they are striving to have with them (Streeck, 2001, p. 223).

The consequences that ensue when therapists disregard this insight and try to remain anonymous nonetheless are quite a different issue (see Renick, 1995; Stolorow & Atwood, 1997). Be that as it may, there are indeed one-sided forms of empathy, and they are not only found in therapy, as we see in the following example taken from everyday life (Box 27).

BOX 27

EXAMPLE

As I settled into a seat on a New York City subway, one of those ambiguous, possibly ominous moments of urban life occurred: I heard a shriek far behind me, from the opposite end of the car.

My back was to the source of the scream. But I faced a gentleman whose face suddenly took on a slightly anxious look.

My mind raced to comprehend what was going on and what—if anything—I should do. Was it a fight? Was someone running amok on the subway? Was danger headed my way?

Or was it merely a shriek of delight, maybe a group of teenagers having a whooping good time?

My answer came swiftly, from the face of the man who could see what was happening: his worried features settled into calm, and he went back to reading his newspaper. Whatever was going on back there, I knew all was well (Goleman, 2006, p. 38)

Here, Goleman describes a situation in which his capacity for empathy helps him to assess what to make of a sound that is coming from a source that he cannot actually see. He empathizes with the man sitting opposite him who can see where the noise is coming from. When this man's face relaxes, Goleman concludes that the event holds no danger and also relaxes.[46] Goleman describes how he *himself* benefits from being able to empathize with another person. This other person, on the other hand, neither relates to nor empathizes with him. Goleman's fellow passenger possibly has not even noticed him—at any rate, his attention is mainly on the event that caused the noise. He is not even aware of the fact that Goleman realizes that he has relaxed, and it makes no difference to him. This situation in the subway is an example of one-sided empathy and also shows how useful it can be.

4.1.1   Mutual Empathy

The situation we have just seen is, however, completely different in structure from the one we find in a therapeutic dialog. Here the client and therapist relate to each other. This involves both the client empathizing with

---

46 I do not wish to elaborate on this any further at this point, but I would simply like to point out that Goleman's act of relaxation could possibly be seen as *confluence* with the relaxation of the man sitting opposite. However, I do not think that this interpretation is correct because his description does not give us reason to assume that he was unable to distinguish clearly between himself and the other passenger.

the therapist and the therapist empathizing with the client. The two of them "together form an intersubjective system of reciprocal mutual influence" (Stolorow et al. 1987, p. 42). The client would not be able to benefit from the empathic attention of the therapist if he were unable to recognize it for what it is. In order to be able to do so, he needs to possess the capacity for empathy himself. Any empathy that the therapist offers him would remain ineffective if it were not recognized as empathy by the client. "When the client has problems resonating effectively with the therapist, then important therapist attitudes like empathy, acceptance, genuineness, and nonpossessive warmth . . . may not be noted" (Dekeyser, Elliott, & Leijssen, 2009, p. 115). The client must take the therapist's empathy on board, at least partially. Otherwise, in the direct contact with the therapist, he will not benefit at all, even if the therapist may be able to gain a clearer picture of him. Also, "my patient is engaged in an empathic process when s/he attempts to describe his/her experience in ways that are understandable to me" (Jacobs in Jacobs, Philippson, & Wheeler, 2007, p. 27).

This is *my* interpretation of Rogers' sixth condition for successful therapy, even if he himself may have had something slightly different in mind. In his words, this condition is that "the communication to the client of the therapist's empathic understanding and unconditional positive regard is to a minimal degree achieved" (1957, p. 96). The way I understand the word "communication" here—and this is my own interpretation—is more than simply understanding the meanings of the words. He is talking about the client understanding and experiencing an important *interpersonal* overture by the therapist because this is the only way that it can unfold its therapeutic effect. In every form of psychotherapy—and *therapy* is my frame of reference—*in which the therapist makes this empathic overture and the client accepts it*, there is empathy in the plural. In the singular, empathy has no therapeutic effect.

In most cases, reciprocal empathy (sometimes referred to as "mutuality"[47]), is taken for granted, even if it assumes various guises and the degree to which it is explicit varies, depending on the school of therapy. This is so, not only because empathy is a fundamental human endowment, but also because it can appear as a chain reaction[48].

> I can remember a memory, expect an expectation, fancy a fancy. And so I can also empathize the empathized, i.e., among the acts of another that I grasp empathically there can be empathic acts in which the other grasps another's acts (Stein, 1917/1964, p. 18).

---

47 Ryback (2001) uses this as a basis for his "mutual affect therapy."
48 Another term for these chain reactions is "iterations."

Not only does this apply to psychotherapy with adults but its "essential features"[49] are evident in early interactions between infants and their mothers. This was demonstrated, quite convincingly, in the experiment of the "visual cliff" (Gibson & Walk, 1960), a "classic" experimental design used in infant research. Its original purpose was to investigate depth perception in infants, but it also proved to be an impressive example of how early reciprocal empathic processes take place between babies and their significant others. "Young children's emotional reactions are often affected by the emotional reactions of those around them" (Boccia & Campos, 1989, p. 25).

In the visual cliff experiment, the babies (mostly aged between 6 and 12 months) are faced with an ambiguous situation. They are crawling on a table, half of which is covered with a checkerboard pattern. On the join to the other half, this pattern drops down steeply, and there is a 1-m gap before it continues on the horizontal plane. Here the tabletop itself assumes more the form of a transparent sheet of glass. Thus, initially the child is uncertain as to whether she can carry on crawling across the glass without being in danger of falling or, if she does proceed, whether she will fall down the "cliff" suggested by the break in the checkerboard pattern.

FIGURE 3
Visual cliff (Graphic-Design: © 2009, Hugo Waschkowski, Freiburg, Germany)

---

49 I use the term "essential features" deliberately because, of course, infants do not yet possess the same fully developed empathic capacities as adults. For more on the developmental psychology of empathy see, for example, Eisenberg und Strayer (1987), Hoffmann (1981), and Thompson (1998).

Because she feels uncertain, when she reaches this spot, the baby will always stop crawling and look at the mother (or indeed any other person present—see Klinnert, Emde, Butterfield, & Campos, 1986). She will look into her face and pay attention to her facial expression and the vocal pointers she gives. If the mother's face is anxious very few children will crawl on, but if the mother is smiling, approximately three quarters of all babies will risk continuing to crawl right across the cliff (see Sorce, Emde, Campos, & Klinnert, 1985, p. 196). To quote Hobson, the obvious conclusions to be drawn from this are that

> the baby's way of experiencing an object or event may be changed through her responses to the feelings of others. She is moved from one way to another way of construing things, as in our example of the visual cliff and its mother-altered meaning for an infant (2002, p. 93).

We can also observe similar reactions in infants in many other situations, for instance, when they are given a new toy that they are not too sure about (see Hornik, Risenhoover, & Gunnar, 1987) or when they start walking (Witherington, Campos, Anderson, Lejeune, & Seah, 2005). What is, of course, particularly interesting is that such processes also occur in the interpersonal triangle between mother, father, and child. If, for example, the child happens to be focusing on the mother while the father is present in the background and there is some disturbance in the relationship between child and mother, then the child will turn to the father for guidance (see Fivaz-Depeursinge & Corboz-Warnery, 1999).

These attunement processes that take place between mother (or any other significant other) and child are known as "social referencing."[50]

BOX 28

SOCIAL REFERENCING "is a process whereby an individual seeks out emotional information in order to make sense of an event that is otherwise ambiguous or beyond that individual's own intrinsic appraisal capabilities" (Sorce et al., 1985, p. 199).

This process, which includes social, emotional, and cognitive dimensions, is extremely complex. The affective aspect is especially important, since it plays an essential part in the development of the child's self.

---

50 It is no coincidence that the inability of autistic people to empathize is also apparent in the fact that it is much rarer for them to look their fellow human beings in the face than other people (see Decety & Jackson, 2004, p. 91).

The expressive areas of the emotions have proved to be the essential building blocks in the learning processes that lead to the development of the self. . . . The child receives information about who he is via the affective signals of the main caregiver, precisely because he himself does not 'know' who he is (Krause, 2001, p. 203).

Although it is not only when the child is confronted with an *unfamiliar* or *uncertain* situation that social referencing takes place, it is in this type of situation that a child is most likely to refer back to its mother. First, it is in such situations that the child will look her in the face more frequently, and second, her reaction will then have the greatest effect on the way he continues to behave (see Klinnert et al., 1986; Walden, 1991). What we find in all such cases of social referencing is that in any given situation, the persons participating will enter into an exchange

in which one person utilizes another person's interpretation of the situation to formulate her own interpretation of it. . . . In referencing, one person serves as a base of information for another and, in so doing, facilitates the other's efforts to construct reality (Feinman, 1992, p. 4).

There are a number of conclusions that may be drawn from the studies of children that also have a bearing on the processes that take place between therapist and client. Of these, there are two that I would like to emphasize in particular: First, like infants, many clients do not yet know who they are. This is one of the many reasons that bring people to psychotherapy, in fact one of the more important reasons, even if it is hidden behind all sorts of symptoms. The social referencing that takes place between them and their therapists contributes significantly to their *becoming* themselves. I am using this unusual form of words rather than saying simply "*finding* themselves,"[51] in order to draw attention to the fact that, to a large extent, the self in question here *comes into being* for the first time in the therapeutic encounter. The self is also a mystery to itself inasmuch as it has never completely and finally formed. I mean this less in the sense of postmodernist analyses, such as Bauman's (1995) description of the "fluid" self (see above), but more as Heraclitus conceptualized it: "One cannot step twice into the same river, nor can one grasp any mortal substance in a stable

---

51 Even this term suggests the (implicit) presence of the Other. "Self-reflexive phrases such as 'understanding oneself' and 'seeking one's identity' hint at a mode of 'intrasubjectivity' that presents itself as intersubjective discourse" (Ziman, 2006, p. 32).

condition, but it scatters and again gathers; it forms and dissolves, and approaches and departs" (1979, p. 53—see also Staemmler, 1997b).

The self as a whole does not preexist somehow (unconsciously, for example) as an entity in such a way that it simply has to be unearthed or "exposed"[52] as many metaphors suggest—e.g., those that describe the therapist as an archaeologist or detective[53] (see Mertens & Haubl, 1996; Haubl & Mertens, 1996).

If we adhere to an interactional idea of the self, then the self that the client becomes in the course of therapy is not stable or lasting either. It remains flexible and constantly reconstructs itself in new forms. What appears to be lasting rests upon an illusion. "At each moment the state of self is constructed, from the ground up. It is an evanescent reference state, so continuously and consistently *re*constructed that the owner never knows it is being *re*made unless something goes wrong with the remaking" (Damasio, 1994, p. 240—original italics). This continuous reformation of the self takes place in dependence on who it happens to be face to face with and also on the characteristics of the joint situation (see Chapter 4.3). "The self," according to the founders of gestalt therapy, "is flexibly various, for it varies with the dominant organic needs and the pressing environmental stimuli; it is the system of responses" (Perls et al., 1951, p. 235).[54]

"When a self does appear it always involves an experience of another; there could not be an experience of a self simply by itself," writes Mead (1934/1963, p. 195) and explains what that means in concrete terms in the context of a conversation:

> That . . . is a process with which we are all familiar. We are continually following up our own address to other persons by an understanding of what we are saying, and using that understanding in the direction

---

52 Jaspers has made the distinction between understanding as "illuminating" and understanding as "exposing," calling the latter "the malicious aspect" (1963, p. 359). "In a mood of scepticism or dislike we think we are always 'seeing through it.' The intended truth of this understanding is the penetration of general dishonesty. . . . In contrast to this, understanding which illuminates and does not expose involves an attitude which is basically positive. It approaches human nature sympathetically. It tries to visualize, it deepens its observation and watches the living substance grow before its eyes. The uncovering psychology which exposes acts reductively and finds, 'this is nothing but . . .'" (Jaspers, 1963, p. 359).

53 "Forced understanding, in the sense of constantly wanting to see through [the client], can result in the therapist assuming the inquisitive attitude of a detective and lead to an attentiveness that is, to some degree, lying in wait, ready to pounce. This must unsettle and worry the patient" (Finke, 2002, p. 221) and it also runs the risk of shaming her.

54 Hannover (1997) gives an overview of empirical studies on this process. See also my comments on neuroplasticity (Box 50) below.

of our continued speech. We are finding out what we are going to say, what we are going to do, by saying and doing, and in the process we are continually controlling the process itself. In the conversation of gestures what we say calls out a certain response in another and that in turn changes our own action, so that we shift from what we started to do because of the reply the other makes (Mead, 1934/1963, pp. 140f.).

In other words, according to this view, the self of the client, and also that of the therapist, continuously forms itself anew in processes of social referencing. "There is no way not to know other subjectivities, but it is only through others that we come to have a subjectivity ourselves" (Jacobs, 2003, p. 91).

These reciprocal influences are very important when one considers the question of what the therapist can know about his client, for in situations where the therapist receives information from her, she is always affected by his presence and her interaction with him. That is to say "the psychotherapist can find out nothing about the patient that is independent of his own person and his own influence on the person with whom he is interacting" (Streeck, 2001, p. 230). The person with whom the therapist empathizes is always the person who comes into being through his participation. What he discovers about her is always a product of his contact with her, and he will always have played a part in creating it (see Mehrgardt, 2005).[55] This also means that what is to be understood is essentially something that only comes into being in dialog.

The second point that can be taken from infant research and applied to therapy concerns the experience of uncertainty that makes social referencing an especially effective process. Unlike small children, adult clients in therapy do not generally have difficulty with simple situations that are optically ambiguous (such as the visual cliff) or unfamiliar objects (like toys), but they do frequently come into therapy with subjective experiences of uncertainty for other reasons. What they hope to get from therapy and the support of the therapist is usually greater clarity and better orientation in their social relationships, their future prospects, and what life means to them.

Moreover, the therapeutic situation is unfamiliar to most clients. Frequently, it will be the first time they have experienced it, and they will

---

55 The fact that the extent to which the therapist is actually able to empathize varies from client to client (see Henry, Schacht, & Strupp 1986), is just one aspect of this.

have only a vague idea about what is expected of them or rather what they can expect of their therapists. Thus, two different kinds of uncertainty come together—the subjective uncertainty that clients arrive with and then the situational uncertainty that arises in the encounter with the therapist. And *these two together*, "*subjective* uncertainty as well as *situational* uncertainty . . . heighten the impact of other people's definitions of the situation" (Feinman, Roberts, Hsieh, Sawyer, & Swanson, 1992, p. 40—original italics).

Whether it is a question of situational or of more complex forms of orientation in therapy, or whether we are looking at a baby testing out how his mother reacts to him in a particular situation, it is always a *reciprocal* process that takes place. To take the example of the visual cliff, the mother empathizes with her child's uncertainty and encourages it with her smile to continue crawling, or conversely, she stops it from doing so by showing an anxious facial expression. The child itself now registers the mother's reaction. To be able do so, it must interpret her smile correctly as encouragement or else it must read her anxious face correctly as a danger signal. It must also construe its mother's reaction as a meaningful and intentional response to its situation (and not simply as a chance facial expression). Finally it must identify the specific point of reference to which the mother's messages relate, i.e., the visual cliff (see Feinman et al., 1992, p. 31). These are all impressive empathic achievements.

There are of course a number of developmental steps through which certain aspects of social referencing in children change and become differentiated over time (see Walden & Ogan, 1988). I do not intend to go into this in detail, but there are two findings that I consider to be of such interest that they deserve mention. They show once more, but in a different way, how extensive the reciprocity of empathic referencing is.

At the beginning of their second year, small children have already acquired the capacity to distinguish whether their mother's reaction in a given context makes sense or whether it is not applicable—in other words, whether their mother is really responding to them empathically or not. If their mother has a *sad* face, for example, as the child is approaching the visual cliff, slightly older children show signs of confusion. They also use the facial expression less as an aid to knowing how they themselves should behave. Sadness in their mother's face does not give them a meaningful answer to their unspoken question as to whether or not they are in danger. Thus, their empathic capacities have clearly increased and they now "do have some notion of appropriate responses to situations" (Walden, 1991, p. 72).

The second finding also relates to the beginning of the second year. This is when a further skill develops, namely, social referencing in the form of *negotiations*. From now on

> there is back and forth emotional signaling in a situation of dyadic uncertainty. The uncertainty concerns the expectations with respect to the response of the other in relation to one's need or intention. Modifications of expectations and intentions occur during the course of the social interaction (Emde, 1992, p. 84).

One person conveys to the other person what she expects or desires from them by using the other person's subtle emotional reactions to the first indications of her own wishes, so as to adjust these wishes (and also the way she expresses them) to the current state of the other person. She does this in such a way that the likelihood of her expectations being fulfilled increases. It is as though the two of them are steering a boat through rapids and must each react to the slightest movement of the other with their own complimentary movements of support or correction, in order to get through.

In adults, such mutual empathic referencing processes are naturally further developed and differentiated. But "despite developmental differences, the social construction of reality operates in infancy in very much the way that it does throughout the rest of the human lifespan" (Feinman et al., 1992, p. 52). In psychotherapy and other social situations, social referencing assumes various and, sometimes, very subtle forms. Nonverbal microprocesses, only a few of which become conscious[56], play an important role (see Merten, 2001).[57] They may also lead to complications and misunderstandings, since the meaning of such microprocesses is often unclear, even when they are consciously perceived, and depend very much on the specific context. "Shown contempt might indicate that the sender is contemptuous of himself, of the object, of a common third person being

---

56 When I speak of "not conscious" or "unconscious" processes, I am not referring to the psychoanalytical concept of the unconscious but to that of cognitive psychology: "If we succeed in proving that human beings receive and store information that later governs their behavior without this information becoming an object of consciousness, then we are ready to speak of 'unconscious processes'" (Perrig, Wippich, &, Perrig-Chiello 1993, p. 25). These and many other researchers have, in my opinion, succeeded in proving this (see, for example, Kihlstrom, 1987).
57 Tepper and Haase (1978) have investigated whether it is more the nonverbal or verbal behavior of therapists that influences the client's feeling of whether or not they have been understood. Nonverbal behavior accounted for twice the amount of variance as verbal behavior.

talked about, or of the interaction partner" (Anstadt, Merten, Ullricht, & Krause, 1997, p. 403).

If the speaker is not aware of his feelings, the danger of a misunderstanding is even greater (see example in Box 29).

BOX 29

EXAMPLE If one person speaks, for instance, about an experience which made him angry without his being aware of it himself, his anger, if conveyed nonverbally in the course of conversation, can easily be construed by the other as a relational signal, because the person cannot and does not establish a connection between his unconscious experience and the experience described. "For the interaction partner the connection cannot but remain unclear, and he will therefore relate the affective sign to the current relationship or to himself and have the corresponding . . . affective reaction" (Benecke, Merten, & Krause, 2000, p. 76).

First, social referencing takes place in an overarching, long-term sense; by referring back to her therapist, a client is able to find a supportive relationship and also a fresh way of approaching those life issues that are important to her. Kohut's language of self psychology referred one-sidedly to the therapist's becoming a "selfobject" for the client (see Jacobs, 1992). Modern psychoanalysts, however, prefer to speak of an "intersubjective field," which moves on from the one-sidedness of Kohut's view, making way for the reciprocity of social referencing. "An intersubjective field is a system of reciprocal mutual influence. . . . Not only does the patient turn to the analyst for selfobject experiences, but the analyst also turns to the patient for such experiences" (Stolorow & Atwood, 1992, p. 3).

Second, social referencing is accomplished on the level of many small, often tiny, interactions that can influence both the course and the success of therapy. One might call them *multiple reciprocal empathic microprocesses*. In the last few years, they have been studied in depth, using modern video technology, for example. This process is summarized by Streeck as follows:

> If what takes place between patient and psychotherapist is examined as if under a magnifying glass for subtle elements of reciprocal behavior, it emerges that both constantly react to each other in a visible and audible way. Each can, therefore, read the reactions of the other by his behavior and regulate his interaction by means of these subtle signals. Krause et al. (e.g. 1983; 1992) have shown that in face-to-face interactions even facial signals that only appear for a fraction of a second

and completely escape conscious perception lead to reactions in the other person and have the function of steering the relationship (2001, p. 226).

These subtle signals are constantly emitted by both participants, and depending on the extent to which the two of them open up to each other, these signals exert effects of varying intensities on the other person. They are unable to escape the effect of the other, not least because many signals do not get past the threshold of awareness—in either the "transmitter" or the "receiver."

4.1.2 The Different Perspectives of Client and Therapist

We must, therefore, take the reciprocity of empathic processes in therapy as our basic starting point. Therapist and client do not differ in their fundamental ability to empathize with the other person. Rather, the capacity for empathy of both participants is often used to advance the therapeutic process. The same is true of the necessity to communicate to the other person how one has understood him or her. Here, too, I am interpreting Rogers' sixth condition slightly differently. For I believe that it is not only important for the therapist to communicate her own empathy and her understanding of the client *to him* but that it is also important for the client to communicate his understanding of the therapist *to her*. Communication is, as the word implies, not a one-way street, but something shared.

The *ability* to empathize with the other person (Kohut's "fundamental ability") is, however, not all that is shared. The equally fundamental human *desire* to be understood by significant others does not differ between therapist and client either. The same can be said for the *basic human need* to understand the other person and the situation in which one finds oneself with her. Grawe refers here to a "basic human need for orientation and control" (2002, p. 312). In Antonovsky's theory of salutogenesis, "comprehensibility" is the most important factor. What is meant is the extent "to which one perceives the stimuli that confront one, deriving from the internal and external environments, as making cognitive sense as information that is ordered, consistent, structured, and clear, rather than as noise" (1987, pp. 16f.).

Regardless of such fundamental skills and motivations, the respective perspectives of therapist and client differ because of their different positions and tasks in the therapeutic dialog. Mutual empathy does not mean that the differences between therapist and client are dissolved. Mutuality is not the same as symmetry. "It is not the patient's job to take care of the therapist. Mutuality is not about equality; roles are different" (Jordan, 2000, p. 1011). For the therapist, empathic communication is not simply spontaneous or reactive behavior. It is also, and most importantly, an aspect of her task that she has to implement in a consistent way. It is a professional *act* and because of this, it can be undertaken or not, just as it can also succeed or fail. In contrast, empathic communication for the client can also be part of his *behavior* (i.e., his reactions or his spontaneous behavior), but there can be no demands made on this behavior or criteria established for its success. It simply happens, to an extent that accords with his personal stage of development or his own personal style.[58]

These differences also determine the perspectives experienced by those involved. What the client experiences as a result of the therapist's empathy is initially something different, in terms of content, from what the client's empathy means to the therapist. The situation is asymmetrical, but there are also parallels. Aron describes this as follows for the psychoanalytic dyad:

> I conceive of the analytic relationship as fully mutual in the sense that mutual regulation needs to be assumed to be occurring at all times between patient and analyst. I view mutual recognition as one of the goals of analysis, and, in addition, I advocate mutual data generation in contrast to unilateral data generation as a general principle of the psychoanalytic method. Nevertheless, I think of the analytic situation as asymmetrical inasmuch as there are clear differences between patient and analyst regarding the purpose for which they are meeting, in their functions and responsibilities, and in the consequences for the two participants if the goals of the analysis are not met (Aron, 1996, p. 99).

Erich Fromm had an even more radical view. In his description, which is reminiscent of Ferenczi's (1988) "mutual analysis," there is hardly any indication of asymmetry:

> The knowledge of another person requires being inside of him, to *be* him. The analyst understands the patient only inasmuch as he experiences in himself all that the patient experiences . . . The analyst analyzes the patient, but the patient also analyzes the analyst, because the analyst, by sharing the unconscious of his patient, cannot help clarifying his own unconscious. Hence the analyst not only cures the patient, but is

58 For more on the systematic distinction between act and behavior, see Hartmann (1998).

also cured by him. He not only understands the patient, but eventually the patient understands him (Fromm, 1960, p. 112).

In order to demonstrate what they have in common and where they differ, the viewpoints of therapist and client could perhaps be expressed as follows, first from the perspective of the therapist: "I experience the client's interest in who I am and who I can be for him, in the role I play for him and the support I offer him. I notice in particular that he is interested in finding out whether my commitment and compassion for him are genuine and reliable. When I give him verbal or nonverbal indications of how I experience and understand him he tries to take my perspective and to understand who he is for me and what he can learn from it. Sometimes he wants to do more than understand and share in what I have uncovered of his mystery. He is also curious or cares about how I am and what I might be feeling as I show commitment to him, and what I feel about being with him in other respects. As I register his recognition of my commitment I feel validated as a human being who can enter into a meaningful relationship, whilst, however, I try not to allow myself to be dependent on this in the individual case."

The perspective of the client can be outlined roughly as follows: "I experience the fact that the therapist is showing commitment to me by trying to empathize with me. She is interested in my world of experience, in my special way of experiencing and being in the world—particularly where I have difficulties and am dissatisfied or unhappy. She tries to participate in that and to communicate her compassion to me in a way that helps me to understand myself better and also dissolves, or at least alleviates, my feeling of being enclosed in my own world of experience. She also perseveres even if difficulties arise in our relationship. By registering her commitment, interest and concern and allowing myself to be affected by them, I feel supported. This support helps me not only to be less of a mystery to myself and to make my own experiences more meaningful, but, because I experience the fact that my feelings are getting through to her and affect her, I also sense that I mean something to her. That helps me to feel a connection with her and other people and thus, as a human being, to experience a sense of belonging."

For the client to have this experience, it is of course necessary for the therapist to express her empathy clearly and not hide behind a professional mask. This is part of the therapist's task and a necessary prerequisite if her empathy is to reach the client and be effective. A *lack* of recognizable emotional resonance in the other person can even be distinctly confusing for the client. I have already mentioned Moser's description of classical analysis as a "deprivation experiment" and its problematic consequences. The famous "still face" experiment of the infancy researchers (Adamson & Frick, 2003; Cohn & Tronick, 1983; Tronick, Als, Adamson, Wise, & Brazelton 1978) speaks volumes. After a period of normal interaction with her baby, the mother was told not to make any facial or bodily movements for a while and not to speak. "The now well-known results were dramatic. Infants attempted to solicit the mother's attention and when their efforts failed they looked away, withdrew, and expressed sad and angry affect" (Tronick, 2007, p. 12).

It is clearly not enough for the therapist to empathize with her client—she must also *show* that she is empathizing. To resolve this, Barrett-Lennard (1981) differentiated between three phases of therapeutic empathy—first, empathic understanding by the therapist herself, second, her communication of what she has understood, and third, the reception of this communication by the client.

In the next section (4.1.3), I will make a few comments about the second phase, communication, describing various ways in which the empathic attitude can be expressed, predominantly *from the perspective of the therapist*. As will be clear from the preceding pages, I am not doing this because I think that only therapists express their empathic understanding in this way. Not at all. Clients often do exactly the same, and mutuality is exactly what social referencing is all about.

There is, however, an essential difference, which is connected to the task of the therapist mentioned above. It is an indispensable part of her task to work hard to communicate her empathic commitment and to keep checking to see whether it has really got through to the client. On the other hand, no such requirement can be placed on clients who, it goes without saying, have the right to behave and to be just as they are at any given time. Naturally, the same goes for how much of their capacity for empathy they communicate to the therapists and how they do it. In such cases where, in the view of the therapist, this capacity for empathy is still undeveloped or perhaps not clearly expressed, it is part of a therapist's job to give the client encouragement and also, by asking for clarification, for example, to make sure that they really understand what is happening.

4.1.3   The Communication of Empathy

For greater clarity, empathic communications can be divided initially into verbal and nonverbal communications and then subdivided into various different nonverbal communications. Communication actually requires attentive, participatory looking and active listening, which

Barrett-Lennard would probably say was still part of the first phase, since these activities carry important messages.

After all, the kind look with which the other person views me and assesses me is not simply coming from an instrument of observation.[59] His living gaze is not identical to the physical functioning of his optical organ of perception, the eye. This is clear in our subjective experience of the look.

> If I apprehend the look, I cease to perceive the eyes. . . . The other's look hides his eyes. . . . To apprehend a look is not to apprehend a look-as-object in the world (unless the look is not directed upon us); it is to be conscious of being looked at (Sartre, 1956, p. 258).

Thus "it is never *eyes* which look at us; it is the other-as-subject" (Sartre, 1956, p. 277—italics added). Being seen is therefore always first and foremost a validation[60] of my existence and personality. When the other person tells me "I see you," he is clearly not just referring to an optical perception but is stating "I recognize that you are *there* and that you are *you*." It is not only in the early years but throughout life that this look of the other has the effect of validating the self. The self sees that it is being seen.

This fundamental recognition comes *before* any understanding. This also presupposes, and this must be seen as a *principle,* not merely a chronological sequence, that every human encounter begins with a greeting. Lévinas stresses that, before establishing common ground with the other by means of understanding, we must first honor our shared humanity by some fitting expression of acknowledgement; this common ground cannot be traced back to the understanding (see 1983, p. 113).

Petzold described this process under the fitting title "dialogues of the gaze."

> *In its unique mutuality,* gazing is of central importance for the development of human communication and personality. . . . Because human eyes can "speak" and convey to the other person the basic recognition— "This is you!—because the other person is reflected in the gaze of one person, and one person is mirrored in the gaze of the other (and this is how in early infancy "self-recognition" and thus all self-knowledge and interpersonal reference begins to take root), in all forms of psychotherapy the look, gazing, recognition, and mirroring are assigned fundamental importance. . . .

---

59 See also Buber's (1947) distinction between observing, looking on, and becoming aware.
60 This term is used by Linehan (1997).

Experiencing the self, certainty of one's identity, a feeling of self and self-esteem are imparted by being looked at in a way that is loving and recognizes one's value and identity (Petzold, 1995, pp. 442f.—original italics).

Thus, it also comes as no surprise that Haase and Tepper (1972) confirm that direct eye contact and the therapist's caring facial expression play an important role in his being experienced by the client as an empathic person. This is underlined further if he leans forward slightly and sits quite close. From time to time, his attentive gaze is complemented by a friendly, validating, or encouraging smile or no, and sometimes by a touch which conveys closeness or support (see Harrigan & Rosenthal, 1986).

This participatory, validating looking is combined with active listening, which involves more than simple perception by the senses. "Active listening" does not simply mean listening in an acoustic sense. It refers rather to an *attitude*—being prepared to take time, to be open and attentive, to appear as approachable and free of fear as possible, and to be receptive to what the other person is saying. This means being receptive not only to the linguistic nuances but also to no-linguistic and atmospheric elements, including the unexpected and perhaps initially unintelligible. It is also important to "read between the lines" without jumping to conclusions too quickly about what appears to be important and what can be discarded as insignificant. It was Theodor Reik (1949) who coined the expression "listening with the third ear" for this attitude, and Gadamer spoke of "uninterrupted listening" that requires the effort "of being negative toward itself." By this he meant willingness, too, "to keep something at a distance—namely everything that suggests itself, on the basis of his own prejudices as the meaning expected" (1989, p. 461). It thus becomes possible

> to experience the Thou truly as a Thou—i.e., not to overlook his claim but to let him really say something to us. Here is where openness belongs. But ultimately this openness does not exist only for the person who speaks; rather, anyone who listens is fundamentally open. Without such openness to one another there is no genuine human bond (Reik, 1949, p. 355).

Not until this open looking and listening has taken place, with as few prejudices and presuppositions as possible and probably accompanied by the occasional sympathetic "mhm," is it the proper time for the therapist to communicate what she has understood to the client. She may do so verbally, for example. In client-centered therapy, this way of expressing empathy is referred to as "verbalizing the client's emotional experiential content." In other words,

> the psychotherapist puts into words the personal-emotional content of the client's experience just as it was expressed . . . by the client . . . Whatever the therapist has understood of the phenomenal world, and feelings that the client has expressed, he then communicates to the client in words, in a concrete, understandable way (Tausch, 1973, pp. 81, 86).

Whether it is understandable to the client depends not only on whether the words chosen by the therapist contain the correct nuances and linguistic exactness, but also often on whether the therapist succeeds in picking up the client's personal style of speaking and combining it with his own. If he does this well, then the client will recognize himself in it and at the same time he will experience a broadening of his self-understanding. The same applies particularly to the metaphorical and symbolic.

BOX 30

EXAMPLE

Client: Since losing my spouse I am lost. I have never been alone like this before. I wish I could find the words to describe it.

Therapist: I have an image of you being untethered in outer space; floating away with nothing to grab onto.

Client: Yes, it feels much like that! It's a frightening experience (Gonzales, 2001, p. 574).

It can be just as useful for the client when

> a therapist finds some way of communicating this embodied experiencing back to her client: for instance, "I experience a tightness in my chest when you talk about your divorce and I'm wondering if you feel that too" (Cooper, 2001, p. 227).

However, the therapist's statements about what she has understood from the client are only one side of the coin. The other side is her asking about aspects that she has not understood initially, in other words, the attempt to fill in gaps in her understanding and also to discriminate more finely and deepen an understanding that was rather rough and superficial to start with. Therapeutic questions of this kind, however, do not merely have the function of nudging the client into revealing information which enables *the therapist* to have a more complete understanding. They mostly also have the function of motivating *the client* to explore himself, which he needs to do first if he wants to answer the therapist's question. Thus "the therapeutically potent question is one that invites the client to search for answers, to think in new ways, to explore new avenues of awareness" (Erskine, Moursund, & Trautmann, 1999, p. 20).

The main reason for asking questions in therapy is not to satisfy the curiosity of the therapist but to encourage the self-exploration of the client and to influence the direction it might take, where it seems helpful to do so. All the same, as a rule, if there is a gap in the therapist's understanding, which he acknowledges and admits to himself, this is sufficient reason for him to ask a question. "In order to be able to ask, one must want to know, and that means knowing that one does not know" (Gadamer, 1989, p. 363). At the same time, it is helpful for the therapist himself to guard against filling in such gaps overhastily, just in his *own* mind and without any exchange with the client. This can easily happen because of the "tendency towards a good gestalt" or "*Prägnanz*," that the Gestalt psychologists have described, and is not necessarily a case of "knowing better." However, if he makes sense of what he hears too soon, the therapist claims the interpretative prerogative—he can certainly make *his own* sense of the information that is still partially unintelligible, but this does not necessarily mean that he has understood *the client*.[61] Even if the sense he has made of the client really is correct, he can only ascertain this by discussing it with the client.

Therapists do not have a monopoly on the truth, even if clients think they have X-ray eyes.

> Therapists . . . can effectively counteract the idea that they have a privileged access to truth by continually asking their clients to help them understand them. They do so by making clear how dependent they are on their clients for feedback about how they perceive the therapy. The way the clients perceive the therapy has proved to be a factor that is absolutely essential for them to find their bearings, and this is the only way a therapist can know what is helpful and what is not (White 1992, p. 60).

"The dialogical connection," writes Waldenfels, with reference to Husserl, "does not thrive where there is premature reconciliation, but

---

61 In a study that caused quite a stir when it was first published, Rosenhan (1973) demonstrated, most impressively, what absurd and also inhuman consequences can result from exerting one-sided control over how something is interpreted, when taken to the extreme.

where there is reluctant harmony in 'communicative agreement out of disagreement, i.e. of correcting each other and thus arriving at a truth to-gether'"(1971, p. 180). It is useful here to adopt an attitude that I refer to as "cultivated uncertainty" (see Staemmler, 2009; see also Spinelli, 1997). This involves first being prepared to accept that the therapist has never before encountered in this particular form what he is now attempting to under-stand. He cannot therefore fall back on any fixed ways of understanding and must, instead, be open to the client's uniqueness and the joint situa-tion that they are sharing. Second, cultivated uncertainty also involves a willingness to allow oneself to be corrected by the client if necessary. This requires continuous checking of one's own empathic understanding in the dialog with the client.[62]

> Any object of knowledge (including man) can be perceived and cog-nized as a thing. But a subject as such cannot be perceived and studied as a thing, for as a subject it cannot, while remaining a subject, be-come voiceless, and, consequently, cognition of it can only be dialogic (Bakhtin, 1986, p. 161).

Third and last, in order to be able to be both curious and thorough in his approach, the therapist needs to accept (provisionally at least) that he may eventually be able to find meaning in and empathize with what initially seemed incomprehensible.

Gadamer calls this the "fore-conception of completeness" (1989, pp. 293f.), but if we are to avoid interpreting this completeness wrongly as a perfect state, we should perhaps, in a psychotherapeutic context, speak not of completeness but of *completion*, or use Davidson's (1984) term of the "principle of charity" (for more on this, see Staemmler, 2010a). Such a "fore-conception of completion" should be understood as a heuristic principle that inspires us to explore together endlessly and check our understanding dialogically. It serves to suggest, charitably, to the other person that his experiential world is meaningful for him, even if from the outside it may appear unintelligible or even bizarre at first glance.

Nevertheless, it is not a question of subscribing to a vision — or should I say illusion — of there being a "one and only correct" or "ultimate" un-derstanding, since it is important to accept "that the meaning of a person's

---

62 Incidentally, this has positive repercussions on the therapist's competence: "The provi-sion of target-generated feedback not only increased the rate at which the perceivers' em-pathic accuracy improved across time for a given target; it also made subsequent targets easier to read, even upon initial exposure to them" (Ickes, Marangoni, & Garcia, 1997, p. 293).

life is always uncertain and inconclusive at any time because the future is open ended and lacking closure" (Guignon, 1998, p. 572). Neither can we assume that there will be no contradictions or that there will be complete consistency, since all human beings, particularly those who enter therapy perhaps, have their conflicts, contradictions, and inconsistencies. Some things only become comprehensible when we let go of the requirement, or perhaps the norm, that it is possible for everything to be brought in line and to be consistent (see Staemmler, 2005).[63]

In order to reach the point where the client's mysterious experience becomes understandable to both, if not "completely," then at least more fully, therapist and client need to enter into a dialog with each other. In the course of this dialog, the therapist puts her thoughts into words and asks questions, thus contributing to the gradual achievement of an increasingly clear empathic understanding of her client. However, the verbal tools only seemingly are opposites of the nonverbal ones, for "one might say that our whole body is an expressive organ of speech" (Matta, 1986, p. 26; see Staemmler, 2003a). It is, therefore, somewhat artificial to describe the verbal and nonverbal aspects of communication separately, even if this is unavoidable if the purpose is to explain them. "Verbal symbols, the behavior and gestures of the body, affects and somatic processes do not each communicate different things. They are parts of communicative actions that belong together. Each interprets the other" (Streeck, 2001, p. 230).

The first nonverbal means of expression is silence. Silence can, of course, fulfill a variety of functions, not all of which are indicative of empathy.[64] Fengler (2004, pp. 180f.) gives many examples of empathic silence, and I would like to mention three in particular. First there is "giving silence as space," which gives the client the opportunity for "the gradual production of thoughts whilst speaking" (Kleist, 1997) and opens up other ways for her to explore herself more deeply and convey what she finds.[65] Kennedy-Moore and Watson explain why this can be so beneficial.

---

63 People differ not only in the amount of mental consistency they possess but also in their tolerance of inconsistency and desire for consistency. The psychological concept of the "consistency principle," defined as "a basic requirement for systems to function" (Grawe, 2002, p. 341), is something different. This is often portrayed, also by Grawe, almost as a kind of law of nature, whereby cultural factors tend to be ignored.

64 The *still-face* experiment, mentioned above, is one of many possible examples of this.

65 Gendlin has observed that the moments of silence are often followed by important steps in the self-exploration of clients. "When somebody is sitting with you *in total silence*, you can focus much more deeply and much more easily than you can alone" (1990, p. 212 — original italics).

The process of trying to explain one's feelings to someone else necessarily involves clarifying these feelings in one's own mind. L. F. Clark (1993) points out that to effectively convey their experience to another person, speakers have to step out of their own perspective enough to be able to consider the listener's viewpoint, which means that they look at their own experience from a new perspective (2001, p. 193),

without the other person having to say a single word.

Second, Fengler speaks of "silence as an invitation," which the therapist uses to invite the client to answer her questions and respond to her suggestions. Third, he mentions "composed silence," whereby the therapist allows herself the freedom not to have to reply to everything the client says immediately (e.g., a personal attack), and, rather, patiently allows her to take her time to hear what she has said and feel the impact of her words. Another aspect of composed silence is that it is an expression of peace, which permits the therapist to trust that the next step of the therapeutic process will be taken when the time is right, rather than having to be produced by actions.

I would like to add another type of silence to Fengler's list—and illustrate it with an example—one that I frequently find important, particularly when I am working with people who tend to react with a feeling of shame. I am thinking of *silence as the expression of tact*, where we prefer not to mention or comment on some of the things that we hear from the other person. We do this first because we want to spare him the embarrassment that (we suspect) he would feel if he were to be aware of the fact that we had noticed them, and second, because in the given situation, there is no particular reason to mention them. To my knowledge, there is no better description of what is meant by "tact" than Gadamer's:

> By tact we understand a particular sensitivity and sensitiveness to situations and how to behave in them, for which knowledge from general principles does not suffice. Hence an essential part of tact is that it is tacit and unformulable inexplicitness and inexpressibility. One can say something tactfully but that will always mean that one will pass over something tactfully and leave it unsaid, and it is tactless to express what one can only pass over. But to pass over something does not mean to avert one's gaze from it, but to keep an eye on it in such a way that rather than knock into it, one slips by it. Thus tact helps one to preserve distance. It avoids the offensive, the intrusive, the violation of the intimate sphere of the person (1989, p. 15).

To remain silent out of tact is a decision *not* to give expression to something that has been perceived or sensed because one wishes to prevent the client from feeling that the empathic attitude of the therapist is invasive, or more importantly, if it is a group situation, that he will feel exposed by it.

BOX 31

EXAMPLE I meet up with a friend for supper and tell him about an experience that I found very moving. Although he listens attentively, because it is the end of a long day and he has had some wine with the meal, he is now perhaps rather tired. I see the beginnings of a yawn pass over his face and also notice that he tries to stifle it. I assume that he wants to avoid my getting the impression that he might be bored by what I am telling him and that he does not want me to be hurt because he has understood that what I experienced was important for me—that he wants to be tactful. Because I do not want to risk disappointing his well-intentioned efforts, I am also tactful and do not let him know that I have noticed his yawn and his attempt to suppress it.

As all forms of silence, by their nature, do *not* name *clearly* the very thing to which they relate, they are a relatively *unspecific* way of expressing empathy. However, the therapist will frequently have cause to communicate her empathy to the client *with a more specific focus in mind*—irrespective of whether or not this addresses an issue that is unpleasant for the client. What is especially important in such cases is the nonverbal way in which the therapist conveys her empathy for the client's *feelings*. This has nothing to do with sentimentality but with the pivotal psychosocial position that feelings occupy as a place where situation, body, and thinking come together.[66]

Here we are concerned not only with those feelings that the client herself already has a clear sense of and either expresses verbally or shows through gesture and facial expression, but also, and especially, with those that are *not* initially in the foreground of the client's awareness. For the "mere concentration of attention, by or with the subject, especially on some parts of the field that are characteristically *out of* awareness, will by definition produce some reorganization of the field—and the potential, at least, for a corresponding behavioral change, of one kind or another" (Wheeler, 1998, p. 39—italics added).

There is empirical evidence for Wheeler's theoretical position:

In the successful treatment, substantial relations between the narrated episodes of the patient and the facial affective behavior of the therapist

---

66 For this reason, Levenson and Ruef believe "that the most useful definition of empathy would emphasize the ability to detect accurately the *emotional* information being transmitted by another person" (1992, p. 234—italics added).

could be found. A closer inspection revealed that the therapist produced those affects that the patient did not tell nor display in the narrated episodes, but which could be expected as adequate emotional responses (Anstadt et al., 1997, p. 414).[67]

The therapist expresses the affects that she has picked up from the other person through a number of mirroring processes which are worthy of closer scrutiny. We must first distinguish between "discrete" or "categorical affects," on the one hand, and "vitality affects" on the other. Discrete or categorical affects (or emotions) are those that can be divided into different categories according to the nature of the feeling and can be specified by nouns. Examples are those that are known as *basic emotions,* such as sadness, anger, surprise, fear, disgust, contempt, and joy, to which I will return in a different context in the next chapter. Shame can also be considered to be an example of a categorical affect.

In contrast, vitality affects have nothing to do with such qualities of *feeling,* but refer to *vitality* contours or "melodies," or *process* qualities that can be observed in connection with all possible categorical affects. These process qualities are best described by present participles, for example welling up, dying away, fleeting, surging, fading, bursting, sweeping, or adjectives such as explosive, wave-like, etc. They can also be clearly represented by time curves. For instance, the feeling of anger can have an explosive course, in the same way as an experience of sadness or joy that comes over one suddenly, in a rush, and which disappears just as quickly (see Diagram 1 in Figure 4). However, feelings can also well up *slowly* and then reach a certain plateau of intensity that is sustained for a while and then *gradually* dies away again (see Diagram 2).

Diagram 1   Diagram 2

FIGURE 4
Vitality affects (contours)

These two curves are just two examples. One can imagine many different curves, i.e., many different vitality affects, as we saw from the list of adjectives above. Vitality affects such as these play an important role in

---

67 An explanation of this association is to be found in Vygotsky's theory (see Chapter 6).

everyday communication between people. They are part of the "how" in the familiar expression, "It's not what you say but how you say it."

BOX 32

VITALITY AFFECTS

are subjective experiences. They consist of the temporal dynamics of changes in feelings consisting of analogic shifts, split second by split second in real time, of affects, thoughts, perceptions, or sensations. For instance, the felt acceleration and the explosion of anger (Stern, 2004, p. 246).

Stern also gives this example:

Imagine that someone you know greets you on the street with a smile. The crescendo time of the smile (is it explosive or does it sneak up?) may indicate spontaneous pleasure or guilty surprise at seeing you. The duration of holding the high point may reflect the level of pleasure. The speed of decomposition may speak to the authenticity of the display, and so on (Stern, 2004, p. 63).

In the same way that categorical affects differ from vitality affects, different too are the methods of communicating to another person the fact that one has understood these various kinds of affects. If someone wants to convey to another person his empathic understanding of categorical affects such as joy or annoyance, he has to follow a different route from someone who wants to show how he has captured the temporal pattern of an emotional movement that he has perceived in another person.

Empathy with another person's categorical feelings can be best conveyed nonverbally by imitating that person's expression as it appears in his face and bodily movements. Many studies show that this already quite often happens spontaneously and unconsciously when we focus on another person. "Facial expressions are contagious" (Lundqvist & Dimberg, 1995).[68] Bodily movements, too, are often mirrored spontaneously and unintentionally, as we will see in more detail in the next chapter under the heading "mimetic synchrony."

When we imitate in this way, unintentionally and unconsciously, it is often not consciously perceived by the person whose expression we are reflecting. Thus, in such cases, there is no danger of the other person feeling that we are mocking them. When we imitate somebody deliberately, it is important to do it in such a way that we do not appear to be aping them.

---

68 There are dramatic consequences if people are unable to show such "infectious" reactions in their faces, for instance, if they suffer from permanent paralysis of the face muscles ("Moebius syndrome"). Cole (1998, 2001) has studied this at length and given us moving descriptions of the fates of these people.

In my experience, it is often helpful to introduce the nonverbal mirroring of a body posture *verbally*. We can also add a suggestion about what the other person may be expressing by this posture.

BOX 33

EXAMPLE For instance, the therapist may preface his feedback on the client's posture (see Figure 5) with the words, "I notice how you are holding your body— rather like this . . . ," and imitate the posture. He can then add, "To me it looks as though you don't really know what to do."

FIGURE 5
Matchstick man shrugging his shoulders (from Sarbin, 1954, p. 231)

If a therapist wants to mirror emotions that she has perceived in the client's facial expression, she needs to be equally careful. In almost all cases, the mirroring will be less marked than the original expression. Particularly where she is reacting to the client's feelings of pain, she will also often mirror a mixture of the pain that she has discerned in the client and compassion for the client's feeling of pain. Thus, imitation is usually supplemented or modified in some way.

This kind of nonverbal communicating of the empathized categorical affects of the client is certainly familiar to most therapists and is frequently practiced—sometimes unconsciously, sometimes consciously. In my experience as a supervisor, the same cannot be said of the vitality affects. The term itself that I have briefly explained above is unfamiliar to many colleagues, even today. Even less well known is the importance of mirroring vitality affects, if the clients are to feel that their therapists are really *with them*. The experience of shared togetherness and connectedness depends to a considerable degree on the successful feedback of vitality affects (see Stern, 1985, p. 157).

Originally, such feedback was investigated in order to better understand the affective referencing between mothers and their toddlers and thus the early forms of intersubjectivity. In successful interactions, processes like those described in the following example were observed. Incidentally, this example corresponds approximately to the second curve in Figure 4. It is taken from Stern's wonderful *Diary of a Baby*.

BOX 34

EXAMPLE

Joey and his mother ... are looking for a stuffed rabbit, his favorite toy, which got hidden under a blanket. Joey finds it. He swings it excitedly into view and looks to his mother with a burst of pleasure. In a smooth crescendo, his face opens up. His eyes grow wider, and his mouth eases into a broad smile, to show her what he found—even more important, to show her how he feels about it. After she sees his face, he lets his face fall back to normal in a smooth diminuendo. She then says "YeaaAAaah!" with a rising, then falling pitch. Joey seems content with her response and goes on playing by himself.

I found it! Here!
A wave of delight rises high in me. It swells to a crest. It leans forward, curls, and breaks into musical foam. The foam slips back as the wave passes, and disappears into the quieter water behind.
Does she feel the wave too?
Yes!
She calls back the rising and falling echo of my wave. I ride her echo up and down. It passes through me, and I sense my delight in her.
It now belongs to both of us (Stern, 1990, pp. 101f.—original italics).

If we analyze this example, we notice, among other things, that the mother mirrors the crescendo and diminuendo in the child's facial expression in a way that corresponds yet is *in a different mode*, i.e., in her tone of voice. Her vocal expression has, however, the same *vitality contour* as the facial expression of the child. The vitality affect is "transposed," as it were, into a different mode—rather like a particular tune can be transposed into a different key without losing its own intrinsic gestalt. It can easily be recognized in the new key. In this way, the child is handed back his *vitality affect, transposed into a different mode.*

What the child gets back is, therefore, *identical in essence* to his own expression but *in a modified form*. Stern refers to this as "transmodal[69] matching." What is the advantage of this? There is just one: The child will feel understood and will sense that his mother is taking an interest. But why does

---

69 This phenomenon is sometimes also called "cross-modal" or "inter-modal" and often used to be called "synesthetic."

it need to be both identical *and* modified? "Better safe than sorry!" The fact that the intrinsic essence is the same in the feedback of the vitality affect (the crescendo and diminuendo) shows the child that his vital experience has been understood by his mother. The modification underlines this as well. The mother thus conveys to the child that she is *not just imitating* him, i.e., that she has just picked up something external, but that she really has *understood* the essence of what he is expressing. Otherwise, she would clearly not have been able to translate it into a different mode.

In a similar way to the mirroring of categorical affects, which, although it is based on imitation, usually contains modifications as well, the feedback of vitality affects also involves the combination of imitation (identical vitality contour) and modification (change in mode). Both aspects find expression in the term "transmodal matching." Here mothers intuitively exploit their children's innate ability spontaneously to "recognize" transmodal matches. "For the senses communicate with each other" (Merleau-Ponty, 1962, p. 225[70]). "There is not one original thing, e.g. an aural event, that is then transposed into a different realm, but there is an interplay between the senses from the outset" (Waldenfels, 2000, p. 94). Therefore even "infants are predesigned to be able to perform a cross-modal transfer of information that permits them to recognize a correspondence across touch and vision" (Stern, 1985, p. 48). In an impressive experiment, Meltzoff and Borton (1979) demonstrated that 3-week-old babies were capable of differentiating, visually, two different types of pacifier that they had never seen before but that they had had in their mouths. Lewkowicz und Turkewitz (1980) showed something similar for the identification of a vitality contour that had initially been perceived visually and which the babies then recognized in an aural form.

One can assume that anything that works reliably in babies will also work in psychotherapy with older children and adults. It is precisely in this way that a therapist can indicate effectively to her client that she has understood his vitality affect. She simply needs to echo in a *different* mode the vitality contour that she has perceived in *the first* mode.

BOX 35

EXAMPLE The therapist hears the pitch in her client's *voice* gradually fall, as he is telling her about a particular experience (mode: aural; contour: falling). She responds to this—instead of, or in addition to, giving a verbal response—by illustrating the vitality contour with a downward *hand movement* (new mode: kinesthetic for the therapist, visual for the client; identical contour: falling).

---

70 "If, then, taken as incomparable qualities, the 'data of the different senses' belong to so many separate worlds, each one in its particular essence being a manner of modulating the thing, they all communicate through their significant core" (Merleau-Ponty, 1962, p. 230).

From this example, moreover, we can easily see that a vitality affect represents a completely different dimension from a categorical affect. The experience that the client is talking about with his voice dropping in pitch (which has purposely not been described more fully here) could either be one where he gradually calmed down in a pleasant way after feeling anxious and disturbed, or one where he slowly gave up hope after a succession of disappointments, or also one where his joy about some good news ebbed away over time.

Naturally, when conveying what she has discovered through empathy, the therapist will not only refer to the current vitality affects of her client but also to his categorical affects (emotions) and the more cognitive aspects of his experience, for instance, the attributions of meaning ("appraisals" — see Scherer, Schorr, & Johnstone, 2001; Staemmler & Staemmler, 2009), which make up his view of relevant situations. Because the client himself also relates empathically to the therapist, albeit often in a rather more implicit and less systematic way than his therapist, *both* contribute to a reciprocal empathic exchange which culminates from time to time in "moments of meeting" (Stern, 2004, pp. 168ff.), "existential moments" (Teschke, 1996), or "tight therapeutic sequences" (Polster, 1991). All of these are similar terms that attempt to describe how reciprocal relatedness in "personal contact" (Staemmler, 1993a) results in episodes of intersubjective intensity and also experiences of togetherness, connectedness, closeness and intimacy, that can have the effect of changing both participants. In the words of a Japanese philosopher:

> My being conscious of you is intertwined with your being conscious of me. . . . Our conscious acts are not determined by ourselves alone, but they are also determined by others. . . . Thus . . . the consciousness of the participants are mutually permeated through one another's. When you are angry, my consciousness is colored by that anger, and when you are grieving, my consciousness is influenced by it (Watsuji, quoted from Arisaka, 2001, p. 200).

The founder of *Focusing*, Eugene Gendlin, used words that are remarkably similar:

> My sense of you, the listener, affects my experiencing as I speak, and your response partly determines my experiencing a moment later.hat occurs to me, and how I live as we speak and interact, is vitally affected by every word and motion you make, and by every facial expression and attitude you show. . . . Thus it is not the case that I tell you about me, and then we figure out how I should change, and then somehow I do

it. Rather, I am changing as I talk and think and feel, for your responses are every moment part of my experiencing, and partly affect, produce, symbolize, and interact with it (1962, pp. 38f.).

The following example of a case study illustrates how closely interwoven are the experiences of the partners in a dialog and how they can influence each successive moment in an interaction.

BOX 36

EXAMPLE My client L.[71] is about 40 years old and has very much withdrawn from social contacts. He has no confidence in himself. He does not believe that anyone could find him interesting as a person, nor does he think that he has any positive qualities at all. Although he has a diploma in business administration he lacks confidence in his ability to work in his profession and earns a relatively low wage as a warehouse worker.

In complete contrast to his expectations, I find being with him stimulating and I look forward to every session with him. For me, the therapeutic sessions always take a surprising turn which arouses my interest. Even if L. almost always manages to come back to his feelings of worthlessness and insignificance—I cannot help liking him.

His experience of inferiority also includes his admiration of me. Not only—and this always comes as a surprise to him—because I view many of the ways in which he behaves and experiences life in a positive way and confirm him, but also because I do many things that he would never dare to do himself, e.g., write books or give lectures. But I do not experience his admiration purely and simply as idealization because whenever he expresses the fact that he is impressed by me, he does not leave it at that. He usually—shaking his head and marveling at the same time—asks how I manage to do things like this that are so completely beyond his own horizons.

His curiosity affects me on several levels. As well as the admiration I have just mentioned, there is something childlike about it. It is the curiosity of a person who is encountering something completely new for the first time, something he has never thought possible before. When he asks about something in this way I feel like a circus performer whose movements he follows with wonder and whom he then bombards with questions about how he could accomplish something similar himself.

When I answer him I usually experience two things. On the one hand I am happy to give information because his interest seems so sincere and I have the impression that what I am telling him opens up new worlds for him, worlds that have not been at all accessible to him so far, but which at least become just about

---

71 Grateful thanks to the client for giving permission for this to be published.

imaginable, thus broadening the horizons of his isolated life. On the other hand I always feel shy as well, because every time I give him information about myself I have a clear sense of how very different our worlds are.

But he questions me at every opportunity, for instance if I can't give him an appointment at the usual time because I am not going to be there. He wants to know what I am going to be doing and often asks about details. When he does this I never have the impression that he wants to violate my personal boundaries or invade my privacy. On the contrary, in his own way, which sometimes appears gauche, he is genuinely interested in me. It was only after we had been working together for some time that I realized that this expression of interest in me was the beginning of the end of his social isolation.

Although for him it is still unthinkable that anyone—including me—could be interested in him, he begins, through becoming interested in me, to relax withdrawal slightly in one direction. As he does this it is extremely important for him to express his interest. For him it is a huge, well-nigh unprecedented step to reveal himself through his interest in me. To do that is diametrically opposed to his old self-image, i.e., that he will only be a burden on others if he allows himself to be seen. With every new question that he asks me he is testing out over and over again whether I really like telling him things and talking to him.

Thus in one of our sessions the question arose as to what it means to him to express himself and reveal himself. He found it hard to put it into words, but during our dialogue it gradually became clear that expressing himself and revealing himself to someone (me) was not simply a way of making contact which can help to overcome his isolation, but that it also gives him a feeling of freedom from his own inhibitions and fears in which he often feels himself so hopelessly trapped in his life outside of therapy.

As we talked about this his eyes suddenly lit up and he began to enthuse about how "fantastic" (and this expression is pregnant with a whole range of meanings) it would be to be able to express himself just once completely freely and without inhibitions. When asked exactly what fantasy he had in his mind's eye at this point, he answered with surprising spontaneity, "I would love to shout at the top of my voice without worrying about what other people might think."

This was right before the end of our session and we were unable to pursue the matter any further. But at the beginning of our next session he raised it straight away, asking whether I remembered where we stopped last time. I had not forgotten, and with unusual directness and decisiveness he said that he would like to pick up where we left off. He would like to make a really loud noise. I indicated that this was fine with me, but now it seemed strange to him to suddenly "have to" make a noise, just like that.

After some dithering he asked me if I would mind joining in with him. He had the idea that we could say a sentence together with each of us taking it in turns to say a word, each one saying the word slightly louder than the previous one.

In this way we would repeat the sentence several times, thus eventually reaching maximum volume. By doing this I would be able to help him to do something that he longed to do, but had never dared to do before.

So we thought of a sentence we could use for the experiment and then we started. During the first few repetitions we didn't get very loud as he did not dare to be louder than me. But after three or four attempts he actually began to grow a little louder than me every time it was his turn. After a while he could no longer stay in his seat and we stood up. We got louder every time and accentuated our words with gestures and movements that we adjusted to fit in with each other just as we did our words. And finally we shouted out the sentence several times— still taking it in turns to say a word each—at the tops of our voices. The effort that we had made in the first few rounds turned more and more into a kind of joyful excitement. As this happened, a beaming smile gradually spread across his face.

Finally, we ended our experiment, rather hoarse and exhausted, but satisfied. L. was elated and could hardly believe what he had experienced. He kept shaking his head in happy disbelief, saying, for example, "I don't believe it!" Once his feelings had died down a bit I asked him what it was that he couldn't believe. What I suspected was something along the lines of his having completely surprised himself by making such a loud noise and revealing himself by doing this. But that was not the most important thing for him at all, although he was also pleased about that. What surprised and impressed him most and what he was most happy about was that I joined in with him, and that we spoke the sentence together. In other words, he had not been left on his own and isolated as he expressed himself.

He continued to stress the importance this experience had for him in the following sessions.

4.1.4   Summary of Chapter 4.1

As we reach the end of this section, I would like to summarize briefly what has been my primary interest here. It is the first building block, as it were, of my new understanding of empathy in psychotherapy.

Empathy is not just a one-sided process, but a process in which "a person who understands himself and others is understanding another person who understands herself and others" (Köhler, 1990, p. 289). Both therapists and clients turn empathically toward the other person and communicate to them what they understand about each other. "Self- and interactive regulation are concurrent and reciprocal processes, each one affecting the success of the other . . .; all behavior is simultaneously unfolding in the individual while at the same time continuously modifying and being modified by the changing behavior of the partner" (Beebe, Lachmann, Feldstein, Crown, & Jasnow, 2000, p. 102). Empathy in psychotherapy should therefore be viewed as a form of social referencing which includes the individual empathic capacities of *both* partners.[72] It should be understood as a process of mutual influencing, in both an overall sense as well as in multiple empathic microprocesses that often remain below the threshold of consciousness and yet nevertheless "are particularly powerful because they occur in the here-and now of the interactive matrix. Thus they possess that special alive quality of something immediate for both" (Beebe & Lachmann, 2002, p. 129).

The mutuality referred to here is to be understood not simply as a model of communication that is like a chess game, where each participant makes a move in turn, one after the other but only one at a time. This erroneous impression is easily inspired by the transcripts of therapy sessions or of other formal dialog. However, it shifts the focus to an essential dimension of empathic communication that is particularly evident on the nonverbal level and which Gendlin was also hinting at above. For "as soon as the verbal domain is left, it becomes obvious that a dyad is in fact a closely knit net of concurrent mutual exchanges across several nonverbal channels. At the same time, each participant is both sender and receiver" (Kappas & Descoteaux, 2003, p. 52).

I would like to emphasize once more that therapists and clients will express their own particular way of empathizing with their partner in different ways that are appropriate to their own roles and tasks. It is the responsibility of the therapists to use their expertise to uphold the offer of personal contact even when the clients at times possibly do not entirely manage to do so. They must also use their expertise to give their clients the support necessary for the mutual empathic relationship to resume.

4.2   BODILY EMPATHY—"ENCORPORATION" (*EINLEIBUNG*)

The author of a book entitled *Embodiment*, a psychologist, states in her introduction: "When people think, feel and act, they do not do so as disembodied ghosts. The body is always involved" (Storch, 2006, p. 37). In the words of the philosopher Friedrich Nietzsche, "behind your thoughts and feelings, my brother, stands a mighty commander, an unknown sage—he is called Self. He lives in your body, he is your body" (2003, p. 62). The neuroscientist Gerald Hüther also stresses that "perceiving and sensing and thinking and feeling and moods and posture and everything that

---

72 See Figure 1, where I showed how I see the relationship between the traditional understanding of empathy and my expanded understanding.

happens in the body are . . . much more closely connected and linked to each other than previously thought" (2006, p. 93).

There is a striking convergence here between psychological research, philosophical insights—particularly those of phenomenology (see Box 6) with its concept of embodiment (see Box 21 and below)—and the insights of the modern neurosciences. In the following section, I shall draw on several studies from these three disciplines to elucidate the embodied nature of empathy.

4.2.1 The Psychological Standpoint

Facial Feedback and Recognition of Basic Emotions

On the one hand, the psychologist mentioned above gives examples[73] of how mental experience affects what happens to the body; e.g., students who have just been awarded good examination grades will walk taller ("more proudly") than those who have just received bad grades. Yet on the other hand, she shows how body processes affect mental experience, using Ekman's theory of *facial feedback* as an example. According to Ekman, "through feedback from the facial muscles . . . changes [are] effected in the brain that produce the emotions that correspond to the facial gestures being made" (Storch 2006, p. 40).[74] The people taking part in the experiment, who are told, for example, to "(A) 'raise your brows and pull them together,' (B) 'now raise your upper eyelids,' (C) 'now also stretch your lips horizontally, back toward your ears'" (Ekman, Levenson, & Friesen, 1983, p. 1208), reported afterward that they had feelings of anxiety, and they also showed corresponding physiological changes (in heart rate, hand temperatures, skin resistance, forearm muscle tension).

Ekman et al. had to admit, however that "with this experiment we cannot rule out the possibility that knowledge of the emotion labels derived from the facial movement instructions or seeing one's own or the coach's face was directly or indirectly responsible for the effect" (Ekman et al., 1983, p. 1210). However, Strack, Martin, and Stepper designed an ingenious study that enabled them to avoid *cognitive* processing of the facial movements. They proved that what is involved is (at least in part) a *direct* and *unconscious* feedback loop and that thought processes are not needed

---

73 Storch is referring to Weisfeld and Beresford (1982) and also to Ekman (1992).
74 "This might occur either through peripheral feedback from making the facial movements or by a direct connection between the motor cortex and hypothalamus" (Ekman et al., 1983, p. 1210).

to produce the effect. "Our findings clearly suggest that recognizing the emotional meaning of the facial response was not a necessary precondition for the effect" (1988, p. 776). In other words, anyone who makes a certain face, completely unconsciously, induces in himself the feeling that this facial expression normally conveys.

One of the things that makes this conclusion interesting is that it is a substantial advance on other, earlier hypotheses that were based on the assumption of there being some *cognitive* link. Bem's "self-perception theory," which might be better named "self-interpretation theory," is one example of these earlier hypotheses. Bem maintained that individuals "come to 'know' their own attitudes, emotions, and other internal states partially by inferring them from observations of their own overt behavior and/or the circumstances in which this behavior occurs" (Bem, 1972, p. 2).[75] Thus, the studies conducted by Strack et al. show that Bem was being suitably cautious when he incorporated the word "partially" into his hypothesis. These studies prove that processes of *self*-experiencing can be both direct and cognitively mediated. This parallels what we learned about how we gain impressions of *other* people under the headings "simulation theory" and "theory theory," above.

These and countless other examples, a few of which I will be giving later on, illustrate how closely body (Descartes' *res extensa*) and mind (*res cogitans* — see Box 4) are linked. They are, in fact, so closely interconnected that separating them into two different concepts is not only useful but also potentially quite problematic because it suggests that they exist primarily as two separate systems and that it is only secondarily that they interact with each other. This view, however, does not do justice to how closely interwoven they are.

We also find a close link between soma and psyche in the phenomenon of empathy, where it is particularly evident, as shown clearly in the two examples given above. The way the successful students in the first example are walking tall makes them appear to the onlooker not only to be *tall*, but also *proud*. He will certainly see them as proud if he also has some knowledge of the context of the situation and is aware, for instance, that the students have just received their examination results. The *embodiment* of the pride experienced by the successful students conveys to the observer the impression of a *feeling* of pride and not simply the impression of a tall *posture*. The second example, the evoking of feelings by activating the associated facial expression by means of *facial feedback*, demonstrates the way in which a person's spontaneous and often unconscious imitation

---

75 Here there is a certain similarity to the James-Lange theory, which I shall come to later.

of the facial expression of the person he is observing (see Lundqvist & Dimberg, 1995) can also produce a similar feeling in him as observer.

> We ourselves take the position that subjective emotional experience is affected by feedback from facial, vocal, and postural movements that are *mimicked* . . . In brief, then, we would argue that the sight of a face that is happy, loving, angry, sad, or fearful can cause the viewer to mimic elements of that face and, consequently, to catch the others' emotions (Hatfield, Cacioppo, & Rapson, 1994, p. 53—original italics).[76]

Perception of other people's facial expressions certainly plays an important role here. Human beings appear to possess the innate capacity to "see"[77] certain emotions in other people's faces, regardless of any cultural or ethnic differences between them. This insight was the final outcome of Paul Ekman's life work (1972, 1992, 2003) and basically confirmed Darwin's (1872) assumptions, although his original intention was to refute them (see Ekman, 2003, p. 2). After extensive research in very different cultures (such as the USA, Brazil, New Guinea, and Japan), he came to the conclusion that the seven basic emotions "each have a distinct, universal, facial expression: sadness, anger surprise, fear, disgust, contempt, and happiness" (Ekman, 2003, p. 58).

> Each of these emotion terms . . . stands for a family of related emotions. Anger, for example, can vary in *strength*, ranging from annoyance to rage, and in *type*, such as sullen anger, resentful anger, indignant anger, and cold anger, to mention just a few. The variations in intensity within each emotion family are clearly marked on the face, but the scientific work has not yet been done to determine if the different types within each emotion family also have unique facial expressions (Ekman, 2003, p. 59—original italics).

For the moment, let us disregard these variations and also feelings such as embarrassment, guilt, shame, and envy, which have not (yet) been

---

76 Dilthey had already made this assumption: "The existence of other people is given us at first only from the outside, in facts available to sense . . . Only through a process of re-creation of that which is available to the senses do we complete this inner experience" (1996, p. 236).
77 I have used the word "see" in order to draw attention to the *immediacy* of the understanding of facial expressions described here. Had I used "recognize," for instance, and not "see," it would have had far too cognitive a connotation because, "when in daily life someone with a radiant face tells us about something, we do not live a piece of knowledge about things intelligible to us which are accompanied, in addition, by movements of the mouth along with characteristic distortion of the facial muscles. From the other's words, instead, we *immediately* and openly witness his joy, see it *directly* in his face" (Gurwitsch, 1979, p. 3—original italics).

FIGURE 6
Faces: Sadness, anger.
© *Photocase*—left: *i make design;* right: *designritter*

proven to have universal facial expressions. With regard to the basic emotions, two things are certain. First, for each of these emotions, there is a standard facial expression that is evidently relatively independent of culture. Ekman has measured and charted these in the minutest detail, right down to the individual face muscles that come into play and the specific way in which each one of them moves. The second finding is linked so closely to the first that they are almost like two sides of the same coin, and that is that when a person expresses one of the basic emotions in her face in a spontaneous, uninhibited and natural way, another person will instantly recognize it even if the two of them belong to completely different cultures. "Despite the translation problems, there has never been an instance in which the majority in two cultures ascribes a different emotion to the same expression. Never" (Ekman, 2003, p. 13). Only 36 hours after birth, babies are able to differentiate between expressions of joy, sadness, and surprise in someone else's face (see Field, Woodson, Greenberg, & Cohen, 1982).

When horror is expressed in another person's face as blatantly as in Edvard Munch's *The Scream* we say, quite correctly, that we "see" the horror in his face. This turn of phrase, which equates the expression with the emotion, might perhaps be termed "crossmodal," but that would be on an explanatory level and does not describe the experience itself. For the observer,

FIGURE 7
Edvard Munch, The Scream (1910?); Tempora and oil on unprimed
cardboard; work of art: © Munch Museum/Munch Ellingsen Group/VG
Bild-Kunst, Bonn 2011; photo: © Munch Museum

facial expression and the feeling that goes with it are *directly* linked, in roughly the same way as the outer shape of a round ball also contains the inner shape within it. We grasp it instantly—we do not first have to think logically about the connections between concave and convex surfaces. Edith Stein writes about "sadness 'being-co-given' in the sad countenance. . . . The sad countenance is . . . at one with sadness. . . . The countenance is the outside of sadness. Together they form a natural unity" (1917/1964, p. 71).

But there are, of course, situations where there are constraints on both the immediacy and the universality of the expression and of the way the observer understands it. In many social situations, cultural conditions and the after-effects of personal life experiences are superimposed on or limit the expression of emotions. It may also be affected by various current contextual factors (see Elfenbein, Marsh, & Ambady, 2002), all of which can be partly responsible for people not always showing their feelings "in a spontaneous, uninhibited and natural way" (see above). Ekman calls some of these many influences "display rules," by which he means

> socially learned, often culturally different, rules about the management
> of expression, about who can show which emotion to whom and when

they can do so. . . . These rules may dictate that we diminish, exaggerate, hide completely, or mask the expression of emotion we are feeling (Ekman, 2003, p. 4).

Ekman demonstrated this most convincingly in a number of studies (see, e.g., Ekman, 1972). Such display rules become second nature, as it were, and it is only when people think they are alone or unobserved or if they are in a situation of intimacy with somebody to whom they feel close, that these rules cease to apply. The extent to which this happens varies.[78] This is true, of course, not only of facial expressions but also postures and gestures, and consequently, "the significance of a posture or gesture is only . . . partially readable across cultural boundaries" (Hall, 1989, p. 76) depending on the extent to which display rules have an effect.

Clearly, empathy involves not only forming a purely *mental* model of the other person but also includes, in a variety of ways, the *bodily* level. This is especially true of the *emotional* aspect of personal interactions. The reason for this is not only the special psychosocial significance that feelings assume, as a kind of "interface" between situation, body, and thinking described above. It is also due to the fact that the emotions are particularly closely connected to the body or, to use the language of the neuroscientists, "in emotions, unlike in cognitions, the brain does not usually function independently of the body. Many if not most emotions involve bodily responses" (LeDoux, 1996, p. 40).[79] They are bodily happenings which reveal themselves on a *bodily* level to anyone who tries to empathize with them.

"Psychological research demonstrates that people have a natural tendency towards mimicking the posture, gestures, expressions or movement of the people they are looking at—a phenomena that Bavelas et al. (1987) term 'mimetic synchrony'" (Cooper, 2001, p. 224), and is sometimes known as "motor mimicry," "behavior matching," or "chameleon effect" (Chartrand & Bargh, 1999). Everyone has presumably experienced how contagious yawning can be, for instance—sometimes you only have to see someone yawn and you are strongly tempted to yawn yourself (see Provine, 1986). Seeing someone else laughing can easily make you want to laugh, too (see Provine, 1992). "Smiles seem to be especially potent,

---

78 Some of these display rules are so much part of people's habitus (Bourdieu 1984) that they become integral parts of their identity and can only be set aside with great difficulty. For example, someone who has been brought up as as English aristocrat will hardly split his sides laughing, and nor would he want to.

79 There are certain exceptions, such as Damasio's "as if loop" (1994), which I will address below.

having the capacity to induce smiles in others directly and almost irresistibly" (Levenson & Ruef, 1997, p. 57). Sometimes someone else's smile forces you to smile back at them even when you do not feel like smiling in the slightest, e.g., because you were just really annoyed with them.[80]

Imitation in Infants

In terms of psychological development, imitation and synchronization of body movements must be the primary, fundamental form of empathy. The two of them together lead to an "apparent unification of two potentially random, unpatterned behavioral elements into a meaningfully described 'whole' or synchronous event" (Bernieri & Rosenthal, 1991, p. 413).[81] Newborn babies are already able to synchronize with and to a certain degree[82] mimic others and also to resonate with what they see (see Trevarthen, 2001, p. 103).

BOX 37

EXAMPLES Condon and Sander (1974) demonstrated how babies that were only a few days old coordinated their movements with adults' speech rhythms—even when they were played a tape, and it was a language that was different to that of their parents (see Kato et al. 1983).

Meltzoff and Moore (1983) showed certain mouth movements to babies who were under 3 days old (mouth opening[83], tongue protusion[84]) and demonstrated that the children repeatedly made these movements themselves. "Evidently the capacity to imitate is available at birth and does not require extensive interactive experience, mirror experience, or reinforcement" (Meltzoff and Moore, 1983, p. 707).

---

80 The inability to empathize with others is considered to be one of the main symptoms of autism, and it is therefore noteworthy that autistic children do not usually respond to their mother's smile with a smile (see Hobson, 1989).
81 In connection with the notion of the "joint situation," which I will be looking at in greater detail below, it is remarkable that "apparently the *nature* of the activity can affect or even determine the length of the predominant behavior rhythms for a given interaction" (Bernieri & Rosenthal, 1991, p. 417—italics added; see also Gottman, 1981): It is what transcends the individual, the whole that determines the individual.
82 Their capacity for motor coordination, in particular, is still undeveloped, and this has a constraining effect.
83 When mothers feed their babies, they often intuitively make use of this, by opening their own mouths to suggest to their babies that they should do the same (see O'Toole & Dubin, 1968).
84 Newborn macaques also have this capacity, but lose it after a few months (Ferrari & Gallese, 2007).

FIGURE 8
Mouth movements of three babies (from Meltzoff and Moore, 1997, p. 187;
with kind permission by A. Meltzoff)

Meltzoff and Moore interpret such imitative behavior as a kind of process of discovery that leads to an understanding of human actions. "Through interactions with others and the concomitant growth in self-understanding infants are engaged in an open-ended developmental process" (1997, p. 190) in which "the imitation of human actions is the first bridge between the infant and others, and that imitation serves the dual functions of differentiating the broad class of 'others' into individuals and providing an early means of communication with them" (Meltzoff and Moore, 1998, p. 49). Imitation is, thus, "a rare ability that is fundamentally linked to characteristically human forms of intelligence, in particular to language, culture, and the ability to understand other minds" (Hurley & Chater, 2005, p. 1). We must not therefore underestimate the importance of this innate skill—it forms the basis of human intersubjectivity.[85]

> Although laymen are often convinced that imitation is a very primitive cognitive function, they are wrong. There is vast agreement among ethologists that imitation, the capacity to learn to do an action from seeing it done . . ., is present among primates, only in humans, and (probably) in apes (Rizzolatti & Craighero, 2004, p. 172).

---

85 It does, however, have its drawbacks: "In recent years the evidence has accumulated that human and some primate young have an innate tendency to imitate whomever they observe . . . Aggressive behaviors are no different than other observable motor behaviors in this regard. Thus, the hitting, grabbing, pushing behaviors that young children see around them or in the media are naturally tried out immediately afterward. The observation of specific aggressive behaviors around them increases the likelihood of children behaving exactly that way" (Huesmann, 2005, pp. 258f.).

It is not simply the fact that these observations of babies were made that is remarkable, but also the conclusions that can be drawn when we consider that the newborn babies that copy the adults' mouth movements have never seen their *own* faces: "There are no mirrors in the womb" (Meltzoff & Decety, 2003, p. 491). However, the experiment quite clearly shows that "neonates can, at some level of processing, apprehend the equivalence between body transformations they see and body transformations of their own whether they see them or not" (Meltzoff & Moore, 1983, p. 708). The question therefore arises as to how they "translate" their visual (but not felt) impressions of the psychologist's mouth movements into their own felt (but not seen) mouth movements. Meltzoff und Moore put forward the hypothesis

> that this imitation is mediated by a representational system that allows infants to unite within one common framework their own body transformations and those of others. According to this view, both visual and motor transformations of the body can be represented in a common form and thus directly compared (Meltzoff & Moore, 1983, p. 708).

This capacity for "crossmodal correspondences" in interpersonal contact, already mentioned above, is already present at birth.[86] It is a starting point for psychological development and not the result of a developmental process. Because they have this capacity, newborns already "know" how *making* a facial movement that will *look* similar to the expression they have just *seen* on the face of an *other* must *feel* in their bodily perception of their *own* faces; and they sense in their *own* faces, in this same way, more or less how the face of the *other* must *feel* when it makes the corresponding facial movement.[87]

We can see from this last sentence and the words I have italicized that the process described is complicated, containing, as it does, a number of changes in perspective and modality. For infants, it is, of course, not a conscious or a deliberate, cognitive achievement but the developmental prerequisite for conscious and intentional changes of perspective to become possible in later stages of development.

---

86 If we look at the results of the studies reported in the preceding paragraphs, together with the observations carried out on babies described further up, we see that the "crossmodal comparisons run in both directions—infants can imitate . . . and can recognize being imitated" (Meltzoff & Brooks, 2001, p. 189).

87 Many studies have now documented the fact that infants imitate not only mouth movements but also very many other simple gestures, e.g., head or hand movements. For an overview, see Meltzoff and Moore (1994, p. 84).

Bråten's[88] term for this is altero-centric participation. It is altero-centric because the baby has not just *observed* his mother's actions from the outside, i.e. perceived things from his own egocentric perspective, but it is rather that perceiving her actions triggers a resonance in him, enabling him to sense how his mother feels as she makes the movement. That is not to say that he already intuits, or even knows, that it is the feeling of the *other*, but simply that he has two 'shades' to his feelings, just as we have when we see someone stumbling . . . and instinctively "stumble with them." We see the process from the outside, but at the same time we "participate" in the experience of stumbling, or rather of the person stumbling, also in that, as we watch, a feeling of what stumbling is like is evoked in us, rather than simply what it is like to watch someone stumble (Dornes, 2006, p. 96—original italics).

BOX 38

ALTERO-CENTERED PARTICIPATION

is the innate capacity to experience, usually out of awareness, what another is experiencing. It is a nonvoluntary act of experiencing as if your center of orientation and perspective were centered in the other. It is not a form of knowledge about the other, but rather a participation in the other's experience. It is the basic intersubjective capacity that makes imitation, empathy, sympathy, emotional contagion, and identification possible. Although innate, the capacity enlarges and becomes refined with development (Stern, 2004, pp. 241f.).

In other words, human beings evidently come into this world with the ability to *simulate* others, an ability which is based on innate skills in forming crossmodal images. Later on, evolving from this, comes a more highly developed cognitive capacity, which enables us to put ourselves deliberately into someone else's shoes and to construct ideas ("theories") about what may be happening in their minds (see de Waal, 2007). Peter Hobson, who has done research on autism, accords a similar importance to imitation as does Rizzolatti, whom we cited above. "There is something about our propensity to imitate others that is as basic as our intellectual prowess, something that makes us *homo imitans* as well as *homo sapiens*. What is the something? It is the capacity to identify with others"[89] (Hobson, 2002, p. 215).

---

88 Dornes is referring to Bråten (1998) and others here.
89 This is the very capacity that autistic people only possess to a limited degree (see also Charman, 2002).

Before the beginning of language development, spontaneous bodily imitation is of particular importance. "It is an avenue for teaching motor skills and also embodies a mutuality and reciprocity that is the essence of communication at the nonverbal level" (Meltzoff & Moore, 1994, p. 83). Just a few weeks after birth, an infant's imitative abilities gain an important dimension—the memory now begins to come into play. From about 6 weeks, babies begin to imitate their caregivers' behaviors without the caregivers having to produce these *directly* in front of their very eyes. Without any prompting, babies imitate behavior that they have observed in the other person *the previous day.*

This transition from purely reactive imitation, which relates to the given moment, to imitation that depends on memory, leads us to suppose that this behavior also serves other purposes. The babies are now testing out for themselves "whether this is a *reencounter* with a familiar person or an encounter with a stranger. . . . Is this the self-same person acting differently, or a different person who merely looks the same?" (Meltzoff & Moore, 1994, p. 96—original italics). The baby can discover this by resuming the imitation game of the previous day and seeing whether she can observe the same behavior in the other person again. She practices with people basically the same exploratory behavior that she engages in with things.

> When infants reencounter a bottle or rattle, they probe whether this "is the one that is suckable/rattleable" as part of making sense of their world. . . . What we are suggesting is that when infants reencounter people, they similarly take action to test the identity of the person before them. Imitation is to understanding people as physical manipulation is to understanding things (Meltzoff & Moore, 1994, p. 96).

Of course the interactive play, with repeated imitations, serves not only to test out the identity of the other person, but also to establish the continuity of the own self. If I can enter into the same physical interaction with the other person as before, then the other person must also have recognized me, which means that I myself am the same person as yesterday, since I can feel the same physical sensations again.

Another impressive finding is how amazingly "creative" young babies are in regulating their imitative behavior. In one study, they were shown a mouth movement that they had not seen before—a sideward rather than a straight tongue protrusion, the tongue appearing in a corner of the mouth at an angle of about 45° off-centre. The babies, who were still too young to be able to control their tongue movements sufficiently accurately, "responded" by producing a straight tongue protrusion coupled with a simultaneous head turn of about 45° (see Meltzoff & Moore, 1997). We can only understand this response if we assume that the babies had realized that there was something like a "goal" of the tongue movement or, in other words, that they had grasped the intention of the act that they had observed and then imitated. "Although the literal muscle movements were very different, the *goal* of the perceived act and the executed act was the same" (Meltzoff & Brooks, 2001, p. 188 — original italics). All these forms of imitation by the body can simply be viewed as precursors of adult empathy, but in the very first few months of life, we see in them the signs of a capacity that will be decisive for the fully developed ability to empathize. This is the capacity to "mentalize," mentioned above, i.e., to apprehend the mental state of another person.

However, we also see clearly (in line with Mead) how human beings' ever-increasing ability to understand the experience and perspective of others is linked to the development of the infantile self.

> Identifying with someone means recognizing the someone as a person with characteristics that one can make one's own—characteristics that come to enrich one's self. . . . If one imagines that this kind of identification is going on all the time, mostly invisibly, one can appreciate that it represents a deeply influential mode of cultural transmission. A child is learning through repeated shifts into the roles of others, doing things and seeing things and adopting attitudes towards the world as "they" do (Hobson, 2002, p. 223).

Mimetic Synchronization

The fact that imitation and synchronization during the first few weeks and months of life are so important for the development of the self in interpersonal interaction does not in any way mean that these behaviors become rarer as we grow older. On the contrary, they can also be seen in many of the postures, movements, and gestures of adults. For example, if we see another person walk into a door and hurt their shoulder, we jerk our own shoulder back. We can often (and not only in therapy) observe how two people sitting opposite each other will take up the same posture. If one of them crosses their legs, for example, it will not be long before the other person does the same. This example also shows particularly clearly that many such congruent body postures may occur in either a direct or mirror-imaged form (Scheflen, 1964, p. 328—see the following illustration).

Direct   Mirror-Imaged

FIGURE 9
Congruent body postures (from Scheflen, 1964, p. 328)

As I understand it, it is still not clear why someone would choose the direct rather than the mirror-imaged form of congruent posture or vice versa. However, LaFrance and Broadbent (1976) have demonstrated that the mirror-image body posture is correlated to the "rapport" between the two people, which tends not to be the case for direct imitation.

Hass (1984) conducted an interesting study that could provide some useful clues for further research on these questions. To half of the subjects participating in an experiment, Hass suggested that there was nobody observing them, whereas he led the other half to believe that they were being observed. Subjects were then asked to mark an imaginary letter E on their foreheads. There was a notable difference between the two groups. Most of those who thought they were being observed wrote the E so that someone facing them would have been able to read it the right way round, but the majority of those who thought they were not being observed wrote it *back to front*, i.e., so that it would be the right way round for them themselves to read, if one imagines them looking out at their foreheads from the inside of their own heads; seen from the outside, however, it would look like this: Ǝ. So, whether someone assumes the direct or the mirror-imaged form of congruent body posture could depend on whether at that particular moment it is their *own* perspective or *the other person's* that is dominant, or, to use Mead's (1934/1963) terms, their "I" or their "Me."

In both cases, the congruence of postures is an indication of an identification process that points not only to a (relative) concurrence in what the participants are currently *thinking* but also to a similarity in social *status* (as they themselves experience it). For "where it is important to indicate different status, congruence is less likely to occur" (Scheflen, 1964, p. 329). Iacoboni's hypothesis is also applicable here:

> If one considers the relevance of goals for this cortical region, the dominance of specular imitation early in development, and the fact that specular imitation substantially means that both the imitator and the model share the same sector of space during imitative behavior, one is led to hypothesize that a general goal of imitating others seems to be "directed

toward" them, a process according to which a certain intimacy between model and imitator is achieved through space and action sharing (2007, p. 442).

There are many more impressive examples of mimetic synchronization through which people pick up and imitate behavioral patterns of others. If this imitation takes place over an extended period of time, it can also take the form of a reciprocal matching of certain rhythms in the behavior of the participants, which is referred to as interactional synchrony; "coordinating temporal patterns is thus one crucial way that social relatedness is organized" (Beebe et al., 2000, p. 100). In research, behavior matching and interactional synchrony are often investigated separately, for methodological reasons (see Bernieri & Rosenthal, 1991). It has only recently emerged how meaningful this distinction is because it is now thought that different neurophysiological mechanisms underlie them. Mimicry is probably more closely related to the activity of mirror neurons (which I shall describe in more detail in section 4.2.3), whereas synchronization demands more the activity of "adaptive oscillators" (see Sethares, 2007, Chapter 6).

> Another thing we are born with that makes this intersubjective matrix are *adaptive oscillators*, which are really like little clocks in different muscle groups that can get into synchronization with something outside and can get reset all the time, so that they synchronize. If we didn't have adaptive oscillators, we could never kick a moving football. In other words, we have to synchronize our movements with the movements of somebody or something else. . . . For instance, if you're washing the dishes and I'm drying them, and you hand me a dish, and then another one, you synchronize, and you do it totally smoothly, because both our adaptive oscillators have gone into synchronization. Think about it: even if you suddenly kiss somebody passionately, why is it that you don't break your front teeth? The answer is that it has to do with this very quick synchronization. It means that you know what the other person is feeling, because you have synchronized your whole body toward that. This is similar to what the mirror neurons do (Stern et al., 2003, p. 24—original italics).

For my purposes, the differentiation between imitation (mirror neurons) and synchronization (oscillators) is of secondary importance, particularly because both are to be found at the same time in many everyday situations. The following box contains examples of studies on both phenomena.

BOX 39

EXAMPLES Watkins, Strafella, and Paus (2003) demonstrated that the muscles activated in speech are reactivated (albeit in a much weaker form) when people are simply watching or listening to others talking, and not speaking at all themselves.

Using an electromyograph (an instrument that registers subtle muscle activity), Berger and Hadley (1975) investigated motor (muscle) activity in the bodies of observers who were watching models carrying out different activities. If they observed a model who was stuttering, their own lip muscle activity increased, whereas if they watched a film showing two men arm wrestling, their own arm muscle activity increased.

Dimberg, Thunberg, and Elmehed (2000) also used electromyography to prove that looking at faces that displayed a particular emotion (e.g., happiness or anger), which required a certain activation pattern of the face muscles, led to the same (but weaker) activation patterns in the observers' faces.

Hsee, Hatfield, Carlson, and Chemtob (1990) showed their subjects a 3-minute film of someone talking either about the happiest or the saddest experience of his life. As they watched, the subjects' faces were secretly filmed, and these recordings were then analyzed. The expressions on the subjects' faces clearly reflected the content of whatever film they had seen. Wallbott (1990) demonstrated that this spontaneous mirroring takes place, not only of the so-called "primary"[90] emotions but also of mixed feelings.

Levenson and Ruef (1992) studied the patterns of cardiovascular arousal of couples or people who were in a relationship with each other to assess how precisely each of them picked up the emotional state of the other at any one time. The more unerring their empathy, the more similar were their physiological readings to those of the target person—interestingly enough, this was more so for negative feelings than for positive ones. The authors coined the term "shared physiology" based on these results.

Condon and Ogston used a very fast movie camera, which recorded 300 images per second, not only to document how someone's body moves, or "dances," as he speaks, but also to show that "the body of the listener dances in rhythm with that of the speaker!" (1966, p. 338).

The terms "emotional contagion"[91] (see Hatfield et al., 1994) and "mood contagion" (see Neumann & Strack, 2000) seem to refer to the emotional level, and yet, they also have a decidedly bodily dimension. The fact that people tend to take on the feelings and moods of whoever they are with is due to "a two-stage mechanism that hinges on the unintentional imitation of another person's emotional behavior, which in turn activates a congruent mood state in the observer" (Neumann & Strack, 2000, p. 211). This is certainly linked to the fact that "the perception of emotional states in others involves the activation of the same brain areas we use to express those emotions" (Iacoboni, 2007, p. 446).[92]

---

90 By "primary" emotions I mean the seven basic emotions (see references to Ekman's research, above), which most experts in this field consider to be anger, fear, disgust, happiness (or joy), surprise, sadness and contempt.
91 This term was also used by Scheler (1916/1954, pp. 12ff.).

These examples will have to suffice, although there are many others that one could add, as we see from the overview provided by Chartrand and Dalton (2009). From some of the examples, it should be clear that "mimetic synchrony is a natural and automatic response to the experience of being with another, as opposed to a conscious and deliberate attempt at imitation" (Cooper, 2001, p. 224). This is essentially because, for the most part, mimetic synchronization takes place subliminally—this is true, at any rate, when it begins. Occasionally, a little later on, one may "catch" oneself in the same posture as the other person.

In social situations, there appears to be something like a *linking of perception and action* that functions separately from (and possibly parallel to) intentional, conscious efforts to understand the other person in the situation in which they happen to be (see Chartrand & Bargh, 1999). Without trying to switch perspectives and irrespective of all one's good intentions to empathize, this linking results in people sensing what they perceive in the other person's body in their *own* body because, spontaneously, they actively reproduce in their own bodies their perception of what is happening in that of the other person. Within themselves, they physically reenact what they have picked up from the other person, and doing this has an effect on how they themselves feel. This spontaneous imitation by the body, that could also be considered to be a form of identification or confluence, is clearly based on the principle of simulation.

This bodily simulation is usually very *specific*. It

> can be observed only in muscles involved in the observed action, not in other muscles. This is true even for muscles of the same body part. . . . The muscle specificity of the effect suggests that this motor resonance behavior is a dynamic, embodied, relational process (Iacoboni, 2007, p. 445).

There is another interesting point that is almost so obvious that it escapes notice: Most of the forms of imitation mentioned are *shown*, i.e., they are not just subjective feelings that also happen to be displayed, but have the character of *expressive* behavior, as Bavelas, Black, Lemery, and Mullett (1986) have demonstrated empirically. Imitation is "not only . . . a nonverbal behavior but also a nonverbal communication . . ., which is expressive *to* another person rather than only expressive *of* the individual's

---

92 Watt assumes "that contagion mechanisms form a poorly understood 'developmental ground' out of which later arriving and more cognitive 'shared representations' or 'mirroring' phenomena develop" (2005, p. 203—see section 4.2.3).

feelings" (Bavelas et al., 1986, p. 323—original italics). In other words, imitations can be seen as being nonverbal *communications* to the person whose expression they are copying.

Let us, for example, suppose that this person first displayed an expression of pain, which could be translated verbally into, "I am in pain." The second person responds with a similar expression of pain, which could similarly be translated into the words, "I also feel the pain." But the important thing is that it is *not* a question of words but of *nonverbal* communication. Perception of people entails partly imitating them physically and synchronizing one's body with theirs. This capacity for *physical* coordination is an important aspect of social skills (see Baron & Boudreau, 1987).

As Watzlawick, Beavin, and Jackson (1967) have convincingly shown, nonverbal (analog) messages address first and foremost the *relational* aspect of communication, as opposed to the *content* aspect, which is conveyed mainly verbally (digitally). *Saying* "I also feel the pain," would therefore be more on the level of content. This verbal statement is primarily an expression that the person has understood cognitively that the other person is feeling pain at this point and not happiness. The nonverbal message, on the other hand, takes effect rather more on the level of the relationship. The mimetic synchronization conveys to the person who is in pain more the message, "I am with you, sharing your pain." Here we see how differently the effects of the so called "hot" and "cold" (or "affective" and "cognitive") forms of empathy described above can develop in communication.[93] Each of these two forms of empathy expresses different relational qualities—the first is warmer and more connected, the second more formal and distant.

The spontaneous and often unconscious imitation of our perceptions of another person's body, together with a synchronization of rhythms, is an essential part of any "warm'" empathy. It creates a direct and sensual connection between the body of the person who is experiencing the body of the other, and the body of the other. The extent to which this imitation takes place is thus also correlated to the intensity of the empathic involvement. Levenson and Ruef report several studies "that found postural mirroring to increase with increasing psychological involvement" (1997, p. 56). LaFrance (1982), too, found a close correlation between the similarity of postures and the extent to which people felt that there was a "rapport" between them. Goleman summarizes some of the results of Levenson and Ruef's (1992) study as follows:

---

93 See Chapter 3.2, under theory theory and simulation theory.

The more strongly a stranger's body *mimicked* that of the person she watched, the more accurate was her sense of what that person felt . . . Empathy—sensing another's emotions—seems to be as physiological as it is mental, built on sharing the inner state of the other person. This biological dance occurs when *anyone* empathizes with someone else— the empathizer subtly shares the physiological state of the person with whom she attunes.

People whose own faces showed the strongest expressions were the most accurate at judging the feelings of others. The general principle: the more similar the physiological state of two people at a given moment, the more easily they can sense each other's feelings (Goleman, 2006, p. 25—original italics).

Apparently, human beings understand each other better if they engage in such imitation and are open to experiencing *shared physiology*, because

perception causes similar behavior, and the perception of the similar behavior on the part of the other creates shared feelings of empathy and rapport. In short, the widely documented automatic link between perception and behavior exists, at least in part, as a kind of natural 'social glue' that produces empathic understanding and even greater liking between people, without their having to intend or try to have this happen (Chartrand & Bargh, 1999, p. 897).

The positive effect of this "social glue" in everyday situations is well documented. Waitresses, for example, can expect more generous tips if they repeat their customers' words exactly, rather than just roughly paraphrasing them, when taking an order (see van Baaren, Holland, Steenaert, & van Knippenberg, 2003). When someone has had the experience of mimetic synchronization of movements with another person, he will be more helpful to her and is more likely to help her if she is in trouble than if he had not had this experience of being imitated beforehand. Interestingly, this prosocial effect becomes generalized and is also noticeable in interactions with a third person who has not previously experienced shared interaction. Thus, if motor mimicry has been experienced, when asked to donate to charity, people will give about twice as much as they would have had they not had this previous experience of rapport (see van Baaren, Holland, Kawakami, & van Knippenberg, 2004).

The authors of these studies conclude "that mimicry increases prosocial behavior and that these behavioral consequences of mimicry are not

BOX 40

EXAMPLES

When one [person] lights a cigarette or gets a drink, he tries to persuade the other to join him. If he fails he is disappointed, not because he really cares if his friend smokes a cigarette or takes a drink, but because if they do not both smoke or drink at the same time, there will be a slight loss of synchrony in their actions. In such situations we frequently see one friend insisting that the other join him, even when it is obvious that he is not interested (Morris, 1977, p. 83).

To explore this, Lynne Murray and Colwyn Trevarthen sat individual two- and three-month-old infants in front of a television. The screen showed the infant's mother live on television, looking towards the infant. The mother herself was facing a camera, sitting in another room. Not only this, but the mother too was watching a television, so that she could see the live image of her infant facing her, relayed over a two-way link-up. This may sound a highly artificial arrangement, but mother and baby were able to engage with each other over video in a surprisingly natural and fluent way. Until the disruption was introduced, that is. In this case, what per- turbed the interaction was a delay of just thirty seconds between events at the two ends of the video link. Now when the baby acted and watched the video monitor, what the baby could see was the mother responding to her actions of thirty seconds ago. It was not that the mother's earlier responses were unpleasant in any way. It was just that they were suited to a different moment, and not in tune with what the infant was expressing now. The effect of introducing the delay was considerable infant distress (Hobson, 2002, p. 38f.).

restricted to behavior directed toward the mimicker. Other people can also benefit from a mimicked person's more prosocial orientation" (van Baaren et al., 2004, p. 73). On the basis of this and many other findings, Chartrand and Bargh consider that it is "plausible that the chameleon effect serves the basic human need to belong" (1999, p. 900).[94] Commensurate with this is the everyday observation that one person will often suggest to others that they should do the same as he does if they seem reluctant to do so of their own accord, or he may become disconcerted if the synchronization does not occur.

---

94 In connection with my thoughts on individualism (above), it is interesting that the au- thors speculate that "there may be greater frequency of chameleon-like social behavior in collectivistic versus individualistic societies, because the former more than the latter are characterized by interdependence. . . . In light of the present experimental findings, this increased perception of others' behavior would be expected to produce greater rapport and smoother social interactions" (Chartrand & Bargh, 1999, p. 907).

Therefore, to sum up, we are not isolated beings enclosed in a "skin sack," as Alan Watts (1967) once put it sarcastically. We participate directly in the other person, and this participation is based on the linking of perception and action described above. We cannot perceive what another person is expressing with their body without synchronizing our own movements with his, while at the same time actively reconstructing them, in one form or another, in ourselves. This may occur almost unnoticeably, e.g., through the subtle innervation of our own muscles, or may be quite patent, e.g., through the adoption of a similar posture.

This is, of course, also likely to play an important role in psychotherapy:

> The success of psychotherapists . . . depend[s] to some extent on the degree of rapport they can achieve in their professional interactions. Their ability to coordinate and synchronize with different people under various circumstances may have a significant effect on their professional competence and effectiveness (Bernieri & Rosenthal, 1991, p. 429).

As should be quite clear by now, I am referring here to *spontaneous, involuntary* imitation and synchronization and not to deliberate copying, which one can do to try to influence the other person, as in "pacing and leading" in Neuro-Linguistic Programming (NLP) (see, e.g., Richardson, 1987). My main concern is to draw attention to the universal human capacity to experience a direct, bodily sense of the other person—a sense that we are born with, that connects us spontaneously with the other, a connection that can become even closer if we become aware of it. In psychotherapy as I understand it, the implication of my becoming aware in this way is not that I might use it to manipulate the client, but that I as therapist should make myself receptive and attentive to what is being mirrored in my own body. In my view, the therapeutic benefit consists mainly in my being able to access the client's experience directly,[95] and thus to gain a bodily understanding of the situation in which she currently finds herself and therefore an important part of how she actually is at this particular moment. This is a helpful prerequisite for being able to support her effectively in really becoming the person that she is at this moment (see Box 2 on Beisser's "paradoxical theory of change").

---

95 When I speak of "direct" access, I am referring to the communication from one lived body to another that is initially not conveyed by conscious thought processes. Thus, "direct" is not the same as "complete," and of course, it certainly does *not* mean being able to read minds.

This empathizing through mimesis does not remain simply physical but becomes *part of the lived body* since the level on which the action takes place does not exist in isolation but in turn affects the perceiving person's own sensations. This is why I referred to having a "sense" of the other person. As I have already indicated, via various feedback loops, the imitative act affects the feeling and mood state of the person who perceives the other (see, for example, the quotation from Iacoboni at the end of Box 39 and also the comments on facial feedback at the beginning of this section).

Digression on the Portrayal of Feelings in Acting

We gain an enlightening insight into these psychological relations if we turn to an area that seems initially to have nothing at all to do with psychotherapy—acting. A brief outline will suffice to show that empathy also plays an important role in dramatic art. The actor, whose facial features are only partially visible to the theater audience, must use her body language in such a way that the audience can recognize and, thus empathize with, the mental state of the character she is playing. This changes constantly during the play, sometimes from 1 min to the next. At the same time, the actor is often required to give an "authentic" performance, i.e., to express the character's moods and feelings as naturally as possible so that they will be taken seriously and appear believable to the audience.

Different drama schools have used various methods to train their students to master this difficult task. The key question for them was, "What can an actor do in order to portray an emotion as accurately as possible?" One answer that had great influence on the acting traditions of Europe and later the United States of America was that of Constantin Stanislavski (1938/1988) in the first 30 years or so of the last century. According to Stanislavski, the actor should no longer, as had previously been customary, portray a given emotion in a stereotypical way by using fixed gestures and modes of speech, the meaning of which was familiar to the audience and which they could therefore recognize. Rather, he should act in a way that gave a much more personal and authentic impression, i.e., he himself should feel, directly, the emotion that he was portraying. Stanislavski believed that this would bridge the gap between the actor's own person and the role he was playing and that it would make the performance more "realistic," which was his goal. In order to do this, the actor was expected to activate his emotional memory and remember, as vividly as he could, experiences of his own where he had felt the same emotion that he now needed to express.

> If the actor could define the emotion that was required of him at any given moment and then stimulate analogous feeling from his own experience then his interpretation could attain a new level of reality and the gap between the actor as individual and the actor as performer could be bridged. The actor and the character would become one (Benedetti, 1982, p. 32).

This method clearly followed a pattern that we would describe today as a *top-down*-procedure. Starting from the higher mental level (*top*), in this case, the memory of an emotional experience, working *down*ward, the associated lower levels of expression are activated. The expression is then produced from the reactivated experience in a way that fits the situation.[96]

Stanislavski's method showed impressive results, but had its limitations. It proved to be relatively laborious and did not meet the need for fast emotional changes required by some roles. Sometimes actors had a strong psychological resistance to activating emotional experiences. Some of them simply did not have enough experiences of their own to draw on, or if they had them, they were either partially forgotten or so buried under other impressions that shades of feeling surfaced that did not fit in with the role to be played.

This last point shows the risks involved in thinking that we can unlock the mystery of the other predominantly by bringing to mind similar experiences of our own. "Certainly 'common sense' does not take 'inference from oneself to others' as a usable means of reaching knowledge of foreign psychic life" (Stein, 1917/1964, pp. 80f.). The special quality of *otherness* in another person's experience often gets lost if we do this, and in the worst scenario, our "empathizing" becomes an intrusive projection of something of our own onto the other person.[97]

---

96 One could see this as an early form of "process activation" (see above). It is interesting to note that in the literature on the skills of professional actors, a similar term—"active experiencing"—is used (Noice & Noice, 2002, p. 7).

97 In my experience, it is just such processes that lead to what is often called "confluence" or identification," in the negative sense. However, this is *not* a merging of *two* ways of experiencing something but is actually a form of self-centeredness. The person who believes he is empathizing uses, whether consciously or not, some impression, or perhaps merely some "stimulus" from the other person that is taken as *a cue* to activate his *own* memory, which then gains control over him. The impression he has of the other person simply triggers an old internal "movie" that is projected on to the other person without having anything at all to do with him.

Toward the end of his career, Stanislavski made some changes based on the disadvantages of his *top-down* method. The conviction grew in him that the actors' feelings could not be produced by force as in the method he had been using, but that they needed to be "lured" or "enticed" (see Benedetti, 1982, p. 66).

> If the intellect can inhibit, and the emotions are fickle, where can an actor begin in his exploration of a role? The answer is, with what is most immediately available to him, with what responds most easily to his wishes—his body (Benedetti, 1982, p. 67).

"The actor must search for actions which will arouse the feeling. This is the bait which the feeling will rise to" (Stanislavski, quoted in the work of Benedetti, 1982).[98]

Stanislavski himself was nearing the end of his life and did not have time to develop this new approach very much further, but he nevertheless considered it to be the fruit of his life work (see Tait, 2002, p. 92). However, years later, the Argentinian neurophysiologist Susana Bloch developed *Alba Emoting*, a training method for actors that builds on this last method of Stanislavski's and attempts to overcome the drawbacks of his early method. *Alba Emoting* does not follow the *top-down* route but works in the opposite direction, i.e. *bottom-up*. The underlying principle is simple:

> We observed . . . that the emotional arousal was accompanied by an ensemble of specific respiratory, postural and facial modifications that were characteristic for each emotion. In other words, we found that *specific emotional feelings were linked to specific patterns of breathing, facial expression, degree of muscular tension, and postural attitudes.* . . . All these observations clearly suggest that during an emotional state there is a *unique interdependence between a specific breathing rhythm, a particular expressive attitude* (both facial and postural) *and a given subjective experience* (Bloch, 1993, pp. 124f.—original italics).

Bloch used the term "emotional effector patterns" for the combinations of patterns of breathing, posture, and facial expression that are typical of any one particular emotion. These are actually "a particular configuration of neurovegetative, hormonal and neuromuscular reactions" (Bloch,

---

98 It should now be clear why I began this digression on acting at this particular point in the development of my argument, where I am considering the way (imitative) actions of the body have repercussions on the feelings of the person who perceives the expressive actions of another.

Orthous, & Santibañez-H., 1987, p. 3), that embraces *more* than these three factors, but "from this complex physiological ensemble, we chose for the purpose of our training only the respiratory-postural-facial components because these can be started and modulated at will and carry with them most of the other features that are not directly under voluntary control" (Bloch et al., 1987).[99] Bloch researched these effector patterns thoroughly and described them in detail so that she could give her drama students exact instructions and then rehearse them with them in a purposeful way. She concentrated on six emotions which she called "basic emotions,"[100] from which she believed all other feelings, as various mixtures, can be derived.

BOX 41

EXAMPLES Bloch defined the emotional effector patterns for the "basic emotions" happiness, sadness, fear, anger, sexual desire, and tenderness and then put the definitions into the form of instructions for acting students. The following are examples of two of them.[101]

Anger: "Breathe sharply in and out through the nose; keep your lips tightly closed and contract the lower jaw; focus your eyes, tensing the lids; put tension in the body and incline it slightly forwards as if ready to attack."

Sadness: "Inhale in brief saccades through the nose and then exhale all the air in one expiratory movement through the open mouth, as in a sigh; keep your body relaxed, arms hanging; let your head drop slightly and point your gaze downwards" (Lemeignan, Aguilera-Torres, & Bloch, 1992, p. 188).

If actors rehearse the emotional effector patterns thoroughly, then, *purely by means of this physical activity*, they will succeed in experiencing the corresponding emotions intensely and will thus be able to express them in a convincing way. Bloch also found empirical evidence "that the correct performance of the effector patterns of emotions is sufficient to evoke the corresponding emotion in the observers (public). At the same time, the reports of the actors show that the correct execution of the effector patterns may trigger in themselves the corresponding subjective feeling"

---

99 "Reproduction of the aspects of those bodily reactions (emotional effector patterns) subject to voluntary control will biochemically stimulate that emotion in the body" (Rix, 1998, p. 69).

100 Only some of these are the same as those posited by Ekman and other emotion researchers.

101 I suggest that you try out these two emotional effector patterns for yourself. Practice them for 2 or 3 min to find out what you experience. Knowing these effector patterns well can help therapists recognize the emotions their clients are expressing. Of course, the less inhibited a client is in expressing his feelings and the purer (less complex) they are, the easier this will be.

(Bloch et al., 1987, p. 17). One could easily believe that Bloch took her inspiration from Nietzsche:

> In order to understand another person, and reproduce in ourselves his feelings, we may probe his feelings to their very depth; but as a rule we abstain from doing this, and produce in ourselves his feelings, not according to their cause, but according to the effects which they exhibit in him; we imitate in ourselves the expression of his eyes, voice, gait, attitude . . . , until we reach a slight resemblance to the play of the muscles and nerves. A similar feeling will thereupon arise within us, in consequence of an old association of movement and sentiment, which is trained to move backwards and forwards. We have developed very highly this art of fathoming the feelings of others, and, in the presence of a human being, we are incessantly and almost unconsciously practising it. One need only watch the play of a woman's features to see how they quiver with animation through the constant imitation and reflection of all that is going on around her (Nietzsche, 1903, pp. 142f.).

End of digression

If we now return to empathy in the context of psychotherapy, we find that several interesting conclusions can be drawn from Bloch's acting techniques. If the therapist[102] occasionally follows her involuntary human inclination to imitate and synchronize her own movements with the client's expressive body movements and if she does not resist this out of a desire to avoid all confluence, then the spontaneous imitation will stimulate those feelings in herself that she has seen expressed in her client. The link between perception and action (that I have already mentioned above) then goes one step further and links the (imitative) behavior to the therapist's feelings. To put it more technically, one could say that feelings are activated by means of a feedback loop which connects the actions of the body to what is experienced on an emotional level, just as we saw in *facial feedback*.

This statement is reminiscent of the "James-Lange theory," according to which the changes in our body come first, and it is only then that we experience the emotions that go with them. In James' famous words: "We feel sorry because we cry, angry because we strike, afraid because we tremble" (1884, p. 190). However, put in such exclusive and, more importantly, such one-sided terms, this theory cannot stand the test. For example Chwalisz,

---

102 I am now more often writing from the perspective of the therapist rather than from that of the client for the same reasons as I mentioned earlier and not because I believe the client has in any way a lesser capacity for empathy than the therapist.

Diener, and Gallagher (1988) conducted a study of patients with spinal cord injuries that were so bad that there were hardly any intact neural pathways between the peripheral nervous system and the brain. They failed to find any marked impairment of the patients' emotionality—at any rate, not in those patients who had *succeeded* in mentally coming to terms with their disability[103] (see also Cobos, Sanchez, Garcia, Vera, & Vila, 2002).[104] These findings can be explained by Damasio's (1994) idea of an "as if loop," according to which the brain creates links between bodily experience and emotion that can later be reactivated on their own. "There are thus neural devices that help us feel 'as if' we were having an emotional state, as if the body were being activated and modified. Such devices permit us to bypass the body and avoid a slow and energy-consuming process" (Damasio, 1994, p. 155).[105]

Taken together, the lessons we have learnt from the training of actors and the results of the studies on paraplegics can be interpreted as indicating a need for a *holistic* view of the emotions, in which feeling, expression, and physical regulation are directly linked and are also closely connected to the cognitive component (appraisal) that weighs up the situation as it has been perceived and evaluates it in terms of what it means for the person.

> We postulate that emotion is not felt experience alone, nor a pattern of neural firing, nor an action such as smiling. Emotion is the process that emerges from the dynamic interaction among these components as they occur in relation to changes in the social and physical context (Fogel et al., 1992, p. 129).

The following sketch shows the different components of an emotion and how they are interconnected (see Figure 10, next page).

In a holistic emotional system such as this, it is not surprising if activating certain components (in *Alba Emoting*, the components of expression and parts of physical regulation) also activates other components at the

---

103 In such cases, a reduction in emotionality must, therefore, be seen as resulting from a failure to come to terms with the illness and not as a direct result of the lesion itself.

104 LeDoux believes that that "does not really prove anything" because "spinal cord injury does not completely interrupt information flow between the brain and body" (1996, p. 294). I am not convinced by this argument because even if the interruption is "not complete" it must surely still result in considerable *impairment.*

105 This is also involved, for instance, in the phantom limb sensation that can be very disturbing for patients. These sensations are, however, the result of a normal process of development through which expressive and body reactions, "along with their real feedback can be transformed into mental expressive and bodily sensations. *Internalization* is the name we have given to this transformation process from an externally perceivable sign form to a mental sign form, that continues to exist only as subjective feeling" (Holodynski & Friedlmeier, 2006, p. 63—italics added). In Chapter 6, I will return to the principle of internalization in connection with Vygotsky, whom Holodynski and Friedlmeier cite.

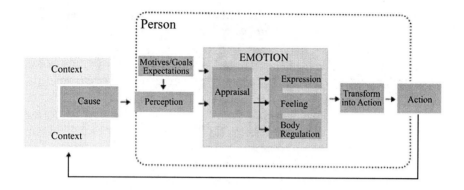

FIGURE 10
Model of emotions (from Holodynski & Friedlmeier, 2006, p. 49—with kind permission by Manfred Holodynski)

same time (in *Alba Emoting*, feeling and other parts of physical regulation). It is equally easy to imagine that paraplegics, whose *appraisal* in any given situation activates a particular feeling along with the facial expression that goes with it, can also activate the *sensations* of physical regulation (in the way that Damasio describes), if these sensations were already neuronally connected to the feeling previously (which would certainly have been unproblematical and possible *before* the injury).

What We Can More or Less Know About Others and What We Cannot Know

This model of emotion also allows us to understand how a therapist who allows herself to feel a spontaneous embodied response to her client's expressive behavior in her own body can experience a connection to the corresponding feeling in herself that should have a certain similarity to the client's feeling. However, this does not indicate that she can read minds, since the cognitive component (*appraisal*) is, as we see in the diagram above, not as closely linked to the other three components of emotion as these are to each other. In order to be able to understand how the client is perceiving and appraising the situation in question (shown in the above diagram as *perception* and *appraisal* of context and cause), she must talk with him, since otherwise she can only arrive at certain conjectures.[106]

---

106 Such conjectures develop out of intuitions (see Lieberman, 2000), conclusions that can be drawn from the context, and from psychological knowledge, e.g., Lazarus' theory of

From this, we can see roughly what the therapist can know more or less directly about the mystery of the client's emotions and what she can only find out by asking him about himself.[107] The following very rough distinction can be made: Those components of the client's emotion that he experiences mainly through the *body*—i.e., expression, feeling, and physical regulation (with the exception, of course, of the biochemical processes, which are inaccessible to consciousness)—are to some degree directly accessible to a therapist through the links between perception, action, and feeling that exist in her. I shall be saying more about this in the next two sections (4.2.2 and 4.2.3). In contrast, the *content* of the client's *appraisal*, which is mainly *cognitive*, can only be assumed, inferred, and explored in verbal exchanges.

Hermann Schmitz has formulated a useful rule of thumb:

> Only what is bodily (*leibhaft*) in the sense that it is itself an embodied impulse or leaves traces in such impulses can be conveyed to the other through direct perception . . . ; feelings become embodied because to be moved by them is to be affected on the level of the lived body . . . But this also applies to thinking and wanting . . . to the extent that one sees that a person is thoughtful or determined, but not what he is thinking or what he wants, and not even what he is attending to when he is listening or "wide-eyed"; you have to ask him about it (1990, p. 151).

This rule is rather basic, and thus, a few more differentiations are necessary.

(1) *Regarding empathy in expression, emotion, and body regulation.* Since I have already said much about this above, what I want here is mainly to emphasize that what a therapist discovers about a client through linking *perception, action, and feeling* is, of course, always subjectively colored from the beginning, at the first step, i.e., perception (and in the next two as well). "*The object as I see it is the meaning I give to the responses the object evokes in my body.* . . . We can see nothing with our eyes detached from the brain" (Polanyi, 1968, pp. 38f.—original italics). There is no "immaculate perception" (Nietzsche) that is free of "motives, aims and expectations," most of which are implicit (see box in Figure 10), prejudices, interests, cultural influences, etc. All forms of empathy are therefore inevitably interpretative (see Stern, 1994). If one takes the concept of resonance

---

"core relational themes" (2001), through which it is possible to deduce a hypothesis about the basic structure of *appraisal* from knowledge of the activated feeling (see also Staemmler & Staemmler, 2009).

107 The thoughts on this issue presented below refer to the conceptual framework that I have developed thus far. I shall expand upon this in Chapters 4.3 and 5.

seriously, the "timbre" of bodily resonances is also, of course, always dependent on the respective "sounding box." This is possibly most evident with respect to the sex difference between a female therapist and a male client, which imposes limitations on bodily resonance which go beyond mere genital sensations.

Thus, when I wrote above that, there were some things that the therapist could "know more or less directly" about her client because she was able to access the more bodily components of the client's emotion "to some degree," I did so deliberately with the intention of leaving room for the therapist's "cultivated uncertainty." This is desirable in this context because, again, it is not an "interpretation-free space," despite the fact that the interpretations that are made must be located more on a micro-level (see Staemmler, 2004, p. 28).[108] However, above all it is

> important to remember that emotional signals do not tell us their source. We may know someone is angry without knowing exactly why. It could be anger at us, anger directed inward at his or her self, or anger about something the person just remembered that has nothing to do with us (Ekman, 2003, pp. 56f.).

Even if bodily resonance is not free of interpretative elements, it can be better exploited the more the therapist has developed her perception of her own body. If her self-perception is well developed, she can make herself aware as often as possible of what initially arises spontaneously within her. She can then also capture the nuances of the sensations she has in contact with the client in a differentiated way and develop an increasingly sensitive perceptual acuity for a broad range of different kinds of resonance.

(2) *Regarding empathy with the other's appraisal.* Empathic access to the cognitive contents of an *appraisal* differs from that of the other three components of emotion in that it is less direct. Cognitive elements are more difficult to access empathically because their bodily manifestations are much weaker—or perhaps one should say *more indirect.* This is because they are strongly dependent on the mediation of the linguistic symbol and how it is interpreted. However, this by no means indicates that the body was not involved. This is also the reason why it is so important to include

---

108 This may not be true of certain "emblems," i.e., nonverbal signals with meanings that are (sub-) culturally clearly defined, e.g., nodding the head, which can completely replace the word "yes." However, this only applies to the meaning "yes" itself. The *way* in which the head is nodded provides further elements of meaning which are not well-defined culturally.

the body in the understanding of empathy or, to put it differently, why its omission from the traditional concept of empathy is so misleading.

Ultimately, verbal dialog about the contents of cognitions is also dependent upon the speaker's (and the listener's) embodiment. The transmission of linguistic symbols is likewise an embodied process of expression. Speech is a "form of organization of the lived body" (Böhme, 1986, p. 9). As Gendlin put it, "language is implicit in the body. The body knows language" (1992, p. 193). This rapidly becomes clear if we imagine a person trying as far as possible to "switch off" his embodiment. He would have to suppress his gestures, inhibit his facial expressions, reduce his lip movements to a mechanically unavoidable minimum, make himself breathe evenly, render his voice monotonous, etc. But what would he achieve? Not the elimination of embodiment that he actually desires, but a certain specific form of machine-like embodiment that would seem very strange to any listener (see Staemmler, 2003a).

The *meanings* of the words and sentences in what the speaker says about how he evaluates a situation and other thoughts are, nonetheless, not themselves transmitted directly via the body. While they are complemented by nonverbal signals of an unmediated, embodied nature (see Staemmler, 1987) and thus commented upon and interpreted, if the listener has no knowledge of the language and does not engage in any other hermeneutic activity, they remain more or less incomprehensible. This hermeneutic effort that the listener makes in her attempt to establish the *sense* of what is being said is a form of interpretation that encompasses more than the mere understanding of direct bodily expression and is therefore associated with a greater risk of misunderstanding.[109]

This form of interpretation of the speaker's intentions is less likely to be relatively accurate than is our understanding of what is taking place in the body, since, in attempting to understand the sense of what has been said, spontaneous *simulation* does not take place as easily as it does with bodily acts and expression. Rather, the emphasis shifts to the necessity of creating a cognitive "theory" about what is in the other person's mind. If we want to reduce the risk of jumping to premature conclusions on the basis of our own motives, goals, expectations, and history and are seriously interested in attempting to understand the other person and his perspective, we need to cultivate our own uncertainty in a special way. We also need to subject the insights we believe we have gained about him to a continuous dialogical examination, i.e., we must constantly be ready to correct ourselves if necessary.

---

109 I have therefore classified this type of interpretation as being on the "macro level" (Staemmler, 2004).

BOX 42

EXAMPLE I was recently present at a live supervision session during which a client reported a dream.[110] In the last sequence of the dream, in the course of which she woke up, she had an encounter with some men, during which the buttons of her dress suddenly burst open and she found herself standing half naked in front of them. Understandably, one of the feelings that she had in that moment was shame. For me as supervisor it was thus not surprising that the therapist responded very empathically to the client, saying "I can understand that!" One could see that as a woman, she would also feel a strong sense of shame if she were to experience such a situation—and in fact that she considered it natural or inevitable that one would experience shame in such a situation. Thus, the way in which she communicated her understanding also conveyed another message that could be expressed as "Yes, in such a situation one must be ashamed"; or, to put it even more succinctly, "There is no alternative but to feel shame."

The identification of one of the women (the therapist) with the other woman (client) went further than the therapist's direct resonance with the client's feeling of shame and reached a totality in which not only a large part of the reference to the client's specific situation got lost, but the therapist also confounded her own perspective with that of the client. In that moment, the therapist was able to see neither the client as the author of her shame nor herself as the author of her own potential shame, let alone to activate the required 'ex-centric' or external stance from which she could have become aware of her identification with the client. Thus she was not able to relate to the other feelings that the client had indicated that she also had.

The example in Box 42 is intended to show how a form of understanding that takes what is assumed to have been understood for granted and fails to sustain any kind of uncertainty can even help to consolidate the other person's experience and thus be counterproductive.

> If the other person is really another, at a certain stage I must be surprised, disoriented. If we are to meet not just through what we have in common but in what is different between us—which presupposes a transformation of myself and of the other (Merleau-Ponty, 1973, p. 142).

(3) *Regarding the understanding of cause and context.* It is not without reason that these reference points of the situation which activated a certain emotion in the client—the cause and the context—are shown in the above diagram (Figure 10) outside of the field representing the "person."

---

110 I am grateful to the client and her therapist for giving me permission to publish this episode.

They point toward the external reality, which must be assumed to exist, even if it is given to a person only in the form of his subjective actuality and he can never have direct knowledge of it (see Staemmler, 2002b).[111]

Basically, two different constellations are conceivable for understanding the cause as perceived by the client and the context that was relevant for her. First, what the client experiences can have to do mainly with something in the *present, joint situation with the therapist* and be within their *shared context of experience.* Second, the reference point for what the client experiences *outside of the therapeutic situation* can be somewhere else in her life. In the following example, the reference point for the client's experiencing during the first session was his family situation, i.e., something external to the therapeutic situation. In contrast, in the second session, the focus of the client's experiencing and the therapist's empathy was what had transpired between the two of them previously.

BOX 43

EXAMPLE In the previous therapy session my client[112] had expressed his dissatisfaction with his family situation, especially with his partner's ever increasing working hours and the double burden of his own work and his bearing the main responsibility for the children and the housework. He had complained about his exhaustion and his frustration about the fact that despite all the effort that he and his partner invested in ensuring the family's well being, neither of them was satisfied, and their marriage was not nearly as happy as he would like.

I had expressed my compassion and said to him, in so many words, "I understand that you are not only exhausted and frustrated that you do not get to do the things you want with your partner. You also seem to have the impression that you and your partner have not managed to attain happiness together by making more and more effort."

He had burst into despairing sobs, but then "pulled himself together" again, as he put it, because he felt that the pain of failure was more than he could bear.

When he came to the next session a week later, he appeared to me to be withdrawn and I thought I could detect an undercurrent of annoyance. I conveyed my impression to him and he confirmed it. He then initially found it difficult to talk about what had caused his feelings. Finally, he plucked up courage and confessed that he was annoyed with me because in the previous session, I had said that his marriage had failed. This was, however, not true—he loved his partner and had no intention of leaving her.

---

111 Reality is never directly accessible to cognition, but it is possible to affect it by acting. Reality and actuality (phenomenal reality) are therefore not hermetically sealed off from each other, but stand in a dialectical relationship with each other (see Mehrgardt, 2005).
112 I am grateful to the client for giving me permission to publish this episode.

At first, I was somewhat surprised at this interpretation, which at first glance seemed to me to have changed the meaning of what I had said. However, after a while, we were able to clarify the misunderstanding. When I had said what I did, I had implicitly assumed that there were other (potentially more promising) ways to arrive at a happy relationship than constantly making a big effort. The client, however, had until then been unable to see any other way to deal with the situation and that he had failed to succeed by making an effort was the same for him as if he had failed to make a go of the relationship. While from my point of view, the fact that he realized that his efforts had failed opened up the prospects of finding new ways, he saw it as the end of all prospects of anything and had had the impression that that was what I meant. Seeing it in this light, I could understand his being annoyed at me.

In the first session, the cause of the client's emotions was an unsatisfactory family situation. The context was the coping strategy of making an effort that he and his partner had used for many years. In the second session, the cause of his emotions was the therapist's previous remark about the failure (of his efforts, or, from his viewpoint, the failure of his marriage). The context was now the attempt made by both client and therapist to find a way out of his frustration. Thus, the first session was mainly concerned with an external reference point and the second with one that was internal to the therapy.

Where the reference points are external, the therapist can focus exclusively on the client's subjective actuality and try to empathize with what he reports about his perception of the reasons and contexts outside of the therapist's office. In other words, the therapist usually has no *personal* impression of the external reference point. He *cannot know* how he himself would experience the family situation or the partner's behavior that the client describes if he were in his place himself or even only a participant observer. Even if he did have such knowledge, it would not be the same as empathizing with the client's experience. Since he does not have his own experience of the external reference point it is relatively easy for him to imagine the client's actuality because there is nothing to distract him from his focus on what the client is experiencing. However, there is also a danger that he may side with the client[113] and take his actuality for reality. This would mean forfeiting the client's changing his actuality.

---

113 I am assuming that I hardly need to mention that "taking sides" is not the same as empathizing with and committing oneself to someone. The confluence that I have already mentioned several times has nothing to do with taking sides, since it arises in relation to the other person's current *experiencing* and is not the same as thinking he is right. How else would it be possible to empathize with the frequent suffering that people have brought upon themselves or with violent people whose actions one finds totally unacceptable?

The situation is different where the reference points are inside therapy. Here the therapist has his own impressions, which are, of course, always also *subjective*. This does not necessarily make it easier to empathize with the client, since here two other risks are involved. The first lies in falling prey to a misapprehension, i.e., in the risk that the therapist may wrongly believe that he has understood the client and his experience of the situation because he is familiar with the external situation (in this case, the therapy) of which the client is speaking.[114] He can, however, only be aware of his own experience of the situation. Under these circumstances, it is therefore probable that he will project his own interpretations of the situation on to the client.

The second risk arises from the opposite situation—if the therapist's impressions are contradictory to those of the client's—which may well happen, as shown in the example above. Such contradictions can limit his willingness to empathize, e.g., when he experiences the client's different perspective as an attack on his own perspective[115] or even when he fails to differentiate the two perspectives clearly from one another. The therapist may at a certain point in time consider it suitable to express his view of the matter. However, this does not render it less necessary or unnecessary to empathize with what the client is experiencing. At all events, these are two different things that can neither replace each other nor cancel each other out or be pitted against each other.

However, if the therapeutic dialog has been relatively successful up to that point, it should be the exception for the two participants to have contradictory impressions of what is going on, since continually checking back with each other, as in social referencing, favors the development of shared perspectives, and thus, in time, they build up a stock of agreements on what they have experienced together. I call these interpretations of situations that have been developed by two people in cooperation with each other, "joint constructions" (Staemmler, 2008). The physicist David Bohm has described how they develop:

> Consider a dialogue. In such a dialogue, when one person says something, the other person does not in general respond with exactly the same meaning as that seen by the first person. Rather, the meanings are

---

114 In everyday life, this kind of pseudo-empathy that relates to the external situation but not to subjective experiencing, is widespread, e.g., A talks about what she has recently experienced with her son, and B answers, "I understand that, my son has done that too . . . "

115 As shown in the example, the client may quite possibly express his different perspective in a reproachful or attacking tone. However, this does not, of course, mean that the therapist also has to *feel* attacked. Although the reproach is an "invitation" to feel attacked, the therapist does not have to accept it. He has the opportunity to conduct his *appraisal* of the situation in such a way that other feelings result (see Staemmler & Staemmler, 2009).

only *similar* and not identical. Thus, when the second person replies, the first person sees a *difference* between what he meant to say and what the other person understood. On considering this difference, he may then be able to see something new, which is relevant both to his own views and to those of the other person. And so it can go back and forth, with the continual emergence of a new content that is common to both participants. Thus, in a dialogue, each person does not attempt to *make common* certain ideas or items of information that are already known to him. Rather, it may be said that the two people are making something *in common*, i.e., creating something new together (2004, p. 3—original italics).

Of course, this creative process does not include only the level of language, but also all aspects of communication, which thus becomes a "creative field" (Burow, 1999). This process of creating joint constructions, through which different meanings come together and are at the same time transcended, can also be referred to as "dyadically expanded states of consciousness" (Tronick, 1998; 2007), which expand the participants' individual states of consciousness and open up for them a more comprehensive view of themselves and the world (see also Chapter 4.3).

4.2.2   The Perspective of Phenomenology

"Toward the things!" was the motto of the phenomenologists. But what was "the thing"? It certainly was regarded as hidden and lost in the tangle of prejudices, grand words, and ideological constructs. . . . To open themselves thus to evidence, that was also what the phenomenologists wanted; their great ambition was to disregard anything that had until then been thought or said about consciousness or the world. They were on the lookout for a new way of letting the things approach them, without covering them up with what they already knew. Reality should be given an opportunity to "show" itself. That which showed itself, and the way it showed itself, was called "the phenomenon" by the phenomenologists.

   The phenomenologists shared . . . the conviction that the real alphabet of perception had first to be relearned. To begin with, everything that had been said before had to be forgotten and the language of reality rediscovered (Safranski, 1998, p. 72).

Whatever the "language of reality" may be, the language that the phenomenologists use is not always easy for the uninitiated to comprehend. However, I believe it is worthwhile making an effort to understand their ideas. I have given some explanations in the hope that they will make it easier to understand those quotes that do not seem to make sense at first sight. The next section (4.2.3) on neuroscientific research, which in many ways provides support for the insights of the phenomenologists, will then be easier to read.

"Towards the things!" was the motto of the "phenomenological movement" (Spiegelberg, 1960) and in principle it has remained so to the present day. Hermann Schmitz, the founder of "New Phenomenology" has defined the *leitmotiv* of this branch of philosophy by posing the following question.

> To what authority do we appeal in order to make clear to ourselves and others what we are actually talking about and to make a distinction between any arbitrary assumptions and foregone conclusions that can be dissolved by interpretation, and that which is obtrusive and indisputable in our constructions, that we can only disavow with mere words and not in earnest? (Schmitz 1980, p. 13)

One of the facts that is most obtrusive and cannot seriously be disputed, on which most phenomenologists basically agree, is the embodiment of the human being. To quote just a few of them briefly: "'Dasein' (*being-there*) is always only incarnated Being . . . For to exist means to be incarnated" (Marcel, 1985, p. 16). This marks the starting point of the phenomenology of embodiment (see Box 21). "The lived body and its forms of movement . . . form a unity of which one can say neither that it is physical, nor that it is psychical" (Plessner & Buytendijk, 1925/1982, p. 83). Each self exists "in the mode of embodiment" (Coenen, 1985, p. 205). "There are no 'psychic phenomena' there to be united with the body. There is nothing behind the body. But the body is wholly 'psychic'"; "it is therefore in no way a contingent addition to my soul; on the contrary it is a permanent structure of my being" (Sartre, 1956, pp. 305, 328).

> In short, my body is not only an object among all other objects, a nexus of sensible qualities among others, but an object which is *sensitive to* all the rest, which reverberates to all sounds, vibrates to all colors, and provides words with their primordial significance through the way in which it receives them (Merleau-Ponty, 1962, p. 236—original italics).

Embodiment and subjectivity are closely and inextricably linked because "the subject . . . forces his ipseity into reality only by actually being a body, and entering the world through that body" (v, p. 408). Kühn says the same thing more enthusiastically: "Only our respective subjectivities can feel incommensurable happiness, so that everywhere where there is bodily sensation there is also subjectivity, in which life tastes its peculiar joy" (2007, p. 603).

This fundamental fact of human embodiment has given rise to a wealth of philosophical considerations that I cannot even begin to address here. I shall therefore restrict myself to presenting a few aspects that I consider helpful if we are to understand the embodied character of empathy. One of these aspects is referred to by philosophers as "mineness." What is meant is that a human being is a being that

> experiences his conscious, inner experiences in a very direct and unmediated sense as *his own*. Pain is not simply painful, it is *my pain*. Also, if I am convinced of a philosophical or scientific theory this does not simply float freely in an internal conscious space, it *is my conviction* (Metzinger, 1993, p. 22—original italics).

Temporality or historicity is another aspect. To be embodied means to be born, grow, fall ill, and recover, become old and die.

> The experiences, the joys and sorrows and the potential of this human being are engraved in the countenance of this lived body. Whoever meets him open-eyed can perceive him as existence, as an embodied potentiality. The lived body is a temporal gestalt . . . It is therefore not enough to say that I am my body. As a living body I am also always my past, and, indeed, my future (Marcel, 1985, p. 63).

Perspectivity is the next aspect of human embodiment to which I turn, and possibly the most important one. I shall therefore discuss it in somewhat more detail.

Perspectivity

Leaving aside out-of-body experiences (which may at first sight appear to be an exception, although on closer scrutiny we find that they are not at all because they also require embodiment[116]), to be a lived body always means to be at the "zero point" (Husserl, 1999, p. 164) or to be in an "absolute location" (Schmitz, 1985, pp. 77f.). Irrespective of our geographical location and also of whether we have a spatial orientation and *know* where we are presently located, or whether we are, on the contrary, perhaps currently

---

116 Out-of-body experiences typically occur in cases of severe physical trauma, e.g., after life-threatening injuries or during epileptic fits (see Brandt, Brandt, Brechtelsbauer, Bien, & Reiners, 2005).

completely disoriented, it is always true to say that our "own body is in the world as the heart is in the organism" (Merleau-Ponty, 1962, p. 203); it is always *here*, i.e., at the place where our embodied self is present.

Thus, human consciousness is "built up around a phenomenal focus" (Metzinger, 1993, p. 25). My body is therefore "the pivot of the world" (Merleau-Ponty, 1962, p. 82), from which alone I can experience what I experience; "the body is our general medium of having a world" (Merleau-Ponty, 1962, p. 146). It is the absolute location that I can never leave and which therefore unequivocally fixes the perspective from which I initially perceive and experience everything to which I turn and that I encounter. In other words, the perspective that is prescribed by my embodiment results in a kind of "centrality" of my self around which the world arranges itself "concentrically," so to speak. While I can shift my geographical location, this does nothing to alter the centrality of my *absolute* location in the world, which is irrevocably given wherever I go.

> The always-standing-somewhere and always-seeing-from-somewhere that we call the standpoint and viewpoint of perspectival awareness are elements of my embodiment . . . That is, each perceived world is related to a center which is me, and is the only location or object of my constantly changing field of view that it is not possible for me to perceive (Graumann, 1960, p. 68).

A view of the world that was not linked to this corporeally defined standpoint would be a "view from nowhere" (Nagel, 1986), perhaps fictional, perhaps godly, but definitely not human.

Nonetheless, because it is taken for granted and because there is no alternative, as a rule embodied perspectivity recedes into the background of our awareness. It is thus something "that I usually leave 'behind me,' for I am [my attention is] initially focused on the things of my world (Graumann, 1960, p. 9), of which I am currently taking note. Graumann calls this the *"phenomenal inconspicuousness of one's own body in perception"* (Graumann, 1960—original italics). In many everyday situations it is this inconspicuousness of the subject's own body, this "self-forgetfulness" of which Husserl speaks, which can lead to the illusion that there is a consciousness that is detached from the body, that would allow one to see the things as they "really are," regardless of one's own perspective.

Another factor that can contribute to this naïvely realistic illusion is the ability to switch perspectives and to view things from different angles, which can easily lead to the mistaken assumption that we have "objective" knowledge of things. We do that constantly in our everyday lives when we investigate an object that we have never seen before. We turn it round and round or walk around it so as to get an impression of it and its various appearances ("adumbrations") from as many perspectives as possible and thus to approximate it in its wholeness. However, *"the Body is,"* of course, *"involved as freely moved sense organ, as freely moved totality of sense organs"* (Husserl, 1989, p. 61 — original italics) and its coincidental and systematic idiosyncrasies codetermine the nature of the experience.

Its characteristics, which are coincidental, include not only the specific physical variables such as, for example, each person's height, but also physical aspects such as sex.[117] As a heterosexual man, how I "see'" a female body is different from how a homosexual man or a bisexual woman would see it. Such individual characteristics merge into the universal ones and thus my current need-state or mood, for example, has an influence on how I perceive something. That is an individual expression of the general fact that the body is "befindlich" (Heidegger)[118], in several different senses of the word: It always "finds" itself at a *location* (see above) and at the same time in a given *situation*; it always finds itself in a certain state, particularly in the form of a *mood*. Both affect what the individual perceives or understands in one way or another, since "understanding always has its mood [Befindlichkeit]" (Heidegger, 1962, p. 182), and this physical *'Befindlichkeit'* is also an aspect of perspectivity.

BOX 44

PERSPECTIVITY The German *Dictionary of Phenomenological Concepts* (*Wörterbuch der phänomenologischen Begriffe*) contains the following entry under "perspective":

> For an ego, spatial existence is only accessible to being seen from different standpoints, in varying orientations, i.e. to different perspectives, appearances and adumbrations. . . . Seeing is perspectival, the perspective being both the means by which objects reveal themselves and the means by which they can hide themselves. The spatial perspective is complemented by the temporal perspective. The individuality of what happens is dependent on the perspective in which it happens. That an object reveals itself in perspectives results from embodiment. None of the perspectival views of the world exhaust this, every perspective indicates further perspectives (Vetter, 2004, p. 409).

---

117 This should perhaps be "gender" and not "sex," but the concept of embodiment also relativizes the sharp distinctions between the two terms (see Butler, 1993).
118 Gendlin (1978/1979) has written some explanations of Heidegger's concept of *"Befindlichkeit"* and the many facets of its meaning (being in a certain mood, finding oneself in a certain situation) that are well worth reading.

Hence, "the body [is] . . . the vehicle of being in the world" (Merleau-Ponty, 1962, p. 82), through it the world reveals itself to me; it is "the general instrument of my 'comprehension'" (Merleau-Ponty, 1962, p. 235). Thus, in a certain sense embodiment and perspectivity are one and the same thing, since if I *am* my body and this provides me with access to the world that is tied to a perspective, then these two conditions are so closely connected that one can, like Merleau-Ponty, link them together and, consolidating them, say that in my embodiment I am "nothing but a view of the world" (Merleau-Ponty, 1962, p. 406), a certain perspective. That is true not only of the functions of my five senses and proprioception, but also of the cognitive processes that develop out of the interactions between my body and the world (see Damasio, 1994). It also applies to language (see Staemmler, 2003a) and even to the basic structures of my thought patterns and theoretical concepts that arise from the conditions of my embodied existence in a three-dimensional space under the influence of gravity and other environmental conditions (see Johnson, 1987; Lakoff & Johnson, 1999).

In view of these implications of embodiment and perspectivity we could, on the one hand, speak of the narrowness of the limitations to which we are subjected as human beings. We can, in fact, never shake off our own perspective. All that we understand we understand from this perspective. In any event, the divine "view from nowhere" remains inaccessible to us. On the other hand, we can view these limitations positively, insofar as they provide the necessary conditions for us to be "in the world" (Merleau-Ponty) at all, i.e. that we are directly related to it and in connection with it through our bodies.

> I am part of the world, I perceive it as one who is situated in it; I have a body and therefore enjoy a permanent membership among the things of the world that surround me, so to speak. *I understand them from the inside, because I am one of them* (Taylor, 1986, p. 208 — italics added).

My body is — as Merleau-Ponty tried to elucidate shortly before he died — part of the "flesh" (French: *chair*) of the world. "Since the world is of the fabric of the lived body and this lived body itself has a subjective quality, the world is revealed in the lived body from the inside" (Waldenfels, 1985, p. 162). The lived body belongs, so to speak, to the same element to which the whole world belongs, to inanimate and animate nature (see Abram, 1997, pp. 66ff.) and of course also and especially to all other human beings. The flesh is neither material, nor spirit, nor substance.

> To designate it, we should need the old term "element," in the sense it was used to speak of water, air, earth, and fire, that is, in the sense of a

general thing, midway between the spatio-temporal individual and the idea, a sort of incarnate principle that brings a style of being wherever there is a fragment of being. The flesh is in this sense an "element" of Being (Merleau-Ponty, 1968, p. 139).

Multiperspectivity, Referential Totality, and Ex-centricity

Thus, despite the limitations associated with it, the perspectivity of the body does not isolate human beings from the world, but *integrates* them into it. The fact that it is impossible to overcome perspectivity does not even mean that human beings are restricted to a *single* perspective forever. Rather, it is precisely the fact, that is given in perception, that I always see an object *from a certain angle* which implicitly 'reveals'[119] that this object also has other aspects which can be accessible to me from a different perspective. "In other words, what *is perceived* in a perspectival adumbration indicates a range of other *possible* associated percepts" (Graumann, 1960, p. 66—original italics). The limitation imposed by the perspective already contains a *reference to the whole* which can be revealed to me if I assume other standpoints, although never completely. Graumann therefore describes the "structure of perspectivity as a *referential totality*" (Graumann, 1960, p. 67—original italics). Merleau-Ponty speaks of a "horizon synthesis" through which "perception is . . . understood as a reference to a whole which can be grasped, in principle, only through certain of its parts and aspects" (1964, p. 18).

> Because we open ourselves up to the world through perception and perceive our respective fields perspectivally, we are never captive to only a *single* perspective. Thus, the world can be apprehended via any number of approaches and from the most widely differing perspectives (Taylor, 1986, p. 208—original italics).

Being able to view something from different points of view enables us to assume countless different perspectives one after the other, making use of our body's ability to move and in the course of the time it takes to move. By so doing we can come closer to capturing the object as a whole on the basis of the sum of perspectives obtained. However, it is often the case that a number of different perspectives are available at a given point

---

119 What is thus additionally presented as a kind of adjunct to all that is perceived Husserl calls "appresentation." It is this that gives perception its "surplus" nature.

in time, given that, for example, an object can be perceived via several different sensory channels at once. When we listen to someone we are not usually restricted to auditory perception, but are also open to visual and possibly also to tactile impressions and to absorbing atmospheres. For the listener, all this is combined to produce a meaningful whole that is more than simply what is understood as the perception of "stimuli." Even within certain individual sensory channels such as the auditory and visual ones, we have *two* ears and *two* eyes, i.e., *two* perspectives in each case, which we then integrate into a more comprehensive sound or image.

Thus, the perspectivity of the lived body is, in fact, a "multi-perspectivity" which has the tendency to go beyond itself and thus (indirectly at least) to allude to the other, who is always assuming one of the other possible perspectives or could potentially do so. "My perceptual objects are not exhausted in their appearance for me; rather, each object always possesses a horizon of coexisting profiles, which although being momentarily inaccessible to me . . . could very well be perceived by other subjects" (Zahavi, 2001, p. 155). And one can imagine these other perspectives of the other, perhaps not always in a really concrete way, but as possibilities that exist in principle, since it is always clear that the other occupies only that space with his body that is currently available to him and that he has his own respective "here" from whence he always has a different view of things from my own (see Thompson, 2001, p. 18).

Although I do not know exactly what an object, for example a table, looks like on its other sides, it is always clear that it does have other sides which are visible to those others who adopt the corresponding perspectives. Since my perspectivity manifests itself in my own perception of the table my attention is directed to the existence of other perspectives that could be adopted by other persons or are in fact adopted by them. "Thus, each object . . . appears in my concrete experience as polyvalent; it is given originally as possessing systems of reference to an indefinite plurality of consciousnesses; it is on the table, on the wall that the Other is revealed to me" (Sartre, 1956, p. 233).

It is also clear that I myself have the ability to adopt the other perspectives, even if for some concrete reason I am not actually able to do so at the moment. Knowing this frees me in a certain sense from the perspective that is given to me, to which, at the same time, I remain tied, since I grasp—from a higher, virtual standpoint, as it were—that from my current perspective I can only capture *part* of that whole (e.g., of the table), namely that part which my current perspective reveals to me. "I cease to be tied to my perspective the moment I become aware of my self in relation to the object while I am looking at it . . . Human beings can represent themselves as bodies-in-the-situation and thus 'see things from above'"

(Fuchs, 2000, p. 264), precisely because they can become aware of the fact that they are and remain centered in the "absolute location" mentioned above. This reflection makes it possible to gain a distance from oneself, a quality which Plessner termed "ex-centricity" and which is something of a paradox: "The life of human beings [is] ex-centric, without being able to escape from the centering and at the same time emerging from it" (Plessner, 1981, p. 364).

Another important dimension opens up when we come to the phenomenon of ex-centricity, since this no longer refers merely to the perception of material things such as tables and simple organisms, which are not considered to have a consciousness of their own and are therefore also not deemed to have a perspective of their own. Ex-centricity is the capacity to adopt a reflective and self-critical perspective *on oneself*, from which it then becomes evident that

> the world in which we live is not only a world of physical bodies but also of experiencing subjects external to us, of whose experiences we know. . . . This [psycho-physical] individual is not given as a physical body, but as a sensitive, living body belonging to an "I," an "I" that senses, thinks, feels, and wills. The living body of this "I" not only fits into my phenomenal world but is itself the center of orientation of such a phenomenal world. It faces this world and communicates with me (Stein, 1917/1964, pp. 5f.).

Only here does the question of empathy arise at all. How could we empathize with the perspective of another person who has her own personal subjective experiences if we ourselves could not, in fact, "slip out of our own shoes and into those of the other," as it were, as individualism and the view of empathy that it espouses assume to be the case? In what I have just been saying about embodiment in general, and specifically about "referential totality" (Graumann), the "flesh of the world" (Merleau-Ponty), perspectivity as a prerequisite for being "in the world" (Merleau-Ponty) and ex-centricity (Plessner), there are a number of pointers as to how the question of empathy could be answered from a phenomenological perspective. For the time being, we can say, to quote Waldenfels, "I understand another person through the world in which I live with him and through the medium of the bodily expression in which he realizes his intentions and mental states" (1976, p. 121). Merleau-Ponty described it as follows:

> It is precisely my body which perceives the body of another, and discovers in that other body a miraculous prolongation of my own intentions, a familiar way of dealing with the world. Henceforth, as the parts of my

body together compromise a system, so my body and the other's are one whole, two sides of one and the same phenomenon (1962, p. 354).

However, these pointers alone are not perhaps sufficient if we do not at least briefly consider the phenomenon of *expression* to which Waldenfels refers. Here I would like to remind the reader of Munch's painting *The Scream* and the photos of the angry man and grieving women above (see Figures 6 and 7 in section 4.2.1). There I pointed out that when one looks at the pictures, one 'sees' the feelings of the people shown in them. What makes the phrase "'see' feelings" seem so strange that I considered it necessary to put the verb in quotes has to do with the fact that "we surely can't 'see' the expression, the shy behaviour, *in the same sense* as we see movement, shapes and colours" (Wittgenstein, 1980, § I-1070—original italics).

Here we have another example of the Cartesian separation of body and consciousness which still has an influence today and according to which the feeling of the person I am looking at is a state or content of consciousness that first exists in his consciousness alone, independently of his body. Only then, in a second step, does he use his body as a *means* of expression with which to externalize his 'internal' feeling, thus rendering it visible for me. If I want to understand him, I must then draw *inferences* about his 'internal' experience on the basis of the expression I perceive. This is the usual theory behind the word "ex-pression."

Bodily Expression and "Encorporation" (Einleibung)

However, the split between internality (or consciousness) and externality (or the body) implied by the word "expression" is not compatible with the nature of embodiment, which encompasses both consciousness and bodily experiencing. On the contrary,

> we must . . . recognize a primary process of signification in which the thing expressed does not exist apart from the expression, and in which the signs themselves induce their significance externally. In this way the body expresses total existence, not because it is an external accompaniment to that existence, but because existence realizes itself in the body (Merleau-Ponty, 1962, p. 166).

Thus, if it is freed from its association with dualism, expression "does not simply mean the emergence of something I already have inside me, but rather, expression *is* the realization of the sense; it does not mean that a sense that is already present internally becomes externally visible" (Waldenfels, 2000, p. 222). In sum, "feeling and expression are related by nature and meaning, not causally" (Stein, 1917/1964, p. 49). This relation also arises from the fact that an expression is linked not only to what is "already present internally," but also to what the external *situation* contributes to the context of meaning. "In itself a clenched fist is nothing and means nothing. But also we never perceive a clenched fist. We perceive a man who *in a certain situation* clenches his fist" (Sartre, 1956, p. 347[120] —italics added).

> For these reasons we need to be cautious about using the word "expression." It is liable to be misunderstood, since 'ex-pression' always sounds as if we had something inside us that is pressed outwards . . . In contrast, Merleau-Ponty's understanding of expression is that what is expressed is *realized* as it is expressed, it is incarnated, an embodied sense and not an external announcement (Waldenfels, 2000, p. 223f.)

of something that is separate from it and exists internally. For example, when I am amused at a funny situation I do not usually first have a feeling and then, in a second step, decide to express it by means of a smile. My amusement and my smile are two intertwined aspects of the humor that I see in the situation. "Expression is everywhere creative, and what is expressed is always inseparable from it" (Merleau-Ponty, 1962, p. 391). I experienced the situation I observed in a *holistic* way, and the funny meaning that I found in it and my amusement and smiling belong together like two sides of the same coin, my "lived-body-soul" (*"Leibseele"* —Scheler, 1973).[121]

What happens when I watch the gestures of *other* people, their "body-things" (*"Leibkörper"* —Scheler, 1973), is similar:[122] I do not first perceive their "expressions" as purely physical, meaningless behaviors and then ascribe corresponding experiences and meaning to them in a second

---

120 Sartre therefore speaks of the "body in situation" (Sartre, 1956, p. 347); a more detailed discussion of the concept of situation is given in Chapter 4.3.
121 Expression can be prevented or faked (see Ekman's "display rules"), and processes of emotional expression can be internalized (see Holodynski & Friedlmeier, 2006). These are *secondary* processes which do not militate against Merleau-Ponty's view. On the contrary, if I suppress my smile at a funny situation, this may be precisely because for me there is not only something funny about the situation, but possibly also something embarrassing. Thus, suppressing a smile is also "embodied meaning."
122 Scheler used these words to distinguish the immediate consciousness we have of our own bodily experiencing ("lived-body-soul"—*"Leibseele"*) from the consciousness that we have of our own bodies when we touch them with our own hands, or from that which we have of the bodies of other people, whom we do not experience as bodies, but as embodied beings ("body-things"—*"Leibkörper"*).

interpretative step. In order to avoid this misunderstanding, Max Scheler speaks of "*expressions* of mind" (1916/1954, p. 239—original italics).

> The apprehension of the human is the apprehension of that person there, who dances, laughs where amused, and chatters, or who discusses something with me in science, etc., is not the apprehension of a spirit fastened to a Body. Instead it is the apprehension, accomplished through the medium of an appearance of a body. . . . Man in his movements, in his action, in his speaking and writing etc., is not a mere connection or linking up of one thing, called a soul, with another thing, the Body. The Body is, as Body, filled with the soul through and through (Husserl, 1989, p. 252).

Thus, empathy is anchored in the experience of our own body, since it is this experience that enables us to perceive another person not as some kind of material body that also, more or less coincidentally, has consciousness, but as a *person* who is just as embodied as we are ourselves. "Intersubjectivity is intercorporeality" (Merleau-Ponty, 1972, p. 248).

> In general I do not surmise fear in him—I *see* it. I do not feel that I am deducing the probable existence of something inside from something outside; rather it is as if the human face were in a way translucent and that I were seeing it not in reflected light but rather in its own (Wittgenstein, 1980, § II-170—original italics).

If we leave the Cartesian split behind us, we can no longer view the mental or psychic aspect exclusively as something 'internal' that exists separately from the body and the world. What a person expresses is now not merely the external manifestation of something that was previously present internally; it is rather that the 'internal' is only fully realized when it is expressed. Expression and behavior always carry meaning. To put it differently, consciousness and experience are not exclusively internal, but have two sides, like a coin, one of which is expression. The overarching whole is the embodiment that is common to all persons.

As Merleau-Ponty puts it:

> The communication or comprehension of gestures comes about through the reciprocity of my intentions and the gestures of others, of my gestures and intentions discernible in the conduct of other people. It is as if the other person's intention inhabited my body, and mine his. . . . Here we must rehabilitate the experience of others which has been distorted by intellectualist analyses (1962, p. 185).

BOX 45

EXAMPLES If someone makes a face like the man in Figure 6 and raises his fist,

> I have no need, in order to understand it, to recall the feelings which I myself experienced when I used these gestures on my own account. . . and what is more, I do not see anger or a threatening attitude as a psychic fact hidden behind the gesture, I read anger in it: The gesture does not make me think of anger, it is anger itself (Merleau-Ponty, 1962, p. 184—original italics).

Scheler gives a similar, more subtle, but no less commonplace example:

> Thus I do not merely see the other person's eyes, for example; I also see that "he is looking at me" and even that "he is looking at me as though he wished to avoid my seeing that he is looking at me" (1916/1954, p. 261).

Wittgenstein speaks of "consciousness in the face of another. Look into someone else's face and see the consciousness in it, and also a particular shade of consciousness. You see on it, in it, joy, indifference, interest, excitement, dullness etc." (1980, § I-927—original italics).[123] Elsewhere, he writes

> We see emotion. . . . We do not see facial contortions and make the inference that he is feeling joy, grief, boredom. We describe a face immediately as sad, radiant, bored, even when we are unable to give any other description of the features.—Grief, one would like to say, is personified in the face. This is essential to what we call "emotion" (1980, § II-570—original italics).

I have taken the last example from Edith Stein because it is so 'physical' and is therefore a good illustration of the embodiment of empathic situations that are seemingly purely bodily. "The hand resting on the table does not lie there like the book beside it. It 'presses' against the table more or less strongly; it lies there limpid or stretched; and I 'see' these sensations of pressure and tension" (Stein, 1917/1964, p. 54).

We know, of course, from experience that it is possible to conduct such analyses, but both chronologically and systematically they come *second*, because the other persons whom we encounter are always primarily "*integral wholes,* whose intuitive content is not immediately resolved in terms of external or internal perception" (Scheler, 1916/1954, p. 261) and needs to be analyzed or interpreted in order to be understandable at all. Other people may keep their secrets to themselves, and some of them may even take them to the grave, but they are not mysterious in the sense that one needs to make a great intellectual effort to understand them (at least in an approximate

---

123 A little further on, Wittgenstein draws attention to the limits of bodily empathy: "Knowledge, opinion, have no facial expression" (Wittgenstein, 1980).

way) in each new everyday situation. Like ourselves, they are embodied "being[s] in the world" (Merleau-Ponty) or "Dasein," to quote Heidegger:

> By "Others" we do not mean everyone else but me—those over against whom the "I" stands out. They are rather those from whom, for the most part, one does *not* distinguish oneself—those among whom one is too. . . . On the basis of this *like-with* being-in-the-world, the world is always already the one that I share with the others. The world of Da-sein is a *with-world*. Being-in is *being-with* others (1962, pp. 154f.—original italics).

Thus, other persons have an original empathic "disclosedness":

> Being-with is such that the disclosedness of the Dasein-with of Others belongs to it; this means that because Dasein's Being is Being-with, its understanding of Being already implies the understanding of Others. This understanding, like any understanding, is not an acquaintance derived from knowledge about them, but a primordially existential kind of Being, which, more than anything else, makes such knowledge and acquaintance possible. Knowing oneself is grounded in Being-with, which understands primordially (Heidegger, 1962, pp. 160f.).

Heidegger's last sentence expresses a view that we have frequently come across, for example in connection with Buber's dialogical theory, in the findings of research on developmental psychology and in the context of symbolic interactionism. The *other* is the *primary* person. *She* is the Thou through whom we become I. Only if we can understand who she essentially is can we understand who we ourselves essentially are, that is, also persons who are acting and feeling as living bodies in the world—just like her.[124] "Thus, taking embodiment as the starting point is an important step on the way to relativizing and overcoming the traditional view of the autonomous, enclosed individual" (Coenen, 1985, p. 218). I understand myself because I first understand the other, and as I begin to fathom her mystery I can also recognize myself.

From a phenomenological viewpoint, on this fundamental level the question as to the mystery of the other does not therefore arise in the same way as it did in the individualistic paradigm. To recapitulate, individualism assumes that individuals are separate to begin with and must then find a way to render the more or less closed 'internal world' of other

---

124 It is therefore no coincidence that empathy (in the specific sense of the word that goes beyond mere imitation) "appears ontogenetically for the first time when the child is able to identify his own mirror image" (Bischof-Köhler, 1994, p. 350), in the second year of life.

people accessible. Phenomenology sees a person's 'Being-with' others[125] as the essential given fact, the "primordially existential kind of Being" (Heidegger). On this basis it then becomes possible, in a second step, to develop one's own individual identity and to understand oneself.

> We are already familiar with ourselves through Nature, which we share, and which is part of our mutual embodiment, and on the other hand through our embodiment we are already familiar with the world in which and through which we encounter the other (Coenen, 1985, pp. 207f.).

Heidegger sums it up as follows: *"'Empathy' does not first constitute Being-with; only on the basis of Being-with does 'empathy' become possible"* (1962, p. 162—italics added).[126]

When we see another person, we do not therefore first need to carry out some complicated thought process and deliberately remind ourselves that her living body "can be the scene of manifold sensations. . . . It is given as a *sensing, living* body" (Stein, 1917/1964, p. 42—italics added), whose sensitivity we take for granted and whose sensations we feel in a special way.

BOX 46

EXAMPLES

I am thinking of the situation where a mother sees that her child, who is playing unsuspectingly in the street, is threatened by something, perhaps an approaching car, but is too far away to go to his aid. In this situation her gaze will be riveted, fixed on the child with horror—so literally that she may not be able to move and even her cry may remain stuck in her throat. She will also feel as if she were in the child's place, . . . but she is far from slipping into the child's role and playing innocently with him in the street (Schmitz, 1989, pp. 189f.).

---

125 One could see this "Being-with" as the fundamental situation of human beings that is repeatedly manifested anew. "Mit-Sein" (Being-with) or "Sich-Befinden" (finding oneself) in situations is therefore an important component of interpersonal understanding. "Everyone knows from experience how uncertain an interpretation remains if it has to rely on an expression alone. Half-closed eyes can express lying in wait, sleepiness, sensuous arousal, pensiveness, smugness or disdain . . . It is only possible to deduce the meaning of an expression from the situation and its purposes or goals or whatever other intentions justify it (Plessner & Buytendijk, 1925/1982, p. 126). I shall address this aspect in more detail in Chapter 4.3.
126 It is surprising how similar such phenomenological statements are to the outcomes of recent research in developmental psychology. *"The recognition of self-other equivalences is the starting point for social cognition—a precondition for infant development, not the outcome of it"* (Meltzoff & Brooks, 2007, p. 166—original italics). "The newborn infant already has an effective interpersonal intelligence" (Trevarthen, 1998, p. 15).

> When I watch a stranger learning to ride a bicycle for the first time, my
> own body, although it is standing solidly on the ground, inadvertently ex-
> periences the uncertain balance of the rider, and when that bicycle teeters
> and falls I feel the harsh impact of the asphalt against my own leg and
> shoulder (Abram, 1997, p. 126).

Hermann Schmitz coined the term *Einleibung* (see end*)* for this, in
analogy to *Einfühlung* (feeling into, empathy) (see Chapter 1). This can
be *one-sided*, as in the example of the mother and child (see Box 46) or as
in certain forms of fascination, for instance when we "watch the daring,
dangerous feats of a tightrope walker, spellbound and with baited breath"
(Schmitz, 1993, p. 132).

Originary and Non-Originary Experience

These examples illustrate how mothers *share* in the bodily actions of the children they are observing. The same applies to people who observe cyclists
and to circus audiences watching acrobats. However, the examples also
show how their experience *differs* from that of the people they are observing.
This is because the fact that we have immediate access to the experience of
others whom we observe and do not have to depend solely on making inferences, by no means implies that we have the same access to the experience
of the other people as we do to our own. To assume this "would lead to an
abolition of the difference between self and other, a negation of the *alterity*[127]
of the other, of that which makes the other other" (Zahavi, 2005, p. 155—
original italics); it would ultimately be an act of violence (Lévinas, 1989b).
    Husserl describes this fundamental difference as follows.

> Yet each has appearances which are exclusively his own, and each has
> lived experiences which are exclusively his own. Only he experiences
> these in their very flesh, utterly originarily. In a certain way, I also expe-
> rience . . . the other's lived experiences . . . To that extent, what we have
> here is thus experience, perception. But this co-existence . . . does not, in
> principle, allow itself to be transformed into immediate originary exis-
> tence (primal presence). It is characteristic of empathy that it *refers* to an
> originary Body-spirit-consciousness but one I cannot myself accomplish
> *originarily*, I who *am* not the other (Husserl, 1989, p. 208—italics added).

127 "Alterity" is a synonym for "otherness" that is frequently used in philosophy.

The "originary experience" of a child, cyclist or acrobat is followed by the "bodily being-*with*" ("*Mitdasein*") of the mother, observer or circus-goer that is accomplished by empathy (or encorporation), since they themselves cannot experience what they are empathizing with "in an *originary way.*" What they can feel right down to the level of their own muscles did not develop primarily (or "originarily") in themselves, however intense it feels, but was evoked by the other persons *via* encorporation. These other persons are the original initiators of the bodily experience, whereas the people who are empathizing with them have only a "non-originary" bodily experience.

In such cases of *one-sided* encorporation the facts can be relatively clearly deciphered, and both Schmitz's example of the child and his mother and Husserl's analysis show how the experiences of the participants differ.[128] In her book entitled *On the Problem of Empathy*, Husserl's student Edith Stein (1917/1964[129]) expresses a remarkable thought which merits closer scrutiny. She asks *in what way* we become aware of the experiences of another person through the medium of empathy. She sees a certain analogy with our own memories of earlier experiences which we can bring to mind but which are currently no longer pertinent. We can still imagine ourselves back in the situation, i.e. we know how it was to be in that situation *at the time*. However, today we immediately assume a perspective that is in a sense distanced from our previous experience, since we are no longer the same person as before, our temporal perspective has changed and "the dimensions of the past are shaped by the present which imposes upon previous events a perspective that is governed by the necessities and the values of the present" (Frank, 1939, p. 301). If we recall something that gave us reason to experience great joy at the time, although this joy may still be accessible, from our current point of view it may arouse different feelings. Our joy may, for example, now seem to us to be silly or even embarrassing or we may enjoy remembering it again.

Whatever feelings we have today, we can conclude from this observation that, despite the continuity of our own histories and the fact that we somehow remain the same person that we always were, we can see our current memories of past joy that remain alive within us as containing two "Is" — the I that is doing the remembering today and the remembered I that experienced joy in the past. "Thus the present 'I' and the past 'I' face each other as subject and object. They do not coincide, though there is a consciousness of sameness" (Stein, 1917/1964, p. 9).

---

128 Husserl paid substantial attention to these cases, in which the differences in the way the respective perspectives are experienced remain relatively clear. In contrast, Schmitz is at least equally as interested in *reciprocal* encorporation (*Einleibung*) in which the differences are not so easy to establish. Thus, the founder of phenomenology is closer to the traditional understanding of empathy than the founder of New Phenomenology.
129 This was Edith Stein's doctoral thesis, which was supervised by Husserl in Freiburg.

In order to capture the difference between these two I's more accurately, Stein introduced the concept of primordiality[130] (*Originarität*), which we have already encountered in Husserl. If we apply this to the *memory of joy*, we can say that "the memory of a joy is primordial as a representational act now being carried out, though its content of joy is non-primordial" (Stein, 1917/1964, p. 8) This is true for today, but *at the time when we had the original experience* the joy was originary. To put it quite simply, at each of the two points in time we are concerned with a different activity. Today it is remembering, while on that past occasion it was being joyful. The joyfulness is no longer originary today, but one can empathize with it originarily by remembering it. It is the empathizing recall that is the originary action today.

It is precisely here that Stein sees an analogy to the situation in empathy, where there are similar structures, i.e., two Is, one of which empathizes with the experience of the other — however, with one important difference: In this case there is no "mineness" but an awareness of *alterity*. But when someone empathizes with the joy of another person, this is also "an act which is primordial as present experience though non-primordial in content" (Stein, 1917/1964, p. 10). The activity of empathizing is the current action of one person, and from her perspective the other's joy (which is not originarily given to her) is the "object" of her empathy.[131]

Phases of Empathy

Here we come back to the subject-object relationship that we encountered in connection with the distinction between the two I's of the person who remembers and the person whom she remembers. Now, where there is no sameness, the subject is the one who empathizes (originarily), while the object of her empathy is the experience of the other person (which is not originary for her). Stein sees this as only the first phase, which she calls "the emergence of the experience" (1917/1964, p. 11). If the empathizing person seriously commits herself, it is soon followed by a second phase in which the separation between subject and object tends to dissolve, "the fulfilling explication" (Stein, 1917/1964, p. 11). As Stein describes it, when the other person's experience presents itself, it faces us as an object (for instance, the sadness that we "read in their face"). However, when we delve more deeply into its implications (i.e., try to make the other person's mood clearly given

---

130 In the English translations of Stein's texts the German "Originarität" (originarity) has been translated as "primordiality."
131 The ability of the therapist to distinguish sensations that are primordial from those that are not is an aspect of the sensitivity of bodily self-awareness described above.

to us), it is no longer an object as such, but has drawn us into it. We are now no longer attending to him, but we are in him, attending to his object, that is, we are in the same place as his subject (see Stein, 1917/1964, p. 10).

This being "drawn into" seems to me to be an important point which merits particular attention, since here we are concerned with the process of "confluence" or "identification," which I have mentioned several times and which in the traditional view of empathy is considered to be so problematic that it is almost taboo—with the negative consequences that I have already described. I believe that Edith Stein's insights are illuminating on this point.

If we pay close attention to her words, we first note that what the empathizing person allows herself to be drawn into is not the other person in an abstract or general way, but *his current experience,* i. e. his joy or sadness. Stein also describes a switch in perspective, a change in 'location,' so to speak, in the empathizing person. In the transition from the first phase to the second this constitutes a shift from a first 'location' which, if we take the subject-object constellation metaphorically, is somewhere 'opposite' the other person. From here it moves to a second 'location,' which is situated "in the same place as his subject." From here, seen from the perspective of the other person, it becomes possible for her to be attending to "*his* object," i.e., to what gives *him* cause to feel joyful or sad. "In my non-primordial experience I feel, as it were, led by a primordial one not experienced by me but still there, manifesting itself in my non-primordial experience" (Stein, 1917/1964, p. 11). Now it is no longer (as it was in the first phase) the current experience of the *other person* that is the object of the person empathizing. Rather, the situation, which he first experienced alone, now becomes a *shared* object of experience, because the empathic person is willing to allow herself to be "drawn in" and to be "in the same place as *his* subject" [that of the other], i.e., at the side of the other person.[132]

If we wanted to put that in terms of confluence and identification, we would have to say that the person who empathizes permits herself to become confluent with the perspective of the other person *in respect of the object of his current experience.* This experience that is empathized with is of a non-originary nature since it did not develop primarily and genuinely within the empathizing person. Her empathy, however, is primordial. Thus, for the empathizing person there are two parallel levels of experience, one of which is, as we might say today, in the non-primordial "format" and the other in the primordial "format." Correspondingly, only one of these levels, i.e. that in the non-originary format, is affected by what we refer to as confluence or identification.

---

132 I should add that Stein also speaks of a third phase, which, however, is of no importance for my argument at this point.

At the same time, on the other level the empathizing person's experience of her empathy with the other person is originary. Moreover, her perception of the other person as another living body remains originary—just as irrevocably as she herself remains rooted in the perspective that her own embodiment prescribes.[133] From there she puts herself in his place and identifies with how he experiences the situation he is focusing on, that is, joyfully or sadly.

> For what do we mean by "transposing ourselves"? Certainly not just disregarding ourselves. This is necessary, of course, insofar as we must imagine the other situation. But into this other situation we must bring, precisely, ourselves. Only this is the full meaning of "transposing ourselves." If we put ourselves in someone else's shoes, for example, then we will understand him—i.e., become aware of the otherness, the indissoluble individuality of the other person—by putting *ourselves* in his position (Gadamer, 1989, p. 305—original italics).

The Middle Mode

The verbs "to be drawn in" and "transposing ourselves" have the same point of reference. They do not, of course, relate to a geographic location, but to the above-mentioned "absolute location." Stein and Gadamer use these verbs to describe what the empathizing person does or allows to happen to her. They differ in one interesting aspect. Stein chooses a *passive* construction, Gadamer an *active* one. I see not only a grammatical difference between them, but also a difference concerning the *attitudes* of which each speaks. Stein talks of something *being* done with her, while Gadamer speaks of his *doing* something.[134] These are also psychologically different modes.

However, neither mode adequately describes what is actually at issue. Stein's description suggests that empathy is something that *happens* to her (see Hartmann 1998 for a discussion of the term "*Widerfahrnis*" (roughly: an experience that befalls one) as distinct from "*Handlung*" (action)). To put it pointedly, she is no longer the agent of her empathy, but its victim. Gadamer's choice of words goes to the other extreme. He is the

---

133 Thus, despite the confluence, a difference remains. The joy of the other person is *originary*, while the joy of the empathizing person is *not originary*. It is the same feeling, but in the one case we might say it is indexed "o," and in the other "non-o." What this means in the neuroscientific context we shall see in the following section.
134 That is perhaps no coincidence if we think of the two in terms of gender.

only agent and remains, to overstate it somewhat, untouched, since he only does something *with his own self*. However, I do not believe that these exaggerated interpretations do justice to these two authors, since other source material and the overall tenor of their works indicate differently. Thus, for example, Stein writes that "empathy is a kind of act of perceiving *sui generis*" (1917/1964, p. 11), and the word "act" does, in fact, refer to an *action*. According to Gadamer, a genuine conversation is characterized by the fact

> that in the Other we encounter something that we have not previously encountered in our experience of the world . . . Conversation has the power to transform. Where a conversation has been successful, something remains in us that has changed us (1993, p. 211).

Thus, Gadamer evidently also had the idea that something *befell* him in encounters with others.[135]

Taken together, all this could be seen as indicating that bodily empathy should rather be understood as something that is *both* an action *and* a being befallen by an experience, and something that takes place *not only* actively, *but also* passively, or — to play with grammar — in the *medium*, i.e. in a mode, or mood, that does not exist in the German or English languages. In gestalt therapy we refer to this as the "middle mode." It describes an attitude that is "both willing and done to."

> Just what the middle mode is not is action *on* the self. . . . The middle mode means, rather, that whether the self does or is done to, it refers the process to itself as a totality, it feels it as its own and is engaged in it (Perls et al., 1951, p. 376 — original italics).

If I really want to "put myself in someone else's shoes," I must also be willing to permit myself to be *"drawn"* into what he is experiencing. I *decide* that I allow something to *happen* to me; my primordial activity consists precisely in this "medial" attitude, which means that I deliberately open myself up to the other person's experience. Thus, "the 'I do' is reduced to an *allowing to happen* . . .; I do not actually do, but participate by acceding and consenting to what arises from me without my willing it and happens to me" (Waldenfels, 1971, p. 159 — original italics). Merleau-Ponty uses the example of falling asleep to give a graphic description of

---

135 This will become clearer in Chapter 4.3 in connection with the concept of the "joint situation" and Gadamer's dance metaphor.

this process (which also serves as a description of the general character of all sensory experiences).

BOX 47

EXAMPLE

Sleep comes when a certain voluntary attitude suddenly receives from outside the confirmation for which it was waiting. I am breathing deeply and slowly in order to summon sleep, and suddenly it is as if my mouth were connected to some great lung outside myself which alternately calls forth and forces back my breath. A certain rhythm of respiration, which a moment ago I voluntarily maintained, now becomes my very being, and sleep, until now aimed at as a significance, suddenly becomes a situation. In the same way I give ear, or look, in the expectation of a sensation, and suddenly the sensible takes possession of my ear or my gaze, and I surrender a part of my body, even my whole body, to this particular manner of vibrating. . . . Sensation is literally a form of communion (Merleau-Ponty, 1962, pp. 211f.—original italics).[136]

Viewed in this way, empathizing with the other is also a sort of communion: One must *want* it, while at the same time *surrendering* to it. Just as one must be willing, when falling asleep, to surrender to one's dreams, whose content and course one cannot determine in advance, empathizing requires a willingness to experience something that one "has not previously encountered in quite that way in one's experience of the world" (Gadamer, see above) and which may not always be pleasant. It will certainly leave traces behind. An empathic conversation "has the power to transform. Where a conversation has been successful, something remains in us that has changed us" (Gadamer, 1993, p. 211).

However, the individualists who shy away from words like "communion" and "loss of control" can be reassured. Just as sooner or later one re-emerges spontaneously from being immersed in a dream, the process of putting oneself into another's place (Stein's second phase) is limited in time, at least in its full intensity. It fades out 'naturally' in what Stein describes as the third phase, which she calls "the comprehensive objectification of the explained experience" (1917/1964, p. 11). What it became possible to experience during the process of empathizing can now, for example, be verbalized, reflected upon, interpreted, placed in other contexts or discussed. Only now does the primarily cognitive, explicitly hermeneutic understanding begin, that plays the main role in the traditional concept of empathy.

---

136 "The perception of qualities is not described here as an activity, nor as a purely passive condition or a merely external process: It cannot be forced into this active-passive dichotomy, but constitutes a very specific way of being into which I fall" (Waldenfels, 2000, p. 85).

One could imagine "the fulfilling explication," the second phase of empathizing with the other, as a transient peak of intensity occurring in the course of a continuous empathic process that (repeatedly) runs through all three of Stein's phases as a never-ending succession of cycles. Each cycle would then roughly follow a pattern, similar to what we experience when we go to a concert. We first enter the auditorium, look around and get our bearings, find our seat and watch the orchestra taking their places and starting to play (Phase 1). As time goes on, we allow ourselves to get carried away by the music, become immersed and lose ourselves in it, so that we are moved and pervaded by it. We may even be moved to tears and in extreme cases temporarily 'become' the music, while at the same time retaining a background awareness that we are in a concert hall and could therefore bring the immersion to an end at any time if, for instance, we arbitrarily decided to watch the conductor (Phase 2).[137] Finally, at the end of the performance, we re-emerge from our immersion in the music and reflect on our impressions, either alone or with the people we came with (Phase 3).

Confluence and Difference

Thus, in the very moment when one empathizes (originarily) with the *other person*, i.e., accesses his (originary) *other*ness, the difference between the (originary) self and the (non-originary) other becomes or remains perceptible. To put it slightly differently, if we are completely confluent with the other person we lose our sense of our own originarity, i.e., we feel different from ourselves, alienated from how we are used to feeling, in any case for as long as we retain at least some trace of a memory of our own selves.[138] If even that trace were to disappear because we no longer had any feeling for what is non-primordial in our experience, then what we experienced would no longer be something "other," but simply what we had just happened to become. However, the real other person would also lose his *vis-à-vis* — there would no longer be a discernible other there empathizing with him, since this other person would have allowed her own way of being to become lost, so as to become completely what was initially the other person.

---

137 This description contains references to states of altered consciousness (which could perhaps be called a "trance" when one is listening to a concert). I shall say more about this later.
138 This typically happens when one permits oneself to be pressed into participating in what is known as projective identification (see Staemmler, 1993b). This can be understood as a process of forced empathy through which one partner forces the other to imitate a feeling or a diffuse mood of which she cannot become aware herself (see Eagle & Wolitzky, 1997, p. 232).

What this shows is that what is our own—the self that gets lost and becomes completely the other—no longer has an originary perspective from which it could benefit the other person. In as far as it is possible, subjectively it becomes the other, i.e., it gives up its own subjectivity. Put this way, it becomes clear that the subject, of whom one can say that he has given up his own subjectivity, remains the agent of his actions, even as he gives up his self, and is therefore the originator of these actions even in the most intense confluence. "Man is nothing else but that which he makes of himself" (Sartre, 1948, p. 18). One cannot lose one's self in the other person, one can only have that precise subjective experience if one blots out the fact that one is an embodied being. For this reason, fear of confluence is a fear that thrives on the soil of Cartesian dualism and the mentalistic understanding of empathy that is based on it.

No amount of identification with the other can abrogate one's own embodiment, which endows the self with its own inescapable perspective and experience of "mineness." At the same time, the other, with whom I empathize so intensely that his feelings become my own, always remains another *body* facing me, which no more dissolves through confluence than my own body does. An actor who identifies completely with his role—and in so doing demonstrates his skill—remains irrevocably 'in' *his own* body, even if it is to a great extent this very body that he uses to actualize the gestures, habitus and feelings of the character he is playing (see my digression on *Alba Emoting* in section 4.2.1).

Reciprocal Encorporation

Up to this point I have been writing mainly about what Schmitz terms "one-sided encorporation." I have accorded it a relatively large amount of space because one might say that it is simpler than encorporation involving more than one person and can therefore be used to illustrate many things more easily. However, at the same time this simplification leads us away from the *mutuality* of empathic processes that I mentioned above. Husserl already drew attention to this:

> If, with my understanding of someone else, I penetrate more deeply into him, into his horizon of ownness, I shall soon run into the fact that, just as his animate bodily organism lies in my field of perception, so my animate organism lies in his field of perception and that, in general, he experiences me forthwith as an Other for him, just as I experience him as *my* Other. Likewise I shall find that, in the case of a plurality

of Others, they are experienced also by one another as Others, and consequently that I can experience any given Other not only as himself an Other but also as related in turn to *his* Others and perhaps—with a mediatedness that may be conceived as reiterable—related at the same time to me (1960, pp. 129f.—original italics).

In psychotherapy, in particular, one must see *encorporation* as something that is initiated by *both* participants together and that affects *both* of them. However, because in this case, too, the whole is more than and different from the sum of its parts, *reciprocal encorporation* is not simply the sum of two one-sided processes of encorporation. Thus, it is no longer as easy to differentiate between the experience of the one participant and the other as it is with one-sided encorporation since now something new is created: We can speak "of a living body, transcending individuals, that comes into being *ad hoc* through encorporation" (Schmitz, 1993, p. 131).

BOX 48

EXAMPLE

In the rush hour on the busy sidewalks of large cities, crowds of people walk past each other in close proximity and in all directions without there being any fixed 'highway' code and yet there are very few collisions to speak of. And that is despite the fact that almost everyone there is pursuing their own personal goal, e.g. something they want to buy, and takes little notice of the others. In order to steer his course, each individual pedestrian must take into account not only where the person coming toward him is likely to go next, but also be aware of the probable next steps of the person behind that person and anyone else who may appear beside him, so that he does not run into one person while trying to avoid another. To accomplish this feat what we need is not to plan in a calculated way, but to build up a vast network of constantly changing encorporations by means of unthinking, fleeting glances that appraise what is suggested by other people's intimated approaching movements and transform them by means of the body schema into movements of the self in the opposite direction (Schmitz, 2005, p. 147).[139]

Schmitz describes reciprocal encorporation as a "merging into each other of attuned or attuning living bodies,[140] e.g., when we look at

---

139 Schmitz' example can also be understood as an illustration of the efficacy of adaptive oscillators (see section 4.2.1) and mirror neurons (see section 4.2.3 and Box 53).
140 Here the word "merging" is associated with "*lived* bodies" and not with "bodies," since merging would be fatal for a body, but not for the lived body. According to Schmitz, this is, "in quite naive and preconceptual terms, to begin with, what a human being *feels* about himself in the region of his body without relying on evidence from the five senses (vision, hearing, touch, smell and taste)" (1993, p. 36—italics added).

each other or shake hands, converse with or make love to each other" (1989, p. 55), and stresses that there can be "no dialogue without encorporation" (1993, p. 131). Psychotherapeutic dialogs are doubtless no exception to this rule. If, as I have justified in detail in Chapter 4.1, empathy in psychotherapy is to be seen as a *mutual* process and if this process is not only a mental, but also a *bodily* one, then we must assume that psychotherapy includes far-reaching processes of *reciprocal* encorporation.

In this context the client and therapist are, of course, much more strongly oriented toward each other and the intensity of the situation, which arises from the importance of the subjects they talk about, and the resulting emotional intensity, is also much greater than on "busy sidewalks."

"The emotional resonance inside the lived body becomes a resonating of expressions and impressions between lived bodies . . . If we keep this double resonance in mind we can better understand how we are able to capture the seemingly completely hidden mental life of the other" (Fuchs, 2000, p. 248). Schmitz refers to this phenomenon as "embodied communication" and even *"participation mystique."*[141] "Human beings lose their personal self-control as a result of encorporation" (1965, p. 343), and hence "their own lived bodies . . . merge into a larger whole that spontaneously forms anew as a larger lived body and encompasses it" (Schmitz, 1989, p. 209). It thereby becomes part of the larger whole, together with the other, who also becomes part of this whole.[142]

"Merging," "bodily communication," *"participation mystique"* and "larger, all-encompassing felt body" are all concepts that go beyond the limitations of individualistic thinking and, for people who are used to thinking in individualistic terms, may even be seen as bordering on the fanciful. Below is an example that shows that we are still within the range of normal interpersonal experience. However, first I want expressly to emphasize what I have already intimated, namely that if we use the concept of the lived body and thus leave body-mind dualism behind us, we also soon find that we have gone beyond the bounds of individualistic thinking.

I would like to conclude this section with a particularly apt phenomenological description of reciprocal encorporation given by Daniel Stern.

---

141 C. G. Jung frequently employed this term. I do not know whether Schmitz is consciously making reference to Jung or not.
142 Schmitz' concept of reciprocal encorporation thus already contains a reference to his concept of the "joint situation" that we shall be looking at more closely in Chapter 4.3.

BOX 49

EXAMPLE

A young man and woman go out together for the first time one winter evening. They barely know each other. They happen to pass a lighted ice-skating rink. On the spur of the moment they decide to go ice-skating. Neither of them is very good at it. They rent skates and stumble onto the ice. They trace a clumsy dance. She almost falls backwards. He reaches out and steadies her. He loses his balance and tilts to the right. She throws out a hand and he grabs it. (Note that each is also participating neurologically and experientially in the bodily feeling centered in the other. And each of them knows, at moments, that the other knows what it feels like to be him or her.) For stretches they manage to move forward together, holding hands with a variety of sudden muscular contractions sent from one hand and arm to the other's to keep them together, steady, and moving. There is much laughing and gasping and falling. There is no space in which to really talk.

At the end of a half hour, tired, they stop and have a hot drink at the side of the rink. But now their relationship is in a different place. They have each directly experienced something of the other's experience. They have vicariously been inside the other's body and mind, through a series of shared feeling voyages. They have created an implicit intersubjective field that endures as part of their short history together. When they now have the physical ease and freedom to look at each other across the table, what will happen (Stern, 2004, pp. 173f.)?

This example shows how "the 'real,' the mundane separation of my psychophysical existence from someone else's," is overcome by *"original communion,"* as Husserl (1960, p. 129—original italics) also concedes. The

> intentional reaching of the other into my primordiality is not irreal in the sense of being dreamed into it or being present to consciousness after the fashion of a mere phantasy. *Something that exists is in intentional communion with something else that exists* (Husserl, 1960—original italics).

4.2.3   The Neuroscientific Viewpoint

The development of imaging techniques and other methods of investigation has led to an enormous number of discoveries in modern neuroscience over the last two decades, greatly increasing its popularity. This has, in fact, opened up new possibilities. On the one hand these have called into question knowledge previously held to be valid, while on the other hand they have led to new insights, one of which is the concept of neuroplasticity.

> ### *BOX 50*
>
> **NEUROPLASTICITY**
>
> is the brain's remarkable capacity constantly to adjust to the exigencies of its use. This process is not limited to a certain phase of life, but continues throughout the entire life of an organism, initially very rapidly and later more slowly . . . The cortex has proven to be a structure with a unique capacity to adjust while at the same time constantly optimizing itself (Spitzer, 1996, p. 148).

Although William James noted in his groundbreaking work *Principles of Psychology* that "organic matter, especially nervous tissue, seems endowed with a very extraordinary degree of plasticity" (1890/1950, p. 105[143]), until only a short time ago the brain was considered to be unmodifiable once it had matured. Today, however, it seems clear that our brains retain "the plasticity of a wax tablet as long as we live" (Spitzer, 1996, p. 335). This applies to all parts of the brain, and especially to those that are younger in evolutionary terms (see Panksepp, in Gallagher, 2008, p. 92).

> Molecular biologists have now collected considerable evidence which shows that the new experiences a person has in the course of her life have an impact right down to the level of the genes. They result, for example, in nerve cells beginning to copy new genetic sequences and to deactivate others. Thus, new experiences alter gene expression. In the brain, this continues to take place up to an advanced age and creates the basis for this organ's lifelong plasticity and capacity to learn (Hüther, 2004, p. 59).

Depending on how a person lives — what he does and what he does not do, what he occupies himself with, etc. — his neuronal structures change: "Thus, experience, a psychological phenomenon, leads to neuronal changes — a material phenomenon — [and] as a result also to changes in information processing" (Gehde & Emrich, 1998, p. 984). Completely new

---

143 James wrote this in connection with the formation of habits, which he attributed to the "plasticity of neural matter" (James, 1890/1950, p. ix) and *repetition*. Here again he anticipated recent insights into neuroplasticity by approximately one hundred years. The fact that changes in neuronal structures require the frequent *repetition* of a certain activity is now beyond doubt. In this connection, James' definition of plasticity is interesting: "Plasticity, then, in the wide sense of the word, means the possession of a structure weak enough to yield to an influence, but strong enough not to yield all at once" (James, 1890/1950, p. 105). This also has *political* consequences: "While the claim that an 'effective psychotherapy' requires only a few hours to modify even those processing mechanisms that have become deeply entrenched over many years . . . is in line with the hopes of some interest groups and health policies, it is not supported by neurobiology or the theory of neuronal networks" (Gehde & Emrich, 1998, p. 999).

nerve cells (see Eriksson et al., 1998), new types of neurons (see Miller, 2006, p. 940) and new connecting pathways between nerves are formed and the strength or the "weight" of these connections changes in accordance with the way in which they are used. This is termed "use-dependent stabilization of synaptic networks."

> Like sand on a beach, the brain bears the footprints of the decisions we have made, the skills we have learned, the actions we have taken. But there are also hints that mind-sculpting can occur with no input from the outside world. That is, the brain can change as a result of the thoughts we have thought (Begley, 2007, p. 9).

Meditative practices which can lead to changes at the neuronal level, even at an advanced age, can be cited as an example of this (see Lazar et al., 2005). However, strictly speaking, in view of their long cultural tradition, meditative practices are just as inconceivable "with no input from the outside world" as "the thoughts that we have thought." We should therefore add that if they are, in fact, sometimes conceivable without this input, it can only be "without *direct* input from the outside world." However, all mental phenomena are primarily social, including those that leave "footprints" in the brain.

> We must regard mind, then, as arising and developing within the social process, within the empirical matrix of social interactions. . . . The processes of experience which the human brain makes possible are made possible only for a group of interacting individuals: only for individual organisms which are members of a society (Mead, 1934/1963, p. 174).

Emergence and Reductionism: The Mind-Body Problem

Thus, the discovery of neuroplasticity is not only important for neurology, but also contains implications that go far beyond the limits of this discipline. Whereas it was previously thought that once it had matured and was no longer modifiable, the brain basically determined the potential of a human being, we must now assume that it is not fixed in such an absolute way. These are insights that affect how we view the nature of the human being. "Perhaps one of the most provocative implications of neuroplasticity and the power of mental training to alter the circuits of the brain is that it undermines neurogenetic determinism" (Begley, 2007, p. 316). Today it is no longer believed that the potential of a human being is determined by the structures of the brain alone. Neurology can no longer claim to have sole hegemony over the psyche—if it ever could—since evidently quite the reverse is the case. Paquette et al. (2003) put it in a nutshell: "Change the mind and you change the brain."

This insight can also be applied to the body—which is, of course, hardly surprising, if body and mind are not isolated from each other. Gerald Hüther writes, "everything that happens in the body leads, if it is sustained over an extended period, to corresponding adjustments in the neuronal feedback systems and synaptic connections" (2006, p. 93). To give a trivial example, anyone who regularly attends a fitness center trains not only his muscles, but also the areas of his brain with which they are connected. Moreover—and this is where the mind comes into play again—it was his mental decision to do fitness training which then led to the muscular and neurological changes.

Thus, the mind and the body (including its neuronal structures) are connected to each other in a complex reciprocal relationship. Because they are intertwined, changes that begin at a certain point also have effects on other areas. This is also reflected in research results associated with the human ability to empathize, to which I would now like to turn. However, before I do so, I think it is necessary to explain the term "mind-body problem."

BOX 51

THE MIND-BODY PROBLEM results from the obvious materiality of the body and the non-material nature of the soul and mind, as described by Descartes and others. What is problematic is not only the dualistic separation of the one sphere from the other, but also the question of how it is conceivable that something material can influence something non-material—and vice versa. Numerous suggestions have been made in the course of the history of philosophy as to how these problems could be solved, which we find under headings such as "dualism," "epiphenomenalism," "materialism," "functionalism," "emergence theories," etc. See Hastedt (1988) for a detailed overview of this debate.

When I write that the mind, body and neuronal structures are connected to each other in a *complex* reciprocal relationship, my intention is to draw attention to the fact that this relationship is not simply linear, since the concepts "mind," "body" and "neuronal structures" (or what they refer to) are not on the same level. One might say, to use Ryle's terminology (1949/2002), that they belong to different "categories." These levels are related to each other in much the same way as H_2O is to water or, to introduce a third level into this comparison, as water is to the sea. While on the molecular level water can be defined as H_2O, when it is filled into a bottle it is more than and something different from simply H_2O. It has properties (for example, it is liquid, wet and has a certain temperature) that one cannot meaningfully ascribe to an H_2O molecule. Similarly, the sea consists of water, but it has properties that go beyond that and which cannot (and this is important!) be derived from the properties of water or H_2O molecules alone. Such properties that presuppose a subordinate subsystem, but cannot be explained on the basis of this level alone, are termed "emergent" (see Bunge, 1977). Thus, it is possible to say (depending on which term one prefers) that consciousness (or mind or the psyche) is an emergent property of a body with complex neuronal structures.[144]

BOX 52

EMERGENCE Properties of a complex whole that are not present in its individual subsystems and cannot be derived from their properties, but only "emerge" with their respective complexities, are termed "emergent." The Encyclopedia Britannica defines emergence as a "surprise-generating mechanism" through which the global properties of the system arise as a result of the interactions between components of subsystems.

Emergence refers to unexpected global system properties, not present in any of the individual subsystems that emerge from component interactions. A good example is water, whose distinguishing characteristics are its natural form as a liquid and its nonflammability—both of which are totally different than the properties of its component gases, hydrogen and oxygen (http://www.britannica.com/bps/search?query=emergence&blacklist=185731—retrieved October 21, 2010).

In Box 7 on Gestalt psychology, I mentioned the example of a melody that is more than and different from the sum of the individual notes of which it is composed. H_2O and water, notes and a melody, brain and consciousness—in each of these cases there are different levels of complexity, each higher level producing new characteristics which were not present in the lower levels. In this sense,

the relationship between the impulses of the brain's physiology and the phenomena of consciousness could be seen in analogy to the relationship between the notes or sounds of a melody as a whole. What a

---

144 For the sake of clarity, I am leaving the natural and social environment aside here, which of course leaves the picture incomplete. "Getting from a physical sequence of causes, to my raising my arm to signal that I want to speak, to wave goodbye, or to command the attention of an orchestra—all these require a larger context *external* to my movement" (Brothers, 2001, p. 88—original italics).

melody is to the notes, the physiological processes of the brain are for consciousness (Müller, 1988, p. 50).

It is clear that the melody (consciousness) cannot exist without the notes (the neurophysiological processes), even if the notes cannot explain the melody completely. The melody contains the notes and goes beyond them. It has different, new, "emergent" properties which cannot be attributed to the notes alone. Thus, likewise,

> the conscious properties of brain excitation are conceived to be something distinct and special in their own right. They are "different from and more than" the collected sum of the neuro-physico-chemical events out of which they are built. . . . The conscious properties of the brain process are more . . . holistic in nature. They encompass and transcend the details of nerve impulse traffic in the cerebral networks in the same way that the properties of the organism transcend the properties of its cells (Sperry, 1969, p. 533).

This is a brief and simple description of how the material level (the processes that can be described in neuroscientific terms) affects the non-material level (consciousness, the processes that can be described in psychological terms). The influence in the opposite direction, from the non-material to the material level, must therefore arise from the emergent, more holistic properties of consciousness.[145] I can *decide* what I am going to do with my time, and my capacity to decide is one of the emergent properties of my consciousness. If I were to decide to stop working on this text for the moment and to go for a jog, that would lead to physical and neurophysiological processes that would be considerably different than if I were to stay sitting in front of my PC. "The subjective mental phenomena are conceived to influence and to govern the flow of nerve impulse traffic by virtue of their encompassing emergent properties" (Sperry, 1969, p. 534).

There is another important aspect that should not be forgotten. With my references to Vygotsky (see Box 8) and Mead (see Box 23) and also to concepts such as "intersubjectivity" (see Box 15) and "altero-centered participation" (see Box 38) I have already drawn attention, from various viewpoints, to the fact that each individual human consciousness always comes into being within a culture and a society and thus in close encounters with other human beings. If we link this fact to the observation made in the paragraph above that mental phenomena influence the structures

---

145 By "consciousness" here I mean the mental or psychological level, not the opposite of "unconscious"; non-conscious processes can, of course, also have physical effects.

of the brain, it seems natural to put two and two together. If the origin and nature of mental processes are to a great extent *social*, this means that "the human brain is inherently dyadic and is created through interactive interchanges" (Tronick, 2007, p. 289). This is why Fuchs (2008) called one of his very readable books *The Brain: A Relational Organ* (original: *Das Gehirn—ein Beziehungsorgan*).

Thus, to sum up, the "level of description of mind and the level of description of brain are very different, but . . . mind depends on brain and without brain there is no mind" (Davidson in Boyce, 2005, p. 41). These are two levels that differ in complexity. Between these levels there are reciprocal effects, but there are also clear differences between the individual mechanisms of action. With the concept of emergence it is possible to differentiate clearly between the body and the psyche. This is important because "the languages of natural science—including neuroscience—and of the mind are fundamentally separate" (Brothers, 2001, p. 11). At the same time, this concept makes it possible to take into account the intertwining of the two levels without splitting the holism of the human being in a dualistic fashion or, conversely, falsely equating the two levels, thus propagating an undifferentiated uniformity in the interests of holism.[146]

I would not have included these remarks on the "mind-body problem" were it not for the fact that the understandable excitement about the neuroscientific innovations has repeatedly been combined with a new faith in the insights of the *natural* sciences. Surely this is a faith that now, in light of Kuhn's (1970) studies on the history of science, can only be considered naïve. Insights do not become truer or more valid *per se* because they have been arrived at by scientific methods. The list of errors made in the natural sciences is long. The value of the insights lies rather in their significance within scientific and philosophical knowledge as a whole, e.g., if they confirm research results obtained through other means by contributing to converging evidence with their special methodology. "We must remember that science only clarifies functional *parts* of a complex phenomenon. Other disciplines, from art to philosophy, are needed to reconstruct an image of the whole" (Panksepp in Gallagher, 2008,

---

146 If we wanted to put a label on this viewpoint on the mind-body problem we could, like Sperry, speak of "emergent interactionism" (1969, p. 534) or use Petzold's (1995, p. 553) term "emergent, differential, interactional monism." In view of the advances in neuroscientific research over the last few years it has become plausible to assume that the relationship between *specific* neuronal activation patterns and *specific* mental states is closer than previously thought. This has led to a continuation in the development of the emergence theory under the heading of "supervenience" (Kim, 2002). I believe that this is not in principle anything new, but only a specification (albeit an interesting one) that I do not wish to go into in any detail.

Me too!

p. 99—original italics). I therefore welcome the fact that much of what developmental and social psychologists, psychotherapists and philosophers have written about embodiment and intersubjectivity, for example, is now also gaining neuroscientific recognition.[147] And the new insights obtained by the neurosciences must, of course, also prove their validity in future interdisciplinary discourse.

Faith in the natural sciences is also often associated with a reductionism which is of questionable epistemological legitimacy (Reichertz & Zaboura, 2006). "To adopt a reductionist strategy is to try to explain the phenomena of the macro-level (psychological characteristics) by those of the micro-level (properties of neuronal networks)" (Churchland, 1996, p. 464). However, this very reductionism has frequently been revealed in headings such as "Empathizing nerve cells discovered—Mirror neurons read other people's thoughts" (Krech, 2001) or "Cells that read minds" (Blakeslee, 2006). In this last article we also read that humans, "it turns out, have mirror neurons that are far *smarter*, more flexible and more highly evolved than any of those found in monkeys" (Blakeslee, 2006—italics added).[148] But that is simply nonsense, since nerve cells cannot, of course, "read," and even less can they read thoughts. They are not "smart," either. "Mirror neurons alone cannot produce empathy at any level" (Preston & de Waal, 2002, p. 10). They simply emit electrical impulses which are no different from those of other nerve cells, due to the "neutrality of the neuronal code."[149] The ability to read, smartness and other mental skills and states are capacities of *whole human beings in social contexts*, not of cells. Neither can empathy simply be equated with a certain pattern of neuronal

---

147 Some of this is, in fact, not new at all. Comparing two books by Grawe that were published a few years apart (*Psychological Therapy* (2002; German original: 1998) and *Neuropsychotherapy* (2007; German original: 2004), except for a revamping of the vocabulary in line with neuroscientific terminology I did not find that much new material relevant to important therapeutic issues had accumulated during this period. At the same time, for some reason unknown to me, Grawe failed to make any reference to mirror neurons and their relevance for therapeutic interactions, although the important discoveries in this area were made between 1998 and 2004.

148 These descriptions are prime examples of the above-mentioned "category mistake" (Ryle). They make about as much sense as the statement that a car engine has exceeded the speed limit and caused an accident. They may be excusable in popular scientific literature, but they frequently also find their way into the discourse between psychotherapists and can even be found in publications by neuroscientists, whose thinking can otherwise be considered to be highly differentiated; see the critical analyses by Brothers (2001) and Gallagher (2006).

149 "The 'language of the brain' . . . [is] the language of the membrane and action potentials, of the neurotransmitters and neuropeptides. This language consists of chemical and electrical signals, which do not as such have any specificity—i.e. they are *neutral* . . . This is the principle of the *neutrality of the neuronal code* and this principle is of the utmost importance for our understanding of how the brain works" (Roth, 1995, p. 80—original italics).

spikes. "The most that can be deduced from observations of the firing of neurons or metabolic or electrical brain activity are the *bases* of psychological processes. These bases are not identical with the psychological phenomena in whose development they are involved" (Klöckner, 2007, p. 18—italics added).[150] Productive and fascinating as the modern neurosciences are, human experiencing, e.g., empathy, cannot be explained by neurological structures and processes alone, since "experiencing" is indicative of a different systematic level from "neurological structures and processes." Experience *emerges* from neurological structures and processes and cannot therefore be reduced to them.

Unfortunately, this is precisely what is often happening in the current discussions. However, "neurons are firing at a *sub*personal level" (Gallagher, 2005, p. 215—italics added); their activity is not the only cause of personal experiencing. Reputable neuroscientists are aware of this: "We should keep different levels of description distinct. We shouldn't imbue neurons with intentional properties. They are just fatty bags letting ions come and go. There is no intentional behavior in a neuron—even a mirror neuron!" (Gallese in de Vignemont, 2006, p. 193). To say, like Ax, for example, that empathy should be understood as "an autonomic nervous system state which tends to simulate that of another person" (1964, p. 11), is wrong, for one thing because this statement makes the category mistake of reducing empathy, i.e., a mental process, to a state of the autonomic nervous system.[151] This also applies to all other mental processes. Siegel uses the example of perception.

> Why not say the neural activity created the visual perception? If we make causal phrases like this, the erroneous idea is reinforced that the mind is only created by the brain. If we are cognitively mindful here, we need to be open to the truth that seeing the picture actually created the neural firing. The directional arrow goes *both* ways: The mind can actually use the brain to create itself (Siegel, 2007, p. 48—italics added).

To explain the mind on the basis of the neuronal level alone would therefore be an inaccurate simplification—a reduction. This does not do justice to the actual facts, even if we are talking about the sensational discovery of the "mirror neurons" and other empathy-related concepts

---

150 Even the word "bases" can easily be misunderstood: "Ontologically, the neural aspect may have some kind of priority, but not of the kind that has the 'right' to marginalize one of its greatest natural products—experience" (Panksepp in Gallagher, 2008, p. 106).
151 It is, of course, also wrong for another reason (which is not, however, what I am referring to here) and that is that empathy is most certainly associated with the activation of other parts of the nervous system, not only the autonomic component.

and neuroscientific findings (see Geuter, 2006, p. 264), which I shall discuss below.

Mirror Neurons

Sometimes researchers are unexpectedly lucky and their hard work is rewarded with a discovery which was not in fact their goal. This happened to a group of Italian neurophysiologists at the University of Parma at the beginning of the 1990s (see di Pellegrino, Fadiga, Fogassi, Gallese, & Rizzolatti, 1992; Gallese, Fadiga, Fogassi, & Rizzolatti, 1996; Rizzolatti, Fadiga, Fogassi, & Gallese, 1996). In the years that followed, their discovery was to cause a furor and trigger a flood of new research studies. Ramachandran even considered them to have the significance of a "second Big Bang" and predicted

> that mirror neurons will do for psychology what DNA did for biology: they will provide a unifying framework and help explain a host of mental abilities that have hitherto remained mysterious and inaccessible to experiments (2001).

Their discovery was said to be more or less a coincidence.

BOX 53

THE DISCOVERY OF THE MIRROR NEURONS

Giacomo Rizzolatti, Vittorio Gallese and Leonardo Fogassi were actually interested in the planning of movement in the brains of mammals. They were investigating the activities of individual nerve cells in the brain of a macaque monkey while it was reaching for various objects such as pieces of fruit, nuts and toys. To do this they had placed a few electrodes in a brain area in the lower portion of the premotor cortex that is referred to as "F5." It is in this region of the cerebral cortex that actions are planned and initiated. Just before beginning with the next measurement, Fogassi reached for a raisin himself. The monkey did not move, but was watching the experimenter. And then there was a small commotion—the measuring device was responding. One of the premotor neurons was firing, exactly as in the previous experiments, when the macaque itself had been reaching for food!

The researchers could not believe their eyes—was this an error, a problem with the apparatus? No, everything was working fine. After they had managed to replicate this result several times they realized that they had discovered something completely new: a premotor neuron that was not only active when the monkey itself reached for the object of its desire, but also when somebody else did . . . ! The Italians were amazed. Finally they had found the long-suspected link between perception and movement. Evidently the monkey's own neuronal circuits that are involved in action—or at least this one cell—were activated by mere observation—and there were likely to be others! The neuron with the dual function seemed to "mirror" what was observed. The researchers therefore called the cells they had discovered "mirror neurons" (Gaschler, 2006, p. 28).

I am not in a position to judge whether the story actually happened exactly as it is described in this popular science magazine.[152] However, the "connection between perception and movement" described in this report is accurate and important.[153] I have already mentioned it—in different forms—in my discussion of spontaneous imitation (see section 4.2.1), as a "link between perception and behavior," and in connection with the phenomenological concept of embodiment (in section 4.2.2). In this context, the mirror neurons evidently fulfill an important function[154] in that their activity links the brain regions responsible for perception with those responsible for the motor functions in a way that can be described in a simplified fashion as follows:

The monkey observes the movement of another monkey (or, coincidentally, that of a researcher[155]) that is reaching for a raisin (or an ice-cream cone). As it does so, the part of its brain that is responsible for processing optical impressions passes on certain information to the mirror neurons. These then re-process the information and send it on to the motor regions of the brain, which then finally transmit motor impulses to the muscles

---

152 There are other versions, e.g., one in which Fogassi did not reach for a raisin, but a student raised an ice-cream cone to his mouth (Blakeslee, 2006). Gallese, who should really know the truth of what happened writes, "one of us brought his hand toward a food-tray to grasp a raisin" (1999, p. 168). However, these differences are not central, merely being an illustration of how scientific myths are created.

153 "Evidence for this perception/action coupling ranges from electrophysiological recordings in monkeys . . . to functional neuroimaging experiments in humans" (Decety & Jackson, 2004, p. 76).

154 In order to avoid misunderstandings, I would point out that there are several differences between macaques and humans, one of which being that, unlike humans, macaques do *not* show imitative behavior—apart from in the first few months of life (see Ferrari & Gallese, 2007). Their mirror neurons therefore have some different functions from those of human beings (see Lyons, Santos, & Keil, 2006).

155 In the excitement over the discovery of the mirror neurons a further sensational aspect of this discovery, i.e., the fact that the gap between two species has evidently been bridged, has frequently been overlooked.

via the efferent neural pathways. The intensity of the motor impulses is simultaneously inhibited[156] and they therefore remain, on balance, relatively weak, so that from the outside no movement or only a weak one is discernible. The *pattern* of these impulses is, however, more or less identical to the pattern that the brain would produce (with far more energy) if it were to cause the muscles to imitate the observed movement and actually to carry it out.[157]

There is now convincing evidence that not only in macaques, but also

> in humans, several brain regions, including the premotor cortex, the posterior parietal cortex and the cerebellum, are activated during action generation and while observing and simulating others' actions.[158] Particularly interesting is the demonstration that action observation activates the premotor cortex in a somatotopic[159] manner—simply watching mouth, hand and foot movements activates the same functionally specific regions of premotor cortex as performing those movements (Blakemore & Decety, 2001, p. 566).

The link between perception and motor functions thus created is the central element in Preston and de Waal's (2002) "perception-action model (PAM)" into which they integrate various results of psychological research (see section 4.2.1) and the neurosciences.[160]

> A Perception-Action Model of empathy specifically states that attended perception of the object's state automatically activates the subject's representations of the state, situation, and object, and that activation of these representations automatically primes or generates the associated autonomic and somatic responses, unless inhibited (Preston & de Waal, 2002, p. 4).

---

156 It is not yet clear by what exact route this inhibition takes place; however, this is of no importance for my reasoning.

157 Recent studies have also shown that there is not only a mirror system oriented towards optical impressions, but also an "echo system" oriented towards auditory impressions. When, for example, human beings hear a noise made by a certain action of another person, their own corresponding neuronal action patterns are also activated (see Keysers et al., 2003; Kohler et al., 2002). When we hear other people speaking, an activation of the motor areas responsible for speech can also be observed (see Buccino et al., 2005; Watkins et al., 2003).

158 "Functional neuroimaging studies in humans have shown that areas of the human brain that are relevant to imitation seem to be the homolog of the mirror neuron areas in macaques" (Iacoboni, 2005, p. 633).

159 Somatotopic = oriented toward the body.

160 This is also a detailed review article which gives a thorough overview of the state of the art of empirical research on empathy and is to be recommended.

Thus, the following two aspects are characteristic of the link described in the PAM: First, an activity is simultaneously elicited in the motor system of the observer by his perception of the other person's action, the main characteristics of which are *qualitatively exactly* the same as if the observer was carrying out exactly the same action. Second, the observed action is not *completely* reproduced *in a quantitative sense*, and because of this the actual *execution* is inhibited to a greater or lesser extent.

The effect of the first aspect is evident in a psychiatric syndrome, echopraxia, in which the second aspect, the process of inhibition, is deficient.

BOX 54

ECHOPRAXIA The neurophysiological linking of perception and action is particularly evident in a syndrome that is described in the psychiatric literature and known as "echopraxia" (and also as "echokinesia"). In this disorder the inhibition of the imitation activated by the mirror neurons is rendered inoperative. People with echopraxia compulsively imitate the movements and actions that they see others making and doing.

Thus, observing other people's actions elicits a (relatively subtle) neurophysiological replication—one could also say a *simulation*—of the corresponding action impulses that goes right down to the level of the observer's musculature. There is a direct inwired link between her perception and her motor system and action tendencies. "By means of such a neural matching system, the observer during action observation is placed in the same 'internal' situation as when actively executing the same action" (Umiltà et al., 2001, p. 155). In short: "Action observation implies *action simulation*" (Gallese, 2001, p. 37—original italics).[161]

The way in which "simulation" is understood in this context indicates that it is "not necessarily the result of a willed and conscious cognitive effort, aimed at interpreting the intentions hidden in the overt behavior of others, but rather a basic functional mechanism of our brain" (Ferrari & Gallese, 2007, p. 74). The observer may also have, through her perception of her own body, a certain awareness of the muscle activity that has been triggered within her in this way (i.e., not originarily). Only if this is so can she experience encorporation, a phenomenon that goes beyond implicit imitation.

---

161 The Gestalt psychologist Arnheim already suspected the existence of such a mechanism. He wrote: "The Gestalt-theoretical thesis would imply that an observer will adequately gauge another person's state of mind by inspection of that person's bodily appearance if the psychical situation of the observed person and the perceptual experience of the observer are structurally similar by means of a number of intermediate isomorphic levels" (1949, p. 163).

The process of mirroring takes place simultaneously, involuntarily and without thinking. An internal neuronal copy of the perceived action is made as if the observer were executing the action himself. Whether he actually executes it or not is up to him. He cannot, however, do anything to prevent the fact that his mirror neurons, which are now resonating, raise the action program stored in them into an internal image. What he observes is re-played on his own neurobiological keyboard in real time. Thus, observing something triggers a kind of internal simulation in a person. It is similar to using a flight simulator. Everything is as if we were flying—we even have a feeling of vertigo during a nosedive, but we are not really flying (Bauer, 2005, p. 26).

In this context, the verb "resonate" that Bauer employs here, and which I myself have also often used, should (like the word "mirroring") not be misunderstood to refer to a completely passive process. That would hardly be plausible from the standpoint of evolutionary psychology and in many situations this would overload the capacities of both animals and humans. Primates, and human beings in particular, are not sounding boards in the sense that they simply resonate with everything they encounter. They choose between the wealth of possibilities open to them. However, there are differences in the criteria upon which human beings and macaques base their choices.

In macaques, mirror neurons do not, for example, react when they observe the movement of someone else's hand (e.g., a grasping movement) without being able to perceive the goal of this movement (e.g., a raisin or an ice-cream cone).[162] Likewise, the mirror neurons remain passive if only a potential goal (the raisin or ice-cream cone) is visible, but no movement toward it (the grasping) (see Rizzolatti, Fogassi, & Gallese, 2001, p. 662).[163] In contrast, in human beings (whose mirror neuron systems are in some respects more advanced), merely observing "intransitive meaningless movements [can] produce mirror-neuron system activation in humans" (Rizzolatti & Craighero, 2004, p. 176). Humans use different

---

162 There is an interesting exception to this rule (see below).
163 It also appears to be important that the action exhibits certain biomechanical characteristics. Mirror neurons do not fire at all, or only weakly, if the action is carried out with the aid of a tool, rather than with the hands (see Gallese et al., 1996, p. 595). However, some become active when the monkey observes biologically plausible movement patterns represented by moving light points, for example (see Oram & Perrett, 1994). In connection with the latter study it is interesting to note that human beings were able to correctly identify basic emotions even when they were expressed in a darkened room by dancers whose body movements could only be discerned with the aid of thirteen light points (see Dittrich, Troscianko, Lea, & Morgan, 1996).

criteria to make their choices. I shall say more about this later on under the heading "Selective Empathy."

Regardless of such differences, mirror neurons seem to play a particularly important role in both macaques and humans when what the individual attention is focused on is not simply a movement, but an *action*.

> What makes a movement into a motor act is the presence of a goal. This distinction is very important since it allows one to interpret the role of the motor system not just in terms of the control of the dynamic variables of movement (like joint torques, etc.), but rather as a possible candidate for the instantiation of mental states such as purpose or intention (Gallese & Goldman, 1998, p. 493; see also Fogassi et al., 2005).

What these authors are alluding to is important in connection with the question of the mystery of the other. In many situations in which we attempt to understand another person, we are trying to establish the intentions that lie behind his actions. With the knowledge we now have of mirror neurons it has become possible to get a more exact picture of this process of understanding. However, to begin with this only applies to actions of another person that are *directly observable*, since it is only in response to such actions that the connection between perception and motor functions via mirror neurons can be activated in the observer.[164]

If, for example, she sees the other person making a grasping movement as described above, the neuronal activity pattern in which the mirror neurons are involved starts when this movement begins. Thus, the observer's own motor programs that she has developed to execute similar grasping movements are simultaneously activated. Since this all occurs synchronously, i.e. she simulates in real time what she sees the other person doing, she implicitly "knows"[165] how the grasping movement she is observing and which is just being initiated, will continue. Iacoboni described this process in an interview with Blakeslee which was published in a popular science magazine:

> When you see me pull my arm back, as if to throw the ball, you also have in your brain a copy of what I am doing and it helps you understand my

---

164 "Deferred imitation necessitates temporary stored action planning, whereas immediate imitation engages on-line control. These two processes are known to rely on different neural networks" (Grèzes, Costes, & Decety, 1998, p. 578).
165 It is important to point out here that the verb "to know" is often associated with knowledge that can be verbalized, whereas here we are concerned with *implicit* knowledge.

goal. Because of mirror neurons, you can read my intentions. You know what I am going to do next (Blakeslee, 2006).

The immediacy with which we are thus able to understand the ongoing actions of other people makes our everyday social interactions considerably easier.

If each time we saw someone perform an activity or express an emotion we would need to mentally imagine their situation and objectives so as to grasp the meaning of their behavior, we would be far too slow to respond . . . Luckily, we grasp the meaning of the behavior of others based on bodily representations that come to us without any conscious effort. We are hard-wired to connect to those around us (de Waal, 2007, p. 64).

BOX 55

EXAMPLE My wife Barbara and I are sitting at the breakfast table. We have already finished our breakfast and are still talking to each other while we drink our tea. My teacup is empty and I reach for the teapot to pour myself some more. There is not much left in it and I am about to put the pot (which is now empty) back onto the tea warmer when I see that the tealight is still burning. I spontaneously take a somewhat deeper breath in order to have enough breath to blow it out, because the tea warmer is about an arm's length away from me. As I do so, I become aware that I probably do not have enough breath to blow out the candle. The movement of my hand, with which I was already 'on the way' to putting the teapot back on the warmer, slows momentarily. The whole process, from the moment that I poured out my tea and decided to put the teapot back on the warmer, took about five seconds.

Barbara, who was telling me about an incident that she had experienced a few days before and which was still preoccupying her, briefly stopped talking, took a breath and blew out the tealight, which was much closer to her than it was to me. She then went on with her story. I speeded up my arm movement, which I had slowed, once more and put the teapot back on the warmer. When I drew Barbara's attention to what had happened, she reported that she had seen me slow my arm movement, but had not been consciously aware that I had drawn a deep breath.

This example is representative of numerous everyday situations in which

we have a direct understanding of another person's intentions because their intentions are explicitly expressed in their embodied actions, and mirrored in our own capabilities for action. For the most part this understanding does not require the postulation of some belief or desire that is hidden away in the other person's mind, since what we might reflectively or abstractly call their belief or desire is expressed directly in their behavior (Gallagher, 2005, p. 224).[166]

How my wife perceived the situation I found myself in with the tealight, registered that I had taken a deep breath, grasped the intention that was associated with it and finally put it into action without having to carry out any intellectual analyses of the situation in order to derive action strategies, is one of countless examples of how the function of the mirror neurons makes it easier for us to negotiate everyday processes.[167] "This *implicit, automatic,* and *unconscious* process of motor simulation enables the observer to use his/her own resources to penetrate the world of the other without the need for theorizing about it" (Gallese, 2001, p. 41 — original italics). Due to the function that mirror neurons have within such processes, Rizzolatti, Fogassi, and Gallese (2000) considered calling them "intentionality detectors." One reason for this was that there are certain situations in which the mirror neurons fire even in macaques, *even though* the goal of the observed movement is *not* visible.[168]

> We showed monkeys actions of which they could see either the entire development or only the beginning, the target being hidden. We found that many mirror neurons discharge when the monkey *understands* the goal of the action even when it *cannot see* it (Rizzolatti et al., 2000, p. 205—italics added).

The fact that macaques 'infer' the goal of an action has been known for some time (see Assad & Maunsell, 1995; Filion, Washburn, & Gulledge, 1996), but was recently reconfirmed.

> A population of mirror neurons is able to represent actions also when crucial parts of these actions are hidden and can only be inferred. This indicates that, even when visual cues are limited, the activation of mirror neurons can place the observer in the same internal state as when actively executing the same action. This would enable the observer to recognize the hidden action (Umiltà et al., 2001, p. 161).

If the word "infer" is problematic in this context, this is particularly true of the words "understand'" and "recognize" with respect to monkeys.

---

166 See footnote 34 in Chapter 3.2 and Ryle's (1949/2002) analysis of the Cartesian category mistake.
167 As mentioned above, adaptive oscillators also play an important role in this.
168 Here I come to the exception mentioned in footnote 162.

It would perhaps be more accurate to say that observed movements that have a biomechanical character which is typically associated with certain goals, activate corresponding action patterns via mirror neurons, which leads to the observed movement being simulated as a directional action, which in turn implies a goal.

Where humans are concerned, however, it is quite possible to use the word "understand." This is evidenced by a study whose findings I find particularly convincing. They indicate that in the course of human evolution it has proven more advantageous to use the mirror neurons not only for imitation, but also in order to understand. Grèzes et al. (1998) presented their subjects with a series of movements and actions that they were to observe, with differing instructions as to what their focus should be. It turned out that the premotor areas in which the mirror neurons investigated are located, showed significantly greater activity when the subjects had been asked to observe the actions *in order to recognize* them, and relatively less activity when they were requested to observe them *in order to be able to imitate* them later.

These two experimental conditions in fact represent the two main functions ascribed to mirror neurons: First, they convey imitative actions and second, they contribute to direct understanding of observed actions. As far as the imitation is concerned, it is perhaps significant that observation of actions whose motor patterns are similar to that of the observer's own action program increases the likelihood that she will also execute this action herself (see Prinz, 2002).[169] As regards direct understanding of observed actions, it should be emphasized how narrowly this understanding associated with the movements of the other person has to be interpreted. "The understanding of action goals does not imply a full grasp of mental states such as beliefs or desires" (Gallese & Goldman, 1998, p. 500). What is understood is, to begin with, only the *immediate* meaning of the *action unit* observed (reaching for a raisin), and not, for instance, what the person who is performing the action intends to do next (does he want to eat something sweet or does he want to find out how a macaque's neurons process its watching him reaching for a raisin?).

Only when the observation is of a sequence of several acts or when the subject knows from experience that a particular act will be followed by another in the sequence, can the observer infer what the person is going to

---

169 To date, we can only speculate on what this may mean for the behavior of persons ready to resort to violence who witness violent actions in the real world or through the media (see, for example, Anderson et al., 2003; Spitzer, 2005), and this is beyond the scope of this book. The question as to the degree to which therapists influence the behavior of their clients, who learn from them as models, or are, *vice versa*, influenced by the patterns of the clients whom they constantly observe is closer to my subject, but I do not wish to go into it further here.

do next. This is due to the activation of chains of "'logically related' mirror neurons" (Iacoboni et al., 2005, p. 5). However, the resulting understanding is not direct, since it is dependent on certain conditions, in particular that what the person intends to do ultimately is identical to the effect of the last act in the sequence (see Gallese, 2006a, pp. 7f.). This, of course, increases the likelihood of a false interpretation. Put differently, the more the action of the other person that is to be understood extends beyond the immediate here-and-now, the more complex and prone to error the corresponding empathic processes of the observer become, and, in the psychotherapeutic context, the more necessary it is to practice "cultivated uncertainty" as described above.

The example of Grèzes' experiment also shows what effects the motivation of the observer (does she want to recognize or imitate?) can have on the activity of her mirror neurons—which in turn illustrates how emergent phenomena of higher levels of a system can affect lower levels (*top-down*). However, the example reveals more than that. "Thanks to this mechanism [of the activity of the mirror neurons], actions done by other individuals become messages that are understood by an observer without any cognitive mediation" (Rizzolatti & Craighero, 2004, p. 183)[170] This is not only one of the many indications of a possible role of mirror neurons in the evolution of language out of gestures (Gallese, 1999), but also one of the many pieces of evidence supporting the validity of the simulation theory.[171]

BOX 56

MIRROR NEURONS AND SIMULATION

Mirror neurons are a primitive version of, or a precursor to, mental simulation (Gallese & Goldman, 1998), insofar as they are a vehicle by which an observer *mimics, resonates with,* or *re-creates* the mental life of a target. . . . Apparently, when observing someone else perform an action, a normal human generates a plan to do the same action, or an image of doing it himself. This plan is inhibited—and thereby taken "off line," as simulationists like to say (Goldman, 2001, p. 221—original italics).

---

170 Although this remark was made in a quite different context, it reminds me of a statement by Merleau-Ponty that I quoted in the previous section. "The communication or comprehension of gestures comes about through the reciprocity of my intentions and the gestures of others, of my gestures and intentions discernible in the conduct of other people. It is as if the other person's intention inhabited my body, and mine his. . . Here we must rehabilitate the experience of others which has been distorted by intellectualist analyses . . ." (1962, p. 185). What is interesting here is the parallel with Mead's views on the importance of gestures for the "mechanism of social consciousness" (1912).
171 This can, of course, not be equated with an argument against the theory theory. "The somatic representation provides scaffolding for more conscious and deliberate reasoning about the actions of the other, leading to the more complex capacity for intersubjective reasoning" (Tucker, Luu, & Derryberry, 2005, p. 710).

The Principles of Mirroring in Neuronal Systems With Relevance for Empathy

The way in which the premotor mirror neurons function seems to be an expression of a mirroring *principle* which the brain also follows in other areas. "The astonishing properties of mirror neurons point to a unique principle that our brains use to link self to nonself" (Nakahara & Miyashita, 2005, p. 645). This principle "is likely a basic organizational feature of our brain" (Gallese, 2001, p. 46). It can be termed "embodied simulation," in reference to the processes that take place in direct contact between human beings (see Gallese, 2006a).

> What is meant is that simulated actions, sensations and emotions are also accompanied by the activation of the bodily states associated with the corresponding real actions, emotions and sensations. The mirror neuron system is therefore closely linked to the somato-sensory regions of the brain so that the observer actually feels how an observed action or emotional expression is felt. The insular cortex, which permits the most complete representation of the state of the body in the brain, plays a particularly important role in these processes (Lux, 2007, pp. 136f.).

The principle of embodied simulation is exemplified in the fact that the areas of activation in brain regions during a person's experience of their own feelings overlap with those activated during the observation of the same feelings in another person. This finding has far-reaching implications.

- De Vignemont (2006) describes it as "sharing the cortical representation of the emotion" (SRE) (I shall come back to this abbreviation later on);
- Goldman and Sripada (2005) speak of "unmediated resonance" and
- Gallese (2001; 2003) calls it the "shared manifold."

Gallese (2003) sees it as no less than "the neural basis of intersubjectivity." Because all human beings have this neuronal "mechanism," "the system of mirror neurons is a *supra-individual neuronal format* through which a *shared interpersonal sphere of meaning* is created," as Bauer (2005, p. 166— original italics) puts it, which is plausible, but inexact.[172] "All human beings"

---

172 In Bauer's account the different levels of description are not clearly differentiated. On the neuronal level, of course, no *"interpersonal sphere of meaning"* is created. Interpersonality and meaning are emergent phenomena on a higher, psychosocial level; the neuronal mechanisms are a necessary, but not sufficient prerequisite.

also includes infants, whose imitative skills we discussed above. In infants it becomes particularly clear that empathic "resonance induced by imitation does *not* require *explicit* representational content and may be a form of 'mirroring' that grounds empathy via an *experiential* mechanism" (Carr, Iacoboni, Dubeau, Mazziotta, & Lenzi, 2003, p. 5502—italics added). The mechanism referred to here is therefore "*not* the result of a hermeneutical process applied to sense data" (Gallese, 2006a, p. 14—italics added), since newborns do not yet have the capacity for such processes. Long

> before we are in a position to explain or predict the behavior of others, to mentalize or mind-read . . . , we are already in a position to interact with and to understand others in terms of their gestures, intentions, and emotions, and in terms of . . . how they act toward ourselves and others in the pragmatically contextualized activities of everyday life (Gallagher, 2005, p. 230).

Due to their innate "neural basis of intersubjectivity," babies are, however, already capable of participating in interpersonal situations to a certain extent at a very young age, although they have not yet become subjects in the full sense of the word. If we do not look at this from the viewpoint of individualism we can see it as a "paradoxical form of inter-subjectivity without subject" (Gallese, 2006a, p. 4) or simply as evidence of the primacy of intersubjectivity (see Box 15), which is, incidentally, also the basis of how the human being is conceptualized in gestalt therapy. "It is the contact that is the simplest and first reality," write Perls et al. (1951, p. 227; see also Staemmler, 2010b); Lynne Jacobs says the same thing in somewhat different words: "The most fundamental proposition is that all subjectivity is intersubjective, that is, all experience is a co-emergent phenomenon of intersecting subjectivities" (2005, p. 45).

The common neuronal basis required for this (the SRE) varies widely, in adults more than in children. To date (March, 2009), the neuronal bases of the following emotions[173] and bodily sensations have been identified: disgust, fear, anger, sadness, happiness, pain[174] and touch[175]

---

173 The end result of direct understanding of emotions through the SRE as described here may be similar to the *facial feedback* mentioned in section 4.2.1, although it is a different kind of process.
174 Singer et al. (2004) found that in pain the mirroring principle applies to the affective components of the experience of pain, but not to the sensory ones.
175 Blakemore reports on a woman whose inhibition system did not work for the mirroring of touch. "If she sees someone else being touched on their face she feels it on her face as if she is being touched. She has always had this and thought it was completely normal. . . . We found that her mirror system for touch is overactive" (in de Vignemont, 2006, pp. 193f.). This is evidently a case of "echo-aesthesia," as one could call it in analogy to the term

(see Avanti, Bueti, Galati, & Aglioti, 2005; Blakemore, Bristow, Bird, Frith, & Ward, 2005; Botvinick et al., 2005; Gallese et al., 2004; Grèzes, Pichon, & de Gelder, 2007; Heberlein & Adolphs, 2007; Hutchison, Davis, Lozano, Tasker, & Dostrovsky, 1999; Jackson, Meltzoff, & Decety, 2005; Keysers et al., 2004; Phillips et al., 1998; Singer et al., 2004; Wicker et al., 2003). It is to be expected that the rapidly advancing research in this field will soon find more resonance systems. The following is true for both pain and the other neural resonance systems already discovered.

> *Brain areas dedicated to subjective experiences of emotions and bodily sensations are activated when observing someone else experiencing the same emotion or sensations* whatever the kind of stimulus that is used. It does not seem to matter whether subjects see an isolated body part being injured (Jackson et al., 2005) or a facial expression of an unknown person (Adolphs, 2002). It does not make a difference whether the study emphasizes the context inducing the sensation (Botvinick et al., 2005) or the specific body location injured (Avenanti et al., 2005) (de Vignemont, 2006, p. 182—italics added).

"Mentalizing," i.e., reflection on the mental states of other people that is one step removed from the here-and-now, also follows the same principle. Certain brain areas have "not only been found to be involved when mentalizing about the thoughts, intentions or beliefs of others but also when people are attending to their *own* mental states" (Singer, 2006a, p. 856—italics added).

All these findings could be summarized as follows: "The way our nervous system is organized and tailored by evolution provides the basic biological mechanism for resonating with others" (Decety, 2007, p. 263). If we now focus on the principle that becomes evident from this we could say that the human neuronal setup creates the conditions for a certain degree of confluence and enables us to enter into relationship with and understand each other. These prerequisites for confluence evidently promote empathic interpersonal contact and thus the sustaining of human relationships. "Empathy is deeply grounded in the experience of our lived-body, and it is this experience that enables us to directly recognize others not as bodies endowed with a mind but as *persons* like us" (Gallese, 2001, p. 43— original italics).

"echopraxia." We could, however, also draw a different parallel if we want to avoid interpreting it in a way that is pathologizing. This woman's situation, which appeared to her to be normal, could then perhaps be called "second touch," in analogy to the expression "second sight," i.e., as a capacity that is generally considered to be "paranormal."

Conversely, to surrender to the fear of confluence or to resist identifying with another person (in therapy or elsewhere) also means taking up
an antagonistic stance toward human empathy and thus also toward sus-
tainable and close (therapeutic and other) relationships. This is the typical
attitude of the individualist self that wants to remain independent and
uninfluenced at all costs (while at the same time not being able to escape
the fear of isolation that goes with it). However, in the end this attitude
will likely prove to be tilting at windmills, since

> obviously immense areas of relatively permanent confluence are indis-
> pensable as the underlying unaware background of the aware back-
> grounds of experience. We are in confluence with everything we are
> fundamentally, unproblematically or irremediably, dependent on . . . : A
> child is in confluence with his family, an adult with his community, a
> man with the universe (Perls et al., 1951, p. 451).

Embodied "being in the world," to belong, as a human being, to the
"flesh of the world" (Merleau-Ponty), "Being-with others" (Heidegger)—
these were the keywords of the phenomenologists whom I presented in
the last section. What the phenomenologists mean by them is reflected
on both the psychological (see section 4.2.1) and the neurophysiological
levels in processes described by terms such as *identification, confluence, imitation, simulation, SRE* and *shared manifold*. The existence of these processes
evidently cannot be seriously denied; without what they are referring to,
empathy is not possible. On the contrary, as we have seen, these are processes that are mainly implicit and automatic and constantly develop their
own dynamics.

Vignemont says that the SRE is "intersubjective" and that its occur-
rence "expresses this *primary* lack of differentiation between self and others" (2006, p. 186—italics added). This is, of course, not meant in the way
that the psychoanalysts once believed that there was a "symbiotic phase" in
early childhood with a "dual unity within one common boundary" (Mahler
et al., 1975, p. 44) and erroneously assumed that infants were not capable
of distinguishing their own bodies from those of their mother or another
baby.[176] We are concerned rather with the neurophysiological processes that
are initially, in these two possible cases, largely the same, i.e., first, when
I perceive a movement or an emotion *in somebody else* and second, when I
carry out this movement *myself* or experience the same emotion *myself.*

---

176 Regarding this view Stern writes, "there is no confusion between self and other in the
beginning or at any point during infancy. . . . There is no symbiotic-like phase" (1985, p. 10—
see also Stern, 1985, pp. 76ff.; Gallagher & Meltzoff, 1996).

Motor intentions are first shared, and only in the second place attributed. As regards the processes involved, the attribution of an action to others doesn't differ from the attribution of an action to oneself: in both cases, the starting point is an . . . *agent-free* representation (Becchio & Bertone, 2005, p. 28—italics added).

Let us think back for a moment to echopraxia (Box 54) or Blakemore's patients with "second touch" or "echo-aesthesia" (see footnote 175). In both examples, the deviation from the norm lay in the fact that the *secondary* inhibition mechanisms that normally ensure that the *primary* tendency toward imitating a movement or experiencing the total sensation of an observed touch is diminished or completely suppressed, failed to function. Here "primary" and "secondary" refer to the specific temporal sequence of activations and counter-activations in neurological circuits (that are measured in fractions of a second). *First* the activation of the common action representation or SRE takes place, and only *then* does the inhibition follow, with the effect that the original activation does not come to full fruition. We can therefore formulate another principle: The shared neuronal activation is primary; what creates a distinction (the inhibition) is secondary.

What that means for bodily movements and actions in concrete terms has, I believe, become sufficiently clear. However, what it means for the SRE needs further explanation. De Vignemont has developed a model that can take the described temporal sequence into account and help to throw further light on the relationship between empathy and confluence: "At a primary level the observation of someone else's emotion triggers the activation of SRE. This activation is automatic and is not inhibited" (de Vignemont, 2006, p. 185). Here something similar is taking place to what happens during the observation of bodily movements of the other person: The corresponding action program of the observer is simultaneously activated. However, just as this does not automatically lead to the observed movement actually being executed, due to the inhibition mechanisms, the automatic activation of the SRE also does not automatically lead to one's having to "carry it out" immediately—and in respect of the SRE this would mean to *experience* the observed feeling oneself.

BOX 57

SHARED REPRESENTATIONS AND THEIR INHIBITION

Actions that are . . . perceived in another . . . seem to activate shared representations. These shared representations may be at the abstract level of meaning, but they are linked downstream with areas responsible for the performance of the action. Activation is thought to spread from the

> representation of the meaning to that of the performance if there is no
> inhibition, but the extent to which motor sequences are activated depends
> on the mode of input, salience of and attention to the stimulus, and extent
> of inhibitory control (Preston & de Waal, 2002, p. 11).

For one to be able to experience the observed feeling oneself, the inhibition mechanisms must be more or less *de*activated or remain relatively
inactive. First, "at a secondary level one has conscious access to the emotion associated with the activation of SRE. It is only then that one *experiences* the emotion of other" (de Vignemont, 2006, p. 185—italics added).
The intensity of the emotion may, of course, vary. If the intensity were not
limited this would be emotional contagion, as happens in small children
whose capacity to inhibit is still immature. In adults one would speak of
unequivocal confluence. Moderated intensity, where the emotion associated with the SRE was more or less inhibited, would then be understood
to be more or less intense empathy, in which a feeling for the difference
between self and other 'remained intact.' However, because the inhibition
is the *secondary* process, it would be more correct to say that it is *created* (if
it is not present primarily, it cannot strictly be 'sustained'). Therefore, "the
essential question is not why do we participate in other people's experiences, but *how do we stop doing it?*" (Stern et al., 2003, p. 24—original italics) or "how can one distinguish one's own actions/intentions from those
of other people" (Becchio & Bertone, 2005, p. 21).

Gallese summarizes the sequence that is discernible here on the neuronal level as follows: "The chain of commands in the head is blocked at a
later stage" (in Klein, 2008, p. 29—italics added). This sequence thus seems
to show similarities with the sequences and rankings assumed—on quite
different levels of description—by developmental and social psychology,
symbolic interactionism and phenomenology. Identification, confluence,
simulation, sharing, and intersubjectivity, etc. are (from a chronological
and systematic viewpoint) *primary* and form the bases or prerequisites for
the development of differentness, distancing, otherness, and individuality
that come into being in a second step. As Heidegger expressed it in the
quotation in the previous section, one person empathizing with another
"does not first constitute Being-with; only on the basis of Being-with does
'empathy' become possible" (1962, p. 162).

A Jungian psychoanalyst writes:

> I am arguing therefore not simply that we can enter into states of merger,
> but that we already exist in a state of merger. From the viewpoint of

consciousness we appear separate individuals with a regrettable tendency to lapse into fantasies of fusion; but if we look through the other
end of the telescope we will see that the fact of our connection is primary
and that our sense of separateness is sustained by a system of defenses
that differentiates us one from another (Field, 1991, p. 97).

If we were to see it from this standpoint, the mystery of the other
person would not originally be a mystery at all, because first there would
be sharing of the cortical representation (SRE) ("merger"). Thus if I were
not to inhibit my spontaneous reaction in a second step, I would be confluent with the other person and able to access *in myself* something analogous
to what was happening *in the other person*. (Incidentally, this could be seen
as a new way of interpreting Kohut's definition of empathy as "vicarious
introspection.") Only in the second step, through the activation of the inhibition, is the mystery of the other person created, because the inhibition
reduces the extent of the confluence. This may go as far as the point where
I no longer clearly feel what the other person is feeling, but only vaguely
sense it. In extreme cases I may no longer notice anything at all and feel
completely distanced and quite "different" from her. Viewed in this way,
the mystery of the other person would not, to start with, be something
that *she* creates—although of course she can do that, if she inhibits the
expression of her own feelings or impulses, e.g., in order to observe some
kind of display rules, but that is something different. Rather, it would be a
mystery that *I* created by *shutting myself off* and suppressing *in myself* what
I have actually already picked up from her.

That also has its neurophysiological correlate, of course. For motor
processes this is described as follows:

> The inhibition of imitation activates the anterior fronto-median cortex
> and the temporal-parietal junction, which are both known to be involved
> in the sense of agency and in perspective-taking. Brass and colleagues
> claim that the distinction between internally generated and externally
> triggered motor representations plays a key role to prevent us to imitate
> someone else's movemens (de Vignemont, 2006, p. 186).

If that also applies to the SRE, and that would seem plausible, one
could, as Singer puts it, speculate that "you would have the same networks
activated, but the magnitude of activation . . . would serve as a tag for
whether you or someone else is experiencing a state" (2006b, p. 37).[177] To

---

177 "It should be noted that the overlap between cortical areas involved in self-related actions and other-related actions is not complete. There are specific subcircuits within the

put it in extreme terms, also if we disregard what was said in footnotes 177 and 178, the extent of the inhibition that I mobilize to prevent the SRE from having an emotional effect is *the same* as my feeling that I am myself and different from the other person.[178] At first sight this idea may seem surprising, but it is remarkably consistent with the millennia-old Buddhist conviction that insistence on one's own ego and compassion with others are contradictory and even antagonistic attitudes. It is also consistent with the equally ancient experience in the same tradition according to which a meditative practice that renders the illusory character of the ego experienceable can lead to the experience of connection with other people and—if it is permissible to draw a link between Buddhism and Merleau-Ponty's phenomenology—to the experience of oneness with the "flesh of the world."

> In the Buddhist philosophical tradition, different levels of attainment are described. At a basic level, compassion . . . is understood mainly in terms of empat—our ability to enter into and, to some extent, share others' suffering. But Buddhists . . . believe that this can be developed to such a degree that not only does our compassion arise without any effort, but it is unconditional, undifferentiated, and universal in scope. A feeling of intimacy toward all other sentient beings . . . is generated. . . . When we enhance our sensitivity toward others' suffering through deliberately opening ourselves up to it, it is believed that we can gradually extend out compassion to the point where the individual feels so moved by even the subtlest suffering of others that they come to have an overwhelming sense of responsibility toward those others. (Dalai Lama, 1999, pp. 123f.).

In light of this, at the upper end of the intensity scale em*pathy* would not necessarily seem to lead to an amorphous merger with what the other person is feeling. If that happens, we are probably concerned with a completely deactivated inhibition. Compassionate commitment is evidently

---

premotor, prefrontal, and parietal cortices that account for either the self or the other" (Decety & Jackson, 2004, p. 77).

178 There also seem to be a few other neuronal patterns that can contribute to the experience of differentness: "Perception of the object's movements may activate the subject's premotor areas, but without peripheral somatosensory cues and efferent motor feedback. Even shared representations are more intensely activated in self-experience than in observation or imagination. Overall, the pattern of activation is different for experiences that originated in the object from ones that originated in the subject" (Preston & de Waal, 2002, p. 20). Moreover, a neuronal system that makes it possible to discriminate "between self-agency and other agency" apparently remains active even in relatively uninhibited simulation (Decety & Grèzes, 2006, p. 12; see also Decety & Sommerville, 2003). Incidentally, this is an interesting parallel to Edith Stein's differentiation between "primordial" (originary) and "non-primordial" (non-originary) experience.

another—more cultivated—option for rendering the SRE emotionally effective. Naturally this is the option to be preferred in the therapeutic context, since it is associated with the capacity and willingness to act. How exactly this can be cultivated is a question that for me remains theoretically open and to which I can, from my own experience, only contribute speculations and intuitions. It seems to me to have something to do with what is referred to as "presence" or "mindfulness" (see Germer, Siegel, & Fulton, 2005; Siegel, 2007). It would also seem to be connected with the important difference between the subjective experience of a person who becomes confluent and in so doing *loses* his feeling of having a separate identity that he would actually rather keep, and the experience of a person who is aware of her connectedness with all other human beings and the world because she has *discovered* that the individual ego existing in isolation is an illusion, which leads her to come to decisions—decisions to participate actively in the suffering of the other person and to do what is possible to relieve it, as expressed in the ideal of Avalokiteśvara[179] (see Box 3).

Our neuronal systems evidently equip us to do this.

> The more that people tend to imitate others, the more that they tend to be empathic and concerned with the emotional states of others. This suggests that the core circuitry for imitation might interact with the limbic system (the neural system concerned with emotions) during social mirroring. (Iacoboni, 2005, p. 635).

I have thus arrived back at the neurosciences, the insights of which, incidentally, converge in some respects with Buddhist insights (see, for example, Begley, 2007; Goleman, 2003).

Selective Empathy

In the last few pages I have focused on processes of involuntary simulation of motor and emotional activation patterns (SRE). These are typical *bottom-up* processes. However, "recent findings suggest that empathic brain responses are modulated by appraisal processes which take into

---

179 According to a legend, Avalokiteśvara was once confluent with human suffering in such a way that he despaired and could only weep. "From one of his tears, Tara [a female Buddha] emerged and encouraged him on the bodhissattva path, saying, 'Do not despair. I will help you to liberate all beings'" (Chodron, 2005, p. 18). (There are also other legends of the origin of the Tara in which she does not arise from the tears of a male being. Avalokiteśvara himself is, as a male figure, possibly a later patriarchal version of an earlier mother goddess—see Wetzel, 1999, pp. 169ff.)

account information about the emotional stimuli, their situative context, characteristics of the empathizer and his/her relationship with the target" (de Vignemont & Singer, 2006, p. 440). Thus, *top-down* processes evidently also play an important role in determining whether a conscious empathic reaction does, in fact, occur (see Decety, 2007, p. 250). This was already evident from the observation that, depending on the superordinate conditions, the emotion targeted by the activated SRE is inhibited to a greater or lesser extent. It can correspondingly be experienced as weaker or stronger. The SRE is activated automatically, but not the feeling that goes with it.

There is a good reason for this, since "in real life, we constantly witness people displaying contradictory emotions. If we were to consciously feel what they feel all the time, we would be in permanent emotional turmoil, leaving no room for our own emotions" (de Vignemont & Singer, 2006, pp. 436f.).

> The emotional state generated by the perception of the other's state or situation needs regulation and control for the experience of empathy. Without such control, the mere activation of the shared representation, . . . would lead to emotional contagion or emotional distress (Decety & Jackson, 2004, p. 87).

People therefore have to select to whom they are going direct their empathy and under what conditions, and they do in fact do this. Some initial research has already been done on some of the selection criteria that are employed. Based on these findings, de Vignemont and Singer (2006, p. 437) propose that future research adopt a "contextual approach," since it is precisely the respective context that takes effect by way of a *top-down* process.

The most important factor is *attention*. Attention also plays a role in many of the other factors, although it is never the only factor because it is itself affected by various possible motivations. I can only be empathic towads a person and the subjective situation of a person to whom I am paying attention. I shall be equally unable to empathize with a person, say in Hong Kong, who is unknown to me as I am with someone who is sitting seven rows behind me at a concert. However, if this person should happen to fall down beside me and injure herself as we leave the auditorium, I can turn my empathic awareness towards her from one moment to the next. The special attention that a baby's cry produces in her mother, who then uses her empathy in a sustained fashion to find out why the baby is crying, is prototypical (see Acebo & Thoman, 1992).

As a rule we can assume that in the psychotherapeutic situation therapists and clients are interested in one another and that they direct their attention towads each other. The client comes to therapy because she is suffering and it is the hope of getting help that makes her therapist important to her (see Chapter 4.1). Sometimes there are exceptions to this rule, either of a more basic nature, for example, where a client has had the therapy 'prescribed' in some way, or of a more situative nature if she is distracted by avoidance tendencies, for instance.

The therapist's attention, on the other hand, is motivated by her professional commitment and her wish to support the client in coping with her difficulties. Here again there are exceptions, of course, for example where the therapist is distracted by her own worries or by loud noises from a nearby building site. However, these exceptions usually remain within the normal human range. A more far-reaching and problematic form of threat to the therapist's attention and thus also to her empathy has to do with her professionality. If she does not take sufficient care of herself, the frequency and intensity of her encounters with suffering people can lead to fatigue, numbing and apathy, and in the extreme case even to cynicism. These are typical symptoms of burn-out (Fengler, 1994) or what is known as compassion fatigue.

BOX 58

COMPASSION FATIGUE is a gradual diminishing of human compassion which can go as far as indifference toward other people's suffering. It can occur not only when people become emotionally numbed by too much information in the media about disasters, wars and other terrible events (Moeller, 1999), but also when over time psychotherapists become emotionally overtaxed by being constantly confronted with clients who are traumatized or suffering severely in some other way. This is referred to as "secondary traumatic stress" (Figley, 1995).

One way to care for oneself is to ensure that one can shift freely between the poles of confluence and empathy, on the one hand, and distancing on the other. Constant and prolonged compassion with the suffering of clients is mentally stressful and therapists need to keep a check on it in order to avoid becoming overburdened. Ultimately it is also useful for clients if therapists keep shifting out of the mode of direct simulation and make use of the mode of reflecting about the client's psychological situation (see Chapter 3.2). Even if therapists sometimes adopt an "ex-centric" perspective (as described by Plessner—see section 4.2.2) in an attempt to obtain an overall view of their joint situation with the client they are working with, this is not only good for their own mental health, but a kind of self-supervision that can have a helpful influence on the therapeutic process.

Doctors and other medical personnel also have to protect themselves from the danger of *compassion fatigue*. One way they do this is by activating their mechanisms that inhibit direct compassion and empathizing with their patients mainly on a cognitive level.

BOX 59

EMPATHIC CONCERN Doctors who have to inflict pain on their patients to help cure them are at risk of suffering from the associated mental stress themselves. Cheng et al. (2007) carried out a study in which they compared laypeople's and doctors' neurophysiological reactions to video clips showing patients being subjected to pain for medical reasons. It turned out that

> doctors develop a protective mechanism in the course of their careers that prevents patients' suffering affecting them too strongly . . . Their pain centers were . . . not activated while they watched the video clips, but a signal increase . . . was found in certain regions of the frontal lobe (Meyer, 2007, p. 111).

These regions are responsible especially for emotional regulation and mentalizing. The researchers did not interpret

> the doctors' lack of response as a lack of compassion . . . Rather, they concluded that instead of empathy the doctors . . . felt empathic concern for their patients. Without this mechanism they could not muster the strength to practice their profession (Meyer, 2007).

Incidentally, the fact that therapists do not respond equally empathically to all their patients' moods can be considered normal. The appraisals that determine what they consider important and worthy of note and what not and to which of their clients' experiences they therefore react with empathy depend not on their respective therapeutic modalities, but on their own personal experiences. "Personality traits can make a big difference. Our own social and cognitive history can make us react to the same stimulus in a different way" (Gallese, 2006a, p. 18) from another person and permit something different to become *figural* from them. In general it can be said that the "shared emotion has to be salient" (de Vignemont, 2006, p. 188); what remains unclear or recedes into the background is not (or no longer) reacted to with particular empathy.[180]

---

180 Of course there is the phenomenon that something about my client begins to attract my attention precisely *because* it always remains in the background or remains unclear. But then it becomes figural for me.

Another factor is *familiarity*—in two different senses: the familiarity of the other person and the familiarity of the experience that is to be empathized with. The rule of thumb is: "The more we care for and love the suffering party, the more potent the resonance induction process is likely to be, *assuming that other variables don't contravene this*" (Watt, 2005, p. 198—original italics), e.g., annoyance with the other person. Singer et al. (2006) showed in a concrete way that the degree of personal familiarity, as exists, for example, between a wife and her husband, leads to stronger activity in the brain regions important for empathic reactions than in persons who do not know each other so well. Similarly, the response is stronger if a person is familiar with the feelings toward which his empathy is shown. If someone has previously experienced something similar to what another person is now experiencing, he finds it easier to be empathic. It is no coincidence that the statement, "That happened to me once, too" is often synonymous with the statement, "I can empathize with that."

In this context, Preston and de Waal (2002, p. 17) report on a study in which the neuronal correlates of empathic reactions were measured in persons watching volunteers being administered an electric shock (of an ethically acceptable strength and painfulness). The intensity of the empathy-related neuronal activity in the subjects who had previously had received such shocks themselves was much higher than in subjects who had not. They simply knew better what a shock feels like and their SRE resonances with the other subjects were easier to activate and more intense. Here again we have parallels between empathy with emotions and bodily movements. Having previously experienced certain movement patterns oneself makes it easier to resonate with similar motor activities that one observes. "If you are skilled in one kind of dance, you recognize it as more familiar [when you see other people dancing it]. This recognition is somehow underpinned by a higher degree of activation of your own motor system" (Gallese in Singer, 2006b, p. 39).

Liking the person with whom one is empathizing is an additional, favorable factor. It overlaps with the familiarity factor to a certain extent. The degree of neuronal activity associated with empathic experiencing is much greater if one finds the other person pleasant and feels affection for them than if the relationship is one of aversion. When this association was investigated with the aid of painful stimuli, an interesting gender-specific difference was also found, incidentally, so to speak.

Both men and women showed increased activation in ACC [the anterior cingulate cortex] and AI [anterior insula] when observing the unfamiliar but likeable person receiving painful stimulation. Interestingly, however, men but not women showed reduced activation in ACC and

AI when they were informed that the player who previously played unfairly in the . . . game received painful shocks (Singer, 2006b, p. 23).[181]

Other feelings for the other person, which cannot be conceived of as liking in the strict sense but may lead to one's being more attentive toward them, also contribute to greater empathy. Examples are illness and (in old people) frailty, which give the impression of neediness and stimulate caring or caregiving impulses (see Batson, Lishner, Cook, & Sawyer, 2005). In contrast, having unpleasant sensations oneself distinctly reduces one's willingness to be empathic. "Simply put, we are typically lousy at empathy when tired and sleep deprived, hungry, or in pain" (Watt, 2005, p. 199).

Finally, the *nature* of the feelings appears to be important for the ease with which they can be empathized with. In general it seems that some people find it easier to empathize with the basic feelings of other people such as sadness, joy or pain than with more sophisticated emotions such as jealousy or shame. However, this probably has much to do with the familiarity factor; most people are familiar with the basic emotions.

If the other person's feelings are directed toward oneself it becomes more difficult to be empathic. This sometimes even applies to the affection that another person feels for us and expresses. It is well known that it becomes even more difficult to empathize with the envy, jealousy or anger of other people if these feelings are directed toward ourselves. Here the empathy is often impeded by defensive reactions. These are *distancing* reactions that emphasize differences and reduce the confluence required for empathy—as the other person's aversive emotions have already done, which we are resisting (see de Vignemont, 2006, pp. 187f.). According to Anderson and Keltner (2002), this may have to do with the evolutionary function of empathy, which could be to maintain and strengthen social attachments—a function that is not associated with aggressive feelings, for example.

It can be similarly difficult (and the reasons for this may also be similar) to empathize with the feelings of another person when we see them in a *context* that makes them appear inadequate. It is difficult to share another person's joy over a perceived success when it is clear to us that it will soon turn out to be a Pyrrhic victory. I sometimes have a similar reaction with some unpleasant feelings that my clients experience and which at a given moment appear to be the whole of reality for them, when my impression is that they will be short-lived and I sense that they will soon dissolve into thin air or even be transformed into positive feelings. My

---

181 Singer connects this finding with feelings of justice and vengeance which men are more likely to feel than women and which then compromise the men's ability to empathize—as in, "He had it coming to him."

compassion for their being imprisoned in a narrow view of things then reduces my empathy for the pain associated with it.

Open Questions

The social neurosciences on which this section focuses constitute an interdisciplinary field of research that has set itself the task of examining

> how nervous (central and peripheral), endocrine, and immune systems are involved in sociocultural processes. Social neuroscience is nondualist in its view of humans, yet it is also nonreductionistic and emphasizes the importance of understanding how the brain and body influence social processes, as well as how social processes influence the brain and body (Harmon-Jones & Winkielman, 2007, p. 4).

Despite its high aspirations and the impressive progress that it has indisputably made in the last 10 to 15 years, this branch of research is in many respects still in its infancy. What I mean is not simply that many of its projects have not been fully completed, but also that there are many questions that have still not been asked—or barely. This is, of course, partly due to the scientific research designs it mainly employs, the methodology of which is limited. If one wishes to "*isolate*" efficacy factors, one must do just that, which frequently means taking them out of their natural and social contexts so as to reduce their vast complexity to manageable proportions. What is gained is insight into how the individual efficacy factors make their presence felt if they are viewed *in isolation*. This only coincides with social reality to a limited extent and the "ecological validity" of these experiments often leaves much to be desired. Moreover, certain limits are also dictated by ethical standards that prohibit the conduct of certain experiments in human beings. These are then carried out in animals, but then it is not possible to give a clear answer to the question as to whether the results are valid for humans or not.

Thus, we now know something about the resonance phenomena that take place in a person when she observes someone else. But we still do not know what effects these phenomena have on her neuronal structure, e.g., if she is a psychotherapist who very frequently pays special attention to other people. To date this has been the subject of only rather general speculations.

> The individual development and fine-tuning of the mirror-neuron system could rely upon similar principles as does any other neuroplastic

development. When the basic requirements for inter-area wiring are fulfilled, the brain self-organizes on the basis of the statistical properties
of the stimuli in the outside world . . . , much more so when the subject
pays attention to the stimuli and interacts actively with her environment
(Hari, 2007, p. 94—see Box 50).

Furthermore, to my knowledge there is still very little research on
what happens to the resonances produced by mirroring systems when
they are expressed and this expression is perceived by the other person
in the next instant. Thus, the original resonance of the observer leads to
further resonance in the observed person. In my view this is where it starts
to become really interesting, but of course also rather complex. However,
social reality is as Husserl described it, such "that I can experience any
given Other not only as himself an Other but also a related in turn to *his*
Others and perhaps . . . related at the same time to me" (1960, p. 130—
original italics).

This "iteration" already takes place when mothers feed their toddlers and open their mouths to get the children to do the same (O'Toole
& Dubin 1968); they intuitively rely on the baby's forging a link between
perception and action. We find similar reactions in adults.

When you are watching another about to perform something, and you
wish for the other to succeed in whatever he or she is doing, you will
tend to show by your own accompanying muscle movements your virtual participation in the other's effort as if you were a helper or a co-
author of the other's effort or doing (Bråten, 2007b, p. 111).

Like mothers feeding their babies, we trust that the other person will
see the movements with which we are supportively mirroring his efforts
and that he will then experience a corresponding muscular activation
which will, so-to-speak, duplicate his efforts and thus assist them. He may
even have the feeling that he is not alone.

Such reciprocal processes on a mainly physical level are still relatively easy to keep track of, but in many other human interactions, particularly those that take place in psychotherapy, they often become much
more complex: "I feel that you have noticed how I perceived that you had
the impression that I had the feeling . . ." In the emotional intensity of the
kind of communication that can arise in therapy sessions such recursive
processes are common—particularly when therapists permit themselves
to become involved in direct bodily I-Thou contact with their clients (see
Boxes 1, 21 and 35) and proceed in a manner oriented toward the here-
and-now (see Grawe's "processual activation," Chapter 3.2).

Then an infinite number of feedback loops develops (see Hofstadter, 1979), the individual sections of which cannot easily be separated from one another and whose interactions are as microscopical as they are diverse. They therefore rapidly become impossible to follow. We are a long way from gaining a more exact understanding of the details of these dynamics. The approaches used to investigate them are still too rudimentary (see, for instance, Bråten, 2007b, p. 118; Bråten, 2007c; Decety, Chaminade, Grèzes, & Meltzoff, 2002; Ferrari & Gallese, 2007, p. 77). For the time being we must make do with concepts such as the "joint situation" (Schmitz) or "dyadically expanded states of consciousness" (Tronick) which are not concerned with microprocesses, but are of a more holistic nature. It is to these, therefore, that I turn in the next chapter.

4.2.4   Summary of Chapter 4.2

In my summary of Chapter 4.1, I spoke of empathy as a process of *mutual social referencing*, since this is the first important building block for my expanded understanding of empathy. I can now add the second building block and characterize empathy likewise as a process of mutual *bodily referencing*. Each insight in fact complements and confirms the other.

In addition to "bringing the other to mind," a primarily mental concept mainly described in the traditional concept of empathy and formulated by the supporters of the theory theory, there is a large range of forms of direct, bodily empathy which follow the principle of imitation and simulation and which are considered particularly important by the proponents of the simulation theory. A large body of neuroscientific, psychological and philosophical phenomenological literature, parts of which I have presented in sections 4.2.1, 4.2.2 and 4.2.3, deals with a different level of this aspect of empathy, respectively.

> By means of embodied simulation we do not just "see" an action, an emotion, or a sensation. Side by side with the sensory description of the observed social stimuli, internal representations of the body states associated with these actions, emotions, and sensations are evoked in the observer. . . . By means of a shared functional state realized in two different bodies that nevertheless obey to same functional rules, the "objectual other" becomes "another self" (Gallese, 2006a, p. 10).

It is in this embodied simulation, in the immediate bodily phenomenon of "Being-with" that I see the foundation of all empathy between human beings, which is operative in all empathic processes and also forms the basis for the more cognitive aspects of empathy and the conscious perspective-taking that is ubiquitous in empathic exchanges between adults. Thus,

> intersubjectivity, then, and its empathic basis, begin to move us away from the simple Cartesian picture of discrete individual consciousnesses inferring one another's existence by a process of analogical reasoning, to one in which subjective realms of experience interpenetrate one another, so that identity and individuality are relative rather than absolute matters (Midgley, 2006, p. 104).

Some readers of this chapter may have gained the impression that I have neglected the aspect of conscious perspective-taking. This impression is both correct and false. It is correct because I have not, in fact, dealt with cognitive perspective-taking in detail. However, it is also false, because (as should be evident from Figure 1) I am taking as understood what is covered by the traditional concept of empathy, which centers mainly on the mental level. In this chapter my aim was to include the bodily level, which has been more or less neglected by the traditional concept of empathy, in order to arrive at an expanded and more accurate concept of empathy.

However, before I can formulate this new concept, we need to consider another dimension that I have hinted at several times, but not yet dealt with sufficiently thoroughly. It therefore merits a chapter of its own.

4.3   Empathy in the Joint Situation

In Chapter 4.1, I pointed out in a number of ways that empathy in psychotherapy is something that takes place largely between *two* people and is not just an activity engaged in by the therapist alone. To a certain extent, the mutuality of empathy described in that section overcomes the individualism that finds expression in the one-sidedness of the traditional concept of empathy. However, this is only partially true, since mutual empathy can still be seen as the product of the empathic activities of two fundamentally separate individuals. However,

> no encounters of fellow human beings are ever given that would be *absolutely* without a horizon such that two "monads" unrelated to the surrounding world would simply confront each other, i.e., "monads" whose being together would not be embedded in a sector of the lived world (Gurwitsch, 1979, p. 36 — original italics).

As became clear in Chapter 4.2, human beings are directly connected with each other through their physical attributes and their embodiment. "I understand another person through the world in which I live with him and through the medium of the bodily expression in which he realizes his intentions and mental states" (Waldenfels, 1976, p. 121). This bodily understanding that is rooted in the world leads to a direct common bond, a *participation mystique* (Schmitz) or a *shared manifold* (Gallese), which can no longer merely be ascribed to a simple interaction between separate monads. The studies of researchers and philosophers such as Meltzoff, Merleau-Ponty and Gallese—to name just three as representative of the many others that I have mentioned—have provided impressive documentation of what human beings can do when they join mental forces.

> This combined power is distinguished not only in quantity but also in quality from that which is solitary. . . . Wit, acumen, imagination, feeling . . . —all these so-called powers of the soul, are powers of humanity, not of man as an individual; they are products of culture, products of human society. Only where man has contact and friction with his fellowman are wit and sagacity kindled . . . Only where man suns and warms himself in the proximity of man, arise feeling and imagination. . . . And only where man communicates with man, only in speech, a social act, awakes reason. . . . It is not until man has reached an advanced stage of culture that he can double himself, so as to play the part of another within himself (Feuerbach, 1855, p. 117f.).

Wherever two people turn to each other and enter into a committed empathic exchange, as in psychotherapy, for example, a whole emerges from their activities that is greater than the sum of its parts and leads to something that is new in quality (see Box 7)—something new that in turn also affects the individual parts of which it is composed. This, too, can be seen as being consistent with the principle of emergence, mentioned above (see Box 52), according to which higher level emergent properties affect and determine the lower levels. In the words of Max Wertheimer, co-founder of Gestalt psychology, there are "wholes, the behaviour of which is not determined by that of their individual elements, but where the part-processes are themselves determined by the intrinsic nature of the whole" (1925/1938, p. 2).

If we apply this to interpersonal situations it simply means that "in certain situations a person is not [only] present as an 'I' but [also] as a characteristic part of a 'we'" (Wertheimer, 1924/1938, p. 362). This "we," however, if the insights of Gestalt psychology are to be taken seriously, is not just the sum of you and I, but, over and above that, also something different. I believe that the psychotherapeutic encounter can be viewed as a clear prototypical example of such "we situations."

> Through the issue of concern to the patient and through the therapist's goodwill, i.e. what is of concern to him as a professional, these two persons clearly form a whole, or, one might say, a joint situation, right from their very first meeting (Marx, 2002, p. 238—italics added).

In the next sections, I will be considering what this really means.

4.3.1   Situation, Situational Circles, and Roles

The term used by phenomenologists such as, for example, Gurwitsch (1979), Rombach (1987), Sartre (1956) and Schmitz (2002) to describe that larger whole that embraces the self and the other is the "situation." This is a term that is also used in social science research (e.g., Arnold, 1981; Graumann, 1975; Magnusson, 1978) and in certain types of psychotherapy (e.g., Robine, 2001; Wiltschko, 2008; Wollants, 2008). The particular situation is, as it were, the microcosm that directly determines human experience and behavior. I have already touched on the concept of the situation in the previous section on social referencing, "in which one person utilizes another person's interpretation of the *situation* to formulate her own interpretation of it" (Feinman, 1992, p. 4—italics added). However, there the situation was seen merely as a point of reference about which the participants reach an agreement. What we are looking at now is what the situation itself contributes to empathic understanding, since, to quote Gallese, "empathy is not something that is simply there—it comes into being as a result of the situation" (in Klein, 2008, p. 29).

BOX 60

THE SITUATION

> Where human Dasein primarily finds itself is the situation. What it responds to is the situation. What it is confronted with is also the situation. Whatever is encountered is encountered in a situation. Whatever is to be undertaken, is undertaken from the starting point of one situation and with other future situations in mind. Clearly, the situation forms the essential ground of our lives and experience, of the way we behave toward one another, gain clarity about our selves, etc. The situation is thus even more primordial than the world, because we only ever experience the world in situations (Rombach, 1987, p. 138).

Thus, on a phenomenological level situations are "the basic objects of our experience of life" (Schmitz, 2002, p. 17) and wholes that are of fundamental significance. I might add that "wholeness" is not the same as "lacking in differentiation." Each particular situation contains various aspects or elements that can be differentiated from each other. The first, and perhaps most important, element is the person who happens to find himself in a situation and experiences and shapes it in his own way. The second point is that, especially when it is brought about deliberately, a situation will have what might be called a "theme." This "theme" is what the situation is about, which will also be one factor influencing how the person or persons behave in the situation. "These situational themes may be doing a job, solving a problem or completing a task, or they can also be purely social, such as conversation" (Dreitzel, 1980, p. 75). The third aspect is the *relatively* discrete nature of the situation in relation to its wider context in time and space, which makes it possible to distinguish it fairly clearly from other situations. And the fourth dimension is that a situation has a "horizon," i.e. a context, that on the one hand lies outside its immediate domain but on the other also has an influence on it.[182]

In the psychotherapeutic situation, each of these four dimensions assumes a specific concrete form. Taken together, these concrete forms characterize the *therapeutic* situation as opposed to other social situations: (1) The subjects of the psychotherapeutic situation, "client" and "therapist," sometimes called "patient" and "analyst," act (2) within the framework of an asymmetrical division of roles which is intended to solve one person's problems and give the other the task of creating conditions which are favorable for doing so. (3) For this, a certain place, e.g., a psychotherapy practice or a clinic, is fixed, and a time frame is laid down (e.g., weekly appointments or a course of hospital treatment lasting several weeks) that seems appropriate for the problematic issues to be addressed. Despite the fact that the therapeutic situation takes place in relative seclusion, so as to allow the work to proceed without being disturbed, to protect the client's confidentiality and to promote the intimacy of the therapeutic relationship, it is not completely isolated from (4) the social context in which it is rooted, because

> there are no situations that are exclusively self-sufficient and thus, so
> to speak, are outside the world. The phenomenological characteristic of

---

182 This fourth element will be explained in more detail below in terms of "situational circles."

worldliness of a situation precisely consists of these references to the "co-included" horizons—horizons that fit the situation in question such that this fittingness itself derives its sense from the references involved" (Gurwitsch, 1979, p. 96).[183]

The "co-included horizons" or respective contexts vary widely and surround the therapeutic situation, relatively directly in both spatial and temporal terms. Rombach (1987, p. 153) describes a context as being "close" or "distant." A close context, for example, has a direct influence on the behavior of the therapist, who has to comply with numerous professional, legal and ethical obligations, and also on the client, who may possibly want to keep the fact that she is in therapy from her partner. The most distant context is the fact that we are "members of the human race; this situation, however, lies pale and imperceptible at the extreme margin of the space of our Dasein" (Rombach, 1987, p. 153). Between closeness and distance are countless levels of context, extending outwards like concentric circles, exerting an influence on the current situation. Their influence may be direct to a greater or lesser degree, depending on how relatively close or distant they are. These "situational circles" always extend to include "*historical* events and eras too and, through them, also the life cycles of *nature* and the *world itself*. . . . Thus the phenomenology of the *situation* expands to become a phenomenology of *history, nature and religion*" (Rombach, 1987, p. 428—original italics).[184]

Both on a general, theoretical level and also in individual concrete situations, it is impossible to catalogue all the situational circles that may be relevant (and I should point out that in Figure 11 the four circles are intended simply to represent the many possible ones—see next page). We cannot distinguish them clearly from one another or capture

---

183 "When, in fact, a case of human being-together is made self-sufficient, then those together withdraw from the world in order to orient themselves toward each other as individuals. They surrender the relations to the surrounding world because their being-together finds its meaning in itself. Precisely on that account it no longer fits into situations of the surrounding world. But just here we find a clue to the *originary* relation to the surrounding world from which one can withdraw when one is together with someone else *exclusively for his own sake*. In other words: because self-sufficient being-together is characterized by having-been-absolved-from-the-surrounding-world, it refers to an originary being-fitted-into-the-surrounding world" (Gurwitsch, 1979, p. 37—original italics).
184 When I consider the theme of spirituality in the next chapter, I will return to "situational circles," since "nature" and "religion" are important among these.

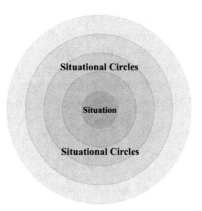

FIGURE 11
Situation and situational circles

how each one may possibly affect the situation,[185] and I shall therefore not even attempt to begin to do so. As long as we are speaking in general terms, we can also only make relatively vague statements about which situational circles have an effect on particular situations and how great that effect might be. This is because their relative proximity does not remain constant but is itself always influenced by what is relevant or important within the situation itself. We can therefore only be more definite about how a *concrete* situation is related to particular situation circles if we subject their reciprocal influences to a rigorous hermeneutic analysis.[186] A further concept, Gurwitsch's (2010) concept of the "field of consciousness," may also prove useful in conducting such an analysis.

A field of consciousness can be defined "as the totality of copresent data. Copresence is understood in a broad sense so as to comprise not

---

185 In my remarks on hermeneutics in the introduction, citing Habermas (1988a, p. 92) and Berlin I indicated that their effect "enters too intimately into our most normal experience, and is a kind of automatic integration of a very large number of data too fugitive and various to be mounted on the pin of some scientific process, one by one, in a sense too obvious, too much taken for granted, to be enumerable" (Berlin, 1996, p. 24).

186 If this statement appears to be rather circular it is because this is in fact an example of a hermeneutic circle: "Any interpretation which is to contribute understanding, must already have understood what is to be interpreted. . . . *But if we see this circle as a vicious one and look out for ways of avoiding it . . ., then the act of understanding has been misunderstood from the ground up.* . . . What is decisive is not to get out of the circle but to come into it in the right way" (Heidegger, 1962, pp. 194f. — original italics).

only data which are experienced as simultaneous but also those which are simultaneously experienced, though not as simultaneous" (Gurwitsch, 2010, p. 2).[187] In order to understand the relationship between situations and their different situational circles, we must also consider the fact "that every total field of consciousness consists of three domains" (Gurwitsch, 2010, p. 4), the "theme," the "thematic field" and the "margin."

BOX 61

THE DOMAINS OF THE FIELD OF CONSCIOUSNESS

The first domain is the theme, that which engrosses the mind of the experiencing subject, or as it is often expressed, which stands in the "focus of his attention." Second is the thematic field, defined as the totality of those data, copresent with the theme, which are experienced as materially relevant or pertinent to the theme and form the background or horizon out of which the theme emerges as the center. The third includes data which, though copresent with, have no relevancy to, the theme and comprise in their totality what we propose to call the margin (Gurwitsch, 2010, p. 4—original italics).

As a rule of thumb, we can say that it is possible to grasp the relationship of a situation to the situational circles surrounding it by looking at the relationship between the theme of the situation and its thematic field or its margin. The situational circles that have a closer thematic connection to the given situation because they belong to its thematic field will have more influence on it than will the circles that are more closely connected to its thematic margin and thus, thematically, are distant from it. Conversely (and in hermeneutic terms in a circular way), the theme of a situation "activates" its thematic field and pushes other situational circles to the margin.

Gurwitsch's concepts make it absolutely clear that even when (and precisely when) it is the role of empathy in psychotherapy that we are considering, we must remember that the participants are not in an isolated space even though the closed doors of the therapy room and the

---

187 This is not unlike Lewin's "principle of contemporaneity": "It is important to realize that the psychological past and the psychological future are simultaneous parts of the psychological field existing at a given time t. The time perspective is continually changing. According to field theory, any type of behavior depends upon the total field, including the time perspective at that time, but not, in addition, upon any past or future field and its time perspectives" (1951, p. 54).

rules of confidentiality might sometimes make this appear to be so. The people who encounter each other in the psychotherapeutic situation have their own "backgrounds" or "horizons" that they bring with them into the joint situation. These might be a person's "customs, beliefs, and opinions held in 'his' country, time, and social environment" (Gurwitsch, 2010, p. 313). The way human beings understand each other is never determined by the effect they have on each other as individuals alone. There are very many factors transcending individuals which contribute to how people understand each other—these might be their social status (see, for example, Billies, 2005), the prevailing "spirit of the time" (Dilthey, 2002), their history (see, for example, Gadamer, 1989) and last, but not least, the language in which they communicate, etc. etc. *"The objective context in terms of which alone social actions can be understood is constituted conjointly by language, labor, and domination"* (Habermas, 1988, p. 174—original italics).

For those concerned, however, all of these factors usually remain in the background and often only come to the fore, as far as is possible for them to do so, when they become problematical. Mostly, the horizon that is consciously in the foreground usually only includes the joint situation that is currently taking place and the thematic field that has direct relevance for the issue that is being addressed. Yet the joint situation is governed by certain rules that emerge from the background, some of which have universal validity and are thus also valid to a greater or lesser degree in any psychotherapeutic situation. Other rather more 'informal' rules are established by the participants in the course of their dialog in a way that is often more implicit than explicit, and these are valid only for that specific situation. Taken together, however, all these sets of rules provide a framework which makes it easier for the participants to understand the other person's statements and behaviors. Without this framework they would be much harder to understand.

> In common situations the partner listens deliberately. While each plays his role, he divines the purposes and tendencies of the other even when the other does not declare them—as is clear from the example of the chessplayer. . . . While I am conversing with my partner, he shakes his head or wrinkles his brow. Shaking the head and wrinkling the brow are not in themselves unambiguous gestures, but they can mean many things. One cannot simply infer what a gesture signifies in a concrete case; it is not "inscribed" as this determinate gesture. . . . Rather it is the case that we understand them by virtue of the whole of the common situation (Gurwitsch, 1979, p. 113).

This kind of understanding also takes place on a simple level in everyday situations. To give an example, here Gurwitsch analyzes two workers who are cobbling a street.

BOX 62

EXAMPLE

In cobbling a street, for instance, one worker lays the stones while the other knocks them into place. . . . Each stands in a situation which is their work-situation and each orients himself to the references in that situation. But because both workers are busied with one and the same job, they stand in a common situation. . . . They work, mutually helping each other; each is related to the other in his dealings and his work. *This relation makes up the meaning of fellow workers.* Precisely because the one is entirely absorbed in the whole work and gears into it, he encounters the other as fellow worker and, more particularly, he encounters him with respect to the function that he possesses in the common, concrete work-situation. . . . But that signifies: the other also belongs to the situation in which I stand; his presence also contributes to the constituting of the situation and to making it what it is *in concreto.* . . . Thus my fellow worker is an integrating and meaningful situational moment (Gurwitsch, 1979, p. 104—original italics).

We can see from this example how participating jointly in a particular situation has an influence on these two people and brings about an understanding between them. This includes, in particular, their commitment to a *task* that makes clearly defined demands on them and which puts the actions they perform to fulfill this task in a meaningful context. This context, which is known to the participants beforehand because they have reached an 'understanding' about it, a context within which they act and behave, offers an overarching frame of reference that helps them to understand each other more easily. One might also say that they *allow themselves to surrender to* the task and the situation that has been structured by it, and that they therefore allow themselves to be *determined* by the common situation and its "affordances" (Lewin), i.e., the way it invites or demands a response. We assume a role and "the situation prescribes a *role* to us which we take over as long as we are in the situation in question" (Gurwitsch, 1979, pp. 107f.—original italics).

The roles are those aspects of the shared situation that are played out by the participating individuals. As the concept of roles is used in very different ways and has very different meanings, I would like at this point to make a few remarks about what the word 'role' means. In some schools of humanistic psychology, in particular, this term has connotations that are directly opposed to the way in which Gurwitsch understands it. And when we are considering the joint situation it is Gurwitsch upon whom I base my views.

In contrast, one representative of humanistic psychology describes roles as follows:

> We behave *as if* we are big shots, *as if* we are nincompoops, *as if* we are pupils, *as if* we are ladies, *as if* we are bitches, etc. It is always the 'as if' attitudes that require that we live up to a concept (Perls, 1970, p. 20 — original italics).

Roles here are clichés, rigid behavior patterns that are practiced in a stereotypical way (living "up to a concept") more or less *irrespective* of the given situation. They serve to create and preserve the *appearance* ("as if") of a permanent identity that remains untouched by the demands of what is currently happening. At the same time, these roles are non-authentic—they are, in a negative sense, "played" and "a sham." Because of that they are a barrier to "good contact" between the person and the other. They therefore need to be overcome so that the person can become "authentic" and live his or her "true self."

For Gurwitsch, it is quite different. For him, the role is the behavior that relates in a concrete way to the given situation and which is, to use his words, "prescribed" by that situation. The more someone fulfills this role, the more he gives up what he previously identified with and becomes caught up in the demands of the current situation, so that he *"gears into the present situation and has his concrete being only as the role he represents in the situation"* (Gurwitsch, 1979, p. 116—original italics). Assuming this role and "playing" it, in a positive sense, means becoming totally involved in the contact with the other in the here and now, since

> we always and necessarily have our role in view of the role of the partner. In that fact are grounded the relation and reference to the partner which . . . we developed as the characteristic of being together in a common situation. *The partners encounter each other in their partnership-situations in these roles constituted by the relationship to one another; they encounter each as the ones who are what they are in the particular common situations* (Gurwitsch, 1979, p. 108—original italics).

In contrast to a situation in general, in a specific *common* situation the participants do more than simply apply themselves to a common issue or task; because of their roles as *persons* they also relate to each other in an intensive way. Compared to the situation of laying cobbles (see Box 62), in psychotherapy, of course, this happens to a much greater extent and is much more likely to be quite explicit. This is in line with the way I have defined "personal contact": "Personal . . . contact is . . . the process of two people becoming aware of each other, their imagining the real[188] on the basis of that and also conveying to each other what they are aware and conscious of, and responding to this" (Staemmler, 1993a, p. 189).[189]

This personal contact, or this "human encounter" (Gurwitsch), acquires its own peculiar distinctiveness through the respective characteristics of the common situation, and this also dictates the participants' individual roles. "Personal contact" and "role" are not mutually exclusive (which is different from Perls' view). Thus

> the other is rather encountered by me as partner in just the concrete sense of partnership in which he is my partner *hic et nunc*. . . . He appears to me as one motivated by the situation which prescribes a role and function to him. Only in this role of his do I have something to do with him. In this situation, his being is exhausted in the role whose bearer he is (Gurwitsch, 1979, p. 108).

Although being *in* a common situation and *in* a role means that you are determined by them it does not mean that you are imprisoned in them, because if you can be "in" a common situation, that also implies that you can get "out" of it, *"as one who is still something outside the situation"* (Gurwitsch, 1979, p. 116—original italics). This

> signifies that the partner, to be sure, gears into the situational encounter, but that he also only has his role just *hic et nunc*. It is, therefore, already indicated that he does not simply exist in this role: a realm of his existence outside the situation as well as outside the role is reported (Gurwitsch, 1979, p. 115).

Therefore, it is not possible to make generalizations about what one can understand about one's partner in a joint situation. My client is in the joint therapeutic situation with me in the role of client and I am with her in the role of therapist. Both of us are different when we assume different roles with different people in different situations, since we are then influenced by the fact that the distinctive features of the situation and the situational circles surrounding it are different. As far as the influences on the joint situation are concerned, what the other person will be like in a joint situation with someone else remains a mystery, and not only to me but, if

---

188 "Imagining the real" is a term coined by Martin Buber which means "a bold swinging—demanding the most intensive stirring of one's being—into the life of the other. This is the nature of all genuine imaging, only that here the realm of my action is not the all-possible, but the particular real person who confronts me, whom I can attempt to make present to myself" (1999, p. 81).
189 On the distinction between awareness and consciousness see Staemmler and Bock (1998, pp. 47ff.).

she has not experienced that other person in joint situations before, it will also remain a mystery to her.

4.3.2 Characteristics of the Joint Situation: Play and Dance

Hans-Georg Gadamer uses the metaphor of *dance* or *play* to elucidate the nature and dynamics of a joint situation. He notes that "every game presents the man who plays it with a task" (1989, p. 107), and points out "that play is not to be understood as something a person does . . . The actual subject of play is obviously not the subjectivity of an individual who, among other activities, also plays but is instead the play itself" (Gadamer, 1989, p. 104). He continues:

> All playing is a being-played. The attraction of a game, the fascination it exerts, consists precisely in the fact that the game masters the players. . . . The real subject of the game . . . is not the player but instead the game itself (Gadamer, 1989, p. 106).

This is true, in particular, of an activity for two—such as two people dancing together—which also involves the dynamics of physical movement and in which the dancers adjust to and cooperate with each other. "As you dance, your motions (if you are a good dancer!) are both continuously influenced by and [have] an influence upon, those of your partner: the two sets of motions 'coevolve' in a highly interdetermined way" (Clark, 1998, p. 42). A common *flow* develops (Csikszentmihalyi, 1997), which can inspire the participants in a special way and enable them to achieve a sporting or creative performance that they would never have been capable of on their own.

BOX 63

THE "CREATIVE FIELD" Burow (1999) used the term "creative field" to describe a similar type of situation which clearly has some features in common with the therapeutic situation. Burow identifies its components as follows:

> Creative fields are characterized by a dialogic relational structure (dialogue), by a shared interest . . . by a multiplicity of different ability profiles . . . , by a concentration on the development of shared creativity (process of synergy) . . . , by participating on an equal basis . . ., and also by a social context . . . that encourages creativity (sustainability) (1999, pp. 123f.—original italics; see also Spagnuolo Lobb & Amendt-Lyon, 2003; Zinker, 1977).

A "creative field," a dance or "play clearly represents an order in which the to-and-fro motion of play follows of *itself*" (Gadamer, 1989, p. 104—italics added). Thus, Gadamer is also referring to the "medial sense" of play (Gadamer, 1989, p. 103), and we can assume that, with his knowledge of

Ancient Greek, he was deliberately alluding to the grammatical Medium, i.e., that "middle" mode in between the Active (to play) and the Passive (to be played), about which he said: "Absorption into the game is an ecstatic self-forgetting that is experienced not as a *loss* of self-possession, but as the free buoyancy of an elevation above oneself" (1977, p. 55).[190]

If he wants to play *well*, when a tennis player[191] is moving toward the ball that his opponent has hit, he has to allow his own movements to be led by the movement of the ball. If he does not want to be accused of cheating he also has to keep to the rules of the game.

> He conforms to the game or subjects himself to it, that is, he relinquishes the autonomy of his own will. . . . The individual self, including his activity and his understanding of himself, is taken up into a higher de-termination that is the really decisive factor (Gadamer, 1977, pp. 53f.).

From this, Gadamer concludes "that play does not have its being in the player's consciousness or attitude, but on the contrary play draws him into its dominion and fills him with its spirit" (1989, p. 109).

BOX 64

PLAY AND SOCIAL COGNITION There are more parallels between empathy and play that Gadamer had presumably not thought of, such as this, for instance: "Play and empathy both powerfully cement social bonds between affective crea-tures" (Watt, 2005, p. 205).

The renowned neuroscientist Jaak Panksepp states:

> I personally believe the play-urge is one of the most important forces that Mother Nature provided for the construction of a pro-social neocortex. And only if we parents guide this construction well, can we expect to have children that can mirror those deeply empathic responses we may need to construct better worlds. . . . The higher social brain is not encoded in our genes, but arises from our intersubjective, societal and cultural interac-tions (in Gallagher, 2008, p. 116).

Mead, too, uses the example of the game to illustrate the connection between the dynamics of the joint situation, the distribution of roles and the taking of other people's perspectives:

---

190 In section 4.2.2, I discussed the term "middle mode" which is described by Perls et al as follows: "Self is spontaneous, middle in mode . . ., and engaged with its situation . . . . as in animated dancing" (1951, pp. 376f.—see also Bocian, 2010, pp. 42f.). "One *is* engaged and carried along, not in spite of oneself, but beyond oneself" (Perls et al., 1951, p. 382—original italics). "That is, the self, aware in middle mode, bursts the compartmenting of mind, body, and external world" (Perls et al., 1951, p. 389).
191 I have chosen this example because Gadamer himself was a passionate tennis player all his life (see Staemmler, 2002c).

> In a game where a number of individuals are involved, then the child taking one role must be ready to take the role of everyone else. If he gets in a ball nine he must have the responses of each position involved in his own position. He must know what everyone else is going to do in order to carry out his own play. He has to take all of these roles. They do not all have to be present in consciousness at the same time, but at some moments he has to have three or four individuals present in his own attitude, such as the one who is going to throw the ball, the one who is going to catch it, and so on. These responses must be, in some degree, present in his own make-up. In the game then, there is a set of responses of such others so organized that the attitude of one calls out the appropriate attitudes of the other (Mead, 1934/1963, p. 151).

> For Schiller, there was an essential connection between play and being a human being: "Man only plays when he is in the fullest sense of the word a human being, and he is only fully a human being when he plays" (1967, p. 107).

These "intersubjective interactions" in joint situations (the term used by Panksepp in discussion with Gallagher) are the necessary conditions for the development of human subjectivity, and here the game can be said to be a prototypical situation, since "the player experiences the game as a reality that surpasses him" (Gadamer, 1989, p. 109). However, his role allows him to participate directly in this reality that surpasses him; he is himself an integral part of it. The game is "a dynamic whole *sui generis* that embraces even the subjectivity of the one who plays" (Gadamer, 1977, p. 53). Although it "can be helpful" to try to understand human beings by explaining them in terms of their individual psychology, without considering the joint situation in which one finds oneself with them, "this is at the same time the product of reductionist thinking, which gets in the way of being open to the autonomy of the particular joint situation—the situation itself can contribute rules of play and problems with dealing with them" (Schmitz, 1993, p. 78).

When the tennis player hits the ball, it is this joint situation involving both him and his opponent that makes it *immediately* obvious to him— instantaneously and without him needing to think about it—why his opponent reacts in the way he does and responds in a particular way to the ball coming toward him: *"The knowledge immanent to the Being in the common situations understands the partner in his particular role with respect to the concrete situation"* (Gurwitsch, 1979, p. 112—original italics). It is clear that assumptions about or knowledge of the different factors motivating the opponent before the game begins are useful when it comes to understanding his behavior. However, what they really do is make it clear what is making him play *in the first place*. What makes him move in a certain way at any given moment can be understood far more as resulting from the totality of the immediate joint situation and the demands it makes on him at this moment: "Empathy . . . is emotional knowledge gained by *participation in a shared reality*" (Orange 1995, p. 21—italics added).

The more the players become involved and caught up in their joint situation, the more their behavior is determined by what happens 'between' them: "Something that obeys its own set of laws gains ascendency in the game" (Gadamer, 1977, p. 53). In this way, the slightest movement one of them makes can be empathized with by the other—and this happens primarily *not* because he is putting himself in her shoes as an *individual* but because she is moved, just as he is, by the joint situation. She feels this movement in her own body and also experiences the other person's movement by means of encorporation. The same applies to the other person and thus mutual encorporation comes about because of the task set by the joint situation and the dynamic that results.[192] "The game is not so much the subjective attitude of the two men confronting each other as it is the formation of the movement as such, which, as in an unconscious teleology, subordinates the attitude of the individuals to itself" (Gadamer, 1977, p. 54). In this way we find

> a joint situation that cannot simply be divided up into the inputs of the individual players, each of whom contributes his own personality and perspective. We can see this in the fact that often a person almost becomes someone else, depending on what the joint situation is that he happens to be in, because, by becoming part of a larger whole, his personal situation becomes a dependent variable in which self-determination and determination by others fluctuate (Schmitz, 2002, p. 27).[193]

The aspect of empathy that I would like to describe using the metaphor of the game and the concept of the joint situation and the roles inherent within it goes beyond the mutual, bodily social referencing described in previous chapters. Here, empathizing and encorporation, sharing and referencing no longer take place simply with reference to the other *person*. Instead, they relate to the *whole therapeutic situation*, of which both persons are part and which at the same time transcends them. Here, it is no longer a question of the mystery of the other person, i.e., what it is like to be

---

192 In section 4.2.2, I quoted Schmitz's observation "that in an encounter one's own lived body, that one feels as such, . . . merges into a larger whole which forms spontaneously as a larger lived body encompassing it" (1989, p. 109).

193 Arisaka informs us that, "unlike English, in which 'I' has a fixed referent (the speaker), the Japanese 'I' points not to the person *per se* but rather indicates a social position in the context of a given situation. . . . It is linguistically transparent that the self is always a self-in-a-situation and a self-with-another in speaking Japanese" (2001, p. 199). Consequently, there are many different words for "I," depending on the situation.

inside her skin, but much more what it is like to be with her "inside the skin of the relationship" (O'Hara, 1997, p. 306) and the joint situation, and to be moved by it as by a "reality that transcends" them.[194] Bozarth (1984) refers to this as "emergent empathy," i.e., empathy on the level of *a more complex* whole (as opposed to the level of interacting individuals), or in other words: the joint situation.[195]

BOX 65

EXAMPLE My client[196] complains about how often she observes, judges, and assesses herself. She finds it hard to let go, relax, and simply 'be.' Instead she permanently pushes herself to do just one more thing. And so she always feels distanced from herself and at the same time helpless and driven. I ask her if she is aware of whether it does her good to assume this observing and driving perspective toward herself. She thinks that perhaps when she is alone with herself she can't stand relaxing and "wasting her time." That seems to me to be a way of identifying with an ethos of achievement, which she says is true. She finds it impossible to simply enjoy her life. And yet she would so love to really relax and feel love and joy.

She remembers her mother, with whom she had a "loving relationship." Shortly before her mother died she had asked her to give her one more hug. But her mother was dismissive and brushed her off brusquely, which came as a real blow to my client. However, she says she still loved her mother and feels that she is still caught up in an endless grieving process. She greatly regrets the fact that she only saw her mother in a negative light at the end. And she says that she is the same toward herself, too: "I can't show my love either."

Following a hunch, and I have no idea myself where it came from, I suggest that she expresses what she is currently feeling by humming something. To begin with, she doesn't find that easy. I describe to her the impression I have of her longing for something carefree, peaceful, and tender and ask her once again if she can think of something to hum to convey this feeling. She suddenly remembers a children's song and tentatively and softly, with tears in her eyes, she sings:

---

194 In certain psychotherapeutic circles, it has become the custom to speak here of a "field" or of a "knowing field." However, I find this terminology rather clumsy and the concepts that lie behind it rather woolly.

195 In my view, there is an overlap here with Lorenzer's concept of "scenic understanding" which he says is centered "in the 'understanding' of the situation . . . [It] addresses . . . the *interaction of the subjects with their social world and environment* . . . It grasps what is happening in the subject only in terms of the subject's actualization in his relationship to the social world and environment. It grasps these happenings only in the way the subject actualizes himself in his relational field" (1970, p. 107f.—italics added).

196 I am grateful to the client for allowing me to publish this.

"I'm happy, so happy
About this day,
I'm happy, so happy
About all I love.
See how the flowers bloom,
See the grass shining green.
See the ball rising to the sky,
Round and beautiful.
I'm happy, so happy
About this day.
I'm happy, so happy
About all I love.
Hear how the bird is singing
And bringing us joy,
The wind is rustling through the leaves on the trees
Quick—sing a song."

After the song has died away I ask my client how she felt while she was singing. In tears she replies, "carefree and childlike." And then she adds how much she would like to have these feelings again. I tell her that she has obviously just experienced these feelings as she was singing. She becomes aware of how, as soon as she has finished singing her song, she has assumed the position of observer again. It is as though she is hearing a voice just behind her head talking her out of the feeling that she longs for, spoiling it for her.

I invite my client to let us hear this voice out loud. This is much easier for her than the singing she did earlier and she says, as though her voice is coming at her from behind: "Who do you think you are? Be quiet! Keep a low profile!" Although these sentences come out quite spontaneously they seem very familiar, as though they have been said a thousand times, and her voice sounds really monotonous. I reflect this back to her. She confirms my impressions, adding that she is reluctant to allow this voice to be more expressive because she is afraid of how destructive it is—destructive not only toward herself but possibly also toward others.

She remembers how once she took part in a seminar and was asked to identify with a "powerful animal," a panther, and to imagine prowling around in the wild. She had felt wonderful acting out this fantasy and felt "on top of the world." But then the seminar leader had told her to approach a village of humans and to be aware of how this made her feel. Then a very unpleasant feeling had come over her and she had imagined all the people screaming and running away in fear when they saw her (the panther). Because she was horrified at this reaction she herself (the panther) had fled up a tree, "and there I still am."

Now I ask her to stop identifying with this destructive voice (or the panther) and to return to what she was feeling before, when she was singing the children's song.

When I sense that she has found her way back to this experience I suggest that she imagine herself going to the tree with the panther up it and singing the song to him.

At the thought of this she really begins to cry. She gets up from her chair and says she has to get up and go and stand under the tree. Amidst her tears she says that she has just sensed a connection with the "cat" in the tree and wants to stroke it. She has the impression that she just has to wait patiently and at some point the cat will come down from the tree.

I ask her if she would like to sing the song to it. But my client says she has not yet quite got the courage "to allow herself to experience joy." And yet she does then cautiously start to sing the song again: "I'm happy, so happy/About this day. I'm happy, so happy/About all that I love. . . ." When she has finished, I ask her what it was like for her to sing the song to the cat in the tree. She replies that the cat listened and occasionally spat a bit. I ask whether it is this spitting that is making her sing so hesitantly and is preventing her from letting her voice ring out freely and clearly.

She says that is not the case, and she herself suggests seeing what it is like to allow her voice to come out freely and sings the song in a carefree, happy and tender way. Now her voice really does seem to sound freer and freer: "I'm happy, so happy/About this day. I'm happy, so happy/About all that I love . . ." She sings for a while, her body becomes more animated and she is clearly enjoying herself more and more.

All at once, she suddenly stops and looks thunderstruck. I ask what has just been going on inside her. She has suddenly remembered another children's song, a Polish one (she spent the first seven years of her life in Poland and then emigrated with her parents). Her mother used to sing it to her and she has not thought about it in years. With great feeling she now sings this Polish song:

"A cat sits on a fence,
with a twinkle in its eye and sings a song,
that's not too short and not too long.
Dear cat, do sing it again."

While she sings, she seems deeply moved. The tears pouring down her face as she sings are now clearly tears of joy. I, too, am moved and have tears in my eyes. Her movements become more and more like a dance—at once strong and graceful. As her emotions slowly ebb away I ask her about what she has experienced. She says the cat "jumped into me, right into my heart. We can't be separated any more." Then she starts to sing again, this time more rhythmically and with no obvious inhibitions. Finally, she says that what she just experienced was "like a miracle."

Clearly, my suggestion that this client should express what she was currently feeling by humming was the key that fit beautifully into the lock of the background of her experience. But if I am honest, I cannot claim that this suggestion was *"my"* idea—it *emerged* from the joint situation. It did not result from my *individual* empathic ability, nor from some theoretical consideration, but rather it took me by surprise myself when it occurred to me because I had no previous knowledge about my client to suggest that music in general or children's songs in particular were somehow significant. The suggestion arose out of our interactions in the joint situation. Certain situational circles that neither of us was consciously aware of crept into our contact and found expression in this suggestion. Evidently, the situational circle of musicality was one of these. It formed a thematic field that had an effect on the subject matter of our joint work and my suggestion.

Consequently, on *this* level what we empathize with is first and foremost *not* the other person, but primarily the joint situation, which certainly includes the other person (as well as the self) but also possesses further qualities that transcend those of the participating individuals (situational circles). And inasmuch as the empathizing on *this* level secondarily also refers to the concrete other, this means that

> the core of another person is neither accessible to this understanding, nor does it disclose such things as the characteristic traits of fellow human beings. . . . Understanding, therefore, concerns the way in which the other plays the role assigned to him by the situation (Gurwitsch, 1979, p. 112).

Gurwitsch concludes that the fellow human being is grasped by this understanding only insofar as he or she is a component of the situation. The empathizing that takes place here occurs as a result of our *allowing ourselves to be become involved in* the joint situation and the resulting assignment of roles, which also means that we each take the "complementary" role to that of the other. We develop a sense of the other person because each of us has allowed ourselves to become involved in the joint situation together and because the other person, just as we have ourselves, has become *part* of this joint situation in which she also plays her role. The shared whole, the *"we"* that embraces both of us, linking us together, permits its parts (the two participants in their respective roles) to experience something of what it is like to be a different part (the other person in her role) in the same whole. On this level, the other person loses some of his mystery to the extent that we play our roles *together* or rather "are played" by the shared game.

Gurwitsch's description shows how the persons participating are influenced by the *whole* of the joint situation and thus are only visible to each other as the persons they are *under the conditions of this particular situation:*

> What exclusively comes into view here is the partner in the sense of partnership in which we have to deal with him in every case. . . . What he might otherwise be, in which sectors he might otherwise exist, in which sense he exists in them—all of this is inaccessible to this understanding immanent in being-together. When I ask someone for something, I then experience the way in which the person asked listens to me, enters into the request, offers resistance, avoids the request, sets conditions, gives in, etc.; I do not experience something like an alien and autonomous will simpliciter. Rather a human being encounters me who comports himself in a certain way in the situation in question (Gurwitsch, 1979, p. 112f.).

Here one might say that empathy with the other person is "a byproduct of participation within the common system. In this sense, it is not the individual who preexists the relationship and initiates the process of communication, but the conventions of relationship that enable understanding to be achieved" (Gergen, 1994, p. 263).[197] Therefore, it is clear that participating in a joint situation has distinct effects on the participants. These effects are a result of its *overarching* dimension. They are not simply to be seen as consequences of reciprocal interaction *between* the participants, such as you would find in questions and answers. The whole of the joint situation is more than and different from the sum of its parts.

BOX 66

THE "JOINT SITUATION" AND THE "BETWEEN" Martin Buber and also several other philosophers and psychologists do not refer to the "joint situation" but to the "between." According to Buber:

> It is basically erroneous to try to understand the interhuman phenomena as psychological. When two men converse together, the psychological is certainly an important part of the situation, as each listens and each prepares to speak. Yet this is only the hidden accompaniment to the conversation itself, the phonetic event fraught with meaning, whose meaning is to be found neither in one of the two partners nor in both together, but only in their dialogue itself, in this between which they live together (Buber, 1999, p. 75).

---

197 The word "byproduct" refers to the lower position within the *system* and certainly does not imply that anything one discovers about the other in this way is of less value.

From this quotation it is evident that Buber understands the "conversation" and its "meaning," i.e, the joint situation, to be the larger whole and the individual mental processes to be parts of this whole. And so when he talks of the "between" it seems to me that what he is describing is the same as the "joint situation." However, I prefer to use the concept of the "joint situation" as it denotes more clearly the overarching dimension. The term "between," on the other hand, suggests that it refers to a third entity that is located on the same plane as one or the other person. The qualitative difference between the whole and its parts is thus not captured by this term.

If we assume that participating in a joint situation always affects the individual participants psychologically, then

> it becomes possible to understand empathy as a *state of consciousness*. It is a way of perceiving and knowing a way of being connected to other consciousnesses by which individual human beings gain access to the inner worlds of other individuals and to the workings of relationships (O'Hara, 1997, pp. 303f.—italics added).

4.3.3 Dyadically Expanded States of Consciousness, Connectedness, and Joint Constructions

In order to clarify what I mean by "dyadically expanded states of consciousness" let me start by reminding you of the visual cliff experiment (see Figure 3 in Chapter 4.1) that led to the concept of social referencing. This concept denotes the mutual communication and cognitive and affective regulation that takes place between the mother and her child and also the ability of both to recognize the significance of the emotional expressions of the respective other and to support the actions of the other so that they both achieve their goals. Using the language of systems theory, Edward Tronick, an infant researcher and member of the *Boston Change Process Study Group* established by Daniel Stern, and colleagues, describes social referencing as follows:

> The internal and external mechanisms [of one of the participants] form a single system made up of two component systems (i. e., infant and mother)—a dyadic system. Moreover, these regulatory processes involve communication among different components of this dyadic system (Tronick, 1998, p. 293).

The mental state of the respective other person expands each participant's individual horizon. "Thus, this dyadic system contains more information, is more complex and coherent than either the infant's (or the mother's) endogenous state of consciousness alone" (Tronick, 1998, p. 296). Tronick calls this "dyadically expanded states of consciousness" and writes:

> Each individual is a self-organizing system that creates its own states of consciousness—states of brain organization—which can be expanded into more coherent and complex states in collaboration with another self-organizing system. When the collaboration of two brains is successful each fulfills the system principle of increasing their coherence and complexity. The states of consciousness of the infant and of the mother are more inclusive and coherent at the moment when they form a dyadic state . . . because it incorporates elements of the state of consciousness of the other. . . . *At the moment when the dyadic system is created both partners experience an expansion of their own state of consciousness* (Tronick, 1998—italics added).

The "dyadic system," or the joint situation, in which the participants operate, can be seen as a level of complexity that transcends the individuals (Wertheimer's "we"), "where the part-processes are themselves determined by the intrinsic nature of the whole" (Wertheimer, 1925/1938, p. 2). This more complex level has (*top-down*) repercussions on the individuals and their respective states of consciousness. These states of consciousness are influenced by the quality of the dyad, which transcends the individual and adds a dimension that would remain inaccessible to the participants on their own if they were not in the joint situation (see the example in Box 65).

So this is "a lived experience, which involves an intersubjective resonance that is irreducible to the consciousness of either participant taken alone" (Neimeyer, 2005, p. 81). Modern developmental psychology considers that such phenomena have particular significance, not just for emotional and cognitive learning but also for growth processes in the brain (see Trevarthen, 2001, p. 98). I agree with Tronick, however, when he says that it is not just between mothers and their babies that such processes can be observed, but "that the therapist and the patient can also achieve these dyadic states" (1998, p. 298). Stern's "moments of meeting," quoted above, give a clear illustration of this.

BOX 67

EXAMPLE

Take, for example, the patient who suddenly sat up to look at her therapist. Right after the patient sat up, the two found themselves looking at each other intently. A silence prevailed. The therapist, without knowing exactly what she was going to do, softened her face slowly and let the suggestion of a smile form around her mouth. She then leaned her head toward slightly and said, "Hello." The patient continued to look at her. They remained locked in a mutual gaze for several seconds. After a moment, the patient laid down again and continued her work on the couch, but more profoundly and in a new key, which opened up new material. The change was dramatic in their therapeutic work together.

The "hello" (with facial expression and head movement) was a "moment of meeting," when the therapist made an authentic personal response beautifully adjusted to the situation immediately at hand (the now moment). It altered the therapy markedly. It was a nodal point when a quantal change in the intersubjective field was achieved. In dynamic systems theory it represents an irreversible shift into a new state.

After a successful moment of meeting, the therapy resumes its process of moving along, but does so in a newly expanded intersubjective field that allows for different possibilities (Stern, 2004, pp. 168f.).

The fact that, after the moment of meeting, Stern's patient was able to continue her therapeutic process "in a new key" leads us to assume that she was able to "take something away with her" from the joint situation intensified in this moment, something that was of use to her later on. Tronick interprets this as resulting from the greater complexity and coherence experienced during the dyadically expanded state of consciousness, which—even after the 'moment of meeting' is over—can then be sustained to a considerable extent by the patient herself. "This increase in the self-organizing capacity of the individual by its participation in a dyadic regulatory system is not unlike Vygotsky's . . . concept of the zone of proximal development" (Tronick, 2007, p. 383), which I shall examine in the final chapter.

The moments of meeting in which the joint situation is intensified will typically have an "I-Thou" quality (as in Buber). They are distinguished not only by the dyadically expanded *state* of consciousness that comes into being in these moments but also by new *contents* of consciousness, and particularly by the emergence of new *meanings*. If my state of consciousness expands by taking on aspects of the other person's state of consciousness, then my views combine with his. In terms of *content*, the dyadic expansion of my consciousness results in a "fusion of horizons"

(Gadamer, 1989), which permits me to see my present concerns in a *different* light, compared to how they seemed to me before in my monadic state of consciousness.[198] The result of the fusion of horizons is, therefore, an integration of the previously existing individual views, which is why the dyadic understanding that emerges from this is "more whole and complex" (Tronick, 2007, p. 503) than each of the two previous individual views.

Thus, "*joint* constructions" (Staemmler, 2008) of meaning come into being, where before there were only *individual* constructions. "In this cocreative process, both partners bring the meanings from all the multiple levels that make up states of consciousness into the interaction that opens up old meanings and transforms them into new ones" (Tronick, 2007, p. 505). With these new constructions of meaning, they will then sooner or later set off on their own individual paths and, depending on what forms of (self-) support are available to them, they will sustain the new constructions even after the therapeutic meeting.

However, it is not only the level of *content,* where meaning is created, that is affected by a dyadically expanded state of consciousness, but also the level of the *relationship.* The *direct* experience of joint situations and joint states of consciousness has a connecting effect on the participants and so too do the resulting joint constructions, which are new and come into existence for the first time. The direct experience in therapy of moments of meeting, with their illuminating effects, induces a feeling of togetherness that culminates in shared "Aha!" experiences, and this goes hand in hand with the impression of community that arises in us when we take pleasure in having understood and achieved something *together.*

> There is some form of recognition that 'we know each other's minds' . . . between patient and therapist, perhaps at the moment when they have cocreated an insight or at the moment when they mutually recognize that they are having the same experience (Tronick, 2007, pp. 443f.).

What I take away with me when our meeting is over is not just the memory of these enriching and uplifting experiences but also the content of our shared discoveries, which I now carry with me. Every time I reactivate them, our joint situation is revived, and along with it the feeling of connectedness that accompanied it.

For Tronick, dyadically expanded states of consciousness, the joint creation of new constructions of meaning and the feeling of connectedness

---

198 See Bohm's (2004, p. 3) description of the dialogic process that I cited at the end of section 4.2.1.

are so closely linked that he says: "Connection *is* the regulation and cocreation of the . . . meanings individuals make of the world and their place in it" (Tronick, 2007, p. 499—italics added). Seen in this way, the desire for empathic understanding between people would be nothing other that the desire to be connected to someone[199]—and it would no longer matter who tried to empathize with whom. If they are prepared to become involved in joint situations, all participants achieve connectedness with another person, regardless of whether convention requires that they be called "therapist" or "client."

BOX 68

EMPATHY AND ALTRUISM, INDIVIDUAL BOUNDARIES, AND THE JOINT SITUATION
The relationship between empathy and altruism has been the subject of much research. There has also been some discussion of whether the willingness to help that springs from our empathy with others in distress can really be called altruistic or whether, ultimately, our apparent selflessness does not conceal self-centered or even egoistical motives. This could be the case if someone commits himself to alleviating the distress of others because he himself cannot bear to be aware of this distress. Helping would then basically be self-centered stress reduction. Or someone might help someone else because he would like to avoid the feeling of guilt that he would experience if he didn't help. Or someone could become involved in helping others so as to raise his own self-esteem. All of these would be forms of "social egoism," i.e., we help others only to the extent that it serves our own sense of well-being (see Batson, 1990, p. 339).

The issues raised here are reminiscent of the discussion of boundaries that I have touched on several times under the headings of "confluence" and "identification." If we interpret helping others (which comes about through empathy) as being self-centered stress reduction this presupposes that the helper is making no clear distinction between herself and the other and consequently experiences in her own person what the other person is actually suffering. The supporters of the altruism theory, on the other hand, assume that there is a clearly felt difference between the self and the other and point out, for example, the fact that we can be fervently and sincerely in favor of the suspension or abolition of the death penalty without having to compromise our perception of the differences between ourselves and a convicted murderer. It would be just as implausible to assume that conservationists fighting to save the whale population in our seas do not sense clear boundaries between themselves and the whales (see Batson et al., 1997, p. 508—and, for the opposite point of view, Cialdini, Brown, Lewis, Luce, & Neuberg, 1997).

---

199 Conversely, this also explains the unbearable, painful feeling of being alone that people can sometimes experience when they feel that they are not understood by significant people in their lives or in matters that are of great importance to them.

The two positions have one thing in common—they do not assume a critical attitude toward the concept of individual boundaries but take it as given and then simply discuss whether the differences experienced between people are distinct or blurred. In this way they remain imprisoned in the individualistic paradigm (see Box 22).

The concept of the joint situation opens up an alternative perspective. A person who finds himself in a joint situation with others—be they whales, murderers or anyone else—can feel concern and compassion toward their sufferings without his own individual boundaries necessarily becoming unclear. The person who is thus affected merges into the *joint situation*—e.g., that of feeling living beings—and therefore is not automatically also identified with the *individual* situation of others.[200]

Viewed in this way, the following statement by Waldenfels can hardly be considered to describe confluence: "I cannot behave altruistically without benefitting myself; I cannot behave egoistically without impoverishing myself" (1971, p. 307). Since then there has been empirical support for Waldenfels' statement:

> The very act of concern for others' well-being, it seems, creates a greater state of well-being within oneself. The finding lends scientific support to an observation often made by the Dalai Lama: that the person doing a meditation on compassion for all beings is the immediate beneficiary (Goleman, 2003, p. 12).

Perhaps it is Nietzsche who has put it most aptly of all: "Look after me, for I have something better to do, namely to look after you" (1997, p. 184).

4.3.4 Summary of Chapter 4.3

The traditional view of empathy is based on the individualist idea that the therapist's psyche exists in isolation. On a virtual level it "roams around" the client's subjective world, which is also thought to exist as an isolated entity, and tries, in so doing, to form a picture of her. In this chapter, I have presented the opposite view in the concept of the joint situation, which can be understood more readily through the metaphor of a game or a dance—a dance that is creatively choreographed by both client and therapist together and which governs how both of them move (see Sucharov, 1998, p. 286).

In this joint situation, which assigns specific roles to the participants, it then becomes possible for one of them to know something *of* (not *about*) the other—not because this other may have conveyed information to her by simply transmitting and receiving it, but because they are both

---

200 This line of thought may perhaps provide the germ of a solution to the dilemma described in section 4.2.3 dealing with deactivated neuronal inhibition and Buddhist ideas of compassion. It is only if we place less importance on individuals as separate entities that it is plausible for us to cultivate participation in joint situations and not primarily compassion for individual others.

integral parts of the same larger whole that encompasses them both. It is this shared whole that is the "carrier" of the information and not the individual person. The empathy that takes place principally involves sensing what it is like to move and be moved *jointly* with the other person in this joint situation. It is only then that something of the current individual situation (the role) of the other 'dance' partner is revealed.

It is especially in the intensive ("I-Thou") episodes of joint situations that dyadically expanded states of consciousness ("fusions of horizons") arise between the participants, through which what they experience and discuss assumes a more complex and coherent shape, so that new, shared constructions of meaning become possible. In this process, a feeling of connectedness can arise that goes beyond the boundaries of the situation itself.

4.4   PROPOSAL FOR AN EXPANDED DEFINITION OF EMPATHY

In the previous chapters, it has become clear in a variety of ways that the individualist view of empathy, which is based on Cartesian dualism, describes only one aspect of what is humanly possible. An impoverished image of humanity results from the traditional form of therapy where the therapist is clearly separate from his client and, through one-sided mental efforts to form a model, tries to bring to mind the mysterious "inner" world of the other person without being influenced by it himself.

I have, therefore, attempted here to extend the traditional concept of empathy by adding those dimensions which in my view are missing, and thus to design an expanded, more holistic conceptualization of empathy in psychotherapy. I am deliberately using the word "expand" because I do not want to exclude the possibility that there are some empathic processes that can be described fairly accurately in terms of the traditional model. However, in my view, it then is a question of *part* processes taking place within a larger whole, which become the *figure* (to use Gestalt psychology terminology), while the other aspects of the whole remain in the background.

Focusing on a partial aspect in this way can be extraordinarily illuminating, which is why there is no point in viewing the addressing of partial aspects as being *an alternative* to addressing the whole. It is undeniable that Carl Rogers and Heinz Kohut, among others, have made important contributions to the understanding of empathy in psychotherapy which remain valid today, even though their *realm* of validity is limited. For, from where we stand today, it is clear that "empathy should not be viewed as a simple apprehension of one person's state by another but as a complex outcome of a number of skilled communicative procedures for querying and decoding another's subjective reality" (Lyons-Ruth, 1999, p. 584).

However, of course my understanding of empathy also has its limitations and ultimately it is a matter of discretion as to where exactly we draw the boundaries, because drawing the boundaries (= "defining") is always a balancing act, a question of choosing between two evils—if the boundaries are too wide then a concept becomes woolly, if they are too narrow it does not describe a large enough section of reality.

One way of achieving this balancing act that seems quite useful, is "to hold both holism and a figural focus together, at the same time, a resolution which creates a new circumstance of understanding and application at a higher level of sophistication" (Latner, 2001, p. 112). This enables the respective advantages of both approaches to interact fruitfully with each other. *As a way of extending and expanding* the traditional concept of empathy, I therefore propose that we understand human empathizing in psychotherapy to be

- an intersubjective *mutual* process (social referencing—see Chapter 4.1),
- which takes place not only on a mental level but also in a multiplicity of ways on a *bodily* level ("encorporation"—see Chapter 4.2.) and
- occurs in the context of a *joint situation* which lends the empathizing an emergent dimension which transcends the individual (Chapter 4.3).

The following diagram gives an overview of these points:

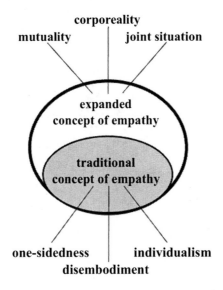

FIGURE 12
Diagram showing the relationship between the traditional and expanded understanding of empathy, with three aspects that are fundamental to each

Drawing the strands of this chapter together, I propose the following definition of empathy in psychotherapy:

BOX 69

EXPANDED UNDERSTANDING OF EMPATHY In addition to what is described by the traditional concept of empathy (see Box 14) I understand **empathy** to be **a form of social referencing that is based on intersubjectivity, takes place on a bodily level and is mutual.** It takes place **between two** (or several) **persons—a referencing of both the experiential world of the other person(s) and also of the joint situation and its emergent characteristics.**[201]

The dyadically expanded states of consciousness described in Chapter 4.3 result from the emergent properties of the joint situation. They are part of the vast number of altered states of consciousness of which human beings are capable. Some of these are related to empathy in one way or another, and it is to these that I shall be devoting the next chapter.

---

201 In my reading, I have only come across one other definition that comes anywhere close to mine. It originates from a feminist psychotherapist who refers to empathy as being a "participatory or relational consciousness, where individual selves are known more through the way they participate in larger wholes than as unique individuals" (O'Hara, 1997, p. 308). This observation contains the ideas of mutuality and the joint situation whereas the embodied nature of empathy is apparently not mentioned.

5

Empathy and Altered
States of Consciousness
Parapsychology and Meditation

M any psychotherapists have addressed the question of how to explain certain phenomena that they experience with their clients, phenomena that are often classed as belonging to the spheres of parapsychology or the esoteric. In their experience, such phenomena are not figments of the imagination, but are just as real as many occurrences that are considered to be normal.

Even Sigmund Freud, "a great, late-born apostle of the enlightenment, [who] presented the naturalism of the enlightenment with a scientific system and thereby with a second flowering" (Buber, 1999, pp. 112f.), could not turn a blind eye to these phenomena: "I am not, however, going to take up the position that I am nothing but a psycho-analyst, that the problems of occultism do not concern me: you would rightly judge that to be only an evasion of a problem" (1922/1975, p. 204). He openly admitted that where the dissolving of the boundary between subject and object was concerned he could not "discover this 'oceanic' feeling in myself" which leads to "men's receiving an intimation of their connection with the world around them" (1931/1975, p. 65), and considered such feelings to be regressive in character. He did not, however, shy away from addressing the topics of "Dreams and telepathy" (1922/1975)[202] and "Psycho-analysis and telepathy" (1921/1975), commenting that "it no longer seems possible to keep away from the study of what are known as 'occult' phenomena—of facts, that is, that profess to speak in favor of the real existence of psychical forces other than the human and animal minds with which we are familiar, or that seem to reveal the possession by those minds of faculties

---

202 He actually maintained in the very first paragraph "that the two have little to do with each other" (Buber, 1922/1975, p. 197).

hitherto unrecognized" (Buber, 1921/1975, p. 177[203]—see also Devereux, 1970). Freud's pupil Sándor Ferenczi wrote in his diary on February 14, 1932: "Cases of thought transference during the analysis of suffering people are extraordinarily frequent. One sometimes has the impression that the reality of such processes encounters strong emotional resistance in us materialists" (1988, p. 33).[204]

In his later years Carl Rogers, too, found the "transcendental" dimension, as he called it, to be increasingly important, saying:

> When I can relax and be close to the transcendental core of me, then I may behave in strange and impulsive ways in the relationship, ways which I cannot justify rationally, which have nothing to do with my thought processes. But these strange behaviors turn out to be *right*, in some odd way: it seems that my inner spirit has reached out and touched the inner spirit of the other. Our relationship transcends itself and becomes a part of something larger (1980, p. 129—original italics).

And a less well-known psychotherapist describes his impressions as follows:

> There are sometimes moments when understanding of the other deepens beyond what I can easily explain. I seem to experience the other's feelings directly in my own body or recognize patterns, history, or meanings that do not appear to come from interpreting the words and gestures that are exchanged . . . [There is] a shift from logical extrapolation to a more direct and spontaneous knowing involving a transcendence of the conventional subject-object dichotomy (Hart, 1999, pp. 112f.).

When we read these comments by Hart, Rogers, and Freud, we are struck by what they have in common, despite the many differences between their views. All have no choice but to recognize that the phenomena they are studying exist, but find it hard to make sense of them. This difficulty seems also to have to do with the question of confluence, which I have mentioned several times before. Hart cannot "easily explain" how the "transcendence of the conventional subject-object dichotomy" that he has observed comes about. Rogers finds the way he behaves "strange

---

203 Niedecken (2001) gives a detailed (psycho-) analysis of Freud's ambivalent attitude toward the "occult."
204 Here as well, Ferenczi was more radical than Freud and added to this comment that it was his impression "that even the intelligence of which we are so proud, though analysts, is not our property but must be replaced or regenerated through the rhythmic outpouring of the ego into the universe, which alone is all knowing and therefore intelligent" (Ferenczi, 1988, p. 33).

and impulsive," and Freud cannot begin to explain the "oceanic feeling" resulting in "men's receiving an intimation of their connection with the world around them" (1931/1975, p. 65). What is missing is clearly a cognitive framework which they could use to classify what appear to be the typical characteristics of "occult" or "transcendental" processes. They do not have direct experience of the connectedness (sometimes also called "oneness") between the self and the world in general, or between the self and the other in particular.

5.1 NORMAL AND PARANORMAL EMPATHY

> *BOX 70*
>
> **Example** One of my clients,[205] a mother, once told me that at a certain point during the previous week she had been surprised to find that she was worried about her grown-up daughter and had been afraid that something might have happened to her. A few hours later she had received a phone call from her son-in-law who told her that her daughter had a car accident and was severely injured. It turned out that the accident had happened exactly at the moment when she had been worrying about her.

While I in no way wish to claim to be able to offer a general explanation for such events, I do think that *some cases* of such phenomena (e.g., some cases of what is known as telepathy or second sight), which are usually considered to be parapsychological, figments of the imagination or trivial coincidences, only appear mysterious or unlikely *under certain circumstances*.[206] It is my belief that some cases of mysterious phenomena are examples of what Wittgenstein meant when he said, in a quote that has become famous, "a *picture* held us captive. And we couldn't get outside it, for it lay in our language, and language seemed only to repeat it to us inexorably" (Wittgenstein, 1958, § 115 — original italics).

The "picture" or "language game" that I am thinking of is that of Cartesian dualism and individualism, which is based on rigid and insurmountable splits — and, in particular, the split between body and mind and that between individual persons. As we have seen, from the contemporary standpoint, these splits, if they are taken as "given," must be seen as

---

205 I am grateful to the client for giving me permission to publish this episode.
206 There are also cases in which the 'mysterious' phenomenon is due to an illness or injury. Here I would remind the reader of the patients with "second touch" mentioned in section 4.2.3.

belonging to a false ideology. While our cultural ways of thinking are for the most part imbued with this ideology, this does not make them truer. Rather, it mystifies certain events and makes them appear incomprehensible or mysterious, whereas they would seem relatively normal if we did not try to view them through the lens of this ideology.

An example of what I mean can be found at the beginning of the passage by Hart cited above. Hart speaks of things "beyond what I can easily explain. I seem to experience the other's feelings directly in my own body" (1999, p. 112). If we assume that feelings belong to the mental sphere (*res cogitans*), which exists in separation from the body (*res extensa*), and if we also assume that two people, even if they are located in the same room and involved in an intense dialog with each other, are two separate bodies who can at most communicate by transmitting and receiving linguistic signals, it is indeed difficult to understand how it might be possible to "experience the other's feelings directly in one's own body."

We remain caught up in the Cartesian picture and cannot help but be amazed or shake our heads and hold some kind of paranormal forces responsible for what is inexplicable in an attempt to provide ourselves with at least a minimal explanation and thus to sustain our familiar worldview. While in the quotation above Hart does not do exactly that, he does fall back on similar strategies and constructs the nebulous concept of "deep empathy,"[207] in which the participants' "subjectivity is suspended" (1999, p. 120). Although his intention is to draw attention to the level that transcends the individual and—unlike Freud—does not seem to have anything against oceanic feelings, he still remains caught up in the individualistic paradigm.

However, "the secret of the world we are seeking must necessarily be contained *in my contact with it*" (Merleau-Ponty, 1968, p. 32—italics added). Thus, if our frame of reference is the psychology of *imitation* and the *linking of perception and action* (see section 4.2.1), which is based on the phenomenological concepts of *intersubjectivity, embodiment,* and *encorporation* (see section 4.2.2), and also take note of the research on *sharing the cortical representation of the emotion* (SRE) and the *shared manifold* (see section 4.2.3)—and possibly also have some idea of what a "joint situation" is (see Chapter 4.3)—*then*, we should rather be surprised if two people who are in intensive contact with each other are *not* physically affected by the

---

207 What I do not like about such concepts is not only that they are nebulous, but also that they sound so essentialist (see Rorty, 1999, pp. 47ff.). Marcel once rightly poked fun at the "sky-blue mantle of initiated gnosis" (1985, pp. 20f.), in which such "depth" psychology wraps itself. Other authors have attempted to define the empathic quality that is meant by coining concepts of their own. Thus, Sterling and Bugental (1993), for example, speak of the "meld experience" and Rowan (1998) of "linking."

feelings of the other since "this relationship of closeness, this contact . . . is the original language, a language without words or sentences, pure communication" (Lévinas, 1983, p. 280). Under these circumstances, none of this seems amazing, paranormal, or occult.[208]

In some other cultures and some spiritual traditions, a similar way of looking at things based on connectedness and community is considered more or less normal and is sometimes expressed even more radically. For example, a leading Zen-Buddhist, Daisetz Suzuki, subscribes to a very radical strategy of empathizing by identification, which evidently does not assume any insurmountable separations or splits, or even a basic difference between human beings and plants:

> To know the flower is to become the flower, to be the flower, to bloom as the flower and to enjoy the sunlight as well as the rainfall. When this is done, the flower speaks to me and I know all its secrets, all its joys, all its sufferings; that is, all its life vibrating within itself (Suzuki, 1960, pp. 11f.).[209]

Another Zen master basically says the same thing, but more with reference to human beings:

> If we want to understand something we should not only observe it. We should immerse ourselves deeply in it and become one with it so as to really understand it. If we want to understand a person, we must feel his feelings, suffer his sufferings and enjoy his joy (Hanh, 2003, p. 29).

I would like to stay with empathy between *human beings* and come back to the issue of "dyadically expanded consciousness" that I introduced in section 4.3.3., since, as suggested by the way in which it is expressed, we find in Tronick's description something similar to what we found in the quotation from Hart. The "normal" state of consciousness that Tronick implicitly takes as his starting point still seems to be the individual, monadic state of consciousness, which is then dyadically *expanded* in a second step and in certain exceptional situations ("joint situations"). Thus, on the one hand, the concept that he has constructed reveals an attempt to leave behind the limitations of individualistic thinking, while on

---

208 Seen in this context, it no longer seems quite so surprising if "collective unconscious, ESP [extra-sensory perception], telepathy and intersubjectivity" are mentioned in the same breath (Sterling & Bugental, 1993, p. 41).

209 I should perhaps mention that at this point I am merely interested in mentioning an alternative cultural concept without approving it straight away. That I cannot do without understanding in what way it makes sense to say that a person "becomes" a flower or to say that the flower "speaks" to him, or even to claim both *at the same time*.

the other, he uses language that "inexorably repeats" this kind of thinking, so that it fails to escape the very same limitations that it was intended to transcend.

Again, on the one hand Tronick had begun to develop his ideas further when, for example, he wrote that "connection *is* the . . . cocreation of . . . meanings (2007, p. 499—italics added). However, if we really take that seriously and take connection, contact, Being-with, and intersubjectivity as our starting point—particularly in our personal contacting—it is the "dyadically expanded state of consciousness" that appears to be what is actually *normal*, while the state of consciousness that is conventionally called "normal" should then (to borrow Tronick's term) actually be referred to as a *"monadically reduced* state of consciousness"—as a mental state that occurs when human beings withdraw voluntarily from the Being-with or the joint situations and meaning constructions, not only physically, but also mentally, and isolate themselves from others. The collective form of withdrawal that prevails in our culture would then have to be sought precisely in the ideological assumption of the *normality* of an individualistic, monadically reduced consciousness—in the fact that it is the *"deficient* mode of Being-with" (Heidegger, 1962, p. 157—italics added) that is considered normal.

In order to avoid becoming embroiled in the potentially confusing terminology ourselves, it would perhaps be helpful to speak of "intersubjective consciousness" rather than "dyadically expanded consciousness" and of "individualist consciousness" instead of "monadically reduced consciousness."[210] It is viewing processes in terms of intersubjective consciousness, which is based on personal contacting between persons in joint situations that helps us to understand how we can, under such circumstances, in fact, come to know something about the mystery of the other person which has not been transmitted via the usual communication channels. However, such phenomena cannot be explained from the perspective of individualistic consciousness and are mystifyingly referred to as "telepathy"[211] or "second sight," for example.

Certain cases of what is known as second sight can be seen in the same way. Second sight is defined as "unexplained information about events in a different place" (see the example in Box 70). As frequently documented in the parasychological literature on such events, to have access to such

---

210 One could, of course, argue that the term intersubjectivity also, in fact, still remains within the confines of individualistic language. I have nonetheless decided to use it because there can be no doubt that the way in which intersubjectivity is defined in phenomenology goes beyond the Cartesian paradigm.
211 One dictionary defines telepathy as "unexplained information about the mental contents of another person."

information typically requires a significant interpersonal *relationship* (e.g., as between close relatives or between client and therapist); Mischo, a parapsychologist (1983), speaks here of an "affective field." The importance of the personal relationship gives the information obtained through second sight a special personal *significance* for the recipient, which leads to its having a stronger or more sustained effect than it would with anyone else. The daughter's car accident understandably had a quite different meaning for the mother and led to a quite different reaction than it would have in some newspaper reader who had no personal relationship to the daughter and read about the accident at the breakfast table without paying further attention to it.

> Thus, the meaning of a piece of information is expressed in the reaction or effect that it produces. A reaction is a change in behavior. In a given situation (such as in our example) it is a measure of the significance of the information. We call this "pragmatic information."[212] The quantity of pragmatic information that a message contains is revealed by its effect on the system. This effect may occur immediately or not until somewhat later (von Lucadou, 1997, p. 144).

The high level of pragmatic information contained in the mother's premonition of her daughter's car accident is a reflection of the close relationship between the two of them, which we can guess is also evidenced in particularly close contact between them when they are together and springs from their long history of shared situations. It can thus be assumed that all the relevant prerequisites of a clear intersubjective state of consciousness were given—apart from one: Mother and daughter were not in the same place!

If we wish to understand the mother's second sight in terms of Tronick's model and not as a parapsychological event, we therefore need to add a further element to his model, which is that one must assume that people can be capable of sustaining or at least sometimes reactivating an intersubjective state of consciousness that has developed in a shared situation even when they are in different places, which may lie far apart. Put another way, it should also be possible to be aware of being in a shared

---

212 This term was introduced by E. von Weizsäcker. One of the sentences in his article on pragmatic information which is noteworthy in this context is, "*the more successfully information creates information, the more difficult it gets to distinguish at all between the transmitter and the receiver,* that is, to say of a system whether it is a transmitter or a receiver" (1974, p. 103— original italics). Here again, the separation between human beings that is so often taken for granted is called into question.

situation and of relating to another person in a significant way when the other person is not in the same place as oneself.

This additional assumption would not appear to me to be too far-fetched. We are all constantly doing something similar with the people we love, for example. We feel connected to them and include them in our thoughts and plans. We also attach meanings to situations in which we find ourselves alone that include meanings of other people, which we either remember or impute to them—irrespective of where we and they happen to be at a given point in time.[213] Ordinarily, the feeling of connect-edness is relatively independent of one's locality. When *both* participants have this feeling of connectedness *simultaneously*, but are *not* in the same place, this is referred to in the terminology of parapsychology as a "nonlo-cal correlation." In everyday language, we could say that two events at different places have something to do with each other without this being due to the transmission of signals (there is no cause-effect relationship). This can also be applied to the case I described above, where the mother became aware that something untoward was happening to her daughter, although she was somewhere quite different, and the two were not in di-rect communication with each other.

In the last few paragraphs, I have introduced all the keywords that are of import in recent parapsychological theories on telepathy, second sight, and other similar psi phenomena. Walther von Lucadou calls his theory "the model of pragmatic information in non-local correlations."

BOX 71

PARAPSYCHOLOGY Von Lucadou defines his entire research project as follows: "Psi effects can be . . . defined as 'meaningful nonlocal correlations' between living systems. Parapsychology could therefore also be redefined as the investiga-tion of 'nonlocal effects in living systems'" (1995, p. 66).

In his view, the "first main thesis of parapsychology" is: "Psi phenomena are nonlocal correlations in psycho-physical systems that are induced by the prag-matic information that the . . . system produces" (1997, p. 162).

Thus, if there is a meaningful and intense relationship between people that develops in meaningful joint situations and has led to im-portant joint constructions of meaning, the intersubjective ("dyadically expanded") states of consciousness associated with them tend to be sus-tained beyond the face-to-face encounters or to be reactivated later, since

---

213 When people cannot do that they have a problem that psychoanalysts refer to as "lack of object constancy."

they *are* the connection, which also remains in existence in the absence of the other person. This is precisely what is meant by von Lucadou's theory. Paranormal phenomena occur mainly in such significant relationships because they imbue the information that is communicated (or rather, that communicates *itself*) with a special significance. The relationship, the joint situation, or the intersubjective state of consciousness, remains in effect after the two persons have parted and are thus able to link two apparently separate events in a very normal, human way.

As I said above, I do *not* think that *all* cases of telepathy or second sight can be thus explained, but it does help me to understand some of them if I view them in this way. There are without doubt also a large number of other events of a similar kind that need to be explained differently,[214] for which parapsychologists have constructed a number of models (see Schmidt, 2002, pp. 127ff., for an overview). Some of these models draw on concepts from modern physics. Thus, for example, the term "nonlocal correlation" is taken from quantum theory.[215]

There are some authors, whom I take seriously, for whom it makes sense to use insights from quantum physics for psychology. They do not give the impression of having simply taken models used in physics and applied them to psychology in an unreflecting and reductionistic way (see, for example, Atmanspacher, 2007; Hill, 1986; Vitiello, 2001). These include, for example, for parapsychology, Walach (2003) and von Lucadou, Römer, and Walach (2007), who suggest using a "weak" or "generalized" quantum theory and hypothesize that "entanglements" may explain the paranormal empathic processes that take place in psychotherapy.

> The overall system of patient and therapist is characterized by openness and awareness. This results, so to speak, from the therapeutic contract. However, locally there are many unconscious elements that complement this, in both the patient and the therapist, those of the patient being of special interest. . . . This state of affairs leads to an entanglement of

---

214 The wholesale rejection of parapsychological studies by some authors who, for example, simply dismiss them as being "hokus pokus," could be understood as a vestige of a mentality that was widespread at the time of the witch hunts (see Lesh, 1970, p. 68), i.e., what does not fit into the prevailing worldview is either demonized or simply ignored (see Habermas, 1971; Kuhn, 1970).

215 Zeilinger, a quantum physicist, explains this as follows: "The name we use to describe the above type of nonlocal connectedness of two particles is entanglement. The idea is that under certain circumstances two particles remain one system even if they are separated by a very large distance" (Zeilinger, 2004, p. 24—original italics). Another physicist draws attention to "the EPR phenomenon, Foucault's pendulum, and Mach's principle. There are mysterious immanent and omnipresent interactions in the universe, which require no force or exchange of energy and which physics is at present incapable of describing" (Thuan in Ricard & Thuan, 2001, p. 214).

the contents of the minds of therapist and patient. . . . Thus, the patient's material can manifest in the therapist "as hers," although when we are concerned with entanglement it does not really make sense to separate it into "yours" and "mine" (Walach, 2003, pp. 35f.).

There are some obvious parallels between such accounts and my own. However, we should not allow ourselves to be taken in by superficial linguistic analogies, since we frequently find that the theories behind them differ widely. I do not feel that I am in a position to make a clear evaluation of the use of models from quantum physics in psychotherapy. First, I know too little about quantum physics and its epistemology to be able to assess its internal consistency; second, it is not clear to me whether or in what way their theorems can be applied to the macroscopic and psychological areas; and third, I do not know what implications the modifications that have been introduced (*weak* and *generalized* quantum theory) may have for the evidential value and applicability of their concepts.

5.2   MEDITATIVE EMPATHY AND EMPATHIC MEDITATION

The English psychiatrist Peter Fenwick . . . tested 11 pairs of people who already knew each other well and who sat quietly together for 20 min before the experiment started, against a control group in which the subjects either did not know each other at all or knew each other only slightly and did not spend time sitting together. In the chosen target parameter [certain correlations in the EEG], in the control group no correlation was found between the two subjects, whereas in the subjects in the experimental group the correlation almost reached significance ($p = 0.06$). When the study was narrowed down to just those pairs who considered themselves to be empathic, on a simple scale of 1–3, then the significance increased to $p < 0.005$ (Schmidt, 2002, pp. 334f.).

"Knowing each other well already" and "sitting quietly together for 20 minutes" are the two variables in this study that to some degree influenced how well the two persons in each pair believed that they understood each other. These two variables can be seen as aspects of what I have called the "joint situation" (see Chapter 4.3). Thus, Fenwick's study can be interpreted as a further indication of how the joint situation can affect the empathic understanding of those who find themselves in it.

Viewed from a different angle, however, this study also suggests that there is a connection between altered states of consciousness that are induced by meditation and empathy. Sitting together quietly may not be seen as a highly developed form of meditation but it is, perhaps, a first step toward it. If so, then it would indeed be remarkable if there were signs of its beginning to affect the subjects' experience of mutual empathy. But true meditation of course goes further than this. Scharfetter has attempted to describe the common denominator of different forms of meditation:

> What they have in common is, perhaps, the experiencing of the ego as less important, the suspension of our egocentric attitude towards the world, which some consider to be a dissolving of the self. This can be encountered as illuminating insight, as an exhilarating, sometimes ecstatic experience of becoming one, of the 'being alone' [literally, being al-one or all one] of the self and of being, or as the cessation of separation in mystic union. It can, however, also be the experience of no-self (*anatta*), transience and the cessation of suffering in Nirvana (1984, p. 35).

In view of all that has been written in previous chapters, these common features, in particular the "experiencing of the ego as less important" or the "dissolving of the self" will easily be recognized as conditions that are conducive to empathy. There are also several studies that back this up, where different forms of meditation were analyzed to determine their influence on the capacities for empathy of those practicing them.

One of the earliest and most comprehensive studies was conducted by Lesh (1970) on "Zen meditation and the development of empathy in counselors," which tested the hypothesis that "counselors who practice zazen ['sitting, opening the hand in thought'; a concept in Zen-Buddhist meditative practice] regularly over a prescribed length of time will develop a higher degree of empathy . . . than counselors who do not practice zazen over the same time span" (Lesh, 1970, p. 48). All the experimental subjects were training to be psychological counselors, and they received half an hour's training per day in meditation over a four-week period, whereas the two control groups did not.[216]

The central hypothesis was confirmed: "The practice of zazen did, in fact, seem to contribute significantly to an increase in their ability to accurately detect and describe the affective states of others" (Lesh, 1970, p. 58). "The group who practiced zazen over the 4-week period improved significantly in their empathic ability. The two control groups did not" (Lesh, 1970, p. 71).

---

216 One of the control groups was made up of people who had said they would be happy to take part in the meditation training but then had not been allocated places in the experimental group. The second control group was made up of people who did not want to take part in the meditation.

Another form of meditation, known as "mindfulness meditation," has attracted special attention over recent years, not only among those practicing it, but in certain medical circles, too, and recently also among psychotherapists, e.g., behavior therapists (Heidenreich & Michalak, 2003; 2004) and client-centered or Rogerian therapists (Bundschuh-Müller, 2007). This is thanks to the work of Jon Kabat-Zinn (1990; see also Santorelli, 1999), who has devoted himself to working with people who are suffering from stress and are chronically ill as well as to the scientific study of the effects of mindfulness meditation on stress reduction, the course of an illness, coping with chronic pain, and many other parameters.[217]

By "mindfulness meditation," Kabat-Zinn means "a particular way of paying attention, one that gives rise to a moment-to-moment, non-judging awareness" (1999, p. 230). In this method, he attempts to bring together two strands. These "two major strands of practice are *samatha*, or *samadhi*, the strand of concentration (including calmness, stability of attention, one-pointedness), and *vipassana*, the strand of insight, mindfulness, awareness, discernment" (Kabat-Zinn, 1999, p. 233). The effectiveness of mindfulness meditation has been demonstrated convincingly in a whole range of applications, but in particular that of stress reduction.[218]

However, I am concerned here not so much with the main applications of mindfulness meditation as with a marginal area—how it affects the capacity for empathy of those practicing it. To illustrate this, I would like briefly to mention two studies that I have picked not only because they prove that there is a general connection between this meditative practice and the ability to empathize but because they also show that regular meditation is especially useful for people in the healing professions. Members of these professions are particularly susceptible to the dangers of burnout and compassion fatigue (see Box 58).

One of these studies was on nurses who took part in an 8-week course in mindfulness-based stress reduction. They did this as a group, and at the same time, they had individual tuition in meditation (Beddoe & Murphy, 2004). As well as a significant fall in anxiety levels, there was clear evidence of an increase in empathy toward the patients they were caring for. Interestingly enough, this was accompanied by a decrease in the likelihood of their being upset by their experiences with their patients.

The second study dealt with the question, "How can we better prepare our future doctors for the stresses of medical practice?" (Shapiro, Schwartz, & Bonner, 1998, p. 581). Here, too, the experimental subjects

---

217 Kabat-Zinn's method is familiar today mainly as "mindfulness based stress reduction—MBSR."
218 Lazar (2005) gives an overview of this research.

(medical students) took part in a formal 8-week meditation course, which also included an introduction into the meditations of "loving kindness" and "forgiveness."[219] In addition, they were given informal support in how to apply what they had learned to everyday practices. For the first time, the parameters measured also allowed for the possible changes in the students' capacity for empathy, since, as Kabat-Zinn suspected, "the ability to perceive interconnectedness and wholeness in addition to separateness and fragmentation can be cultivated through mindfulness practice" (1990, p. 157). The results showed not only reductions in levels of depression and anxiety but also a significant increase in the subjects' general level of empathy. In summarizing their results, the authors refer expressly to the study on the effect of zazen, mentioned above: "This [result] is consistent with Lesh's study (1970), which demonstrated that reducing stress and anxiety through meditation led to greater compassion and empathy" (Shapiro et al., 1998, pp. 592f.).

These indications that meditation has positive effects on our capacity to empathize have also been confirmed in recent studies of a quite different kind, carried out by Paul Ekman, whose research on the spontaneous recognition of the facial expressions of basic emotions was described in section 4.2.1. In those earlier studies, he had shown people photographs of faces and asked them to say what emotions they recognized in the facial expression. Now, he added to his earlier research design, adapting it to a new research initiative that he called the *Extraordinary Persons Project.* This project concerned the differences, in terms of certain cognitive skills, between "normal" people and those with advanced skills in meditation, including a high Tibetan Lama (I should add here that in Tibetan Buddhism, one meditative practice is meditation of compassion.).

One of the experiments used a video in which, for split seconds (in one for 1/5 of a second and in another for 1/30 of a second), the faces showing the basic emotions flashed past. Although the faces appeared for such a short time that they could not be perceived consciously, the experimental subjects were invited to say which facial expression they had seen at any one time. The ability to perceive such fleeting emotional signals subliminally and then assess them accurately is considered to be a sign of a particularly highly developed capacity for empathy.

Goleman witnessed the results of Ekman's experiments:

> Both Oser [the Lama] and another advanced Western meditator he had been able to test were two standard deviations above the norm in

---

219 These meditations have certain similarities with the "meditation of compassion," described below.

recognizing these superquick facial signals of emotion . . . They both scored far higher than any of the five thousand other people tested. "They do better than policemen, lawyers, psychiatrists, customs officials, judges—even Secret Service agents," the group that had previously distinguished itself as most accurate. "It appears that one benefit of some part of the life paths these two have followed is becoming more aware of these subtle signs of how other people feel," Ekman noted (2003, pp. 14f.).

To follow that life path involves years of meditation, often for several hours a day.[220] For Buddhist monks, the subjects of this study, a special form of this meditative practice is "meditation of compassion," referred to above, which, as the name suggests, naturally has a particular affinity with the development of empathy. In saying this, I do not wish to imply that this practice has a *special* effect on a meditator's capacity for empathy. At any rate, it is not possible to deduce this from the studies on the "extraordinary persons," since meditation of compassion represents just *one* of several forms of meditation that they have practiced extensively over the course of many years. It was probably not even the one they practiced most frequently.

I am assuming that the main factor contributing to empathic skills is the "experiencing of the ego as less important," which is a requirement of *all* forms of Buddhist meditation (and many other spiritual practices), i.e., the more people learn to dissolve their belief in their own ego, the more empathic they become—probably completely irrespective of which form of meditation they actually practice:

> If you are not trapped in the bubble of self-centeredness and do not always see everything in relation to yourself, then your ego ceases to feel threatened. You no longer constantly have the feeling of having to defend yourself, you are less fearful and do not keep worrying about yourself. The more this feeling of insecurity vanishes the more too do the walls that the ego had built up around itself. You become more open to other people and are ready to act for their good. Compassion destroys the bubble of the ego (Ricard in Singer & Ricard, 2008, p. 99).

Because meditation of compassion has proved to be a relatively easily accessible form of meditation for people in the Western world, I shall now describe it in more detail.

---

220 Lutz, Brefczynski-Lewis, Johnstone, & Davidson (2008) proved that because of neuroplasticity (see Box 50), practicing meditation over several years also results in clearly demonstrable alterations in the brain.

BOX 72

Meditation of compassion Oser, who took part in Ekman's studies studies mentioned above, explained meditation of compassion (Sanskrit: metā) as follows:

> In generating love and compassion, bringing to mind the suffering of living beings and the fact that they all aspire to achieve happiness and be free from suffering is a vital part of the training. So does the idea to "let there be only compassion and love in the mind tor all beings—friends and loved ones, strangers and enemies alike. It's a compassion with no agenda, that excludes no one. You generate this quality of loving, and let it soak the mind" (in Goleman, 2003, p. 32).

The following is an abridged version of Anthony Matthews' practical instructions for Western readers:

> Prepare yourself for meditation by sitting still for a few minutes—"be fully present," gather your thoughts and get in touch with your feelings . . .

> Now allow yourself to feel loving kindness and goodwill towards yourself, and seek a sense of well-being. You may find it helpful to hear your inner voice saying "Be happy and content." . . .

> After a few minutes turn your attention to a good friend. . . . Become aware of your reaction to your friend—how you feel about him or her at this moment—and try to allow yourself to experience powerful feelings of loving kindness and caring. . . .

> After a few more minutes . . . think of someone you might refer to as a "neutral" person. This is someone you neither like nor dislike. Again, become aware of what thinking of this person feels like. . . . Wish this person well. . . .

> Then turn your attention to a difficult person. This "difficult person" is someone you do not currently get on with particularly well. Anybody you don't like or who doesn't like you will do here. Again, be aware of what your actual inner reaction to this person in your meditation is like. . . . Try to simply let go of all feelings of hostility and dislike. Remain attentive to the feeling of goodwill in this reaction.

> Then concentrate on all four people (yourself, your friend, the neutral person and the difficult person), and let metta arise equally for all of them, so that you feel no less kindly towards one than another. . . . Spend a few minutes doing this (and don't forget yourself!).

> In this way allow metta to expand in all directions—so that eventually it embraces the whole world. . . . Include everyone—in your own country, in your part of the

> world and in others, all over the world and the universe. Think of all these people
> and what they are experiencing at this very moment while you are here meditat-
> ing. Include all animals and all sentient beings. Try to think of them all and love
> them all with equal goodwill and kindness (Matthews, 2004, pp. 33ff.).[221]

However, naturally, we have to ask how these findings about the empathic abilities of such extraordinary persons can be explained. At the current time, any answers we may have to this question must remain more
or less pure speculation. One aspect of a possible answer, however, most
probably has to do once more with the separation of subject and object
because the state of consciousness induced by meditation leads to insight
into self as process. As this insight grows

> we begin to see the folly of accepting our naive adherence to the idea
> that the "I" is fixed, enduring, or even truly "mine." This insight greatly
> reduces our concerns for self-protection or self-aggrandizement and al-
> lows us to respond compassionately to others as we perceive our genu-
> ine interdependence with all of creation (Fulton & Siegel, 2005, p. 41).

In such a state of consciousness, we have direct experience of the
impression of a clearly defined, enduring self and, consequently, also of
the fact that the separation of self and other is an illusion and that being
interdependent in an all-embracing common situation is very much more
real.[222] This is what leads to the compassion that Oser and other meditators describe. From a Buddhist viewpoint, "true compassion does not
come from wanting to help out those less fortunate than ourselves but
from realizing our kinship with all beings" (Chödrön, 1994, p. xi).[223]

An effect of meditation can be "that the distance or separation between myself and my senses, on the one hand, and the external world,
on the other, seemed to disappear. I was no longer a detached observer"
(Watts, 1960, p. 138). The distinction between self and others becomes
blurred or even dissolved by meditation, and this can clearly lead to a
special kind of intersubjective consciousness where the aspects of subjectivity and mutuality carry less weight. Instead, it is the third aspect of
intersubjective consciousness that is experienced more intensely, i.e., the

---

221 Sweet and Johnson (1990) have attempted to systematize this form of meditation, with
some success, transforming it into *Meditation Enhanced Empathy Training* (*MEET*).
222 See the references to Heraclitus and the concept of the self in gestalt therapy, mentioned
in Chapter 4.1.
223 This was also mentioned above in the context of the neurosciences in section 4.2.3, under
the heading "The principles of mirroring in neuronal systems with relevance for empathy."

fact that people are in a common or joint situation, which otherwise occurs mainly in personal contact that is actually taking place (see Chapter 4.3).

But the consciousness of which we are talking here does not need *personal* contact in which the boundaries between the self and a *concrete* other person become fluid. It is rather a question of global connectedness with "*all* sentient beings." In addition to the fact that the ego and the boundaries between it and others become less important, there seems to be a further essential element, which is that meditation opens us to the effects of those wider situational circles to which Rombach is perhaps alluding when he speaks of "nature" and "religion" (1987, p. 428—see Chapter 4.3, Figure 11).[224]

BOX 73

Example I once experienced such a state of consciousness relating to nature when my wife and I were meditating in the countryside.

An all-encompassing feeling of being one with nature seized us, and also a clarity that we experienced visually as a kind of 'radiance' as we watched a flock of swallows darting across the bright blue summer sky in Provence. As the swallows entered our field of vision there was also the scarcely audible gentle whirring sound of the birds' wings as they flew through the hot air. The air vibrated gently and our bare skin tingled.

In the very same moment that we noticed the swallows with our eyes, ears and bodies, coinciding with that external impression, the image of swallows darted through our minds. This image was accompanied by a tingling of our skin and by a subtle sensation in our ears such as is usually associated with the perception of a whirring sound.

In this moment, which seemed to last an eternity, the external events coincided with what was happening inside us. Or to be more precise, our sensations and thoughts were one aspect and the external events the other aspect of one and the same happening. It was not that the swallows had come along first, generating our thoughts and perceptions, nor was it our thoughts and perceptions that had preceded or even caused the appearance of the swallows. Everything happened at absolutely the same time and seemed both spontaneous and natural. The whole situation seemed to be a work of art, the creation of which involved our participation in exactly the same way as that of the swallows, the sun, the air and the landscape.

The relevant situational circle may be nature or the divine, but unlike empathy in psychotherapy, here it is not basically a question of grasping

---

224 Abram (1997) refers to the "more-than-human world."

how a concrete other person is feeling in a concrete way. One might also say that it is of no particular interest to *recognize* another individual—it is not a question of airing his personal secret. That is why Ricard, whom I mentioned in this context at the end of Chapter 2, speaks of

> many kinds of compassion. Some are focused on a particular person or group who suffers and go together with empathy—that is, imagining vividly the feeling that the other is experiencing. Some are related to a state of benevolence that pervades the mind and is accompanied by a complete readiness to act for the benefit of others without necessarily trying to 'feel' the suffering of others (in Harrington & Zajonc, 2006, p. 167).

In this second approach, the main aim is to alleviate the *general* suffering of the *many* others,[225] and is therefore rather more an *ethical* attitude, since "the foundation of Buddhist practice is ethics" (Wallace, 2006, p. 39), which can also have political consequences and can result in actions of solidarity (see Norberg-Hodge, 1999). This energy arising from compassion is symbolized in the thousand arms of Avalokiteśvara (see Box 3), who symbolically expresses what is considered to be the most important area of *"practical* philosophy," to use the Western categories of branches of philosophy, i.e., ethics.

In order to take up such an ethical attitude, it is not necessary to have an exact understanding of the psychological details of individual suffering. One only needs to grasp the suffering in its totality in approximate terms. Perhaps it is even enough just to have a sense of the Being-with that exists before any kind of empathy is felt, the connectedness in the shared condition of being human. Before establishing common ground with the other by means of understanding, we must first honor our shared humanity by some fitting expression of acknowledgement; this common ground does *not* arise from the understanding (see Lévinas, 1983, p. 113).

In psychotherapy, which is concerned with the *specific* changing of the particular constellations of mental characteristics of *concrete* individuals, although this kind of compassion often helps to motivate people to become psychotherapists, it is not enough when it comes to actually working as a psychotherapist. For practical work, there is also a requirement

---

225 With reference to the fluidity of boundaries between the self and others, which plays a significant role in empathy and compassion, it is perhaps important to point out: "In the classical Buddhist perspective the sufferings endemic to human life are ultimately brought about by the construction of and a deep-seated attachment to our sense of a permanent identity, what we mistakenly take to be a unitary, autonomous entity, independent of and isolated from the dynamically changing and contingent world around us" (Waldron, 2003, p. 147).

for "*client*-centered'" empathy, which strives to understand the unique human being who is present in the role of "client."

However, this also brings with it a danger, which becomes greater the more the therapist follows the traditional model of empathy that maintains the separation between individuals, a model which can therefore, in exceptional cases, even get by without empathy. The danger is that the client becomes the pure "*object*" of empathic understanding, with intersubjectivity retreating into the background and the client appearing to the therapist simply as an "*object* of study." When this happens, empathy ultimately becomes an "act of *violence*," which in seeking to understand the other person seizes possession of her and incorporates what has been understood into its own frame of reference. It thus "assimilates" the other to the self and "suppresses and extinguishes the very otherness of the other" (Wenzler in Lévinas, 1989b, p. 71). Empathy that wants to avoid this kind of appropriation that blots out differences requires the therapist to have an ethically responsible attitude, which includes compassion. "The authentic encounter with the other is not perceptual or epistemic, but *ethical* in nature" (Zahavi, 2001, p. 159—original italics).

If empathic understanding takes place in the way that is described in the expanded concept of empathy, i.e., if the empathic person *experiences in his body* what he has picked up from the other person, then there should be no risk of this happening. This is because, despite the differences between empathy and compassion described above, both are based on that temporary or partial confluence (which I have already mentioned several times) that makes it hard to imagine empathizing with another person without experiencing something of their suffering in one's own body and without experiencing along with them their desire for their suffering to be relieved. In other words, *the dividing line between empathy, in its expanded form, and compassion, is narrow* and is most successful the more the participants can push the importance of their own self and their own boundaries into the background (and in therapy this is initially the task of the therapist).

At this point, it is interesting to note that the results of extensive research carried out by Daniel Batson (1990) show that people's motives for caring about other people are only genuinely altruistic when they feel a clear empathic response to them. If this response is weak or non-existent then, although people will do a great deal for each other, their motives will be largely selfish, i.e., helping others serves a purpose that is ultimately related to one's own needs. However,

> altruists seem to conceive of themselves as part of all mankind rather than as members of any particular group or subgroup. . . . Altruists have

a particular perspective in which all mankind is connected through a common humanity, in which each individual is linked to all others and to a world in which all living beings are entitled to a certain humane treatment merely by virtue of being alive (Monroe, 1996, pp. 204, 206).

There is what one might call a logical line that can be drawn between primary human intersubjectivity and empathy and, from there, between empathy and compassion: "At its essence, compassion requires that we develop a sense of connectedness to others, which will give us empathy for them, he [the Dalai Lama] explains. 'If we are genuinely able to feel empathy for others, then compassion is the natural outcome'" (Davis, 2010, p. 3).

If you feel what another person feels, and if you want to feel a sense of well-being, then you will want that person to experience a sense of well-being. Therefore, you will act to promote that person's well-being. The morality of empathy is not merely that of the Golden Rule ("Do unto others as you would have them do unto you"), because others may not share your values. Moral empathy requires, instead, that you make their values your values. This constitutes a much stronger principle, namely, "Do unto others as they would have you do unto them" (Lakoff & Johnson, 1999, p. 309).

Compassionate empathy can tend to assume a temporary form that is sometimes referred to as "mystical experience." Blackstone, who adheres to Buddhist traditions, speaks of "nondual realization,"

the emergence of a nonconceptual experience of self/other unity. It is the basis of deepened contact with oneself, one's environment, and with other people. . . . Nonduality does not refer to the numerical oneness of subject and object, but to the experience that the nature of the subject and the nature of the object are the same; they are "one taste" (2007, pp. 17, 23).

What he is referring to here is perhaps the direct experience of that "'element'" that Merleau-Ponty calls "the flesh of the world." This experience no longer only encompasses all of humankind, all other sentient beings, flowers, etc., but it also embraces the situational circle of the divine or spirituality (of which there are certainly also atheist forms). In this experience, a horizon opens up that transcends the individual, and this allows the subject to have the experience of being connected to all that surrounds her.

Thich Nhat Hanh (1992) called this form of intersubjective consciousness "inter-being." As has been mentioned above, this is characterized firstly by a particular emphasis on the joint situation and, second, by the way that there is a particular resonance with the situational circle of the numinous.

Compassionate empathy (developed by meditating or other methods) that attains this spiritual dimension has numerous positive effects, not only on its recipients[226] but also on those practicing it. What I am thinking of here is initially the finding already mentioned in Box 68 that an "act of concern for others' well-being [brought about, for example, by meditation of compassion] . . . creates a greater state of well-being within oneself" (Goleman, 2003, p. 12), for which there is even objective evidence (see Rilling et al., 2002). Here the spiritual aspect seems to play an especially important role, as was seen in a study in which the effects of spiritual meditation were compared with those of "secular" meditation and relaxation techniques: "The addition of the spiritual focus to a meditation task not only resulted in better mental health, but it was more beneficial than the secular meditation and relaxation techniques" (Wachholtz & Pargament, 2005, p. 380). Psychological findings included a lower anxiety level, more frequent positive moods, and a greater pain tolerance. This last point is particularly interesting because it turned out that the markedly raised tolerance for feelings of pain (those engaging in *spiritual* meditation were able to bear pain for about *twice* as long as the two control groups!) was due not to an altered *perception* of the intensity of the pain but to the fact that the subjects were able to *deal better* with the pain, even though it was felt just as intensely.[227]

---

226 An intriguing and highly controversial study by Leibovici (2001), published in a very respectable scientific journal, investigated the effects of praying (in the sense of intercessions, i.e., the Christian form of meditation of compassion). The results showed that even praying for people who had been ill *in the past*, retrospectively (!) had a significant positive influence on the course of their illness. The methodology used in this study is considered to be fairly reliable. The controversy over this study has been mainly about the explanation of the surprising results.

227 It would be interesting to compare Wachholtz and Pargament's findings to those of Singer et al., who discovered that the empathic sharing of others' pain "does *not* involve the activation of the *whole* pain matrix, but is based on activation of those second-order representations containing the subjective *affective* dimension of pain" (2004, p. 1161—italics added). One of the interesting questions arising from such a comparison is whether the raising of the pain threshold induced by spiritual meditation, which also increases the ability to empathize, does not perhaps have to do with the fact that the meditators become more empathic toward *themselves* and are therefore concentrating more on the *affective* dimension of their own experience of pain while pushing the physical components into the background. Andersen describes meditation as "self-directed empathy" (2005, p. 495). This is certainly a very one-sided way of looking at it, but it may contain a grain of truth that goes some way toward answering the question.

Furthermore, being prepared to empathize with another person through compassion, which means opening ourselves to an expanded intersubjective state of consciousness, results in our sensing *in ourselves* something of what, in a "normal'" monadically reduced state of consciousness, appears to exist completely *outside of* ourselves. If we approach this experience discerningly and attentively and allow ourselves to be led by it, then, as Tronick has shown (see section 4.3.3), this results in an expansion of our *own* experience, i.e., in a change in ourselves whereby we become more complex and coherent, which is usually felt to be enriching.[228] These positive feelings spring from (at least) two sources. The first is quite generally our experiencing of the expansion of the possibilities contained within us, i.e., our own personal development. The second is more specific and has to do with the development of something that is especially valuable to human beings—the feeling of connectedness (see Baumeister & Leary, 1995). From a neuroscientific viewpoint, one might add that this state of consciousness "not only feels good in the moment, it likely alters the self-regulatory integrative fibers of the brain, especially in the middle aspects of the prefrontal cortex" (Siegel, 2007, p. 291). It is this that strengthens our ability to feel *connected* with ourselves and with others (see Siegel, 2007, p. 355).

As we have seen, intersubjective states of consciousness result essentially in development, connectedness, and expanded constructions of meaning. This last aspect becomes especially important when it extends beyond the purely interpersonal realm to help to *make life meaningful* in an all-pervasive way. Along with "comprehensibility" and "manageability" (see Antonovsky, 1987), the experience of "meaningfulness" is one of the three decisive elements in mental (and, to a certain extent, physical) health. And the positive effects of meaningfulness, particularly when it results in us having a clear sense of the meaning of life, are not merely short-lived. These positive effects also help to give us a feeling of well-being in the long term because they allow us to be more resilient, equipping us to recover relatively quickly from the occasional negative frame of mind and get back into a positive mood (see Goleman & Schwartz, 1976): "Spirituality may provide us with an inspiring perspective when our lives are going

---

228 In some cases, the intersubjective state of consciousness can also result in unpleasant feelings that weigh us down when the other person's suffering that we are experiencing along with him becomes too strong (see Boxes 58 und 59). In view of the above-mentioned findings by Wachholtz and Pargament (2005) about meditators' pain tolerance and those findings of Beddoe and Murphy (2004) showing a reduction in negativity in nurses who meditate, we can assume that people who practice spiritual meditation can bear these unpleasant feelings far more easily than other empathic people. I would suggest that this is also connected with the experiencing of the ego as less important. It probably does not occur in non-spiritual forms of meditation that are primarily intended to serve one's own (!) well-being.

well, but it is nothing if [we] cannot also find meaning in life that has gone very wrong" (Solomon, 2002, p. 75).

5.3   SUMMARY OF CHAPTER 5

The expanded understanding of empathy outlined in Chapter 4.4 permits us to understand some of the phenomena that are commonly referred to as belonging to parapsychology and are often consigned to the realm of the mysterious. We can begin to understand them if we put aside the separation of self and other that is a prerequisite on which the traditional understanding of empathy is based and rather take intersubjective Being-with as our starting point, which can be intensified in joint situations. Occasionally, in individual cases, such joint situations have an impact on intersubjective states of consciousness, which can be sustained after the joint situation is over or reactivated later. This can explain many "non-local correlations."

Intersubjective states of consciousness, in which the rigid separation of self and other becomes more fluid or ceases to exist, are promoted by meditative practices, as can be seen in the case of zazen, mindfulness meditation, or Tibetan Buddhist meditation of compassion. There are a number of reliable indications that practicing meditation in this way helps us to develop our abilities to empathize and thus "could [also] help therapists to grasp intuitively their clients' communications and experiences with greater ease, clarity, and fluidity" (Schuster, 1979, p. 76).

In addition to their empathic dimension, intersubjective states of consciousness that arise in joint situations and are related to religious or spiritual situational circles also gain a quality of intense compassion, which can open up an ethical or spiritual dimension. Then, as Lakoff and Johnson put it so concisely, "empathy links moral values to spiritual experience" (1999, p. 566).

I therefore support the plea that follows, which I would very much like to see realized not only in the field of psychotherapy but in general:

> We need to give a strong place in our society to people who cultivate advanced contemplative states of empathy and compassion. We should foster them so they're able to bring the benefits of that kind of mental training to those of us who lead more ordinary lives. Having individuals with that kind of skill present in and respected by our society, and having those skills developed as part of our education, could have all sorts of benefits (Thompson in de Waal et al., 2005, p. 51).

6

Why Is Empathy Healing?
Some Considerations Inspired by Vygotsky

My fellow-man is the bond between me and the world. . . . If I did not need man, I should not need the world. . . . Only through his fellow does man become clear to himself and self-conscious. . . . The first object of man is man. The sense of Nature, which opens to us the consciousness of the world as a world, is a later product; for it first arises through the distinction of man from himself. . . . The *ego*, then, attains to consciousness of the world through consciousness of the *thou* (Feuerbach, 1855, p. 117 — original italics).

Today, Ludwig Feuerbach is only rarely cited in the psychological and psychotherapy literature, although there is considerable evidence of his influence on modern psychology.[229] This applies particularly to the effects that Feuerbach's theories had on Vygotsky[230] (see Box 8). Keiler comments that

Vygotsky's opinions are neither reducible to Feuerbach's psychology, nor can they be directly derived from them — but if we see Feuerbach's psychology as a "subtext" to all conceptualizations in Vygotsky's later work on the psychology of language, development, and personality this certainly helps us to understand them better, as should be clear from the debate on his tenet that "cooperation" is the source of "higher" mental functions (1999, p. 116).

---

229 Feuerbach also had a certain influence on Martin Buber, despite their disparate theological ideas and other differences between them (see Wehr, 1991). Buber refers to him and writes: "By man, whom he considers as the highest subject of philosophy, Feuerbach does not mean man as an individual, but man with man — the connexion of I and Thou. 'The individual man for himself,' runs his manifesto, 'does not have man's being in himself . . . Man's being is contained only in community, in the unity of man with man — a unity which rests, however, only on the reality of the difference between I and Thou'" (1947, p. 175).

230 Vygotsky's name can be spelt in a number of different ways, i.e., Vygotsky, Vigotski, Vygotskij, in German also Wygotski. I have chosen to use the first spelling. However, in the list of references Vygotsky appears under both "V" and "W," depending on how his name is spelt in the publication in question.

Keiler's heading of a section of his book *Lev Vygotskij — Ein Leben für die Psychologie* (*Lev Vygotsky: A Life for Psychology*) makes the links particularly clear: "'We become ourselves through others.' This is the law of transition from social to individual behaviors" (2002, p. 195). The "law" that Keiler refers to in this heading is decisive for Vygotsky's developmental psychology. Vygotsky himself calls it "interiorization."[231]

6.1   INTERIORIZATION AND THE ZONE OF PROXIMAL DEVELOPMENT

By "interiorization" Vygotsky means "that in the process of development, children begin to use the same forms of behavior in relation to themselves that others initially used in relation to them. Children master the social forms of behavior and transfer these forms to themselves" (1988, p. 69). Basically, this means "that the relations among higher mental functions were at some earlier time actual relations among people. I shall relate to myself as people relate to me" (Vygotsky, 1988, p. 70). To be more precise:

> The very mechanism underlying higher mental functions is a copy from so-
> cial interaction; all higher mental functions are internalized social relation-
> ships. These higher mental functions are the basis of the individual's social
> structure. Their composition, genetic structure, and means of action — in
> a word, their whole nature — is social. Even when we turn to mental pro-
> cesses, their nature remains quasi-social. In their own private sphere, hu-
> man beings retain the functions of social interaction (Vygotsky, 1988, p. 74).

What was originally "divided between two people" and a "reciprocal mental process" (Keiler, 2002, p. 196) between persons shifts to the 'inside' in the course of human development and thus becomes a *mental* process. This view evidences a non-individualist way of thinking — just as Feuerbach had outlined it previously.

> The image of the other is so closely knit into my self-awareness, my im-
> age of myself, that even the expression of what is most peculiarly mine
> and of my most intimate self . . . is an expression of socialism, of commu-
> nality, that I cannot withdraw into even the most secret, hidden corner
> of my house, of my self without at the same time bearing witness to the
> existence of the other (Feuerbach, 1868/1994, p. 422).

---

231 I shall continue to use this word when I am referring specifically to this concept of Vygotsky's, despite the fact that today it is relatively uncommon.

Thus, for Vygotsky "the true direction of the development . . . is not from the individual to the social, but from the social to the individual" (Vygotsky, 1986, p. 36). The mental processes over which human beings can dispose autonomously—one could also say originarily—at a later point in the course of their development were, at an earlier point in their lives, *interactions* between them and their significant others. To put it even more succinctly, in this model of development, an individual (originary) mental process is understood essentially as the internalized form of a previous social relationship in which the (non-originary) modes of experience and behavior of the other people played a decisive role.

> Higher psychological processes unique to humans can be acquired only through interaction with others, that is, through interpsychological processes that only later will begin to be carried out independently by the individual. When this happens, some of these processes lose their initial, external form and are converted into intrapsychological processes (Leont'ev, 1981, p. 56).

Vygotsky studied this in depth, focusing on speech, which is without doubt a "higher mental function" (Vygotsky, 1986; 1988). Lyons-Ruth gives a nice example (see Box 74).

BOX 74

EXAMPLE

The parent actively scaffolds the infant's ability to articulate and communicate his mental states somewhat ahead of the infant's ability to do so himself. Thus, the parent inducts the infant into the role of communicative partner . . . by responding carefully to infant nonlinguistic initiatives as communications and by taking the infant's turn in conversation until the infant can fill the turn himself, for example, to a 2-month-old: "Does that noise mean you're hungry? Maybe you're hungry. Let's see if you want this water? No? No water? How about juice? Ok, you like that!" (Lyons-Ruth, 1999, pp. 583f.)

Following the same pattern, children begin to carry on conversations with themselves *after* they have learned to talk a little with their mothers. In a second interiorizing step, they begin to think without the need to articulate their thoughts.[232]

---

232 However, Vygotsky was not a cognitivist, as one might suppose at first sight. He spoke of "the existence of a dynamic system of meaning in which the affective and the intellectual unite" (1986, p. 10) and argued *against* the blind alley that we finish up in if we separate cognition and affect. "The door is closed on the issue of the causation and origin of our thoughts, since

If we understand the example of speech not in the strict verbal sense, but more as an aspect of a general process of interpersonal communication, in Vygotsky's developmental model and following his "law of interiorization," we must assume that the higher mental function of being able to understand oneself is what takes form in shared processes of communication and understanding which have taken place in significant relationships. Kohut's definition of empathy as "vicarious introspection" could therefore be reversed, and introspection would then have to be interpreted as interiorized empathic interactions.

Imitative behavior in early childhood (Meltzoff & Moore, 1983), the coordination of vitality affects between mother and child (Stern, 1985), motor and emotional mirroring processes (Gallese, 2001; 2003) and many of the other observations that I have reported in the previous chapters can be seen as evidence in favor of Vygotsky's law of development. They all illustrate not only the "individuating power" of the "gaze of others" (see Box 15), but also show the *prime importance of what we share* (see Chapters 4.1 and 4.3) and emphasize the major role played by exchanges between the other and the self, out of which the higher mental functions of the self develop (see Box 1).

There is much evidence to show that people who have been treated in a sensitive way behave empathically themselves. Some of the studies on this issue were conducted in research on attachment theory (Ainsworth, Blehar, Waters, & Wall, 1978; Bowlby, 1969) and show that people who are securely attached are able to behave altruistically toward others—including strangers—much more easily and that they are more willing to help them without being motivated by self-interest than persons with an anxious-ambivalent or anxious-avoidant attachment style (see Mikulincer, Shaver, Gillath, & Nitzberg, 2005). Further evidence has come from various contexts (see, for example, Berkowitz & Grych, 1998; Bryant, 1987; Hojat, 2005). The following is just one example of many:

> Mothers observed to be affectionate and sensitive in interaction with their children in the first years of life had children who were also more likely to express concerned behavior patterns. Moreover, mothers who explained clearly, and with considerable conviction, the importance of kindness, of regard for the rights of others, and of restraint from harming others had the more concerned children (Zahn-Waxler & Radke-Yarrow, 1990, p. 118).[233]

---

deterministic analysis would require clarification of the motive forces that direct thought into this or that channel. By the same token, the old approach precludes any fruitful study of the reverse process, the influence of thought on affect and volition" (Vygotsky, 1986, p. 10).

233 It is even possible to predict people's (particularly girls') empathic behavior over 25 years later, i.e., when they have long grown up, from their mothers' efforts to curb their aggressive behavior at the age of five (see Koestner, Franz, & Weinberger, 1990).

It can be assumed that a person's capacity to empathize with and understand himself has been nurtured by empathic relationships. If a person has once experienced and internalized empathic interactions with other people, even when he is on his own, he retains the functions of social interaction, as Feuerbach postulates and Vygotsky has explored by research. He has interiorized it as a *mental* function and now enters into an understanding conversation with himself, into an "internal dialog," which one could perhaps better describe as a *soliloquy with a dialogical character*. This is also how the mutual empathy of therapeutic relationships is able to exert an effect. Where people have not yet been able to develop an understanding of themselves, where they fail to appropriate experiences of understanding dialogs, the therapeutic relationship can provide the joint process between the two participants that forms the starting point for subsequent transformations into subjective processes.

However, if we take Vygotsky's model seriously, *this* kind of transformation is *not* what we generally mean by the term "introjection" or learning from models, i.e., the adoption of certain behaviors, communications, or attitudes of another *individual* into our own repertoire. The logic of such individualistic theories is often roughly as follows: In a therapeutic interaction, the therapist represents for the client someone who is external and empathic, while for himself, the client is a person who experiences. The client then internalizes the therapist's empathic attitude, following which he likewise adopts an empathic attitude toward what he experiences himself.

Such processes of unidirectional internalization do, of course, also take place, but these are processes between two separate *individuals*, which is *not* what Vygotsky is referring to. What is interiorized, according to his theory, is the *interaction* between the other person and the self, the joint situation, the intersubjective ("dyadically expanded") state of consciousness—irrespective of what it is called—i.e., something in which the self was involved from the start.[234] It was already involved with its own "lower" mental functions, which were then, following the interaction experienced in personal contact and then interiorized, expanded by the novel exchanges that took place in this interaction. In other words,

the "boundaries" between people who are in communication are already permeated;[235] it is impossible to say "whose" an object of joint focus is,

234 We have already seen in connection with social referencing that this self is actively involved in interactions when it is still very young.
235 Rogoff puts the word "boundaries" in quotes, because it is a problematic concept (see Staemmler, 1996b; 2002a); As revealed by the material on intersubjectivity, confluence and mirror neurons presented above, human existence is always so fundamentally and in such a

or "whose" a collaborative idea is. An individual participating in shared problem solving or in communication is already involved in a process beyond the individual level. Benefiting from shared thinking thus does not involve *taking* something from an external model. Instead, in the process of participation in social activity, the individual already functions with the shared understanding. The individual's later use of this shared understanding is not the same as what was constructed jointly; it is an appropriation of the shared activity by each individual that reflects the individual's understanding of and involvement in the activity (Rogoff, 1990, p. 195—original italics).

"Higher" mental functions, which are higher by virtue of the fact that they contain within them a Being-with, which is qualitatively superior to, i.e., has more nuances and is more complex than, what had previously been interiorized, then arise from this process. Thus, a qualitative change in the person's intersubjectivity takes place. When this mutual, expanded understanding is later interiorized by the person, what becomes their mental function is not something primarily foreign that is only secondarily brought in line with the self through "assimilation" or "accommodation" (see Piaget, 1950). Rather, it is something that was co-created from the start, which expands the person's own potentials, so that they become complex, while at the same time the continuum of that person's own development is maintained.

Here Vygotsky sees a systematic process: "There is a learning process. It has its own inner structure, its own sequence, its own developmental logic" (Wygotski, 1972, p. 235).[236] This logic consists essentially in the transformation of an *inter*personal process into an *intra*personal process. However, this structural sequence logically results from the necessity that an *inter*personal process must first take place if a higher mental function is to develop later. In the therapeutic context, only if empathy becomes possible between the therapist and the client to an extent that goes qualitatively *beyond* the client's previous understanding of herself can a higher level of mental functioning be expected to develop.

At this point, the question arises, of course, as to how it can come about that a person actively enters into an exchange with another person that reaches a level of complexity that *goes beyond* his own level of mental development. Here Vygotsky's well-known concept of the "zone of proximal development" supplies a response that immediately makes sense if

---

far-reaching sense always Being-with that it is only possible to speak of boundaries between people in a very relative sense, if at all.
236 This passage is not included in the English edition (Vygotsky, 1986).

we think, for example, of small children who are just beginning to learn to walk. At some stage, a mother notices that her child has developed to a point that she can hold his hands and help him to take his first steps, which he has been unsuccessfully attempting to do for some time without external support. By helping their children to take their first steps in this way, mothers also help them to learn, so that they are able to exercise their muscles and practice motor coordination and balance. They are thus able to learn to walk *sooner* and *better* than they would have without their mothers' support and encouragement. In this way, the supportive interaction with the mother promotes the child's development.

Thus, the child's developmental status at this point has two aspects. The first is what the child has already learned to do *on its own* (e.g., sit, push itself away from something with its legs), and the second is what the child is not yet able to do alone, but *can* do *with its mother's support* (take its first shaky steps).

> Just as a gardener who wants to find out about the state of his garden would be acting wrongly if he judged it only by the apple trees that are fully developed and have carried fruit, instead of considering also the ripening trees, so the psychologist when judging the level of development, should consider not only the ripe, or mature functions but also the maturing ones, not only the present level but also the zone of proximal development (Vygotsky, 1986, p. 212).

Vygotsky calls this gap between what is possible without help and what has as yet only been possible with support of the "zone of proximal development."

BOX 75

THE "ZONE OF PROXIMAL DEVELOPMENT"

is the distance between the actual developmental level as determined by independent problem solving and the level of potential development as determined through problem solving under adult guidance, or in collaboration with more capable peers (Vygotsky, 1978, p. 86).

EXAMPLE

Having found that the mental age of two children was, let us say, eight, we gave each of them harder problems than he could manage on his own and provided some slight assistance: the first step in a solution, a leading question, or some other form of help. We discovered that one child could, in cooperation, solve problems designed for twelve-year-olds, while the other could not go beyond problems intended for nine-year-olds. The discrepancy between a child's actual mental age and the

> level he reaches in solving problems with assistance indicates the zone of
> his proximal development; in our example, this zone is four for the first
> child and one for the second. . . . Experience has shown that the child with
> the larger zone of proximal development will do much better in school.
> This measure gives a more helpful clue than mental age does to the dy-
> namics of intellectual progress (Vygotsky, 1986, p. 187—original italics).

The mother in my example furthered her child's development by encouraging and helping him to do precisely what he could not yet do of his
own accord, but what she suspected that he could gradually manage to do
with her help. She thus adjusted her behavior exactly to the child's proximal zone of development. She entered into an interaction with the child in
which she contributed support and the child the abilities he had developed
up to that point. In this interaction, the child was able to perform a psycho-
motor act, which he could not achieve without help and which he could
now gradually begin to accomplish independent of his mother. This is what
Vygotsky means when he writes in general terms, "any function in the child's
cultural development appears twice or on two planes. First it appears *between people* as an *inter*psychological category, and then *within the child* as an
*intra*psychological category" (Vygotsky, 1988, p. 163—italics added). To
put it even more generally and somewhat (more) pointedly: All subjectivity is interiorized intersubjectivity.

This example also illustrates what I meant when I drew attention
to the difference between Vygotsky's developmental concept and introjection viewed as an individual process. However, the main thing here
is *not* that the child internalizes the mother's ability to walk. This may
have occurred previously as it watched her walking and the appropriate
neuromotor patterns for the imitation that it was about to initiate were
established with the aid of its mirror neuron system. But this alone is not
sufficient. Only when the child enters into a social action, a concrete *interaction* with its mother, and later interiorizes this interaction, does it actually learn to walk on its own.[237] What then becomes a higher mental
function is the child's experience of what it is like to stand on its own two
feet and find its footing and balance, *together* with the mother's support.

Support—and this also applies to the therapeutic context—is not, in
the strict sense, a "one-way street." It is "that which enables" and "always

---

237 The child might learn to walk without having experienced such an interaction, but this
would certainly not happen until later on and not be so well coordinated. In the case of other
aspects of development, such as learning to speak, the supportive interactions are probably
indispensable (see Box 74).

involves an *interaction between the individual's resources and the resources of the environment"* (Jacobs, 2006, p. 12—italics added), as we saw in connection with social referencing and the joint situation. Jacobs' statement therefore also applies to the support that a client experiences through the empathic interaction *with* his therapist.[238] This support arises from "a crucial match between a *support system* in the social environment and an *acquisition process* in the learner" (Bruner, 1985, p. 28—original italics), a process for which the learner has already developed certain skills. This support *system* is a *shared* one, and its transformation into a mental function therefore has the intersubjective format of the "self with other," which is a *dialogical* format: "In their own private sphere, human beings retain the functions of social interaction" (Vygotsky, 1988, p. 74).

This concept of Vygotsky's can also be applied to empathic relationships. In other words, after the end of therapy, in situations where they are on their own again, clients (and their therapists) can also practice alone any empathic understanding that they have developed for themselves and interiorized in the course of the therapy. "Being listened to by an understanding person makes it possible for him to listen more accurately to himself, with greater empathy toward his own visceral experiencing, his own vaguely felt meanings" (Rogers, 1975, pp. 8f.; see also Barrett-Lennard, 1997). However, as Rogers' description illustrates, the client's understanding of himself retains its original dialogical, intersubjective format and reveals itself in the way in which the client's process of coming to understand himself develops: "It is the dialectical, almost dramaturgic quality of dialogue that provides a model for pursuing our own thoughts in the privacy of our own consciousness" (Bruner, 1979, pp. VIIf.).

Thus, the healing effect of empathic exchanges between a client and her therapist arises not only from the fact that *as* they occur, they allow both participants to expand their understanding of their worlds of experience; it is correct to say, like Anna and Paul H. Ornstein, that "feeling understood is the adult equivalent of being held, which strengthens or consolidates the self at the experiencing level" (2001, p. 19). But in my view, the therapeutic effect is more comprehensive and sustained because each process of gaining empathic understanding can help to induce that state that Tronick referred to as a dyadically expanded state of consciousness. The individuals involved are then able to construct more complex and more coherent meanings. Finally, the subsequent processes of interiorization create the higher mental functions of which Vygotsky speaks.

---

238 I am deliberately *not* talking one-sidedly about the support that the client receives as a result of her therapist's empathy. This support between individuals does exist but it is not what I am talking about when I refer to Vygotsky (see above).

Bohart therefore goes as far as to claim that "what one learns about oneself is far less important than how one learns to relate to oneself" (1991, p. 41).

Thus, one could say that self-understanding in terms of content, i.e., what one learns about certain mental patterns and processes, is only the initial, most concrete level of the therapeutic effects of empathy. It is important enough, since it helps clients to give meaning to what they experience. The second level is learning to treat oneself empathically through experiencing numerous concrete empathic interactions. The empathy that clients experience helps them to treat themselves more empathically and compassionately. But there is also a third level, to which I have already alluded several times, most recently in connection with the "intersubjective format" of self-understanding. In previous chapters, I have also talked about the reciprocal encorporation that is experienced in empathic interpersonal contact, about the "joint constructions of meaning" that develop in intersubjective states of consciousness. Other related concepts that I have mentioned are the *shared manifold* or "SRE" discussed by neuroscientists and the "Being-with" of the phenomenologists, the concrete expression of which is empathic intersubjectivity.

All of these concepts relate in some way to the feeling of connectedness that arises in empathic contact between human beings and on which human beings depend just as vitally as they do on food (Baumeister & Leary, 1995, p. 498), since in such resonant states, we "feel good as we feel 'felt' by another, no longer alone but in connection. This is the heart of empathic relationships, as we sense a clear image of our mind in the mind of another" (Siegel, 2007, p. 290). Without intersubjective resonance, we feel unbearably isolated, and this feeling is not only responsible for emotional suffering in a general way (see Jordan, 2000), but also, specifically, involved in almost all forms of mental disorder in some way. "Cutting oneself off, isolating oneself, closing oneself off, those are the basic reasons for loss of self" (Bakhtin, quoted in Todorov, 1984, p. 96), of a self that needs the other in order to constitute itself. It is for this reason that the "sense of intimate intersubjectivity can itself serve as a powerful counter to a client's sense of isolation and alienation" (Neimeyer, 2005, p. 82).

Jordan therefore emphatically criticizes the subordinate role that has traditionally been assigned to empathy:

> Empathy has often been relegated to a supporting role, as necessary to establish rapport so that the "real" work of uncovering, exposing conflict, and working on transference distortions and interpretation can take place. It has also been seen as facilitating a therapeutic context in which a person can learn coping skills. . . . [This] model suggests that isolation is one of the (if not *the*) primary sources of suffering in people's lives and also points to movement out of isolation as one of the main achievements of therapeutic

intervention. Thus, empathy becomes not just a way of knowing another's subjective experience but a way of actually experiencing connectedness. In empathic joining, one comes out of isolation and begins to believe that one is worthy of empathy, connection, and love (2000, p. 1008).

Such experiences of intense intersubjective encounters—the third level of the therapeutic effect of empathy—elicit a sustained feeling of connectedness in two different ways. On the one hand, of course, there is a conscious memory that one has directly experienced a quality of "sharedness" with the other person and was evidently able to establish such a connection. Thus, a new potential of which one had not previously been aware has entered one's own horizons of experience. This potential opens up the hopeful perspective that intersubjective encounters of this kind can in fact also happen again in the future. It shows that we are right to be confident that it really is possible to satisfy human basic needs for connectedness with other people.

The second aspect is perhaps even more important. I would remind the reader of the passage from Tronick's book that I quoted in Chapter 4.3, "Connection *is* the regulation and cocreation of the . . . meanings individuals make of the world and their place in it" (2007, p. 499—italics added). During the therapeutic explorations of the client's world of experience, this precise co-creation of meanings has taken place and led to shared constructions, to meanings that were created by both participants in the joint situation and to the connectedness experienced in it. Inherent in these shared constructions is the "dialogical format" that I described above. The interactions from which they emerged are implicitly embedded in them, and thus Tronick can say, "Connection *is* the cocreation of meanings."

If we now link this fact to Vygotsky's concept of interiorization and assume that the persons who were originally involved in the empathic dialogue interiorize their shared experiences, then their current perceptions of a shared empathic situation are transformed into a permanent higher mental function which is available to these persons later on when they are alone again or in new social situations. Thus, the feeling of connectedness can be sustained after the two have parted—for example, after the end of therapy—even if no one else is around or if the people that they encounter are at first unfamiliar.

6.2   RUPTURES AND "REPAIRS" OF EMPATHY

Efforts to create empathy between human beings can, of course, fail—not only in everyday situations, but also in psychotherapy. "Miscommunications are normal events. They occur when one of the partners fails to accurately appreciate the meaning of the other's emotional display and in turn reacts inappropriately" (Tronick, 1998, p. 294). As a rule, the failures are just as mutual and shared as successes. Usually, *both* partners feel misunderstood when empathy fails.

However, due to their personal situations and role in therapy, for clients, there is more at stake because they are necessarily dependent on empathy and achieving understanding for the success of their change processes. However, if the desired empathy that is required for a successful therapeutic outcome does not come about, the helpful processes of joint construction of meaning, the interiorization, and connectedness described above also fail. In extreme cases, what is interiorized *is* the failure. As a result, not only does the client's development stagnate, but the familiar experience of separation and isolation may also be confirmed: "If even my therapist doesn't understand me. . . ."

Fortunately, the consequences are not usually so extreme, since although empathic failures are a challenge for those concerned, they are by no means always too much of a challenge. Rather, the challenge presents a special opportunity, i.e., the opportunity to overcome it.

BOX 76

EXAMPLE

David was intense and easily injured. He had been coming to see me for three months while his therapist took maternity leave. In our first meeting, he asked if we could arrange a regular weekly session. He said it would help to anchor him during this difficult time. He was feeling bereft and abandoned by his therapist and frightened that the therapist's new baby portended a loss of his place in his therapist's heart and mind. As our discussion unfolded, I told him that although there would be occasional exceptions, we could meet regularly on Friday mornings.

A few weeks later, I told him, in a rather matter-of-fact tone, that I would have to reschedule three of our subsequent sessions. In our next session he expressed hurt and righteous anger at my casual attitude. He said it meant to him that I did not take our interim work seriously, that I was just biding my time with him. Frankly, I was surprised by the intensity of his reaction. I felt a flash of reciprocal anger, saying to myself, 'How dare he attack me, I have gone out of my way to accommodate him, surely he must know it was not easy to carve out a regular time at such short notice!'

My angry reaction was defensive. I had experienced his righteousness as shaming to me, and wished to defend myself against my rising shame by shaming him for shaming me! I also recognised that I had presumed that he was aware of the demands he had made upon my schedule. I had simply been so absorbed in my own perspective that I had not noticed that his vantage point was quite different from mine. In the course of our explorations, he described how he had never had any impact on his parents and how they had been dismissive of his aims and desires. I asked him how I had dismissed him. He said I had ignored his need to plan and his feelings about needing an anchor and needing me to see our work as important. He said he felt like he was just a 'flat line,' someone I did not need to contend with. I told him, appreciatively, that he had now brought himself to me as someone to contend with. I also said I had been insensitive to his needs and had been preoccupied with my own. He was excited and relieved that we could work/fight this problem out between us.

This exchange laid the groundwork for later therapeutic work. There were other times when he came upon limits of my availability. One example was that I ended our sessions on time and 'coldly,' whereas his primary therapist tended to run overtime quite regularly. . . . For my part, I acknowledged that my stricter time boundaries must be a surprising insult, given how his regular therapist worked and that he was not the only one who was distressed by my apparent coldness at the end of sessions.

When he settled into a more reflective state of mind, I drew his attention to the pattern I had noticed: whenever he came upon someone else's limits he felt deeply wounded and reacted with self-protective withdrawal. He smiled and said he didn't just withdraw, he tried to hurt the other person as well! He laughed at himself. As we continued to explore, it became clear that someone else's limits were intensely shaming to him. He had taken them as a personal rejection because he felt he was not worthy of more serious consideration, whereas he now saw that I was not *intentionally* shaming him, even though he felt ashamed. This was an exciting revelation to him. He began to understand that another's self-centred behaviour may have little or nothing to do with the other's feelings toward him (Jacobs, 1995, pp. 87f.—original italics).

This example shows how the contact between therapist and client is transformed from a miscoordinated form into a coordinated form (see Tronick, 1998, p. 294). The therapist contributes to this by assuming responsibility for her role in the empathic rupture and enters into a discussion with the client about what happened between them and what went wrong. In this way, the client experiences that he actually does have an impact on his therapist. He has the experience that his concerns are important and are taken seriously. For his part, the client helps to clarify the situation by rendering transparent what he has experienced, what triggered it, and what was the context for it, so that the therapist can understand what meanings the failed communication had for him. It is precisely in discussing the failure together in this way that they succeed in empathizing with each other again.

Tronick calls this process of restoring empathic relating "interactive repair" (1998, p. 294). The word "repair" is a term that has become common in psychoanalytic circles since Heinz Kohut's seminal publications in the 1960s and 1970s. However, whether one understands repair more technically in the sense of "fixing" or in a more human sense as "correcting" or "restoring," these words always imply that the participants revert to a state that they were already in *previously*.

While this is true inasfar as the empathic attunement that was lost is recovered, it is by no means all that happens in such situations! Talking *about* the rupture empathically is a kind of empathic *meta*communication which, if it succeeds, does so on precisely this *meta*level. Thus, the effect of this interaction does not lie only in the fact that the empathic attunement is reinstated, and therapist and client can simply pick up again where they left off. It also arises from the experience that the temporary rupture does not necessarily have to result in a lasting estrangement and that the participants do manage to cope with relationship problems that arise.

Such experiences are decisive, since they convey the hope that future ruptures in empathic attunement can also be repaired. Experiences like this can (if they are repeated, which, given human failings, is unavoidable) lead to the development of skills in coping with relationship crises and also to confidence in such skills. Thus, what happens is much more than simply a return to how things were before. Relationships become less vulnerable and more resilient. Clients can develop a capacity for relationship that is strong enough to withstand stress. "The creation of an empathic bond and its continual repair by empathic understanding of empathic failures is . . . an important curative agent" (Greenberg & Elliott, 1997, p. 175).

This healing development can only occur if the efforts of therapist and client to empathize do, in fact, fail from time to time. Thus, these occasional failures are not only normal, but actually to be welcomed—of course, only on the condition that both client and therapist do succeed in coping with the crisis as described above.

> Nonoptimal interactions have a therapeutic value of their own. Although such events are not specifically planned by an analyst, they do occur with some frequency. Disruption and nonoptimal interactions are ubiquitous and an essential constituent of all communication. They are mutually regulated both in their unfolding and in their repair. Establishing expectations that disruptions and mismatches can be repaired is an essential mode of therapeutic action (Lachmann & Beebe, 1998, p. 309).

Disturbances in empathic resonance between therapist and client are usually more difficult to cope with in the initial phase of therapy than they are in later phases and may even lead the client to drop out of therapy. Although, as Lachmann and Beebe write, "such events are not specifically planned," it is possible to discern a certain analogy with Winnicott's description of the "good enough mother," who likewise does not use a plan to tell her when to frustrate her children.

> The good-enough mother . . . starts off with an almost complete adaptation to her infant's needs, and as time proceeds the adapts less and less completely, gradually, according to the infant's growing ability to deal with her failure. . . . *If all goes well* the infant can actually come to gain from the experience of frustration (Winnicott, 2005, p. 14—original italics).[239]

There is also no need for empathic attunement between therapists and their clients to be perfect. It is sufficient if it is simply "good enough" or, as Bacal puts it, "optimal." "'Optimal' does not mean 'perfect' . . . 'Optimal' denotes the 'most favourable (natural) conditions for growth . . .' (Oxford Dictionary); and 'a condition, degree, amount or compromise that produces the best possible result'" (1998a, pp. 3f.).

Crises that can be coped with are such optimal conditions, likewise the support that makes the coping possible. An effective psychotherapy is, as in the earlier quote from Perls et al., a "safe emergency" (1951, p. 286). Challenging and promoting go hand in hand.

6.3 SUMMARY OF CHAPTER 6

Vygotsky formulated the principle of interiorization, which he put in a nutshell as, "I shall relate to myself as people relate to me" (1988, p. 70). This principle helps us to understand how it happens that empathic interpersonal relationships can have a healing effect. From the client's perspective it looks roughly like this:

"To start with it simply does me good to empathize with my therapist and, as I do so, to understand that he is empathizing with me and understanding me. Because we see our empathic encounter in part as a bodily event and also practice it as such, it helps me to understand myself better, not only in a cognitive sense, but also 'to be what I am—to be fully invested in my current positions' (Beisser, 1970, p. 77). The way we are in contact with each other therefore has a therapeutic effect on my current

---

239 Winnicott's description still has a strong individualist tone and thus it is only compatible with my views to a limited extent. I am not so much interested in drawing an analogy between mothers and therapists, particularly in connection with Vygotsky's ideas, but in the parallel between the child-mother *interaction* and the therapist-client *interaction*.

problems (see Box 2). We can also both feel understood and experience a direct connection between us. I can recall this later on and thus be certain that I am able to come to an understanding with another person in such a way that he has access to what I am experiencing, and I have access to what he is experiencing and we can feel connected to each other.

"I can also absorb ('interiorize') the repeated experiences of this understanding and connection, and so I am able to be more empathic with myself than I was before. What I have experienced with my therapist increasingly becomes something that I practice with myself (a 'higher mental function'). I can now 'listen more accurately to myself, with greater empathy toward my own visceral experiencing, my own vaguely felt meanings,' as Rogers (1975, p. 9) put it. This way of treating myself also includes the feeling that I have an attentive and empathic companion constantly with me, even if I am sometimes alone and nobody else is paying attention to me.

"Although I do not always manage to feel this—and when I do, it is not always complete, that was my experience with my therapist, too. Sometimes we were off target. That was painful to start with, and in some cases, also hurtful, and we had to make an effort to discover how that could happen and what we needed to do to get back on track. But usually we managed it. These experiences have helped me to trust that relationships can still carry on even if there are sometimes misunderstandings, and that the odd misunderstanding need not be the final word, but that it can be resolved and that it is thus possible to arrive at a broader understanding on a new level. In this way, we remain connected even in difficult situations—in fact, the connection to the other person can even take on a new quality.

"I now have similar experiences with myself. Sometimes I don't understand myself and am not quite in touch with what is going on inside me. But then I am confident that that can change and that I can sustain a loving attitude towards myself. Usually after a while what's going on in me becomes clearer and I feel connected with myself again."

7

Conclusion

I began this book with two quotations: "Encountering a human being means being kept awake by an enigma" (Lévinas, 1983, p. 120), and "The mystery of the person lures us for its own sake into ever new and deeper attempts at understanding" (Dilthey, 2002, p. 233).

These two quotations accurately describe what is important to me as a psychotherapist in my work with my clients. It is also what motivates me to spend many hours reading in libraries and writing at my computer. The former kind of work is especially strenuous and demanding, since it is—at least for me—not easy to expose myself to the constantly changing atmospheres, moods, feelings, looks, sounds, touches, and smells that the people who come to me bring with them. But what Martin Buber said about the philosophical anthropologist is valid for anyone who wishes to make empathy possible in the expanded sense that I have described. He must

> stake nothing less than his real wholeness, his concrete self. . . . He can know the *wholeness* of the person and through it the wholeness of *man* only when he does not leave his *subjectivity* out and does not remain an untouched observer. . . . In other words, he must carry out this act of entry into that unique dimension as an act of his *life* . . . ; that is, he must expose himself to all that can meet you when you are really living (Buber, 1947, p. 148—original italics).

I also always find it a challenge to make the transition between the moments of intense intimacy that arise in the joint situations with my clients, on the one hand, and the necessary phases of relative distancing and reflexion on the other. What I find stimulating and inspiring is the fact that there is always something new to discover—not only when I begin a new therapy with someone, but also in each new session with a person I have been working with for some time.

Max Frisch wrote in one of his diaries that the "mystery that human beings are, [is] ultimately, an exciting riddle that we [tend to] tire of." When we get tired, we create an "image for ourselves. We are loveless, betraying" (1958, p. 32), replacing what the other person really is with a likeness of him.

That is sometimes comforting; the other person is now defined and predictable, apparently no longer a mystery. Of course I, too, sometimes tend to get tired and commit the kind of betrayal that Frisch describes. But it never stays like that for long because it is simply too stimulating and enriching to discover something new about the mystery of the other person. Feeling tired and feeling excited are both equally part of the human condition. As Gendlin writes,

> the essence of working with another person is to be present as a living being. And that is lucky, because if we had to be smart, or good, or mature, or wise, then we would probably be in trouble. But, what matters is not that. What matters is to be a human being with another human being, to recognize the other person as another being in there. . . . If they happen to look into my eyes, they will see that I am just a shaky being. I have to tolerate that. They may not look. But if they do, they will see that (Gendlin, 1990, p. 205).

It is not a question of having to be perfect or achieving absolute empathy. In spite of all the discoveries that enable me to empathize with another person, part of his mystery will always remain, since he is also not perfect or complete.

> *That which is meaningful* is itself inconclusive because it borders on the ununderstandable, on what is given, on human existence and on the freedom of Existence itself. *Understanding* must be related to the nature of the meaningful and therefore must itself be inconclusive (Jaspers, 1963, p. 357—original italics).

However empathically understanding we are, the other thus retains his mystery and simply remains irrevocably *different*. Yet at the same time, this also makes him familiar to us and *similar*, since who does not remain a mystery even to themselves—notwithstanding all self-searching and insight? Ultimately, it is not a question of unravelling the mystery of the other, but of allowing him to keep us awake and, for his sake, making ever new and deeper attempts to achieve "good enough" understanding. Then, we pave the way for what really counts: human connection.

References

Abram, D. (1997). *The spell of the sensuous: Perception and language in a more-than-human world*. New York: Vintage.

Acebo, C., & Thoman, E. B. (1992). Crying as social behavior. *Infant Mental Health Journal, 13*, 67–82.

Adamson, L. B., & Frick, J. E. (2003). The still face: A history of a shared experimental paradigm. *Infancy, 4*(4), 451–473.

Ainsworth, M. D. S., Blehar, M. C., Waters, E., & Wall, S. (1978). *Patterns of attachment: Assessed in the strange situation and at home*. Hillsdale, NJ: Erlbaum.

Altmeyer, M. (2003). *Im Spiegel des Anderen — Anwendungen einer relationalen Psychoanalyse*. Gießen: Psychosozial-Verlag.

Andersen, D. T. (2005). Empathy, psychotherapy integration, and meditation: A Buddhist contribution to the common factors movement. *Journal of Humanistic Psychology, 45*(4), 483–502.

Anderson, C. A., Berkowitz, L., Donnerstein, E., Huesmann, L. R., Johnson, J. D., Linz, D., Malamuth, N. M., & Wartella, E. (2003). The influence of media violence on youth. *Psychological Science in the Public Interest, 4*(3), 81–110.

Anderson, C. A., & Keltner, D. (2002). The role of empathy in the formation and maintenance of social bonds. *Behavioral and Brain Sciences, 25*, 21–22.

Anstadt, T., Merten, J., Ullrich, B., & Krause, R. (1997). Affective dyadic behavior, core conflictual relationship themes, and success of treatment. *Psychotherapy Research, 7*(4), 397–417.

Antonovsky, A. (1987). *Unraveling the mystery of health: How people manage stress and stay well*. San Francisco & London: Jossey-Bass.

Arisaka, Y. (2001). The ontological co-emergence of "self and other" in Japanese philosophy. *Journal of Consciousness Studies, 8*(5–7), 197–208.

Arnheim, R. (1949). The gestalt theory of expression. *Psychological Review, 56*, 156–171.

Arnold, K. H. (1981). *Der Situationsbegriff in den Sozialwissenschaften*. Weinheim & Basel: Beltz.

Aron, L. (1996). *A meeting of minds: Mutuality in psychoanalysis*. Hillsdale, NJ: Analytic Press.

Assad, J. A., & Maunsell, J. H. R. (1995). Neuronal correlates of inferred motion in primates posterior parietal cortex. *Nature, 373*, 518–521.

Atmanspacher, H. (2007). Contextual emergence from physics to cognitive neuroscience. *Journal of Consciousness Studies, 14*(1–2), 18–36.

Avenanti, A., Bueti, D., Galati, G., & Aglioti, S. M. (2005). Transcranial magnetic stimulation highlights the sensorimotor side of empathy for pain. *Nature Neuroscience, 8*(7), 955–960.

Ax, A. A. (1964). Goals and methods of psychophysiology. *Psychophysiology, 1,* 8–25.

Bacal, H. A. (1998a). Optimal responsiveness and the therapeutic process. In H. A. Bacal (Ed.), *Optimal responsiveness: How therapists heal their patients* (pp. 3–34). Northvale, NJ & London: Aronson.

Bacal, H. A. (1998b). Optimal responsiveness and the specificity of selfobject experience. In H. A. Bacal (Ed.), *Optimal responsiveness: How therapists heal their patients* (pp. 142–170). Northvale, NJ & London: Aronson.

Bakhtin, M. M. (1986). *Speech genres and other late essays* (C. Emerson & M. Holquist, Eds.). Austin: University of Texas Press.

Balint, M. (1968). *The basic fault: Therapeutic aspects of regression.* London: Tavistock.

Bar-On, R., Tranel, D., Denburg, N. L., & Bechara, A. (2003). Exploring the neurological substrate of emotional and social intelligence. *Brain, 126,* 1790–1800.

Baron, R. M., & Boudreau, L. A. (1987). An ecological perspective on integrating personality and social psychology. *Journal of Personality and Social Psychology, 53,* 1222–1228.

Barrett-Lennard, G. T. (1981). The empathy cycle: Refinement of a nuclear concept. *Journal of Counseling Psychology, 28,* 91–100.

Barrett-Lennard, G. T. (1997). The recovery of empathy—toward others and self. In A. C. Bohart & L. S. Greenberg (Eds.), *Empathy reconsidered: New directions in psychotherapy* (pp. 103–121). Washington, DC: American Psychological Association.

Basch, M. F. (1983). Empathic understanding: A review of the concept and some theoretical considerations. *Journal of the American Psychoanalytic Association, 31*(1), 101–126.

Batson, C. D. (1990). How social an animal? The human capacity for caring. *American Psychologist, 45*(3), 336–346.

Batson, C. D., Ahmad, N., & Stocks, E. L. (2004). Benefits and liabilities of empathy-induced altruism. In A. G. Miller (Ed.), *The social psychology of good and evil* (pp. 359–385). New York & London: Guilford Press.

Batson, C. D., Lishner, D. A., Cook, J., & Sawyer, S. (2005). Similarity and nurturance: Two possible sources of empathy for strangers. *Basic and Applied Social Psychology, 27*(1), 15–25.

Batson, C. D., Sager, K., Garst, E., Kang, M., Rubchinsky, K., & Dawson, K. (1997). Is empathy-enduced helping due to self-other merging? *Journal of Personality and Social Psychology, 73*(3), 495–509.

Bauer, E., & von Lucadou, W. (Eds.) (1983). *Spektrum der Parapsychologie—Hans Bender zum 75. Geburtstag.* Freiburg/Br.: Aurum.

Bauer, J. (2005). *Warum ich fühle, was du fühlst—Intuitive Kommunikation und das Geheimnis der Spiegelneurone.* Hamburg: Hoffmann & Campe.

Bauman, Z. (1995). *Life in fragments: Essays zu postmodernen Lebensformen.* Oxford, UK, & Malden, MA: Blackwell.

Bauman, Z. (1997). *Postmodernity and its discontents.* New York University Press.

Baumeister, R. F., & Leary, M. R (1995). The need to belong: Desire for interpersonal attachments as a fundamental human motivation. *Psychological Bulletin* *117*(3), 497–529.

Bauriedl, T. (1998). Ohne Abstinenz stirbt die Psychoanalyse—Über die Unvereinbarkeit von Psychoanalyse und Körpertherapie. *Forum der Psychoanalyse, 14*(4), 342–363.

Bavelas, J. B., Black, A., Lemery, C. R., & Mullett, J. (1986). "I *show* how you feel": Motor mimicry as a communicative act. *Journal of Personality and Social Psychology, 50*(2), 322–329.

Becchio, C., & Bertone, C. (2005). Beyond Cartesian subjectivism: Neural correlates of shared intentionality. *Journal of Consciousness Studies, 12*(7), 20–30.

Becker, K., & Sachse, R. (1998). *Therapeutisches Verstehen.* Göttingen: Hogrefe.

Beddoe, A. E., & Murphy, S. O. (2004). Does mindfulness decrease stress and foster empathy among nursing students? *Journal of Nursing Education, 43*(7), 305–312.

Beebe, B., Jaffe, J., Lachmann, F., Feldstein, S., Crown, C., & Jasnow, M. (2000). Systems models in development and psychoanalysis: The case of vocal rhythm coordination and attachment. *Infant Mental Health Journal, 21*(1–2), 99–122.

Beebe, B., & Lachmann, F. M. (2002). *Infant research and adult treatment: Co-constructing interactions.* Hillsdale, NJ: Analytic Press.

Begley, S. (2007). *Train your mind and change your brain: How a new science reveals our extraordinary potential to transform ourselves.* New York: Ballantine.

Beisser, A. R. (1970) The paradoxical theory of change. In J. Fagan & I. L. Shepherd (Eds.), *Gestalt therapy now* (pp. 77–80). New York: Harper Colophon.

Beisser, A. R. (1989). *Flying without wings: Personal reflections on being disabled.* New York: Doubleday.

Bellah, R., Madsen, R., Sullivan, W., Swidler, A., & Tipton, S. M. (1985). *Habits of the heart: Individualism and commitment in American life.* Berkeley: University of California Press.

Bem, D. J. (1972). Self-perception theory. *Advances in Experimental Social Psychology, 6*, 2–62.

Benecke, C., Merten, J., & Krause, R. (2000). Über die Bedeutung des intersubjektiven Feldes in der Psychotherapie. *Psychotherapie, 5*(2), 73–80.

Benedetti, J. (1982). *Stanislavski – The system: An introduction.* London: Methuen.

Berger, S. M., & Hadley, S. W. (1975). Some effects of a model's performance on an observer's electromyographic activity. *American Journal of Psychology, 88*, 263–276.

Berkowitz, M. W., & Grych, J. H. (1998). Fostering goodness: Teaching parents to facilitate children's moral development. *Journal of Moral Education, 27*(3), 371–391.

Berlin (1996). *The sense of reality: Studies in ideas and their history.* London: Chatto & Windus.

Bernieri, F. J., & Rosenthal, R. (1991). Interpersonal coordination: Behavior matching and interactional synchrony. In R. S. Feldman & B. Rimé (Eds.), *Fundamentals of nonverbal behavior* (pp. 401–432). Cambridge, MA: Cambridge University Press.

Billies, M. (2005). Therapist confluence with social systems of oppression and privilege. *International Gestalt Journal, 28*(1), 71–92.

Bischof-Köhler, D. (1994). Selbstobjektivierung und fremdbezogene Emotionen – Identifikation des eigenen Selbstbildes, Empathie und prosoziales Verhalten im 2. Lebensjahr. *Zeitschrift für Psychologie, 202*(4), 349–377.

Bischof-Köhler, D. (2001). Zusammenhang von Empathie und Selbsterkennen bei Kleinkindern. In M. Cierpka & P. Buchheim (Eds.), *Psychodynamische Konzepte* (pp. 321–328). Berlin & Heidelberg: Springer.

Blackstone, J. (2007). *The empathic ground: Intersubjectivity and nonduality in the psychotherapeutic process.* Albany, NY: State University of New York Press.

Blakemore, S.-J., Bristow, D., Bird, G., Frith, C., & Ward, J. (2005). Somatosensory activations during the observation of touch and a case of vision-touch synaesthesia. *Brain, 128,* 1571–1583.

Blakemore, S.-J., & Decety, J. (2001). From the perception of action to the understanding of intention. *Nature Reviews: Neuroscience, 2*(8), 561–567.

Blakeslee, S. (2006). Cells that read minds. *The New York Times, 10.* January.

Bloch, S. (1993). Alba Emoting: A psychophysiological technique to help actors create and control real emotions. *Theatre Topics, 3*(2), 121–138.

Bloch, S., Orthous, P., & Santibañez-H., G. (1987). Effector patterns of basic emotions: A psychophysiological method for training actors. *Journal of Social and Biological Structures, 10*(1), 1–19.

Blum, L. (1980). Compassion. In A. Oksenberg Rorty (Ed.), *Explaining emotions* (pp. 507–517). Berkeley, CA: University of California Press.

Boccia, M., & Campos, J. J. (1989). Maternal emotional signals, social referencing, and infants' reactions to strangers. In N. Eisenberg (Ed.), *Empathy and related emotional responses* (pp. 25–49). San Francisco: Jossey-Bass.

Bocian, B. (2010). *Fritz Perls in Berlin 1893–1933 — Expressionism, Psychoanalysis, Judaism.* Bergisch-Gladbach: Edition Humanistische Psychologie.

Böhme, G. (1986). *Natur, Leib, Sprache — Die Natur und der menschliche Leib.* Delft: Eburon.

Bohart, A. C. (1991). Empathy in client-centered therapy: A contrast with psychoanalysis and self psychology. *Journal of Humanistic Psychology, 31*(1), 34–48.

Bohart, A. C., & Greenberg, L. S. (1997). Empathy and psychotherapy: An introductory overview. In A. C. Bohart & L. S. Greenberg (Eds.), *Empathy reconsidered: New directions in psychotherapy* (pp. 3–31). Washington, DC: American Psychological Association.

Bohm, D. (2004). *On dialogue.* New York: Routledge.

Bonn, R. (2008). Luzifers Sturz — Oder: Die Angst, nicht dazuzugehören. In F.-M. Staemmler & R. Merten (Eds.), *Therapie der Aggression — Perspektiven für Individuum und Gesellschaft* (pp. 185–200). Bergisch-Gladbach: Edition Humanistische Psychologie.

Botvinick, M., Jha, A. P., Bylsma, L. M., Fabian, S. A., Solomon, P. E., & Prkachin, K. M. (2005). Viewing facial expressions of pain engages cortical areas involved in the direct experience of pain. *Neuroimage, 25,* 312–319.

Bourdieu, P. (1984). *Distinction: A social critique of the judgement of taste.* Cambridge, MA: Harvard University Press.

Bowlby, J. (1969). *Attachment and loss — Vol. 1: Attachment.* New York: Basic Books.

Boyce, B. (2005). Two sciences of mind. *Shambala Sun, 9*, 34–43, 93–94.

Bozarth, J. D. (1984). Beyond reflection: Emergent modes of empathy. In J. Shlien & R. Levant (Eds.), *Client-centered therapy and the person-centered approach: New directions in theory, research and practice* (pp. 59–75). Boston: Praeger.

Bozarth, J. D. (1997). Empathy from the framework of client-centered theory and the Rogerian hypothesis. In A. C. Bohart & L. S. Greenberg (Eds.), *Empathy reconsidered: New directions in psychotherapy* (pp. 81–102). Washington, DC: American Psychological Association.

Brandt, C., Brechtelsbauer, D., Bien, C. G., & Reiners, K. (2005). "Out-of-body experience" als mögliches Anfallssymptom bei einem Patienten mit rechtsparietaler Läsion. *Nervenarzt, 76*(10), 1259–1262.

Bråten, S. (1992). The virtual other in infants' minds and social feelings. In A. H. Wold (Ed.), *The dialogical alternative: Towards a theory of language and mind* (pp. 77–97). Oslo: Scandinavian University Press.

Bråten, S. (1998). Infant learning by altercentric participation: The reverse of egocentric observation in autism. In S. Bråten (Ed.), *Intersubjective communication and emotion in early ontogeny* (pp. 105–124). Cambridge, MA: Cambridge University Press.

Bråten, S. (Ed.) (2007a). *On being moved: From mirror neurons to empathy.* Amsterdam: Benjamins.

Bråten, S. (2007b). Altercentric infants and adult: On the origins and manifestations of participant perception of others' acts and utterances. In S. Bråten (Ed.), *On being moved: From mirror neurons to empathy* (pp. 111–135). Amsterdam: Benjamins.

Bråten, S. (2007c). On circular re-enactment of care and abuse, and on other-centred moments in psychotherapy: Closing comments. In S. Bråten (Ed.), *On being moved: From mirror neurons to empathy* (pp. 303–314). Amsterdam: Benjamins.

Brodley, B. T. (1991). Empathic understanding and feelings in client-centered therapy. http://www.adpca.org/Journal/Vol1_1/empatheticund.htm. Retrieved August 19, 2007.

Brodley, B. T., & Brody, A. F. (1990, Summer). *Understanding client-centered therapy through interviews conducted by Carl Rogers.* Paper prepared for the panel Fifty Years of Client-Centered Therapy: Recent Research, at the American Psychological Association Convention in Boston, MA.

Brothers, L. (2001). *Mistaken identity: The mind-brain problem reconsidered.* New York: State University of New York Press.

Bruner, J. S. (1979). *On knowing: Essays for the left hand.* Cambridge, MA & London: Belknap Press.

Bruner, J. S. (1985). Vygotsky: A historical and conceptual perspective. In J. V. Wertsch (Ed.), *Culture, communication, and cognition: Vygotskian perspectives* (pp. 21–34). Cambridge, MA & London: Cambridge University Press.

Bryant, B. K. (1987). Mental health, temperament, family and friends: Perspectives on children's empathy and social perspective taking. In N. Eisenberg & J. Strayer (Eds.), *Empathy and its development* (pp. 245–270). Cambridge: Cambridge University Press.

Buber, M. (1947). *Between man and man.* London: Kegan Paul.

Buber, M. (1957). Distance and relation. *Psychiatry: Journal for the Study of Interpersonal Processes 20*(2), 97–113.

Buber, M. (1958). *I and Thou*. New York: Scribner's Sons.

Buber, M. (1965). *The knowledge of man: A philosophy of the interhuman* (M. Friedman, Ed.). New York: Harper.

Buber, M. (1999). *Martin Buber on psychology and psychotherapy: Essays, letters, and dialogue* (J. Buber Agassi, Ed.). New York: Syracuse University Press.

Bundschuh-Müller, K. (2007). Von Augenblick zu Augenblick, von Angesicht zu Angesicht – Gesprächspsychotherapie als achtsamkeitsbasiertes personzentriertes Verfahren. *Gesprächspsychotherapie und Personzentrierte Beratung 38*(2), 75–83.

Burow, O.-A. (1999). *Die Individualisierungsfalle—Kreativität gibt es nur im Plural.* Stuttgart: Klett-Cotta.

Butler, J. (1993). *Bodies that matter: On the discursive limits of "sex."* New York: Routledge.

Buccino, G., Riggio, L., Melli, G., Binkofski, F., Gallese, V., & Rizzolatti, G. (2005). Listening to action-related sentences modulates the activity of the motor system: A combined TMS and behavioral study. *Cognitive Brain Research 24,* 355–363.

Buirski, P., & Haglund, P. (2001). *Making sense together: The intersubjective approach to psychotherapy.* Northvale, NJ & London: Jason Aronson.

Bunge, M. (1977). Emergence and the mind. *Neuroscience, 2,* 501–509.

Burow, O.-A. (1999). *Die Individualisierungsfalle—Kreativität gibt es nur im Plural.* Stuttgart: Klett-Cotta.

Carr, J. L., Iacoboni, M., Dubeau, M.-C., Mazziotta, J. C., & Lenzi, G. L. (2003). Neural mechanisms of empathy in humans: A relay from neural systems for imitation to limbic areas. *Proceedings of the National Academy of Sciences of the United States of America 100*(9), 5497–5502.

Carruthers, P., & Smith, P. K. (Eds.) (1996). *Theories of theories of mind.* Cambridge: Cambridge University Press.

Charman, T. (2002). Understanding the imitation deficit in autism may lead to a more specific model of autism as an empathy disorder. *Behavioral and Brain Sciences, 25,* 29–30.

Chartrand, T. L., & Bargh, J. A. (1999). The Chameleon effect: The perception-behavior link and social interaction. *Journal of Personality and Social Psychology, 76*(6), 893–910.

Chartrand, T. L., & Dalton, A. N. (2009). Mimicry: Its ubiquity, importance, and functionality. In: J. Bargh, P. Gollwitzer & E. Morsella (Eds.), *Psychology of action, Vol. 2* (pp. 458-483). New York: Guilford.

Cheng, Y., Lin, C.-P., Liu, H.-L., Hsu, Y.-Y., Lim, K.-E., Hung, D., & Decety, J. (2007). Expertise modulales the perception of pain in others. *Current Biology, 17,* 1708–1713.

Chödrön, P. (1994). *Start where you are: A guide to compassionate living.* Boston, MA: Shambala.

Chodron, T. (2005). *How to free your mind: Tara the liberator.* Ithaca, NY: Snow Lion Publications.

Churchland, P. S. (1996). Die Neurobiologie des Bewußtseins—Was können wir von ihr lernen? In T. Metzinger (Ed.), *Bewußtsein—Beiträge aus der Gegenwartsphilosophie* (pp. 463–490). Paderborn: Schöningh.

Chwalisz, K., Diener, E., & Gallagher, D. (1988) Autonomic arousal feedback and emotional experience: Evidence from the spinal cord injured. *Journal of Personality and Social Psychology, 54*, 820–828.

Cialdini, R. B., Brown, S. L., Lewis, B. P., Luce, C., & Neuberg, S. L. (1997). Reinterpreting the empathy-altruism relationship: When one into one equals oneness. *Journal of Personality and Social Psychology, 73*(3), 481–494.

Clark, A. (1998). Embodiment and the philosophy of mind. In A. O'Hear (Ed.), *Current issues in philosophy of mind* (pp. 35–51). Cambridge: Cambridge University Press.

Cobos, P., Sanchez, M., Garcia, C., Vera, M. N., & Vila, J. (2002). Revisiting the James versus Cannon debate on emotion: Startle and autonomic modulation in patients with spinal cord injuries. *Biological Psychology, 61*, 251–69.

Coenen, H. (1985). Leiblichkeit und Sozialität—Ein Grundproblem der phänomenologischen Soziologie. In H. G. Petzold (Ed.), *Leiblichkeit—Philosophische, gesellschaftliche und therapeutische Perspektiven* (pp. 197–228). Paderborn: Junfermann.

Cohn, J. F., & Tronick, E. Z. (1983). Three-month-old infants' reaction to simulated maternal depression. *Child Development, 54*, 185–193.

Cole, J. (1998). *About face*. Cambridge, MA &V London: MIT Press.

Cole, J. (2001). Empathy needs a face. *Journal of Consciousness Studies, 8*(5–7), 51–68.

Colvin, C. R., Vogt, D., & Ickes, W. (1997). Why do friends understand each other better than strangers do? In W. Ickes (Ed.), *Empathic accuracy* (pp. 169–193). New York & London: Guilford Press.

Condon, W. S., & Ogston, W. D. (1966). Sound film analysis of normal and pathological behavior patterns. *The Journal of Nervous and Mental Disease, 143*(4), 338–347.

Condon, W. S., & Sander, L. W. (1974). Synchrony demonstrated between movements of the neonate and adult speech. *Child Development, 45*, 456–462.

Cooper, M. (2001). Embodied empathy. In S. Haugh & T. Merry (Eds.), *Empathy: Rogers' therapeutic conditions: Evolution, theory and practice* (pp. 218–229). Ross-on-Wye: PCCS.

Cozolino, L. J. (2006). *The neuroscience of human relationships: Attachment and the developing social brain*. New York: W. W. Norton.

Csikszentmihalyi, M. (1997). *Finding flow: The psychology of engagement with everyday life*. New York: Basic Books.

Dalai Lama (1999). *Ethics for the new millenium*. New York: Riverhead.

Damasio, A. R. (1994). *Descartes' error: Emotion, reason and the human brain*. New York: Putnam's Son.

Damasio, A. R. (2003). *Looking for Spinoza: Joy, sorrow and the feeling brain*. London: Hartcourt.

Darley, J. M., & Latané, B. (1968). Bystander intervention in emergencies: Diffusion of responsibility. *Journal of Personality and Social Psychology, 8*, 377–383.

Darwin, C. (1872). *The expression of the emotions in man and animals.* (s.l.) Murray.

Davidson, D. (1984). *Inquiries into truth and interpretation*. Oxford: Clarendon Press.

Davies, M., & Stone, T. (Eds.) (1995). *Mental simulation: Evaluations and applications*. Oxford: Blackwell.

Davis, J. L. (2010). The Dalia Lama's advice on depression. http://www.webmd.com/depression/features/the-dalai-lama-and-depression-treatment. Retrieved November 1, 2010.

de Vignemont, F. (2006). When do we empathize? In G. Bock & J. Goode (Eds.), *Empathy and fairness* (pp. 181–196). Chichester: John Wiley & Sons.

de Vignemont, F., & Singer, T. (2006.) The empathic brain: How, when, and why? *Trends in Cognitive Science, 10*(10), 435–441.

de Waal, F. (2007). The 'Russian doll' model of empathy and imitation. In S. Bråten (Ed.), *On being moved: From mirror neurons to empathy* (pp. 49–69). Amsterdam: Benjamins.

de Waal, F., Thompson, E., & Proctor, J. (2005). Primates, monks and the mind: The case of empathy. *Journal of Consciousness Studies, 12*(7), 38–54.

Dean, C. J. (2004). *The fragility of empathy after the Holocaust.* Ithaca & London: Cornell University Press.

Decety, J. (2007). A social cognitive neuroscience model of human empathy. In E. Harmon-Jones & P. Winkielman (Eds.), *Social neuroscience: Integrating biological and psychological explanations of social behavior* (pp. 246–270). New York: Guilford Press.

Decety, J., Chaminade, T., Grèzes, J., & Meltzoff, A. N. (2002). A PET exploration of the neural mechanisms involved in reciprocal imitation. *Neuroimage, 15,* 265–272.

Decety, J., & Jackson, P. L. (2004). The functional architecture of human empathy. *Behavioral and Cognitive Neuroscience Reviews, 3*(2) 71–100.

Decety, J., & Sommerville, J. A. (2003). Shared representations between self and other: A social cognitive neuroscience view. *Trends in Cognitive Sciences, 7*(12), 527–533.

Dekeyser, M., Elliott, R., & Leijssen, M. (2009). Empathy in psychotherapy: Dialogue and embodied understanding. In J. Decety & W. Ickes (Eds.), *The social neuroscience of empathy* (pp. 113–124). Cambridge, MA: MIT Press.

Descartes, R. (1924/2008). *Discourse on the method.* New York: Cosimo.

Devereux, G. (Ed.) (1970). *Psychoanalysis and the occult.* New York: International Universities Press.

di Pellegrino, G., Fadiga, L., Fogassi, L., Gallese, V., & Rizzolatti, G. (1992). Understanding motor events: A neurophysiological study. *Experimental Brain Research, 91*(1), 176–180.

Dilthey, W. (1996). *Hermeneutics and the study of history: Selected works, Vol. IV* (R. A. Makkreel & F. Rodi, Eds.). Princeton, NJ: Princeton University Press.

Dilthey, W. (2002). *The formation of the historical world in the human sciences.* Princeton, NJ.: Princeton University Press.

Dimberg, U., Thunberg, M., & Elmehed, K. (2000). Unconscious facial reactions to emotional facial expressions. *Psychological Science, 11*(1), 86–89.

Dittrich, W. H., Troscianko, T., Lea, S. E. G., & Morgan, D. (1996). Perception of emotion from dynamic point-light displays represented in dance. *Perception, 25,* 727–738.

Dornes, M. (1993). *Der kompetente Säugling—Die präverbale Entwicklung des Menschen.* Frankfurt/M.: Fischer.

Dornes, M. (2006). *Die Seele des Kindes—Entstehung und Entwicklung.* Frankfurt/M.: Fischer.

Downing, G. (1996). *Körper und Wort in der Psychotherapie—Leitlinien für die Praxis.* München: Kösel.

Dreitzel, H. P. (1980). *Die gesellschaftlichen Leiden und das Leiden an der Gesellschaft — Eine Pathologie des Alltagslebens* (3., neubearb. Aufl.). Stuttgart: Enke.

Eagle, M., & Wolitzky, D. L. (1997). Empathy: A psychoanalytic perspective. In A. C. Bohart & L. S. Greenberg (Eds.), *Empathy reconsidered: New directions in psychotherapy* (pp. 217–244). Washington, DC: American Psychological Association.

Eisenberg, N. (2000). Empathy and sympathy. In M. Lewis & J. M. Javiland-Jones (Eds.), *Handbook of emotions* (pp. 677–691). New York: Guilford Press.

Eisenberg, N., & Strayer, J. (Eds.) (1987). *Empathy and its development*. Cambridge: Cambridge University Press.

Eisenberg, N., Valiente, C., & Champion, C. (2004). Empathy-related responding: Moral, social, and socialization correlates. In A. G. Miller (Ed.), *The social psychology of good and evil* (pp. 386–415). New York & London: Guilford Press.

Ekman, P. (1972). Universals and cultural differences in facial expressions of emotion. In J. Cole, (Ed.), *Nebraska Symposium on Motivation, 1971* (pp. 207–283). Lincoln, NE: University of Nebraska Press.

Ekman, P. (1992). Facial expressions of emotion: New findings, new questions. *Psychological Science, 3*(1), 34–38.

Ekman, P. (2003). *Emotions revealed: How recognizing faces and feelings improves communication and emotional life*. New York: Times Books.

Ekman, P., Levenson, R. W., & Friesen, W. V. (1983). Autonomic nervous system activity distinguishes among emotions. *Science, 221*, 1208–1210.

Elfenbein, H. A., Marsh, A. A., & Ambady, N. (2002). Emotional intelligence and the recognition of emotion from facial expressions. In L. F. Barrett & P. Salovey (Eds.), *The wisdom in feeling: Psychological processes in emotional intelligence* (pp. 37–59). New York & London: Guilford Press.

Emde, R. (1992). Social referencing research: Uncertainty, self, and the search for meaning. In S. Feinman (Ed.), *Social referencing and the social construction of reality in infancy* (pp. 79–94). New York & London: Plenum Press.

Eriksson, P. S., Perfilieva, E., Björk-Eriksson, T., Alborn, A.-M., Nordborg, C., Peterson, D. A., & Gage, F. H. (1998). Neurogenesis in the adult human hippocampus. *Nature Medicine, 4*, 1313–1317.

Erskine, R. G., Moursund, J. P., & Trautmann, R. L. (1999). *Beyond empathy: A therapy of contact-in-relationship*. Philadelphia & London: Brunner/Mazel.

Etzioni, A. (1997). *Die Verantwortungsgesellschaft — Individualismus und Moral in der heutigen Demokratie*. Frankfurt/M., & New York: Campus.

Feinman, S. (1992). In the broad valley: An integrative look at social referencing. In S. Feinman (Ed.), *Social referencing and the social construction of reality in infancy* (pp. 3–13). New York & London: Plenum Press.

Feinman, S., Roberts, D., Hsieh, K.-F., Sawyer, D., & Swanson, D. (1992). A critical review of social referencing in infancy. In S. Feinman (Ed.), *Social referencing and the social construction of reality in infancy* (pp. 15–54). New York & London: Plenum Press.

Fengler, J. (1994). *Helfen macht müde — Zur Analyse und Bewältigung von Burnout und beruflicher Deformation*. München: Pfeiffer.

Fengler, J. (2004). Das Schweigen in der Psychotherapie. In M. Hermer & H. G. Klinzing (Eds.), *Nonverbale Prozesse in der Psychotherapie* (pp. 177–190). Tübingen: dgvt.

Ferenczi, S. (1988). *The clinical diary of Sándor Ferenczi* (J. Dupont, Ed.). Cambridge, MA: Harvard University Press.

Ferrari, P. F., & Gallese, V. (2007). Mirror neurons and intersubjectivity. In S. Bråten (Ed.), *On being moved: From mirror neurons to empathy* (pp. 73–88). Amsterdam: Benjamins.

Feuerbach, L. (1855). *The essence of Christianity.* New York: Blanchard.

Feuerbach, L. A. (1868/1994). Zur Moralphilosophie. In H.-J. Braun (Ed.), *Solidarität oder Egoismus – Studien zu einer Ethik bei und nach Ludwig Feuerbach* (pp. 353–429). Berlin: Akademie-Verlag.

Field, N. (1991). Projective identification: Mechanism or mystery? *Journal of Analytical Psychology, 36*(1), 93–109.

Field, T. M., Woodson, R., Greenberg, R., & Cohen, D. (1982). Discrimination and imitation of facial expressions by neonates. *Science, 218,* 179–181.

Figley, C. R. (Ed.) (1995). *Compassion fatigue: Coping with secondary traumatic stress disorder in those who treat the traumatized.* NY: Brunner/Mazel.

Filion, C. M., Washburn, D. A., & Gulledge, J. P. (1996). Can monkeys (*Macaca mulatta*) represent invisible emplacement? *Journal of Compariative Psychology, 110,* 386–395.

Finke, J. (2002). Grenzen und Möglichkeiten des Verstehens in der Psychotherapie. In G. Kühne-Bertram & G. Scholtz (Eds.), *Grenzen des Verstehens — Philosophische und humanwissenschaftliche Perspektiven* (pp. 216–229). Göttingen: Vandenhoeck & Ruprecht.

Fivaz-Depeursinge, E., & Corboz-Warnery, A. (1999). *The primary triangle — A developmental systems view of mothers, fathers, and infants.* New York: Basic Books.

Fogassi, L., Ferrari, P. F., Gesierich, B., Rozzi, S., Chersi, F., & Rizzolatti, G. (2005). Parietal lobe: From action organization to intention understanding. *Science, 308,* 662–667.

Fogel, A., Nwokah, E., Dedo, J. Y., Messinger, D., Dickson, K. L., Matusov, E., & Holt, S. A. (1992). Social process theory of emotion: A dynamic systems approach. *Social Development, 1*(2), 122–142.

Fonagy, P., Gergely, G., Jurist, E. L., & Target, M. (2002). *Affect regulation, mentalization and the development of the self.* New York: Other Press.

Fosshage, J. L. (1994). Toward reconceptualising transference: Theoretical and clinical considerations. *International Journal of Psycho-Analysis, 75,* 265–280.

Foucault, M. (1970). The order of things: An archaeology of the human sciences. London: Tavistock.

Frank, L. K. (1939). Time perspectives. *Journal of Social Philosophy, 4,* 293–312.

Freud, S. (1901/1975). The dynamics of transference. In J. Strachey (Ed.), *The standard edition of the complete psychological works of Sigmund Freud, Vol. 6* (pp. 97–108). London: Hogarth Press.

Freud, S. (1905/1975). Psychical (or mental) treatment. In J. Strachey (Ed.), *The standard edition of the complete psychological works of Sigmund Freud, Vol. 7* (pp. 283–302): London: Hogarth Press.

Freud, S. (1921/1975). Psycho-analysis and telepathy. In J. Strachey (Ed.), *The standard edition of the complete psychological works of Sigmund Freud, Vol. 18* (pp. 173–194). London: Hogarth Press.

Freud, S. (1922/1975). Dreams and telepathy. In J. Strachey (Ed.), *The standard edition of the complete psychological works of Sigmund Freud, Vol. 18* (pp. 195–220). London: Hogarth Press.

Freud, S. (1931/1975). Civilization and its discontents. In J. Strachey (Ed.), *The standard edition of the complete psychological works of Sigmund Freud, Vol. 21* (pp. 57-145). London: Hogarth Press.

Friedman, M. (1990). Dialogue, philosophical anthropology and gestalt therapy. *The Gestalt Journal, 13*(1), 7–40.

Frisch, M. (1958). *Tagebuch 1946–1949*. Frankfurt/M.: Suhrkamp.

Frith, U., & Frith, C. D. (2003). Development and neurophysiology of mentalizing. *Philosophical Transactions of the Royal Society of London, Series B: Biological Sciences, 358*, 459–473.

Fromm, E. (1960). Psychoanalysis and Zen-Buddhism. In E. Fromm, D. T. Suzuku, & R. de Martino, *Zen Buddhism and psychoanalysis* (pp. 77–141). New York: Harper.

Fuchs, T. (2000). *Leib, Raum, Person—Entwurf einer phänomenologischen Anthropologie*. Stuttgart: Klett-Cotta.

Fuchs, T. (2008). *Das Gehirn—Ein Beziehungsorgan—Eine phänomenologisch-ökologische Konzeption*. Stuttgart: Kohlhammer.

Fuhr, R. (1999). Praxisprinzipien—Gestalttherapie als experientieller, existentieller und experimenteller Ansatz. In R. Fuhr, M. Sreckovic & M. Gremmler-Fuhr (Eds.), *Handbuch der Gestalttherapie* (pp. 417–437). Göttingen: Hogrefe.

Fulton, P. R., & Siegel, R. D. (2005). Buddhist and Western psychology: Seeking common ground. In C. K. Germer, R. D. Siegel & P. R. Fulton (Eds.), *Mindfulness in psychotherapy* (pp. 28–51). New York & London: Guilford Press.

Gadamer, H.-G. (1977). *Philosophical hermeneutics* (D. E. Linge, Ed.). Berkeley, CA: University of California Press.

Gadamer, H.-G. (1989). *Truth and method—Second, revised edition*. New York: Crossroad.

Gadamer, H.-G. (1993). *Wahrheit und Methode—Ergänzungen, Register* (Vol. II). Tübingen: Mohr.

Gallagher, S. (2005). *How the body shapes the mind*. Oxford: Clarendon.

Gallagher, S. (2006). *Perceiving others in action*. Paris: Collège de France.

Gallagher, S. (2008). How to undress the affective mind: An interview with Jaak Panksepp. *Journal of Consciousness Studies, 15*(2), 89–119.

Gallagher, S., & Meltzoff, A. N. (1996). The earliest sense of self and others: Merleau-Ponty and recent developmental studies. *Philosophical Psychology, 9*(2), 211–233.

Gallese, V. (1999). From grasping to language: Mirror neurons and the origin of social communication. In S. R. Hameroff, A. W. Kazniak & D. J. Chalmers (Eds.), *Towards a science of consciousness III: The third Tucson discussions and debates* (pp. 165–178). Cambridge, MA: MIT Press.

Gallese, V. (2001). The 'shared manifold' hypothesis: From mirror neurons to empathy. *Journal of Consciousness Studies, 8*(5–7), 33–50.

Gallese, V. (2003). The roots of empathy: The shared manifold hypothesis and the neural basis of intersubjectivity. *Psychopathology, 36*(4), 171–180.

Gallese, V. (2006a). Embodied simulation: From mirror neuron systems to interpersonal relations. In G. Bock & J. Goode (Eds.), *Empathy and fairness* (pp. 3–19). Chichester: John Wiley & Sons.

Gallese, V. (2006b). Intentional attunement: A neurophysiological perspective on social cognition and its disruption in autism. *Brain Research, 1079*, 15–24.

Gallese, V., Fadiga, L., Fogassi, L., & Rizzolatti, G. (1996). Action recognition in the premotor cortex. *Brain, 119*, 593–609.

Gallese, V., & Goldman, A. I. (1998). Mirror neurons and the simulation theory of mind-reading. *Trends in Cognitive Sciences, 2*(12), 493–501.

Gallese, V., Keysers, C., & Rizzolatti, G. (2004). A unifying view of the basis of social cognition. *Trends in Cognitive Sciences, 8*(9), 396–403.

Gaschler, K. (2006). Spiegelneurone—Die Entdeckung des Anderen. *Gehirn & Geist 10*, 26–33.

Gehde, E., & Emrich, H. M. (1998). Kontext und Bedeutung—Psychobiologie der Subjektivität im Hinblick auf psychoanalytische Theoriebildungen. *Psyche, 52*(9–10), 963–1003.

Gendlin, E. T. (1962). *Experiencing and the creation of meaning: A philosophical and psychological approach to the subjective.* New York: Free Press of Glencoe.

Gendlin, E. T. (1978/79). Befindlichkeit: Heidegger and the philosophy of psychology. *Review of Existential Psychology and Psychiatry, 16*(1–3), 43–71.

Gendlin, E. T. (1990). The small steps of the therapy process: How they come and how to help them become. In G. Lietaer, J. Rombauts & R. van Balen (Eds.), *Client-centered and experiential psychotherapy in the nineties* (pp. 205–224). Leuven: Leuven University Press.

Gendlin, E. T. (1992). The wider role of bodily sense in thought and language. In M. Sheets-Johnstone (Ed.), *Giving the body its due* (pp. 192–207). Albany, NY: State University of New York Press.

Gendlin, E. T. (1994). *Körperbezogenes Philosophieren—Gespräche über die Philosophie von Veränderungsprozessen.* Würzburg: DAF.

Gergen, K. J. (1994). *Realities and relationships: Soundings in social construction.* Cambridge, MA & London: Harvard University Press.

Germer, C. K., Siegel, R. D., & Fulton, P. R. (Eds.) (2005). *Mindfulness in psychotherapy.* New York & London: Guilford Press.

Geuter, U. (2006). Körperpsychotherapie: Der körperbezogene Ansatz im neueren wissenschaftlichen Diskurs der Psychotherapie—Teil 2. *Psychotherapeutenjournal, 5*(3), 258–264.

Gibson, E. J., & Walk, R. D. (1960). The "visual cliff." *Scientific American, 202*(4), 67–71.

Goldman, A. I. (2001). Desire, intention, and the simulation theory. In B. F. Malle, L. J. Moses & D. A. Baldwin (Eds.), *Intentions and intentionality: Foundations of social cognition* (pp. 207–224). Cambridge, MA: MIT Press.

Goldman, A. I., & Sripada, C. S. (2005). Simulationist models of face-based emotion recognition. *Cognition, 94*, 193–213.

Goldner, C. (2003). *Der Wille zum Schicksal—Die Heilslehre des Bert Hellinger.* Wien: Ueberreuther.

Goleman, D. (1995). *Emotional intelligence.* New York: Bantam.

Goleman, D. (2003). *Destructive emotions and how we can overcome them: A dialogue with the Dalai Lama.* London: Bloomsbury.

Goleman, D. (2006). *Social intelligence: The new science of human relationships*. London: Hutchinson.

Goleman, D., & Schwartz, G. (1976). Meditation as an intervention in stress reactivity. *Journal of Consulting and Clinical Psycholology, 44*(3), 456–66.

Gonzales, D. M. (2001). Client variables and psychotherapy outcomes. In D. J. Cain & J. Seeman (Eds.), *Humanistic psychotherapies: Handbook of research and practice* (pp. 559–578). Washington, DC: American Psychological Association.

Gottman, J. M. (1981). *Time-series analysis: A comprehensive introduction for social scientists*. Cambridge: Cambridge University Press.

Graumann, C. F. (1960). *Grundlagen einer Phänomenologie und Psychologie der Perspektivität*. Berlin: de Gruyter.

Graumann, C. F. (1975). Person und Situation. In U. M. Lehr & F. E. Weinert (Eds.), *Entwicklung und Persönlichkeit — Beiträge zur Psychologie intra- und interindividueller Unterschiede* (pp. 15–24). Stuttgart: Kohlhammer.

Grawe, K. (2002). *Psychological therapy*. Cambridge, MA: Hogrefe & Huber.

Grawe, K. (2007). *Neuropsychotherapy: How the neurosciences inform effective psychotherapy*. Mahwah, NJ: Erlbaum.

Greenberg, L.S., & Elliott, R. (1997). Varieties of empathic responding. In A. C. Bohart & L. S. Greenberg (Eds.), *Empathy reconsidered: New directions in psychotherapy* (pp. 167–186). Washington, DC: American Psychological Association.

Grèzes, J., Costes, N., & Decety, J. (1998). Top-down effect of strategy on the perception of human biological motion: A PET investigation. *Cognitive Neuropsychology, 15*(6–8), 552–582.

Grèzes, J., Pichon, S., & de Gelder, B. (2007). Perceiving fear in dynamic body expressions. *NeuroImage, 35*(2), 959–967.

Gruen, A. (1997). *Der Verlust des Mitgefühls — Über die Politik der Gleichgültigkeit*. München: dtv.

Guignon, C. (1998). Narrative explanation in psychotherapy. *American Behavioral Scientist, 41*(4), 558–577.

Gurwitsch, A. (1979). *Human encounters in the social world*. Pittsburgh, PA: Duquesne University Press.

Gurwitsch, A. (2010). *The collected works of Aron Gurwitsch (1901–1973), Vol. III: The field of consciousness: Theme, thematic field, and margin*. New York: Springer.

Haase, R. F., & Tepper, D. T. (1972). Nonverbal components of empathic communication. *Journal of Counseling Psychology, 19*, 417–424.

Habermas, J. (1971). *Knowledge and human interests*. Boston: Beacon Press.

Habermas, J. (1984). *The theory of communicative action — Vol. 1: Reason and the rationalization of society*. Boston: Beacon Press.

Habermas, J. (1988). *On the logic of the social sciences*. Cambridge, MA: MIT Press.

Habermas, J. (2008). *Between naturalism and religion: Philosophical essays*. Cambridge, UK, & Malden, MA: Polity Press.

Hakansson, J., & Montgomery, H. (2003). Empathy as an interpersonal phenomenon. *Journal of Social and Personal Relationships, 20*(3), 267–284.

Hall, E. T. (1989). *Beyond culture*. New York: Doubleday.

Hanh, T. N. (1992). *Peace is every step*. New York: Bantam.

Hanh, T. N. (2003). *Mit dem Herzen verstehen*. Berlin: Theseus.

Hannover, B. (1997). *Das dynamische Selbst — Die Kontextabhängigkeit selbstbezogenen Wissens*. Bern: Huber.

Hari, R. (2007). Human mirroring systems: On assessing mind by reading brain and body during social interaction. In S. Bråten (Ed.), *On being moved: From mirror neurons to empathy* (pp. 89–99). Amsterdam: Benjamins.

Harmon-Jones, E., & Winkielman, P. (2007). A brief overview of social neuroscience. In E. Harmon-Jones & P. Winkielman (Eds.), *Social neuroscience: Integrating biological and psychological explanations of social behavior* (pp. 3–11). New York & London: Guilford Press.

Harrigan, J. A., & Rosenthal, R. (1986). Nonverbal aspects of empathy and rapport in physician-patient interaction. In P. D. Blanck, R. Buck & R. Rosenthal (Eds.), *Nonverbal communication in the clinical context* (pp. 36–73). University Park & London: Pennsylvania State University Press.

Harrington, A., & Zajonc, A. (2006). *The Dalai Lama at MIT*. Cambridge, MA: Harvard University Press.

Hart, T. (1999). The refinement of empathy. *Journal of Humanistic Psychology, 39*(4), 111–125.

Hartmann, D. (1998). *Philosophische Grundlagen der Psychologie*. Darmstadt: Wissenschaftliche Buchgesellschaft.

Hasenhüttl, G. (2006). Zivilcourage bei Jesus und Sartre. In F.-M. Staemmler & R. Merten (Eds.), *Aggression, Selbstbehauptung, Zivilcourage — Zwischen Destruktivität und engagierter Menschlichkeit* (pp. 107–125). Bergisch Gladbach: Edition Humanistische Psychologie.

Hass, R. G. (1984). Perspective taking and self-awareness: Drawing an E on your forehead. *Journal of Personality and Social Psychology, 46*(4), 788–798.

Hastedt, H. (1988). *Das Leib-Seele-Problem — Zwischen Naturwissenschaft des Geistes und kultureller Eindimensionalität*. Frankfurt/M.: Suhrkamp.

Hastedt, H. (1998). *Der Wert des Einzelnen – Eine Verteidigung des Individualismus*. Frankfurt/M.: Suhrkamp.

Hatfield, E., Cacioppo, J. T., & Rapson, R. L. (1994). *Emotional contagion*. Cambridge: Cambridge University Press.

Haubl, R., & Mertens, W. (1996). *Der Psychoanalytiker als Detektiv — Eine Einführung in die psychoanalytische Erkenntnistheorie*. Stuttgart: Kohlhammer.

Heberlein, A. S., & Adolphs, R. (2007). Neurobiology of emotion recognition: Current evidence for shared substrates. In E. Harmon-Jones & P. Winkielman (Eds.), *Social neuroscience: Integrating biological and psychological explanations of social behavior* (pp. 31–55). New York & London: Guilford Press.

Heidegger, M. (1962). *Being and time*. San Francisco: Harper.

Heidenreich, T., & Michalak, J. (2003). Achtsamkeit ("Mindfulness") als Therapieprinzip in der Verhaltenstherapie und Verhaltensmedizin. *Verhaltenstherapie, 13*, 264–274.

Heidenreich, T., & Michalak, J. (Eds.) (2004). *Achtsamkeit und Akzeptanz in der Psychotherapie — Ein Handbuch*. Tübingen: dgvt.

Hellinger, B. (1998). *Love's hidden symmetry: What makes love work in relationships* (with G. Weber and H. Beaumont). Phoenix, AZ: Zeig, Tucker.

Henry, W. P., Schacht, T. E., & Strupp, H. H. (1986). Structural analysis of social behavior: Application to a study of interpersonal process in differential psychotherapeutic outcome. *Journal of Consulting and Clinical Psychology, 54,* 27–31.

Heraclitus (1979). *The art and thought of Heraclitus: An edition of the fragments with translation and commentary* (C. H. Kahn, Ed.). Cambridge: Cambridge University Press.

Hill, O. W. (1986). Further implications of anomalous observations for scientific psychology. *American Psychologist, 41*(10), 1170–1172.

Hobson, P. (1989). On sharing experiences. *Development and Psychopathology, 1,* 197–203.

Hobson, P. (1991). Against the theory of "Theory of Mind." *British Journal of Developmental Psychology, 9,* 33–51.

Hobson, P. (2002). *The cradle of thought.* London: Macmillan.

Hoffmann, M. L. (1981). The development of empathy. In J. P. Rushton & R. M. Sorrentino (Eds.), *Altruism and helping behavior: Social, personality, and developmental perspectives* (pp. 41–63). Hillsdale, NJ: Erlbaum.

Hofstadter, D. R. (1979). *Gödel, Escher, Bach: An eternal Golden Braid.* New York: Basic Books.

Hojat, M. (2005). Development of prosocial behavior and empathy in the hand that rocks the cradle. http://www.worldcongress.org/wcf3_spkrs/wcf3_hojat.htm. Retrieved October 12, 2006.

Holodynski, M., & Friedlmeier, W. (2006). *Development of emotions and emotion regulation.* New York: Springer.

Hornik, R., Risenhoover, N., & Gunnar, M. (1987). The effects of maternal positive, neutral, and negative affective communications on infant responses to new toys. *Child Development, 58,* 937–944.

Hsee, C. K., Hatfield, E., Carlson, J. G., & Chemtob, C. (1990). The effect of power on susceptibility to emotional contagion. *Cognition and Emotion, 4,* 327–340.

Huesmann, L. R. (2005). Imitation and the effects of observing media violence on behavior. In S. Hurley & N. Chater (Eds.), *Perspectives on imitation: From neuroscience to social science — Vol. 2: Imitation, human development, and culture* (pp. 257–266). Cambridge, MA: MIT Press.

Hüther, G. (2004). *Die Macht der inneren Bilder — Wie Visionen das Gehirn, den Menschen und die Welt verändern.* Göttingen: Vandenhoeck & Ruprecht.

Hüther, G. (2006). Wie Embodiment neurobiologisch erklärt werden kann. In M. Storch, B. Cantieni, G. Hüther & W. Tschacher, *Embodiment — Die Wechselwirkung von Körper und Psyche verstehen und nutzen* (pp. 73–97). Bern: Hans Huber.

Hunter, M., & Struve, J. (1998). *The ethical use of touch in psychotherapy.* London: Sage.

Hurley, S., & Chater, N. (2005). Introduction: The importance of imitation. In S. Hurley & N. Chater (Eds.), *Perspectives on imitation: From neuroscience to social science — Vol. 1: Mechanisms of imitation and imitation in animals* (pp. 1–52). Cambridge, MA: MIT Press.

Husserl, E. (1960). *Cartesian meditations: An introduction to phenomenology.* Dordrecht, Netherlands: Kluwer.

Husserl, E. (1973). *Zur Phänomenologie der Intersubjektivität; Texte aus dem Nachlass, Erster Teil: 1905–1920 — Gesammelte Werke, Vol. XIII.* (I. Kern, Ed.). Den Haag: Nijhoff.

Husserl, E. (1989). *Ideas pertaining to a pure phenomenology and to a phenomenological philosophy* —Second book. Dordrecht, Netherlands: Kluwer.

Husserl, E. (1999). The essential Husserl (D. Welton, Ed.). Bloomington, IN: Indiana University Press.

Hutchison, W. D., Davis, K. D., Lozano, A. M., Tasker, R. R., & Dostrovsky, J. O. (1999). Pain-related neurons in the human cingulate cortex. *Nature Neuroscience, 2*(5), 403–405.

Iacoboni, M. (2005). Neural mechanisms of imitation. *Current Opinion in Neurobiology, 15,* 632–637.

Iacoboni, M. (2007). The quiet revolution of existential neuroscience. In E. Harmon-Jones & P. Winkielman (Eds.), *Social neuroscience: Integrating biological and psychological explanations of social behavior* (pp. 439–453). New York: Guilford Press.

Iacoboni, M., Molnar-Szakacs, I., Gallese, V., Buccino, G., Mazziotta, J. C., & Rizzolatti, G. (2005). Grasping the intentions of others with one's own mirror neuron system. *Public Library of Science: Biology, 3*(3), e79, 1–7.

Ickes, W. (Ed.) (1997). *Empathic accuracy.* New York & London: Guilford Press.

Ickes, W., Marangoni, C., & Garcia, S. (1997). Studying empathic accuracy in a clinically relevant context. In W. Ickes (Ed.), *Empathic accuracy* (pp. 282–310). New York & London: Guilford Press.

Jackson, P. L., Meltzoff, A. N., & Decety, J. (2005). How do we perceive the pain of others? A window into the neural processes involved in empathy. *NeuroImage, 24,* 771–779.

Jacobs, L. (1992). Insights from psychoanalytic self-psychology and intersubjectivity theory for gestalt therapists. *The Gestalt Journal, 15*(2), 25–60.

Jacobs, L. (1995). Shame in the therapeutic dialogue. *British Gestalt Journal, 4*(2), 86–90.

Jacobs, L. (1998). Optimal responsiveness and subject-subject relating. In H. A. Bacal (Ed.), *Optimal responsiveness: How therapists heal their patients* (pp. 191–212). Northvale, NJ, & London: Aronson.

Jacobs, L. (2003). Ethics of context and field: The practices of care, inclusion and openness to dialogue. *British Gestalt Journal, 12*(2), 88–96.

Jacobs, L. (2005). The inevitable intersubjectivity of selfhood. *International Gestalt Journal, 28*(1), 43–70.

Jacobs, L. (2006). That which enables: Support as complex and contextually emergent. *British Gestalt Journal, 15*(2), 10–19.

Jacobs, L., Philippson, P., & Wheeler, G. (2007). Self, subject, and intersubjectivity: Gestalt therapists reply to questions from the editors and from Daniel Stern and Michael Mahoney. *Studies in Gestalt Therapy: Dialogical Bridges, 1*(1), 13–38.

James, W. (1884). What is an emotion? *Mind, 9,* 188–205.

James, W. (1890/1950). *The principles of psychology.* New York: Dover.

Jaspers, K. (1963). *General psychopathology.* Manchester: Manchester University Press.

Johnson, M. (1987). *The body in the mind: The bodily basis of meaning, imagination, and reason.* Chicago & London: University of Chicago Press.

Jordan, J. V. (1997). Relational development through mutual empathy. In A. C. Bohart & L. S. Greenberg (Eds.), *Empathy reconsidered: New directions in psychotherapy* (pp. 343–351). Washington, DC: American Psychological Association.

Jordan, J. V. (2000). The role of mutual empathy in relational/cultural therapy. *Journal of Clinical Psychology, 56*, 1005–1016.

Kabat-Zinn, J. (1990). *Full catastrophe living: How to cope with stress, pain and illness using mindfulness meditation.* New York: Delacorte.

Kabat-Zinn, J. (1999). Indra's net at work: The mainstreaming of Dharma practice in society. In G. Watson, S. Batchelor & G. Claxton (Eds.), *The psychology of awakening: Buddhism, science and our day-to-day lives* (pp. 225–249). London: Rider.

Kappas, A., & Descoteaux, J. (2003). Of butterflies and roaring thunder: Nonverbal communication in interaction and regulation of emotion. In P. Philippot, R. S. Feldman & E. J. Coats (Eds.), *Nonverbal behavior in clinical settings* (pp. 45–74). New York: Oxford University Press.

Kato, T., Takahashi, E., Sawada, K., Kobayashi, N., Watanabe, T., & Ishii, T. (1983). A computer analysis of infant movements synchronized with adult speech. *Pediatric Research, 17*, 625–628.

Keiler, P. (1999). *Feuerbach, Wygotski & Co. — Studien zur Grundlegung einer Psychologie des gesellschaftlichen Menschen* (3., erw. Aufl.). Hamburg: Argument.

Keiler, P. (2002). *Lev Vygotskiy — Ein Leben für die Psychologie.* Weinheim & Basel: Beltz.

Kennedy-Moore, E., & Watson J. C. (2001). How and when does emotional expression help? *Review of General Psychology, 5*(3), 187–212.

Keysers, C., Kohler, E., Umiltà, M. A., Nanetti, L., Fogassi, L., & Gallese, V. (2003). Audiovisual mirror neurons and action recognition. *Experimental Brain Research, 153*, 628–636.

Keysers, C., Wickers, B., Gazzola, V., Anton, J.-L., Fogassi, L., & Gallese, V. (2004). A touching sight: SII/PV activation during the observation and experience of touch. *Neuron, 42*, 335–346.

Kihlstrom, J. F. (1987). The cognitive unconscious. *Science, 237*, 1445–1452.

Kim, J. (Ed.) (2002). *Supervenience.* Aldershot, Hampshire: Ashgate.

Klein, S. (2008). Mitgefühl ist Eigennutz. *Zeit Magazin Leben, 21*, 26–33.

Kleist, H. v. (1997). On the gradual production of thoughts whilst speaking. In H. v. Kleist, *Selected writings* (D. Constantine, Ed.) (pp. 405-409). London: J. M. Dent.

Klinnert, M. D., Emde, R. N., Butterfield, P., & Campos, J. J. (1986). Social referencing: The infant's use of emotional signals from a friendly adult with mother present. *Developmental Psychology, 22*(4), 427–432.

Klöckner, D. (2007). Wo (k)ein Wille ist . . . —Anmerkungen zur neurophysiologischen Hirnforschung. *Gestalttherapie, 21*(2), 11–21.

Köhler, W. R. (1990). Intentionalität und Personenverstehen. In Forum für Philosophie Bad Homburg (Ed.), *Intentionalität und Verstehen* (pp. 273–309). Frankfurt/M.: Suhrkamp.

Koelbl, C. (2006). *Die Psychologie der kulturhistorischen Schule—Vygotskij, Lurija, Leont'ev.* Göttingen: Vandenhoeck & Ruprecht.

Koestner, R., Franz, C., & Weinberger, J. (1990). The family origins of empathic concern: A 26-year longitudinal study. *Journal of Personality and Social Psychology, 58*, 709–717.

Kohler, E., Keysers, C., Umiltà, M. A., Fogassi, L., Gallese, V., & Rizzolatti, G. (2002). Hearing sounds, understanding actions: Action representation in mirror neurons. *Science, 297*(5582), 846–848.

Kohn, A. (1990). *The brighter side of human nature: Altruism and empathy in everyday life*. New York: Basic Books.

Kohut, H. (1971). *The analysis of the self: A systematic approach to the psychoanalytic treatment of narcissistic personality disorders*. New York: International Universities Press.

Kohut, H. (1977). *The restoration of the self*. New York: International Universities Press.

Kohut, H. (1980). *The search for the self: Selected writings of Heinz Kohut 1950-1978* (P. H. Ornstein, Ed.). New York: International University Press.

Kohut, H. (1984). Introspection, empathy, and the semicircle of mental health. In J. Lichtenberg, M. Bornstein, & D. Silver (Eds.), *Empathy I* (pp. 8–100). Hillsdale, NJ: Analytic Press.

Krause, R. (2001). Affektpsychologische Perspektiven. In M. Cierpka & P. Buchheim (Eds.), *Psychodynamische Konzepte* (pp. 201–207). Berlin & Heidelberg: Springer.

Krech, H. (2001). Ursache für Sprache und Kultur? Einfühlende Nervenzellen entdeckt—Spiegelneuronen lesen Gedanken anderer. www.wissenschaft.de/wissenschaft/news/ 155366.html. Retrieved December 31, 2007.

Kühn, R. (2007). Der unsichtbare Leib—Affektivität und Fleisch in phänomenologischer Sicht. In P. Geißler & G. Heisterkamp (Ed.), *Psychoanalyse der Lebensbewegungen—Zum körperlichen Geschehen in der psychoanalytischen Therapie—Ein Lehrbuch* (pp. 595–613). Wien & New York: Springer.

Kuhn, T. S. (1970). *The structure of scientific revolutions*. Chicago: Chicago University Press.

Lachmann, F. M., & Beebe, B. (1998). Optimal responsiveness in a systems approach to representational and selfobject transference. In H. A. Bacal (Ed.), *Optimal responsiveness: How therapists heal their patients* (pp. 305–326). Northvale, NJ, & London: Aronson.

LaFrance, M. (1982). Posture mirroring and rapport. In M. Davis (Ed.), *Interaction rhythms: Periodicity in communicative behavior* (pp. 279–298). New York: Human Sciences Press.

LaFrance, M., & Broadbent, M. (1976). Group rapport: Posture sharing as a nonverbal indicator. *Group and Organization Studies, 1*, 328–333.

Lakoff, G., & Johnson, M. (1999). *Philosophy in the flesh: The embodied mind and its challenge to Western thought*. New York: Basic Books.

Latner, J. (2001). The sense of gestalt therapy: Holism, reality, and explanation. *British Gestalt Journal, 10*(2), 106–113.

Lazar, S. W. (2005). Mindfulness research. In C. K. Germer, R. D. Siegel & P. R. Fulton (Eds.), *Mindfulness in psychotherapy* (pp. 220–238). New York & London: Guilford Press.

Lazar, S. W., Kerr, C. E., Wasserman, R. H., Gray, J. R., Greve, D. N., Treadway, M. T., McGarvey, M., Quinn, B. T., Dusek, J. A., Benson, H., Rauch, S. L., Moore, C. I., & Fischl, B. (2005). Meditation experience is associated with increased cortical thickness. *NeuroReport, 16*(17), 1893–1897.

Lazarus, R. S. (2001). Relational meaning and discrete emotions. In K. R. Scherer, A. Schorr & T. Johnstone (Eds.), *Appraisal processes in emotion: Theory, methods, research* (pp. 37–67). Oxford & New York: Oxford University Press.

Leder, D. (1998). A tale of two bodies: The Cartesian corpse and the lived body. In D. Welton (Ed.), *Body and flesh: A philosophical reader* (pp. 117–129). Malden, MA: Blackwell.

LeDoux, J. (1996). *The emotional brain: The mysterious underpinnings of emotional life.* New York: Simon & Schuster.

Leibovici, L. (2001). Effects of remote, retroactive intercessory prayer on outcomes in patients with bloodstream infection: Randomised controlled trial. *British Medical Journal, 323,* 22.–29. Dezember, 1450–1451.

Lemeignan, M., Aguilera-Torres, N., & Bloch, S. (1992). Emotional effector patterns: Recognition of expressions. *European Bulletin of Cognitive Psychology, 12*(2), 173–188.

Lenzen, M. (2005). *In den Schuhen des anderen—Simulation und Theorie in der Alltagspsychologie.* Paderborn: Mentis.

Leont'ev, A. N. (1981). The problem of activity in psychology. In J. V. Wertsch (Ed.), *The concept of activity in Soviet psychology* (pp. 37–71). New York: Sharpe.

Lesh, T. V. (1970). Zen meditation and the development of empathy in counselors. *Journal of Humanistic Psychology, 10,* 39–83.

Levenson, R. W., & Ruef, A. M. (1992). Empathy: A physiological substrate. *Journal of Personality and Social Psychology, 63*(2), 234–246.

Levenson, R. W., & Ruef, A. M. (1997). Physiological aspects of emotional knowledge and rapport. In W. Ickes (Ed.), *Empathic accuracy* (pp. 44–72). New York & London: Guilford Press.

Lévinas, E. (1983). *Die Spur des Anderen—Untersuchungen zur Phänomenologie und Sozialphilosophie.* Freiburg & München: Alber.

Lévinas, E. (1989a). *The Levinas reader* (S. Hand, Ed.). Malden, MA: Blackwell.

Lévinas, E. (1989b). *Die Zeit und der Andere.* Hamburg: Meiner.

Lévinas, E. (2006). *Entre nous: Essays on thinking-of-the-other.* London: Continuum.

Lewin, K. (1951). *Field theory in social science: Selected theoretical papers* (D. Cartwright, Ed.). New York: Harper & Brothers.

Lewkowicz, D., & Turkewitz, G. (1980). Cross-modal equivalence in early infancy on the neonate. *International Review of Psychoanalysis, 8,* 35–52.

Lieberman, M. D. (2000). Intuition: A social cognitive neuroscience approach. *Psychological Bulletin, 126*(1), 109–137.

Linehan, M. M. (1997). Validation and psychotherapy. In A. C. Bohart & L. S. Greenberg (Eds.), *Empathy reconsidered: New directions in psychotherapy* (pp. 353–392). Washington, DC: American Psychological Association.

Lipps, T. (1913). Zur Einfühlung. In T. Lipps, *Psychologische Untersuchungen II* (pp. 111–491). Leipzig: Engelmann.

Lorenzer, A. (1970). *Sprachzerstörung und Rekonstruktion—Vorarbeiten zu einer Metatheorie der Psychoanalyse.* Frankfurt/M.: Suhrkamp.

Luborsky, L., Crits-Christoph, P., Mintz, J., & Auerbach, A. (1988). *Who will benefit from psychotherapy? Predicting therapeutic outcomes.* New York: Basic Books.

Lundqvist, L.-O., & Dimberg, U. (1995). Facial expressions are contagious. *Journal of Psychophysiology, 9,* 203–211.

Lutz, A., Brefczynski-Lewis, J., Johnstone, T., & Davidson, R. J. (2008). Regulation of the neural circuitry of emotion by compassion meditation: Effects of meditative expertise. *PLoS ONE, 3*(3), e1897. doi:10.1371/journal.pone.0001897.

Lux, M. (2007). *Der Personzentrierte Ansatz und die Neurowissenschaften.* München: Reinhardt.

Lyons, D. E., Santos, L. R., & Keil, F. C. (2006). Reflections of other minds: How primate social cognition can inform the function of mirror neurons. *Current Opinion in Neurobiology, 16*, 230–234.

Lyons-Ruth, K. (1999). The two-person unconscious: Intersubjective dialogue, enactive relational representation, and the emergence of new forms of relational organization. *Psychoanalytic Inquiry, 19*, 576–617.

Macann, C. (1995). Ein-fühlung—Schlüsselbegriff der persönlichen Beziehung. In M. Großheim (Ed.), *Leib und Gefühl—Beiträge zur Anthropologie* (pp. 97–108). BerlIn Akademie-Verlag.

Magnusson, D. (1978). On the psychological situation. *Reports from the Department of Psychology, University of Stockholm, Vol. 544.*

Mahler, M. S., Pine, F., & Bergman, A. (1975). *The psychological birth of the human infant: Symbiosis and individuation.* London: Hutchinson.

Mahrer, A. R. (1997). Empathy as therapist-client alignment. In A. C. Bohart & L. S. Greenberg (Eds.), *Empathy reconsidered: New directions in psychotherapy* (pp. 187–213). Washington, DC: American Psychological Association.

Mahrer, A. R., Boulet, D. B., & Fairweather, D. R. (1994). Beyond empathy: Advances in the clinical theory and methods of empathy. *Clinical Psychology Review, 14*(3), 183–198.

Marcel, G. (1985). Leibliche Begegnung—Notizen aus einem gemeinsamen Gedankengang. In H. G. Petzold (Ed.), *Leiblichkeit—Philosophische, gesellschaftliche und therapeutische Perspektiven* (pp. 15–46). Paderborn: Junferman.

Marx, G. (2002). Sprechenlernen über die erfahrbare Wirklichkeit—Anregungen der Neuen Phänomenologie für die Psychotherapie. In H. Schmitz (Ed.), *Begriffene Erfahrung—Beiträge zur antireduktionistischen Phänomenologie* (pp. 235–249). Rostock: Koch.

Matta, M. C. (1986). *Die Beziehung von Körperlichkeit und Sprachlichkeit im psychoanalytischen Prozess.* Zürich: ADAG.

Matthews, A. (2004). *Buddhistische Meditation—Der Weg zu Glück und Erkenntnis.* Berlin: Theseus.

Mayer, J. D.; DiPaolo, M., & Salovey, P. (1990). Perceiving affective content in ambiguous visual stimuli: A component of emotional intelligence. *Journal of Personality Assessment, 54*(3–4), 772–781.

Mead, G. H. (1912). The mechanism of social consciousness. *Journal of Philosophy, Psychology and Scientific Methods, 9*, 401–406.

Mead, G. H. (1934/1963). *Mind, self and society—From the standpoint of a social behaviorist* (C. W. Morris, Ed.). Chicago: University of Chicago Press.

Mealey, L. (1995). The sociobiology of sociopathy: An integrated evolutionary model. *Behavioral and Brain Sciences, 18*, 523–599.

Mehrgardt, M. (2005). Dialectic constructivism: An epistemological critique of gestalt therapy. *International Gestalt Journal, 28*(2), 31–65.

Meltzoff, A. N., & Borton, W. (1979). Intermodal matching by human neonates. *Nature, 282,* 403–404.

Meltzoff, A. N., & Brooks, R. (2001). "Like Me" as a building block for understanding other minds: Bodily acts, attention, and intention. In B. F. Malle, L. J. Moses & D. A. Baldwin (Eds.), *Intentions and intentionality: Foundations of social cognition* (pp. 171–191). Cambridge, MA: MIT Press.

Meltzoff, A. N., & Brooks, R. (2007). Intersubjectivity before language: Three windows on preverbal sharing. In S. Bråten (Ed.), *On being moved: From mirror neurons to empathy* (pp. 149–174). Amsterdam: Benjamins.

Meltzoff, A. N., & Decety, J. (2003). What imitation tells us about social cognition: A rapprochement between developmental psychology and cognitive neuroscience. *Philosophical Transactions of the Royal Society B: Biological Sciences, 358,* 491–500.

Meltzoff, A. N., & Moore, M. K. (1983). Newborn infants imitate adult facial gestures. *Child Development, 54,* 702–709.

Meltzoff, A. N., & Moore, M. K. (1994). Imitation, memory, and the representation of persons. *Infant Behavior and Development, 17,* 83–99.

Meltzoff, A. N., & Moore, M. K. (1997). Explaining facial imitation: A theoretical model. *Early Development and Parenting, 6,* 179–192.

Meltzoff, A. N., & Moore, M. K. (1998). Infant intersubjectivity: Broadening the dialogue to include imitation, identity and intention. In S. Bråten (Ed.), *Intersubjective communication and emotion in early ontogeny* (pp. 47–62). Cambridge: Cambridge University Press.

Merleau-Ponty, M. (1962). *Phenomenology of perception.* London: Routledge & Kegan Paul.

Merleau-Ponty, M. (1964). The primacy of perception, and other essays on phenomenological psychology, the philosophy of art, history and politics (J. M. Edie, Ed.). Evanston, IL: Northwestern University Press.

Merleau-Ponty, M. (1968). *The visible and the invisible. Followed by working notes.* Evanston, IL: Northwestern University Press.

Merleau-Ponty, M. (1972). *Vorlesungen I.* Berlin: de Gruyter.

Merleau-Ponty, M. (1973). *The prose of the world.* Evanston, IL: Northwestern University Press.

Merten, J. (2001). *Beziehungsregulation in Psychotherapien—Maladaptive Beziehungsmuster und der therapeutische Prozess.* Stuttgart: Kohlhammer.

Merten, R. (2008). Auf dem Weg zur gesellschaftlichen Veränderung—Wie die Gestalttherapie durch die Philosophie Jean-Paul Sartres erweitert werden kann. In F.-M. Staemmler & R. Merten (Eds.), *Therapie der Aggression—Perspektiven für Individuum und Gesellschaft* (pp. 201–227). Bergisch-Gladbach: Edition Humanistische Psychologie.

Mertens, W., & Haubl, R. (1996). *Der Psychoanalytiker als Archäologe—Eine Einführung in die Methode der Rekonstruktion.* Stuttgart: Kohlhammer.

Metzinger, T. (1993). *Subjekt und Selbstmodell—Die Perspektivität phänomenalen Bewußtseins vor dem Hintergrund einer naturalistischen Theorie mentaler Repräsentation.* Paderborn: Schöningh.

Meyer, R. (2007). Wie Ärzte ihr Mitgefühl kontrollieren. *Deutsches Ärzteblatt, 104*(42), 111.

Midal, F. (2002). *Tibetische Mythen und Gottheiten—Einblick in eine spirituelle Welt.* Berlin: Theseus.

Midgley, D. (2006). Intersubjectivity and collective consciousness. *Journal of Consciousness Studies, 13*(5), 99–109.

Mikulincer, M., Shaver, P. R., Gillath, O., & Nitzberg, R. A. (2005). Attachment, caregiving and altruism: Boosting attachment security increases compassion and helping. *Journal of Personality and Social Psychology, 8*(5), 817–839.

Milgram, S. (1974). *Obedience to authority: An experimental view.* New York: Harper & Row.

Miller, G. (2006). New neurons strive to fit in: Neurons born in the adult brain are highly adaptable, but what are they good for? *Science, 311*, 938–940.

Mischo, J. (1983). Parapsychische Erfahrungen und Psychodiagnostik im "affektiven Feld." In E. Bauer & W. von Lucadou (Eds.), *Spektrum der Parapsychologie—Hans Bender zum 75. Geburtstag* (pp. 167–192). Freiburg/Br.: Aurum.

Moeller, S. D. (1999). *Compassion fatigue—How the media sell disease, famine, war and death.* New York & London: Routledge.

Monroe, K. R. (1996). *The heart of altruism: Perceptions of a common humanity.* Princeton, NJ: Princeton University Press.

Morris, D. (1977). *Manwatching: A field guide to human behaviour.* London: Cape.

Moser, T. (1987). *Der Psychoanalytiker als sprechende Attrappe—Eine Streitschrift.* Frankfurt/M.: Suhrkamp.

Moser, T. (1989). *Körpertherapeutische Phantasien—Psychoanalytische Fallgeschichten neu betrachtet.* Frankfurt/M.: Suhrkamp.

Moore, C. (1996). Theories of mind in infancy. *British Journal of Developmental Psychology, 14*, 19–40.

Müller, K. (1988). Gestalttheorie, Emergenztheorie und der Neofunktionalismus. *Gestalt Theory, 10*(1), 46–56.

Nagel, T. (1974). What is it like to be a bat? *Philosophical Review, 83*(10), 435–450.

Nagel, T. (1986). *The view from nowhere.* New York: Oxford University Press.

Nakahara, K., & Miyashita, Y. (2005). Understanding intentions: Through the looking glass. *Science, 308*, 644–645.

Neimeyer, R. A. (2005). The construction of change: Personal reflections on the therapeutic process. *Constructivism in the Human Sciences, 10*, 77–98.

Neumann, R., & Strack, F. (2000). "Mood contagion": The automatic transfer of mood between persons. *Journal of Personality and Social Psychology, 79*(2), 211–223.

Neville, B. (1996). Five kinds of empathy. In R. Hutterer, G. Pawlowsky, P. F. Schmid & R. Stipsits (Eds.), *Client-centered and experiential psychotherapy: A paradigm in motion* (pp. 439–453). Frankfurt/M.: Peter Lang.

Niedecken, D. (2001). *Versuch über das Okkulte—Eine psychoanalytische Studie.* Tübingen: edition diskord.

Nietzsche, F. (1903). *The dawn of day.* London: Unwin.

Nietzsche, F. (1997). *Untimely meditations.* Cambridge, UK: Cambridge University Press.

Nietzsche, F. (2003). *Thus spoke Zarathustra.* London: Penguin.

Noice, T., & Noice, H. (2002). The expertise of professional actors: A review of recent research. *High Ability Studies, 13*(1), 7–19.

Norberg-Hodge, H. (1999). Compassion in the age of the global economy. In G. Watson, S. Batchelor & G. Claxton (Eds.), *The psychology of awakening: Buddhism, science and our day-to-day lives* (pp. 55–67). London: Rider.

Norcross, J. (Ed.). (2002). *Psychotherapy relationships that work: Therapist contributions and responsiveness to patient needs.* New York: Oxford University Press.

Oberman, L. M., Hubbard, E. M., McCleery, J. P., Altschuler, E. L., Ramachandran, V. S., & Pineda, J. A. (2005). EEG evidence for mirror neuron dysfunction in autism spectrum disorders. *Cognitive Brain Research, 24,* 190–198.

O'Hara, M. (1997). Relational empathy: Beyond modernist egocentricism to postmodern holistic contextualism. In A. C. Bohart & L. S. Greenberg (Eds.), *Empathy reconsidered: New directions in psychotherapy* (pp. 295–319). Washington, DC: American Psychological Association.

O'Toole, R., & Dubin, R. (1968). Baby feeding and body sway: An experiment in George Herbert Mead's "Taking the role of the other." *Journal of Personality and Social Psychology, 10*(1), 59–65.

Oram, M. W., & Perrett, D. I. (1994). Responses of anterior superior temporal polysensory (stpa) neurons to 'biological motion' stimuli. *Journal of Cognitive Neurosciences, 6*(2), 99–116.

Orange, D. M. (1995). *Emotional understanding: Studies in psychoanalytic epistemology.* New York & London: Guilford.

Ornstein, A., & Ornstein, P. H. (2001). *Empathie und therapeutischer Dialog—Beiträge zur klinischen Praxis der psychoanalytischen Selbstpsychologie* (H.-P. Harmann, Ed.). Gießen: Psychosozial-Verlag.

Paquette, V., Levesque, J., Mensour, B., Leroux, J.-M., Beaudoin, G., Bourgouin, P., & Beauregard, M. (2003). "Change the mind and you change the brain": Effects of cognitive-behavioral therapy on the neural correlates of spider phobia. *NeuroImage, 18,* 401–409.

Perls, F. S. (1969). *In and out the garbage pail.* Lafayette, CA: Real People Press.

Perls, F. S. (1970). Four lectures. In J. Fagan & I. L. Shepherd (Eds.), *Gestalt therapy now* (pp. 14–38). New York: Harper Colophon.

Perls, F. S. (1973). *The gestalt approach & Eye witness to therapy.* Palo Alto, CA: Science & Behavior Books.

Perls, F. S., Hefferline, R. F., & Goodman, P. (1951). *Gestalt therapy: Excitement and growth in the human personality.* New York: The Julian Press.

Perner, J. (1996). Simulation as explicitation of predication-implicit knowledge about the mind: Arguments for a simulation-theory mix. In P. Carruthers & P. K. Smith (Eds.), *Theories of theories of mind* (pp. 90–104). Cambridge, UK: Cambridge University Press.

Perrig, W., Wippich, W., & Perrig-Chiello, P. (1993). *Unbewußte Informationsverarbeitung.* Bern: Huber.

Petzold, H. G. (1986). Konfluenz, Kontakt, Begegnung und Beziehung als Dimensionen therapeutischer Korrespondenz in der Integrativen Therapie. *Integrative Therapie, 12*(4), 320–341.

Petzold, H. G. (1995). Integrative Therapie in der Lebensspanne—Zur entwicklungspsychologischen und gedächtnistheoretischen Fundierung aktiver und leibzentrierter Interventionen bei "frühen Schädigungen" und "negativen Ereignisketten" in unglücklichen Lebenskarrieren. In: H. G. Petzold

(Hg.), *Psychotherapie und Babyforschung—Vol. II: Die Kraft liebevoller Blicke—Säuglingsbeobachtungen revolutionieren die Psychotherapie* (pp. 325–490). Paderborn: Junfermann.

Petzold, H. G., & Orth, I. (1999). *Die Mythen der Psychotherapie—Deologien, Machtstrukturen und Wege kritischer Praxis.* Paderborn: Junfermann.

Petzold, H. G., & Sieper, J. (2005). Vygotskij, Lev Semjonovic. In G. Stumm, A. Pritz, P. Gumhalter, N. Nemeskeri & M. Voracek (Eds.), *Personenlexikon der Psychotherapie* (pp. 488–491). Wien & New York: Springer.

Petzold, H. G., van Beek, Y., & van der Hoek, A.-M. (1995). Grundlagen und Grundmuster "intimer emotionaler Kommunikation und Interaktion"—"Intuitive Parenting" und "Sensitive Caregiving" von der Säuglingszeit über die Lebensspanne. In H. G. Petzold (Ed.), *Psychotherapie und Babyforschung—Vol. II: Die Kraft liebevoller Blicke—Säuglingsbeobachtungen revolutionieren die Psychotherapie* (pp. 491–645). Paderborn: Junfermann.

Phillips, M. L., Young, A. W., Scott, S. K., Calder, A. J., Andrew, C., Giampietro, V., Williams, S. C., Bullmore, E. T., Brammer, M., & Gray, J. A. (1998). Neural responses to facial and vocal expressions of fear and disgust. *Proceedings of the Royal Society B: Biological Sciences, 265*(1408), 1809–1817.

Piaget, J. (1950). *The psychology of intelligence.* Longon: Routledge & Kegan Paul.

Pieper, A. (2003). Individuum. In H. Krings, H. M. Baumgartner & C. Wild (Ed.), *Handbuch philosophischer Grundbegriffe.* Berlin: Xenomos, 61/1–61/8.

Plessner, H. (1981). *Gesammelte Schriften IV—Die Stufen des Organischen und der Mensch—Einleitung in die philosophische Anthropologie.* Frankfurt/M.: Suhrkamp.

Plessner, H., & Buytendijk, F. J. J. (1925/1982). Die Deutung des mimischen Ausdrucks—Ein Beitrag zur Lehre vom Bewußtsein des anderen Ichs. In H. Plessner, *Gesammelte Schriften VII—Ausdruck und menschliche Natur* (pp. 67–129). Frankfurt/M.: Suhrkamp.

Poe, E. A. (1902). *The complete works of Edgar Allan Poe—Vol. VI* (J. A. Harrison, Ed.). New York: Sproul.

Polanyi, M. (1968). Logic and psychology. *American Psychologist, 23,* 27–43.

Polster, E. (1991). Tight therapeutic sequences. *British Gestalt Journal, 1*(2), 63–68.

Preston, S. D., & de Waal, F. B. M. (2002). Empathy: Its ultimate and proximate bases. *Behavioral and Brain Sciences, 25,* 1–20.

Prinz, W. (2002). Experimental approaches to imitation. In A. N. Meltzoff & W. Prinz, *The imitative mind: Development, evolution and brain bases* (pp. 143–162). Cambridge, UK: Cambridge University Press.

Provine, R. R. (1986). Yawning as a stereotyped action pattern and releasing stimulus. *Ethology, 72,* 109–122.

Provine, R. R. (1992). Contagious laughter: Laughter is a sufficient stimulus for laughs and smiles. *Bulletin of the Psychonomic Society, 30,* 1–4.

Quitmann, H. (1985). *Humanistische Psychologie—Zentrale Konzepte und philosophischer Hintergrund.* Göttingen: Hogrefe.

Ramachandran, V. S. (2001). Mirror neurons and imitation learning as the driving force behind "the great leap forward" in human evolution. www.edge.org/3rd_culture/ramachandran/ ramachandran_p1.html. Retrieved January 1, 2008.

Reichertz, J., & Zaboura, N. (Eds.) (2006). *Akteur Gehirn—Oder das vermeintliche Ende des handelnden Subjekts. Eine Kontroverse.* Wiesbaden: Verlag für Sozialwissenschaften.

Reik, T. (1949). *Listening with the third ear: The inner experience of a psychoanalyst.* New York: Farrar, Straus & Co.

Renick, O. (1995). The ideal of the anonymous analyst and the problem of self-disclosure. *Psychoanalytic Quaterly, 64*(3), 466–495.

Ricard, M., & Thuan, T. X. (2001). *The quantum and the lotus: A journey to the frontiers where science and Buddhism meet.* New York: Crown.

Richardson, J. (1987). *The magic of rapport: How you can gain personal power in any situation.* Capitola, CA: Meta Publications.

Richardson, F. C., Fowers, B. J., & Guignon, C. B. (1999). *Re-envisioning psychology: Moral dimensions of theory and practice.* San Francisco: Jossey-Bass.

Rilling, J. K., Gutman, D. A., Zeh, T. R., Pagnoni, G., Berns, G. S., & Clinton D. Kilts, C. D. (2002). A neural basis for docial cooperation. *Neuron, 35,* 395–405.

Rix, R. (1998). Learning Alba Emoting. *Theatre Topics, 8*(1), 55–71.

Rizzolatti, G., & Craighero, L. (2004). The mirror-neuron system. *Annual Review of Neuroscience, 27,* 169–192.

Rizzolatti, G., Fadiga, L., Fogassi, L., & Gallese, V. (1996). Premotor cortex and the recognition of motor actions. *Cognitive Brain Research, 3,* 131–141.

Rizzolatti, G., Fogassi, L., & Gallese, V. (2000). Mirror neurons: Intentionality detectors? *International Journal of Psychology, 35,* 205.

Rizzolatti, G., Fogassi, L., & Gallese, V. (2001). Neurophysiological mechanisms underlying the understanding and imitation of action. *Nature Reviews: Neuroscience, 2*(9), 661–670.

Robine, J.-M. (2001). From field to situation. In J.-M.Robine (Ed.), *Contact and relationship in a field perspective* (pp. 95–107). Bordeaux: L'Exprimerie.

Rogers, C. R. (1951). *Client-centered therapy: Its current practice, implications, and theory.* Boston: Houghton Mifflin.

Rogers, C. R. (1957). The necessary and sufficient conditions of therapeutic personality change. *Journal of Consulting Psychology, 21,* 95–103.

Rogers, C. R. (1959). A theory of therapy, personality, and interpersonal relationships, as developed in the client-centered framework. In S. Koch (Ed.), *Psychology: A study of a science—Vol. 3: Formulations of the person and the social context* (pp. 184–256). New York: McGraw-Hill.

Rogers, C. R. (1975). Empathic: An unappreciated way of being. *The Counseling Psychologist, 5*(2), 2–11.

Rogers, C. (1980). *A way of being.* New York: Houghton Mifflin.

Rogoff, B. (1990). *Apprenticeship in thinking: Cognitive development in social context.* New York & Oxford: Oxford University Press.

Rombach, H. (1987). *Strukturanthropologie—"Der menschliche Mensch."* Freiburg & München: Alber.

Rorty, R. (1999). *Philosophy and social hope.* London: Penguin.

Rosenhan, D. L. (1973) On being sane in insane places. *Science, 179,* 250–258.

Rosenthal, A. M. (1999). *Thirty-eight witnesses: The Kitty Genovese case.* Berkeley: University Press.

Roth, G. (1995). *Das Gehirn und seine Wirklichkeit—Kognitive Neurobiologie und ihre philosophischen Konsequenzen.* Frankfurt/M.: Suhrkamp.

Rowan, J. (1998). Linking: Its place in therapy. *International Journal of Psychotherapy, 3*(3), 245–254.

Ryback, D. (2001). Mutual affect therapy and the emergence of transformational empathy. *Journal of Humanistic Psychology, 41*(3), 75–94.

Ryle, G. (1949/2002). *The concept of mind* (with an introduction by D. Dennett). Chicago: University of Chicago Press.

Safranski, R. (1998). *Martin Heidegger: Between good and evil.* Cambridge, MA: Harvard University Press.

Santorelli, S. (1999). *Heal thy self: Lessons on mindfulness in medicine.* New York: Random House.

Sarbin, T. R. (1954). Role theory. In G. Lindzey (Ed.), *The handbook of social psychology—Vol. I: Theory and method* (pp. 223–258). Reading, MA: Addison-Wesley.

Sartre, J.-P. (1948). *Existentialism and humanism.* London: Methuen.

Sartre, J.-P. (1956). *Being and nothingness: An essay on phenomenological ontology.* New York: Philosophical Library.

Scharfetter, C. (1984). Über Meditation—Begriffsfeld, Sichtung der "Befunde", Anwendung in der Psychotherapie. In H. G. Petzold (Ed.), *Psychotherapie, Meditation, Gestalt* (pp. 27–52). Paderborn: Junfermann.

Scheflen, A. E. (1964). The significance of posture in communication systems. *Psychiatry, 27,* 316–331.

Scheler, M. (1916/1954). *The nature of sympathy.* Routledge & K. Paul.

Scheler, M. (1973). *Formalism in ethics and non-formal ethics of values: a new attempt toward the foundation of an ethical personalism.* Northwestern University Press.

Scherer, K. R., Schorr, A., & Johnstone, T. (Eds.) (2001). *Appraisal processes in emotion: Theory, methods, research.* Oxford & New York: Oxford University Press.

Schiller, F. (1967). *On the aesthetic education of man—In a series of letters, English and German facing.* (E. M. Wilkinson & L. A. Willoughby, Eds.) Oxford: Clarendon Press.

Schmidt, S. (2002). *Außergewöhnliche Kommunikation? Eine kritische Evaluation des parapsychologischen Standardexperimentes zur direkten mentalen Interaktion.* Oldenburg: Bibliotheks- und Informationssystem der Universität Oldenburg.

Schmitz, H. (1965). *System der Philosophie—2. Band, 1. Teil: Der Leib.* Bonn: Bouvier.

Schmitz, H. (1980). *Neue Phänomenologie.* Bonn: Bouvier.

Schmitz, H. (1985). Phänomenologie der Leiblichkeit. In H. G. Petzold (Ed.), *Leiblichkeit—Philosophische, gesellschaftliche und therapeutische Perspektiven* (pp. 71–106). Paderborn: Junfermann.

Schmitz, H. (1989). *Leib und Gefühl—Materialien zu einer philosophischen Therapeutik* (H. Gausebeck & G. Risch, Eds.). Paderborn: Junfermann.

Schmitz, H. (1990). *Der unerschöpfliche Gegenstand—Grundzüge der Philosophie.* Bonn: Bouvier.

Schmitz, H. (1993). *Die Liebe.* Bonn: Bouvier.

Schmitz, H. (2002). *Begriffene Erfahrung—Beiträge zur antireduktionistischen Phänomenologie.* Rostock: Koch.

Schmitz, H. (2003). The 'new phenomenology'. In A.-T. Tymienicka (Ed.), *Phenomenology world-wide* (pp. 491-494). Durdrecht: Kluwer Academic Publishers.

Schmitz, H. (2005). *Situationen und Konstellationen—Wider die Ideologie totaler Vernetzung*. Freiburg & München: Alber.

Scholz, O. R. (1999). Wie versteht man eine Person? Zum Streit über die Form der Alltagspsychologie. *Analyse & Kritik, 21*, 75–96.

Schuster, R. (1979). Empathy and mindfulness. *Journal of Humanistic Psychology, 19*(1), 71–77.

Scotti, R. (2001). Die moderne Bohème—Moderne, Individualismus und Isolation. In M. M. Moeller (Ed.), *Ernst Ludwig Kirchner—Gemälde, Zeichnung, Druckgraphik—Neuerwerbungen des Brücke-Museums Berlin seit 1988* (pp. 16–22). Köln: Dumont.

Segal, G. (1996). The modularity of theory of mind. In P. Carruthers & P. K. Smith (Eds.), *Theories of theories of mind* (pp. 141–157). Cambridge, UK: Cambridge University Press.

Sethares, W. A. (2007). *Rhythm and transforms*. London: Springer.

Shapiro, S. L., Schwartz, G. E., & Bonner, G. (1998). Effects of mindfulness-based stress reduction on medical and premedical students. *Journal of Behavioral Medicine, 21*(6), 581–599.

Shapiro, T. (1981). Empathy: A critical reevaluation. *Psychoanalytic Inquiry, 1*, 423–448.

Siegel, D. J. (2007). *The mindful brain: Reflection and attunement in the cultivation of well-being*. New York: W. W. Norton.

Simmel, J. M. (1975). *Niemand ist eine Insel*. Locarno: Droemer Knaur.

Singer, T. (2006a). The neuronal basis and ontogeny of empathy and mind reading: Review of literature and implications for future research. *Neuroscience and Biobehavioral Reviews, 30*, 855–863.

Singer, T. (2006b). The neuronal basis of empathy and fairness. In G. Bock & J. Goode (Eds.), *Empathy and fairness* (pp. 20–40). Chichester: John Wiley & Sons.

Singer, T., Seymour, B., O'Doherty, J., Kaube, H., Dolan, R. J., & Frith, C. D. (2004). Empathy for pain involves the affective but not sensory components of pain. *Science, 303*, 1157–1162.

Singer, T., Seymour, B., O'Doherty, J., Stephan, K. R., Dolan, R. J., & Frith, C. D. (2006). Empathic neural responses are modulated by the perceived fairness of others. *Nature, 439*, 466–469.

Singer, W., & Ricard, M. (2008). *Hirnforschung und Meditation—Ein Dialog*. Frankfurt/M.: Suhrkamp.

Soderstrom, H. (2003). Psychopathy as a disorder of empathy. *European Child and Adolescent Psychiatry, 12*, 249–252.

Solomon, R. C. (2002). *Spirituality for the skeptic: The thoughtful love of life*. New York: Oxford University Press.

Sorce, J. F., Emde, R. N., Campos, J., & Klinnert, M. D. (1985). Maternal emotional signaling: Its effect on the visual cliff behavior of 1-year-olds. *Developmental Psychology, 21*(1), 195–200.

Spagnuolo Lobb, M., & Amendt-Lyon, N. (Eds.) (2003). *Creative license: The art of gestalt therapy*. Wien & New York: Springer.

Sperry, R. W. (1969). A modified concept of consciousness. *Psychological Review, 76*(6), 532–536.

Spiegelberg, H. (1960). *The phenomenological movement—Vols. I & II*. Den Haag: Nijhoff.

Spinelli, E. (1996). *Demystifying therapy*. London: Constable.

Spinelli, E. (1997). *Tales of un-knowing: Eight stories of existential therapy*. New York: New York University Press.

Spitzer, M. (1996). *Geist im Netz—Modelle für Lernen, Denken und Handeln*. Heidelberg: Spektrum.

Spitzer, M. (2005). *Vorsicht Bildschirm! Elektronische Medien, Gehirnentwicklung, Gesundheit und Gesellschaft*. Stuttgart: Klett.

Staemmler, F.-M. (1981). Bitte berühren! *Psychologie heute, 8*(6), 34–37.

Staemmler, F.-M. (1987). Jenseits von Wörtern und Zeit—Über Inhalt und Prozeß in der Gestalttherapie. *Gestalt-Publikationen* 4 (Würzburg: Zentrum für Gestalttherapie).

Staemmler, F.-M. (1989). "Etiketten sind für Flaschen, nicht für Menschen"—Anmerkungen zur Diagnostik-Diskussion in der Gestalttherapie. *Gestalttherapie, 3*(1), 71–77.

Staemmler, F.-M. (1993a). *Therapeutische Beziehung und Diagnose—Gestalttherapeutische Antworten*. München: Pfeiffer.

Staemmler, F.-M. (1993b). Projective identification in gestalt therapy with severely impaired clients. *British Gestalt Journal, 2*(2), 104–110.

Staemmler, F.-M. (1995). *Der, leere Stuhl'—Ein Beitrag zur Technik der Gestalttherapie*. München: Pfeiffer.

Staemmler, F.-M. (1996). Grenze?—Welche Grenze?—Zur Problematik eines zentralen gestalttherapeutischen Begriffs. *Integrative Therapie, 22*(1), 36–55.

Staemmler, F.-M. (1997a). Towards a theory of regressive processes in gestalt therapy—On time perspective, developmental model and the wish to be understood. *The Gestalt Journal, 20*(1), 49–120.

Staemmler, F.-M. (1997b). Prozeß und Diagnose – Einführende Gedanken zur Eröffnung der 10. Münchner Gestalttage, 1996. In M. Billich, H. Koch & R. Merten (Eds.), *Dokumentation der 10. Münchner Gestalttage 1996—Prozeß und Diagnose—Gestalttherapie und Gestaltpädagogik in Praxis, Theorie und Wissenschaft* (pp. 9–23). Eurasburg: GFE.

Staemmler, F.-M. (1998). Körperorientierte Psychotherapien. In C. Kraiker & B. Peter (Eds.), *Psychotherapieführer—Wege zur seelischen Gesundheit* (pp. 231–239). München: C. H. Beck.

Staemmler, F.-M. (1999a). Déjà vu?: Klaus Grawes "Psychologische Therapie"—Eine Rezension und Evaluation aus gestalttherapeutischer Sicht. *Gestalttherapie, 13*(2), 86–124.

Staemmler, F.-M. (1999b). Der Geist der Gestalttherapie in Aktion—Methoden und Techniken. In R. Fuhr, M. Sreckovic & M. Gremmler-Fuhr (Eds.), *Handbuch der Gestalttherapie* (pp. 439–460). Göttingen: Hogrefe.

Staemmler, F.-M. (2002a). The here and now: A critical analysis. *British Gestalt Journal, 11*(1), 21–32.

Staemmler, F.-M. (2002b). Realität und Wirklichkeit: Innen oder außen?—Zur Klärung einiger Verwirrungen an der gestalttherapeutischen "Grenze." *Gestalt-Publikationen* 37 (Würzburg: Zentrum für Gestalttherapie).

Staemmler, F.-M. (2002c). Hans-Georg Gadamer: An obituary. *International Gestalt Journal, 25*(1), 129–131.

Staemmler, F.-M. (2003a). *Ganzheitliches ,Gespräch,' sprechender Leib, lebendige Sprache*. Bergisch Gladbach: Edition Humanistische Psychologie.

Staemmler, F.-M. (2003b). Körperliche Mikroprozesse im Hier und Jetzt – Gestalttherapeutische Zugänge zur prozessualen Aktivierung. In P. Geissler (Ed.), *Körperbilder—Sammelband zum 3. Wiener Symposium "Psychoanalyse und Körper"* (pp. 127–139). Gießen: Psychosozial.

Staemmler, F.-M. (2004). Dialogue and interpretation in gestalt therapy: Making sense together. *International Gestalt Journal, 27*(2), 33–57.

Staemmler, F.-M. (2005). Cultural field conditions: A hermeneutic study of consistency. *British Gestalt Journal, 14*(1), 34–43.

Staemmler, F.-M. (2006). A Babylonian confusion?: On the uses and meanings of the term 'field.' *British Gestalt Journal, 15*(2), 64–83.

Staemmler, F.-M. (2008). Joint constructions: On the subject matter of gestalt couple therapy, exemplified by gender-specific misunderstandings with regard to intimacy. In R. G. Lee (Ed.), *The secret language of intimacy: Releasing the hidden power in couple relationships* (pp. 205–248). New York: Routledge, Taylor & Francis.

Staemmler, F.-M. (2009). Cultivated uncertainty: An attitude of gestalt therapists. In F.-M. Staemmler, *Aggression, time and understanding: Contributions to the evolution of gestalt therapy* (pp. 335–357). New York: Routledge, Taylor & Francis (GestaltPress).

Staemmler, F.-M. (2010a). The willingness to be uncertain: Preliminary thoughts about interpretation and understanding in gestalt therapy. In L. Jacobs & R. Hycner (Eds.), *Relational approaches in gestalt therapy* (pp. 65–110). New York: Routledge, Taylor & Francis (GestaltPress).

Staemmler, F.-M. (2010b). Contact as first reality: Gestalt therapy as an intersubjective approach. *British Gestalt Journal, 19*(2), 28–33.

Staemmler, F.-M., & Bock, W. (1998). *Ganzheitliche Veränderung in der Gestalttherapie* (Neuausg.). Wuppertal: Hammer.

Staemmler, F.-M., & Merten, R. (2006). Vorwort. In F.-M. Staemmler & R. Merten (Eds.), *Aggression, Selbstbehauptung, Zivilcourage—Zwischen Destruktivität und engagierter Menschlichkeit* (pp. 7–13). Bergisch Gladbach: Edition Humanistische Psychologie.

Staemmler, F.-M., & Staemmler, B. (2009). Ego, anger, and attachment: A critique of Perls's aggression theory and method. In F.-M. Staemmler, *Aggression, time and understanding: Contributions to the evolution of gestalt therapy* (pp. 3–184). New York: Routledge, Taylor & Francis (GestaltPress).

Stanislavskij, K. S. (1938/1988). *An actor prepares*. London: Methuen.

Stein, E. (1917/1964). *On the problem of empathy*. The Hague: Nijhoff.

Sterling, M. M., & Bugental, J. F. T. (1993). The meld experience in psychotherapy supervision. *Journal of Humanistic Psychology, 33*(2), 38–48.

Stern, D. B. (1994). Empathy is interpretation (and who ever said it wasn't?). *Psychoanalytic Dialogues, 4*(3), 441–471.

Stern, D. N. (1985). *The interpersonal world of the infant: A view from psychoanalysis and developmental psychology*. New York: Basic Books.

Stern, D. N. (1990). *Diary of a baby*. New York: Basic Books.

Stern, D. N. (1999). Vitality contours: The temporal contour of feelings as a basic unit for constructing the infant's social experience. In P. Rochat (Ed.), *Early social cognition: Understanding others in the first months of life* (pp. 67–80). Mahwah, NJ & London: Erlbaum.

Stern, D. N. (2004). *The present moment in psychotherapy and everyday life.* New York: Norton.

Stern, D. N., & the Boston Change Process Study Group (2003). On the other side of the moon: The import of implicit knowledge for gestalt therapy. In M. Spagnuolo Lobb & N. Amendt-Lyon (Eds.), *Creative license: The art of gestalt therapy* (pp. 21–35). Wien & New York: Springer.

Stolorow, R. D., & Atwood, G. E. (1992). *Contexts of being: The intersubjective foundations of psychological life.* Hillsdale, NJ: Analytic Press.

Stolorow, R. D., & Atwood, G. E. (1997). Deconstructing the myth of the neutral analyst: An alternative from intersubjective systems theory. *Psychoanalytic Quarterly, 66,* 431–449.

Stolorow, R. D., Brandchaft, B., & Atwood, G. E. (1987). *Psychoanalytic treatment: An intersubjektive approach.* Hillsdale, NJ: Analytic Press.

Storch, M. (2006). Wie Embodiment in der Psychologie erforscht wurde. In M. Storch, B. Cantieni, G. Hüther & W. Tschacher, *Embodiment—Die Wechselwirkung von Körper und Psyche verstehen und nutzen* (pp. 35–72). Bern: Hans Huber.

Strack, F., Martin, L. L., & Stepper, S. (1988). Inhibiting and facilitating conditions of the human smile: A nonobstrusive test of the facial feedback hypothesis. *Journal of Personality and Social Psychology, 54*(5), 768–777.

Streeck, U. (2001). Agieren, Interaktion und gestische Verständigung. In M. Cierpka & P. Buchheim (Eds.), *Psychodynamische Konzepte* (pp. 201–233). Berlin & Heidelberg: Springer.

Sucharov, M. S. (1998). Optimal responsiveness and a systems view of the empathic process. In H. A. Bacal (Ed.), *Optimal responsiveness: How therapists heal their patients* (pp. 273–287). Northvale, NJ & London: Aronson.

Sullivan, H. S. (1953). *The interpersonal theory of psychiatry.* New York: Norton.

Suzuki, D. (1960). Lectures on Zen Buddhism. In E. Fromm, D. T.Suzuki & R. de Martino, *Zen Buddhism and psychoanalysis* (pp. 1–75). New York: Harper.

Sweet, M. J., & Johnson, C. G. (1990). Enhancing empathy: The interpersonal implications of a Buddhist meditation technique. *Psychotherapy, 27*(1), 19–29.

Tait, P. (2002). *Performing emotions: Gender, bodies, spaces, in Chekhov's drama and Stanislavski's theatre.* Burlington, VT: Ashgate.

Tausch, R. (1973). *Gesprächspsychotherapie.* Göttingen: Hogrefe.

Taylor, C. (1986). Leibliches Handeln. In A. Métraux & B. Waldenfels (Eds.), *Leibhaftige Vernunft – Spuren von Merleau-Pontys Denken* (pp. 194–217). München: Fink.

Taylor, C. (1992). *Sources of the self: The making of the modern identity.* Cambridge, MA: Cambridge University Press.

Tepper, D. T., & Haase, R. F. (1978). Verbal and nonverbal communication of facilitative conditions. *Journal of Counseling Psychology, 25,* 35–44.

Teschke, D. (1996). *Existentielle Momente in der Psychotherapie—Eine empirische Untersuchung mit gestalttherapeutischer Perspektive.* Münster: LIT.

Thompson, E. (2001). Empathy and consciousness. *Journal of Consciousness Studies, 8*(5–7), 1–32.

Thompson, R. A. (1998). Empathy and its origins in early development. In S. Bråten (Ed.), *Intersubjective communication and emotion in early ontogeny* (pp. 144–157). Cambridge, MA: Cambridge University Press.

Todorov, T. (1984). *Mikhail Bakhtin: The dialogical principle.* Manchester: Manchester University Press.

Trevarthen, C. (1993). The self born in intersubjectivity: The psychology of an infant communicating. In U. Neisser (Ed.), *The perceived self: Ecological and interpersonal sources of self knowledge* (pp. 121–173). Cambridge, MA: Cambridge University Press.

Trevarthen, C. (1998). The concept and foundations of infant intersubjectivity. In S. Bråten (Ed.), *Intersubjective communication and emotion in early ontogeny* (pp. 15–46). Cambridge, MA: Cambridge University Press.

Trevarthen, C. (2001). Intrinsic motives for companionship in understanding: Their origin, development, and significance for infant mental health. *Infant Mental Health Journal, 22*(1–2), 95–131.

Triandis, H. C. (1995). *Individualism and collectivism.* Boulder, CO: Westview Press.

Tronick, E. Z. (1998). Dyadically expanded states of consciousness and the process of therapeutic change. *Infant Mental Health Journal, 19*(3), 290–299.

Tronick, E. Z. (2007). *The neurobehavioral and social-emotional development of infants and children.* New York: W. W. Norton.

Tronick, E. Z., Als, H., Adamson, L., Wise, S., & Brazelton, T. B. (1978). The infant's response to entrapment between contradictory messages in face-to-face interaction. *Journal of the American Academy of Child and Adolescent Psychiatry, 17*, 1–13.

Tucker, D. M., Luu, P., & Derryberry, D. (2005). Love hurts: The evolution of empathic concern through the encephalization of nociceptive capacity. *Development and Psychopathology, 17*, 699–713.

Umiltà, M. A., Kohler, E., Gallese, V., Fogassi, L., Fadiga, L., Keysers, C., & Rizzolatti, G. (2001). I know what you are doing: A neurophysiological study. *Neuron, 31*(1), 155–165.

van Baaren, R. B., Holland, R. W., Kawakami, K., & van Knippenberg, A. (2004). Mimicry and prosocial behavior. *Psychological Science, 15*(1), 71–74.

van Baaren, R. B., Holland, R. W., Steenaert, B., & van Knippenberg, A. (2003). Mimicry for money: Behavioral consequences of imitation. *Journal of Experimental Social Psychology, 39*, 393–398.

Varela, F. J. (1999). Steps to a science of inter-being: Unfolding the dharma implicit in modern cognitive science. In G. Watson, S. Batchelor & G. Claxton, G. (Eds.), *The psychology of awakening: Buddhism, science and our day-to-day lives* (pp. 71–89). London: Rider.

Vetter, H. (Ed.) (2004). *Wörterbuch der phänomenologischen Begriffe.* Hamburg: Meiner.

Vitiello, G. (2001). *My double unveiled: The dissipative quantum model of the brain.* Amsterdam: John Benjamin.

von Lucadou, W. (1995). The model of pragmatic information (MPI). *European Journal of Parapsychology, 11*, 58–75.

von Lucadou, W. (1997). *Psi-Phänomene—Neue Ergebnisse der Psychokinese-Forschung.* Frankfurt/M.: Insel.

von Lucadou, W., Römer, H., & Walach, H. (2007). Synchronistic phenomena as entanglement correlations in generalized quantum theory. *Journal of Consciousness Studies, 14*(4), 50–74.

von Weizsäcker, E. (1974). Erstmaligkeit und Bestätigung als Komponenten der pragmatischen Information. In E. von Weizsäcker (Ed.), *Offene Systeme I— Beiträge zur Zeitstruktur von Information, Entropie und Evolution* (pp. 82–113). Stuttgart: Klett.

Vygodskaja, G. L., & Lifanova, T. M. (2000). *Lev Semjonovic Vygotskij—Leben, Tätigkeit, Persönlichkeit* (J. Lompscher & G. Rückriem, Eds.). Hamburg: Kovac.

Vygotsky, L. S. (1978). *Mind in society: The development of higher psychological processes* (M. Cole, V. John-Steiner, S. Scribner & E. Souberman, Eds.). Cambridge, MA & London: Harvard University Press.

Vygotsky, L. S. (1986). *Thought and language* (A. Kozulin, Ed.). Cambridge, MA: MIT Press.

Vygotsky, L. S. (1988). The genesis of higher mental functions. In K. Richardson & S. Sheldon (Eds.), *Cognitive development to adolescence* (pp. 61–80). Hove, UK: Psychology Press.

Wachholtz, A. B., & Pargament, K. I. (2005). Is spirituality a critical ingredient of meditation? Comparing the effects of spiritual meditation, secular meditation, and relaxation on spiritual, psychological, cardiac, and pain outcomes. *Journal of Behavioral Medicine, 28*(4), 369–384.

Walach, H. (2003). Generalisierte Quantentheorie (*Weak Quantum Theory*)—Eine theoretische Basis zum Verständnis transpersonaler Phänomene. In W. Belschner, L. Hofmann & H. Walach (Eds.), *Auf dem Weg zu einer Psychologie des Bewusstseins* (pp. 13–46). Oldenburg: Bibliotheks- und Informationssystem der Universität Oldenburg.

Walden, T. A. (1991). Infant social referencing. In J. Garber & K. A. Dodge (Eds.), *The development of emotional regulation and dysregulation* (pp. 69–88). Cambridge, MA: Cambridge University Press.

Walden, T. A., & Ogan, T. A. (1988). The development of social referencing. *Child Development, 59*, 1230–1240.

Waldenfels, B. (1971). *Das Zwischenreich des Dialogs—Sozialphilosophische Untersuchungen in Anschluss an Edmund Husserl.* Den Haag: Nijhoff.

Waldenfels, B. (1976). Die Verschränkung von Innen und Außen im Verhalten— Phänomenologische Ansatzpunkte zu einer nicht-behavioristischen Verhaltenstheorie. In Deutsche Gesellschaft für phänomenologische Forschung (Ed.), *Die Phänomenologie und die Wissenschaften* (pp. 102–129). Freiburg/Br.: Alber.

Waldenfels, B. (1985). Das Problem der Leiblichkeit bei Merleau-Ponty. In H. G. Petzold (Ed.), *Leiblichkeit—Philosophische, gesellschaftliche und therapeutische Perspektiven* (pp. 149–172). Paderborn: Junfermann.

Waldenfels, B. (2000). *Das leibliche Selbst—Vorlesungen zur Phänomenologie des Leibes.* Frankfurt/M.: Suhrkamp.

Waldron, W. S. (2003). Common ground, common cause: Buddhism and science on the afflictions of identity. In B. A. Wallace (Ed.), *Buddhism and science: Breaking new ground* (pp. 145–191). New York: Columbia University Press.

Wallace, B. A. (2006). Buddhist training in enhanced attention skills. In A. Harrington & A. Zajonc (Eds.), *The Dalai Lama at MIT* (pp. 37–45). Cambridge, MA: Harvard University Press.

Wallbott, H. G. (1990). *Mimik im Kontext — Die Bedeutung verschiedener Informationskomponenten für das Erkennen von Emotionen*. Göttingen: Hogrefe.

Watkins, K. E., Strafella, A. P., & Paus, T. (2003). Seeing and hearing speech excites the motor system involved in speech production. *Neuropsychologia, 41*, 989–994.

Watson, J. C. (2001). Re-visioning empathy. In D. J. Cain & J. Seeman (Eds.), *Humanistic psychotherapies: Handbook of research and practice* (pp. 445–471). Washington, DC: American Psychological Association.

Watt, D. F. (2005). Social bonds and the nature of empathy. *Journal of Consciousness Studies, 12*(8–10), 185–209.

Watts, A. (1960). *This is IT and other essays on Zen and spiritual experience*. New York: Pantheon.

Watts, A. (1967). *The book on the taboo against knowing who you are*. New York: Collier.

Watzlawick, P., Beavin, J. H., & Jackson, D. D. (1967). *Pragmatics of human communication: A study of interactional patterns, pathologies, and paradoxes*. New York: Norton.

Wehr, G. (1991). *Martin Buber — Leben, Werk, Wirkung*. Zürich: Diogenes.

Weisfeld, G. E., & Beresford, I. M. (1982). Erectness of posture as an indicator of dominance or success in humans. *Motivation & Emotion, 6*, 113–131.

Wertheimer, M. (1924/1938). An approach to a gestalt theory of paranoic phenomena. In W. D. Ellis (Ed.), *A source book of gestalt psychology* (pp. 362–369). London & New York: Kegan Paul & Harcourt, Brace & Company.

Wertheimer, M. (1925/1938). Gestalt theory. In W. D. Ellis (Ed.), *A source book of gestalt psychology* (pp. 1–11). London & New York: Kegan Paul & Harcourt, Brace & Company.

Wetzel, S. (1999). *Das Herz des Lotos — Frauen und Buddhismus*. Frankfurt/M.: Fischer.

Wheeler, G. (1998). *Gestalt reconsidered: A new approach to contact and resistance* (2nd edition). Cambridge, MA: GIC Press.

Wheeler, G. (2000). *Beyond individualism — Toward a new understanding of self, relationship, and experience*. Hillsdale, NJ: Analytic Press (Gestalt Press).

White, M. (1992). Therapie als Dekonstruktion. In J. Schweitzer, A. Retzer & R. Fischer (Eds.), *Systemische Praxis und Postmoderne* (pp. 39–63). Frankfurt/M.: Suhrkamp.

Whiten, A. (Ed.) (1991). *Natural theories of mind: Evolution, development and simulation of everyday mindreading*. Oxford: Basil Blackwell.

Wicker, B., Keysers, C., Plailly, J., Royet, J.-P., Gallese, V., & Rizzolatti, G. (2003). Both of us disgusted in *my* insula: The common neural basis of seeing and feeling disgust. *Neuron, 40*, 655–664.

Wiltschko, J. (Ed.) (2008). *Focusing und Philosophie — Eugene T. Gendlin über die Praxis körperbezogenen Philophierens*. Wien: Facultas.

Winnicott (2005). *Playing and reality*. New York: Routledge.

Wispé, L. (1986). The distinction between sympathy and empathy: To call forth a concept, a word is needed. *Journal of Personality and Social Psychology, 50*(2), 314–421.

Witherington, D. C., Campos, J. J., Anderson, D. I., Lejeune, L., & Seah, E. (2005). Avoidance of heights on the visual cliff in newly walking infants. *Infancy*, 7(3), 285–298.

Wittgenstein, L. (1958). *Philosophical investigations*. Oxford: Blackwell.

Wittgenstein, L. (1980). *Bermerkungen über die Philosophie der Psychologie—Remarks on the philosophy of psychology, Vols. 1 & 2*. Oxford: Basil Blackwell.

Wollants, G. (2008). *Gestalt therapy: Therapy of the situation*. Turnhout, Belgien: Faculteit voor Mens en Samenleving.

Wygotski, L. S. (1972). *Denken und Sprechen*. Frankfurt/M.: S. Fischer.

Zahavi, D. (2001). Beyond empathy: Phenomenological approaches to intersubjectivity. *Journal of Consciousness Studies*, 8(5–7), 151–167.

Zahavi, D. (2005). *Subjectivity and selfhood: Investigating the first-person perspective*. Cambridge, MA & London: MIT Press.

Zahn-Waxler, C., & Radke-Yarrow, M. (1990). The origins of empathic concern. *Motivation and Emotion*, 14(2), 107–130.

Zeilinger, A. (2004). Experiment and paradox in quantum physics. In A. Zajonc (Ed.), *The new physics and cosmology—Dialogues with the Dalai Lama* (pp. 11–30). Oxford: Oxford University Press.

Ziman, J. (2006). No man is an island. *Journal of Consciousness Studies*, 13(5), 17–42.

Zimbardo, P. (2007). *The Lucifer effect: Understanding how good people turn evil*. New York: Random House.

Zinker, J. (1977). *Creative process in gestalt therapy*. New York: Brunner/Mazel.

Zwiebel, R. (1992). *Der Schlaf des Analytikers—Die Müdigkeitsreaktion in der Gegenübertragung*. Stuttgart: Verlag Internationale Psychoanalyse.

Author Index

Subject Index